Büttner · Meissner   Town Houses of Europe

St. Martin's Press
New York

Town Houses of Europe

by Horst Büttner/ Günter Meissner

End-papers: Vicke Schorler, A True and
Faithful Counterfeit of the Most Estimable
and Far-Famed Seaport and Hanseatic City of
Rostock . . ., 1578–1586 (Rostock, municipal
archives).

Translated from the German by Peter and
Betty Ross

Copyright © 1982 by Edition Leipzig
For information, write: St. Martin's Press,
175 Fifth Avenue, New York, N.Y. 10010
Design: Gert Wunderlich
Drawings: Britta Matthies
Manufactured in the German Democratic
Republic
Library of Congress Catalog Card Number
81–52467
ISBN 0-312-81157-8

Table of Contents

Some Necessary Words of Introduction

By comparison with other architectural assignments the middle class town house would appear to be of scant importance. Situated, as often as not, in the shadow of burghs and castles, and a humble neighbour of sumptuous châteaux and palaces, not only was it dwarfed by mighty cathedrals and overtopped by such monuments to civic pride as town halls, city churches and guildhalls, but long remained concealed up to the very tips of its gables behind a protective ring of city walls and watch-towers. Thus it goes virtually unnoticed in major histories of art, while town guides seldom accord it more than a brief mention.

And yet the visual experience, however cursory, of an ancient city reveals, behind this ill-defined and diffident image, a distinct world of pride and grandeur wholly capable of competing with the architecture of spiritual and temporal potentates. This does not, of course, by any means apply in every individual case (although certain examples or certain impulses—the development of the villa and the palace, for instance—are of truly splendid dimensions), but rather to the effect created by the whole ensemble, an effect characteristic of and inseparable from the middle class town house as such. It is primarily in the market square and the tortuous thoroughfares adjoining it that one can experience the peculiar fascination of seeing, reproduced on a monumental urban scale, the otherwise marked individualism of this type of building. That collective impulse—infinitely diverse and imposing in the powerful trading metropolis, patriarchically well-to-do in the medium-sized town and cosily intimate in the smaller agricultural settlement—finds expression in each individual work. Just as cells go to make up an organism, so middle class town houses are the *sine qua non* of the European city. On their own, town houses are unassuming, but as a group they dominate the urban scene. As private buildings they merge with newer public buildings to produce a unity and grandeur so impressive as to make castles and châteaux seem insignificant by comparison. In this book, we have aimed primarily at presenting the multiplicity of types by looking at individual examples and we ask the reader to accept as a given the idea that the middle class town house is a part and a germ-cell of the totality of the European town from which modern civilization has sprung.

Few, however, of the thousands of towns on the continent of Europe can still convey any real idea of the multiplicity that once prevailed. Since the nineteenth century the population explosion, the growth of industry and the spread of irresponsible construction have done more to sweep away the original stock than the many fires and wars of preceding centuries had succeeded in doing. But there is another reason for this destruction whose origins lie in the nature of the middle class town house itself, no other sphere of architecture having, perhaps, been so closely and organically bound up with the whole range of man's changing living conditions. Like the farmstead, the middle class homestead was not only a dwelling; it was also a place of production and trade. Almost every new generation, however, was impelled to adapt and rebuild not only by the rapid growth of the productive forces but also by changes in the mode of production, by the effect of numerous social contradictions, by the spur of competition and by new requirements, including the pursuit of a better style of living. Not until the end of the Middle Ages, when the transition to stone and brick architecture became general, was there a sharp increase in the number of houses which were, besides, of such artistic distinction and merit as to have survived subsequent periods and styles as the expression of traditional prosperity. It is upon these, therefore, that we shall concentrate our attention, with the assistance of illustrations drawn from contemporary sources; this will necessarily entail an imbalance, since there are few surviving examples of earlier houses which were mostly constructed out of wood.

Because of its multifunctional nature and the consequent changes in design the middle class house constitutes one of the most interesting and complex subjects of study. Various social, ethnic, material, technological, climatic and, finally, artistic factors and considerations have to be taken into account, as do the actual requirements of a particular country, region or town, and the specifically personal circumstances of the patron. Nor is it a question of chance that virtually no one middle class town house should be an exact replica of any other. Again, it is almost impossible to keep track of the profusion of specialized treatises in many languages, for not only is the history of art involved here, but also to an increasing extent economic, social, cultural and constitutional history, not to mention ethnology, architectural studies and other such disciplines. The optimal goal—the presentation of the middle class town house in all its complexity, as a place of trade and industry, a house and a meeting place, as a capital investment, a status symbol, a witness to the rule of law and as proof of the social standing, wealth, power and culture of its occupants—could not be achieved in this survey. What we are primarily concerned with here are those aspects that appertain to the history of art and architecture, not forgetting, of course, the factors by which these were determined. Our emphasis, combined with the fact that a lot of detailed research in this field is still needed, necessarily vitiates the picture. Similarly, our account

leaves something to be desired in that more attention is paid to certain countries and certain types of house. Compared with other parts of Europe, the German-speaking region has the lion's share. In the same way, the large proportion of patrician houses—theirs being the most important architectural contribution—fails to reflect the quantitative relationship to the far greater number of houses, having little or no artistic merit, of artisans and urban farmers, or to the primitive dwellings of the urban poor, though it is a moot point whether these last may properly form a part of the subject under discussion. The literature on the middle class town house consists of widely divergent views expressed in many languages, as the important survey *Storia della Casa* (published by Ettore Camesasca, Milan, 1968), goes to show.

To clarify what is meant by the use of the term "middle class town house", a word of explanation is required. In other countries it is customarily referred to as *maison bourgeoise*, *casa di borghese*, *dom burzua*, *dom mieszczanina*, etc. True, this invariably denotes a private town house, though there is not always any clear indication as to whether the owner belonged to the middle classes or to the nobility; nor are palazzi, town palaces, villas and country houses (which bear a strong middle class imprint) generally subsumed under this heading. In certain works the very term "middle class town house" is called into question, the term "middle class homestead" being proposed as a substitute, since house, yard and ancillary buildings invariably constituted a single unit. In fact, the idea that there is a single type of middle class town house is as much a fiction as the idea of a middle class community in which all the citizens have equal rights and obligations. The distinction drawn between, say, the patrician and the lower middle class type of house, or that of the artisan or urban farmer—a distinction frequently based on external characteristics—can only serve as a loose classification.

Admittedly, classification of this kind is indispensable in a survey. This being so, A. Bernt's brief definition of a middle class town house as "the historical term for the urban domestic dwelling with or without workshop and business premises, from the rise of the middle classes in the twelfth century up to the inception of the most recent developments in domestic architecture in the early part of the nineteenth century" would seem apposite. It conceives of the middle class homestead as a building type with its own unmistakable characteristics—a type that should be seen as wholly distinct from aristocratic building (e.g. a prince's town residence), and a type that came into being with the emergence of the middle class and developed out of the latter's urban mode of existence and production. However, it gives no indication of the many and highly contradictory shades of meaning attached to the term "middle class". As far as civil rights are concerned, the term "middle class" also applies to the proletarian masses who, though no longer serfs or bondsmen, were unpropertied and played no part in municipal government, unlike the middle classes whose role in this respect varied widely in accordance with their standing. However, the shacks and hovels of the urban poor can hardly be said to fall within the category of the middle class town house. Lower class housing is not disqualified because of its primitive nature, but rather because those who lived in such housing did not fulfill the definition of the middle class. They did not own the means of production.

The term "middle class town house" is applicable to the buildings of all other middle class strata—the privileged burgesses, patricians or long-established families, as to those of that section of the middle and lower middle classes which, while they had fewer rights, were nevertheless economically independent and/or propertied. These homesteads, however, and their location within the city, reflect very plainly the differences that existed in the matter of economic and political power and their owners' share in the production and the distribution of goods. It was undoubtedly these last, crucial questions which determined, not only the architectural appearance, type and size of the middle class town house, but also the diversity of rooms, the degree of domestic comfort and the pretensions to elegance and culture which manifested themselves above all in the wealth of ornamentation and the choice of motifs. The social position of the patron may also be gauged from his ability to introduce better materials and technical innovations as soon as they were available. Finally, it might be asked whether the evolution of the middle class town house may be legitimately confined to a term of seven centuries. Even if we subscribe to this, it would not be inappropriate to invoke certain parallels in the cities of Antiquity and in the post-classical era, or to discuss in passing palazzi and villas which are not generally regarded as middle class town houses. The middle class did not cease to exist; nor is there anything absolutely conclusive about the splitting up of what was once a single functional unit into the multitude of individual building types of modern civilization, such as tenements, single and multi-family houses, suburban villas, separate offices, and commercial and industrial premises. The recent history of architecture shows that the middle class private house has also played its part in the evolution of architecture. However the material has now assumed unmanageable proportions, while fresh problems are constantly being posed. Accordingly we shall keep within the limits we have set. There can

9

be no doubt that that idiosyncratic, creative achievement, the historic middle class town house, is clearly distinct from its successors as a field of study.

We shall here endeavour to convey facts, combined with an appreciation of the beauties of architecture. For, especially recently, there has been a tremendous revival of interest in the subject. Following the appalling destruction wrought by the Second World War and the often ruthless demolition brought on by the construction of new streets, warehouses and office blocks, the number of middle class houses in many European countries has been drastically reduced. This has highlighted the fact that they are both desirable to live in and worthy of preservation. The retention of the historical plan of Lübeck in the rebuilding of that city and the restoration of the Old Market Place in Warsaw are just two examples among many that bear eloquent witness to the great need felt by people today to maintain their links with the past. Despite all the modern domestic amenities which, together with industrial technology, have spelled such great advances in private and public building (even though they may also have led to the anonymity and uniformity of standardized architecture in concrete and glass), the need for historically mature, unstereotyped urban areas cannot be dismissed as mere nostalgia. As a means of implementing new concepts of housing in such historic city centres, restoration and the demarcation of pedestrian precincts have increasingly taken the place of demolition. The research, documentation and questions of conservation this has involved have undoubtedly increased the knowledge and increased the sense of responsibility of those concerned with the preservation of the middle class town house. We therefore hope that the contents of the present book will be construed accordingly.

Although no complete evidence has survived, there would now seem to be a reasonable consensus about the birth of the middle class town house. Our earliest pictorial examples derive from the twelfth century, but its origins undoubtedly go back much farther, indeed, in some parts of Europe, to the ninth and tenth centuries when, under the aegis of feudalism, towns began to develop. However, it was not until the urban middle classes had, after many a struggle, established themselves as an independent economic and political force in medieval society that the wealth of architectural types was able fully to deploy itself. This applies particularly to central and western Europe where the development of the productive forces could proceed more rapidly than anywhere else because they remained unhampered by invading armies. Not for several centuries do large tracts of eastern and southern Europe enter our sphere with contributions of their own, a time-lag in which the Mongolian incursions into Russia and the Turkish occupation of the Balkans played a crucial part.

Aside from this, however, the factors influencing the evolution of the middle class town house might vary even from one district to the next. In our introductory chapter we shall try to show what specific circumstances were conducive to the development of this type of building.

Background to the Evolution of the Middle Class Town House

As the tenth century drew to a close, the general appearance of the countryside in central Europe began to change. Up till that time the sparse population had been widely spread. People lived in small hamlets and farms in forest clearings, princely palaces, castles, episcopal sees, monasteries and, here and there, a more or less ruinous town—all that was left of the long defunct Roman Empire. Now, however, settlements began to form at nodal points, usually where protection was afforded by the fortified seats of temporal or spiritual princes, but also at the junctions of important trade routes, at favourable places on the coast and beside much-used bridges and fords. At first the low houses and farmsteads (as a rule timber-framed, because stone and brick were seldom used) were built at random, but later became concentrated in enclosures formed by palisades or earth walls. Rather than cattle or agricultural implements, the inhabitants' possessions consisted of objects which they made, bartered or sold. So alluring did existence seem in the shelter of these communities that it attracted newcomers. Many such market settlements thus became the nuclei of new towns.

This process of urbanization which began in the ninth and tenth centuries was a result of the rapid development of productive forces. The advances made in agriculture had increased profits to such an extent as to emancipate the craftsman and promote specialization. This, in turn, gave a considerable fillip to commerce. The increasing demand for goods of all descriptions shifted the emphasis to foreign trade, a development which called for entrepôts and halting places, usually where protection was given by a castle. It was here that goods were bartered and sold on regular market days. Temporary trading posts gave way to market settlements where, because of the favourable conditions these offered, artisans also came to live. Market centres and merchants enjoyed the special protection of the king's ban whereby he guaranteed the peace of the market, the safety of the roads and the personal liberty of the traders. Either the local feudal lord or the king's immediate representative, the *praefectus* or *comes*, stood surety for the maintenance of order—not, of course, without having to pay a tidy sum in return for the concomitant privilege of collecting market dues, taxes and seigniorage. Once a market settlement of this kind had become a viable, productive centre as a result of the strengthening of ties with the surrounding countryside and the influx of handicraftsmen, urbanization quickly set in. Most towns grew out of what had once been market places. Hence their lay-out was often determined by two centres of settlement—on the one hand the middle class *nova civitas*, *suburbium* or *oppidum* and, on the other, the *civitas* or *urbs*, this being usually an older nucleus adjoining a nobleman's fortified residence that was inhabited by *burgenses*. At this stage it was customary for each centre to have its own fortifications. Marked inequalities in legal status were a cause of constant strife until, with the growth in population, unification became imperative. However, in districts such as northern Italy and the South of France where the remains of old Roman cities provided the inhabitants with a flying start, urbanization proceeded more rapidly, though not always along the same lines. In France the *citoyens* of certain ancient *cités* looked down with contempt upon the *bourgeois*, as the inhabitants of the more recent feudal boroughs were called. The boroughs, like new foundations everywhere, would long have to rely for their protection on wooden palisades or earth walls,

whereas the *cités* had possessed early on a stone-built city wall—the first visible sign of their prosperity and of the fulfilment of their civic aspirations to independence.

The struggle against exploitation by the nobility, ministerials, *advocati* and other officers of the Crown gave impetus to the communal movement which grew apace and was to set its own peculiar stamp on the course of events between the eleventh and the thirteenth centuries. This could not have happened had it not been for the huge rise in productivity in the towns, continued industrial specialization, the transition to the production of commodities and, above all, the growing power of the patrician caste of big merchants engaged in the home and foreign trades who now sought to gain control over the destiny of the towns. In the course of some two hundred years, against a background of a general population explosion, towns proliferated, as did the number of their inhabitants. In Germany the number of towns rose from some two hundred in the eleventh century to approximately a thousand in the thirteenth while, in the fourteenth century, the almost unbelievable figure of four thousand was reached. Meanwhile the country's population had more than doubled, rising from five to eleven million (at which level it was to remain for several centuries), at least a quarter of whom lived in the towns. However, the majority of these communities were small towns of one or two thousand inhabitants, while those with between two and ten thousand must be accounted middle-sized towns and anything in excess of ten thousand being cities. In Germany there were some twenty-five of the latter. Such differences in size were not, of course, without effect upon the structure of the town and the evolution of the house. In fortified places congestion led to the building of tall and narrow houses and to an enforced closeness which in turn brought about the

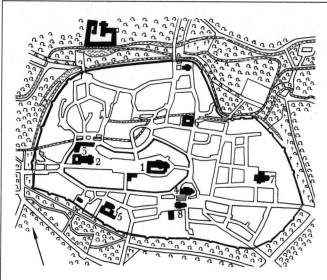

HALBERSTADT. *Town plan redrawn in 1861.*

An example of the organic growth of an important medieval town. At the centre, on the Domplatz, the Bischofsburg, dating from the ninth century, immured in 1018 (1. Cathedral, 2. Liebfrauenkirche, 3. Peter-hof, 7. Cathedral deanery) and, to the southeast, a market settlement (described after 1108 as *civitas*), from which sprang the Altstadt (Old Town: Goslar Statutes, 1184) and with it the Martinikirche (4) and the Town Hall (8)—(known to date from 1241). In the northern part of the Bischofsburg there came into being during the thirteenth century a *nova civitas* of artisans which, at the beginning of the fourteenth century, merged with the Old Town. Also, 5. Andreaskirche, 6. Katharinenkirche.

fusion of *urbs* and *suburbium.* It was not unusual for a town to expand its city walls more than once within a comparatively short space of time and thus, in larger communities, there grew up alongside the principal market place smaller centres for the practice of each individual trade. The character of a town was further determined by social and industrial circumstances which, as a rule, also exerted some influence on its size. Most small towns belonged to the category *Ackerbürgerstadt* or agricultural settlement, largely self-sufficient as far as agricultural produce was concerned. Here, too, specialized branches of agriculture, such as viticulture and animal husbandry, were also practised. Next in size came the manufacturing towns, while the largest were all of them primarily engaged in foreign trade. If some of the latter never attained any great size, it was because the trade routes on which they lay diminished in importance. Favourable conditions were created either by a long-standing monopoly (such as that of the Baltic and North Sea trades in the case of the Hanse ports and of the eastern trade in the case of Venice, Genoa, etc.), or else by a combination of merchant's capital and productive industry. Even in the thirteenth century this latter combination could give rise to cities with as many as fifty or a hundred thousand inhabitants, a size attained in Flanders and Brabant, centres of the European cloth trade, by Ghent, Antwerp, Bruges and Brussels, and in Tuscany by its metropolis, Florence. It was here that the first banks came into being, while the expansion of early industry and the outworker system ushered in the era of capitalist production.

Finally, the shape taken by a town depended to a very great extent upon the date of its founding and the intentions of the founders. 13 Early towns grew organically; skilfully exploiting topographical features, they expanded without any definite plan, with tortuous streets and a maze of alleyways winding around, or radiating out from, the centre. By comparison, the many towns founded towards the end of the twelfth and during the thirteenth centuries were based on a deliberate design; at the centre itself, roughly square or circular in shape, lay the quadrangular market place from whose corners wide main streets led to the four gates. Between them, the network of side streets created a regular pattern of rectangles, which permitted the building of tall, narrow houses on plots of equal width. Individually fortified residences belonging to the feudal nobility are, on the whole, comparatively rare. As Germany expanded eastwards into the Slavic territories, colonial towns were built in accordance with this principle so that they might serve as military bases. When the English attacked France in the thirteenth century, ushering in a long period of hostilities, that country, too, saw the building of a number of towns on similarly rigid lines and with strong fortifications. These were known as *villes-neuves* or *bastides* (e.g. Aigues-Mortes, Montauban, Sauveterre-de-Guyenne) and were of military and economic importance to the monarch and the local feudal rulers. In order to attract inhabitants, they were often granted privileged charters together with subsidies of building materials and money.

Generally speaking, the relationship of the feudal ruler to his city had already undergone a radical change and the time of the early defensive alliance was over. By the twelfth century, the communal movement had become a power to be reckoned with as it struggled to free itself from increasingly oppressive taxation (market dues, imposts, safe-conduct money, seigniorage, levies on Jews and on inheritance, etc.) and from tutelage in matters of jurisdiction, fortification, etc. It would take us too far from our subject were we to

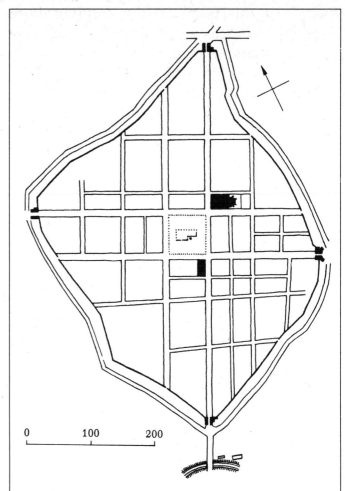

0   100   200

SAUVETERRE-DE-GUYENNE. *Town plan, example of a "ville neuve" on a regular plan laid out in 1281 by King Edward I of England as a means of asserting his sovereignty in France.*

At the centre, the rectangular market place, the proportions of which determine the quadrature of the network of streets. In the northeast corner of the market place, St Catherine's Church. For reasons of defence the plan has been kept very compact.

14

discuss at this point all the configurations assumed by those early middle-class attempts at emancipation. Though alliances between towns were common during this initial period, they were seldom strong enough to combat feudal power by force of arms as successfully as the cities of the Lombard League which defeated the German Emperor Frederick I at the Battle of Legnano in 1176. Quite often a city would obtain partial emancipation by exploiting the struggle for power between King and Pope, the quarrels between warring territorial princes or the latter's feuds with the Crown. In the conflicts of the twelfth and thirteenth centuries, which brought a large measure of independence to the big centres of foreign trade, the lead was taken by the patricians who often formed confederacies or *coniurationes* in which the city's communal spirit manifested itself as a new collective force. This did not apply to the same extent in countries with a strong central government which guaranteed order and security. In France, the towns grew up in alliance with a strong monarchy and, in the Estates General, participated alongside the great nobles in important decisions of state. Citizens and burgesses were also represented in the first English Parliament of 1265. In Germany, the decline of imperial power in the thirteenth century compelled many towns to form defensive alliances. At the same time the Imperial cities on Crownland reneged on virtually all their obligations. In a country torn with strife, they represented a power in their own right as did the great federation of the German Hanseatic League which, in the fourteenth century, successfully challenged the power of the Danish Crown. At that time the Hanseatic League was still a monopolistic commercial federation of patrician towns which expelled refractory members or cities such as Brunswick where the patrician régime had been overthrown in 1374.

This transition to independent if despotic rule was earliest in evidence in the cities of northern and central Italy. Here the conflict between Guelphs and Ghibellines involved the towns in a changing pattern of alliances which, once the territorial supremacy of the feudal lords had been destroyed, competed against each other for power and for spheres of influence. The leading caste, the *popolo grasso*, joined the nobility in the city republics to form a patrician élite. In the end, these great families ruled their cities even more despotically than the erstwhile enemies of the communes had done.

The events briefly outlined above show that in the Middle Ages the urban middle classes, even when wholly victorious, never succeeded in transcending the limitations of the feudal order. Nevertheless, an important advance made as a result of the communal movement was the relative autonomy attained by the towns and the codification of this autonomy in the municipal statutes. These municipal constitutions, in many different versions, were first set down in writing in the twelfth century and, in all important matters, these laws were to safeguard for centuries to come the further development of the communes and the interests of their ruling classes. Such was the case even in the many small towns which remained under feudal rule. One of the most important victories over feudalism occurred in the twelfth century with the right to grant freedom to the serfs and bondsmen, hordes of whom had come flocking into the towns.

The emergence of the urban middle classes as a significant social force was also to have enduring effects in the intellectual and artistic fields. The new wave of self-confidence and pragmatism brought with it a new art oriented towards things worldly and towards personal displays of wealth. This in turn began to undermine the teaching of the church and set the rudiments of a middle class culture against the culture of the Court. This manifested itself primarily in the representational arts and, most clearly of all, in architecture. It enriched Gothic with significant stylistic impulses, created in Late Gothic a form of its own and, with the dawning of Humanism and the Renaissance, finally left the Middle Ages behind. In the twelfth century it began to imprint its own image upon that of the town, as is evident from churches that are larger and loftier than ever before, richly ornamented town halls and other public and communal buildings, vast fortifications with numerous towers and imposing gates and, last but not least, the middle class town house.

The Early Social Structure of the Urban Middle Classes

Needless to say, our survey of urban development can do no more than contribute towards a general appreciation of the middle class town house, for the latter was invariably a private building. Later on, reference will frequently be made to certain correlations between, say, the size and power of a commune and its middle class houses, or the influence exerted on house-design by the economic, political and cultural links between cities. Of greater importance is the question of the marked difference between middle class houses in any one town; a question that directs our attention to conditions within the city walls. Here the citizens may all have been free—at any rate after a year and a day—but they were not all equal. The relative standing enjoyed by the different professions, an individual's position therein, the extent of his taxable property and—most crucial question of all—of his share in the means of production and in the article produced—all these gave rise to

social inequality which in its turn naturally found expression in varying degrees of social prestige and, ultimately, in different political rights as far as the government of the town was concerned. Early on, and as long as feudal dependence continued to prevail, the contradictions remained hidden. With the advent of autonomy, better conditions and a more broadly based division of labour, they became plainly evident. The social stratification created within the towns is illuminating in that it has left its mark on the various basic types of middle class house, and for this reason we propose to depict it in broad outline.

. Handicrafts and trade were, from the beginning, the twin pillars of urban existence. But the period during which they went hand in hand, i.e. when a product was sold, either by the producer himself or through a small retailer, gradually drew to a close in the twelfth and thirteenth centuries with the expansion of commodity production, of the money economy and, most important of all, of foreign trade. As a result, trade became divorced from production. In this process merchants, especially the large wholesalers dealing in substantial quantities of important foreign goods or of commodities in great demand, such as spices, dye-stuffs, perfume and much else, rapidly secured a controlling position. This stratum, namely the patricians or old-established families, together with the clergy and the officials in the service of the aristocracy, constituted a class which, more than any other, needed to be able to read, write and do math. No one had a less parochial outlook than these patricians who were, besides, accumulators rather than consumers of wealth which they regularly invested in new, potentially profitable, enterprises. Since the risks inherent in the use of long trade routes by land and sea were considerable, they joined together to form the first Hansas or guilds as a means of mutual

JOST AMMAN, "The Merchant", woodcut from the "Stände-buch" of 1567, with verses by Hans Sachs and Hartmann Schopper.

A patrician merchant, wearing a sword, is clinching a bargain in a typical setting. In his house are to be seen securely roped bales of merchandise stored in vaults with barred windows. With such nicety does the woodcut hit off the merchant's calling that, apart from the sixteenth century garb, the scene here depicted might have taken place at any time during the preceding two hundred years.

support in time of trouble. From the thirteenth century onwards they rarely accompanied their caravans in person, but instead set up offices with their own representatives, discharged their obligations one to another, drew bills of exchange, and developed the banking system as a new source of wealth. As a result, they were able to acquire the best sites in their towns and even buy up villages and estates, while securing such highly lucrative privileges as the right to brew beer. One source of particular profit proved to be the financial transactions of the money changers. Thanks to the extensive patronage of the Italian patricians in particular, they effected the transition, by granting credit, of merchant's capital to usurer's capital. Through the out-worker system they also exerted a direct influence on the handicraftsmen and, in so doing, took the first step from the simple to the capitalist production of commodities. In Florence, at the beginning of the fourteenth century, approximately thirty thousand workers were employed by some two hundred patricians in the textile industry. The families of the *meliores*, *maiores*, and *richen* were few in number, were often interrelated and wanted to preserve their privileges. These patricians were at most prepared to admit into their *cercle d'élite* persons of equal standing such as noblemen (this was frequently done in Italy, for example, and in the Rhenish towns), rich masters of guilds, shipowners, brewers and owners of salt works. The multitude of small traders and other merchants, who had combined to form their own guilds and fraternities, were excluded, as were the great majority of the artisans. By their nature, the patricians were primarily interested in security and the consolidation of their position. As a result, they frequently provided the main impetus in the struggle for emancipation from feudalism, besides being spokesmen in the town council or *conventus civium*.

17

But once the goal had been achieved, the latter dwindled in importance and control passed to small councils largely drawn from the patriciate and headed by one or two burgomasters or *consules*. Town councils of this kind, consisting of *consules*, were already in existence in the towns of northern Italy round about 1100, some hundred years before they made an appearance north of the Alps. From the thirteenth century onwards, the craft guilds fought strenuously for the control of these councils which enacted laws, supervised the guilds themselves, levied taxes and were responsible for all important decisions concerning the town as a whole. In the big mercantile cities the struggle came to nothing, but elsewhere the craft guilds frequently achieved the right to a voice in the council, if not actual supremacy.

It was in these guilds, or craftsmen's associations, each one representing a separate or closely allied trade, that the main element of the numerically substantial urban middle and lower classes confronted the patriciate. In Germany the organization of that element began in the twelfth century and earlier still in Italy, France and England. The resulting bodies were organs for vocational self-administration, for collective social representation and for protection against undesirable competition, having precise rules governing qualification, and the quality and quantity of goods produced. All problems were discussed and resolved by the masters in conclave. While journeymen and apprentices were compelled to join a craft guild, they had no voice in its affairs. However, the journeymen subsequently formed clubs for the purpose of mutual social aid. In most cases, one journeyman and one apprentice worked and lodged with their master who was required to own a house and be a full citizen. Only rarely were masters such as these able to accumulate riches, since

TOBIAS STIMMER, "Locksmith's Workshop", pen drawing, Staatliche Museen zu Berlin, Kupferstichkabinett.

This portrayal, dating from the third quarter of the sixteenth century, of the world of the guild handicraftsman, shows master and apprentices working as a patriarchal group. The workshop, situated on a level with the street, has an unglazed window equipped with wooden shutters, one of which is lowered to form a counter for the display and sale of their products.

their commercial existence consisted of simple reproduction. The members of a craft guild normally lived in specific quarters or alleyways and, with the increase in specialization in the craft trades and the new tasks this entailed, their number rapidly increased. Thus, with the general adoption of stone as a building material, for example, the masons' and roofers' fraternities grew in importance at the expense of the supra-regional master builders' associations. When a town was threatened with attack, the defences were largely manned by the craft guilds. As their economic importance grew, they came, with the support of the other, lower strata, to be the decisive force in the struggle against the patrician-dominated councils. True, the influence of the craft guilds varied greatly, as did the financial circumstances of the masters who belonged to them. Some fell on hard times and, once deprived of their own means of production, became dependent on their wealthier brethren who then proceeded to engage further journeymen. In the fifteenth century, moreover, the restrictive practices of the guilds began to hamper the development of early capitalist production. They made it increasingly difficult for the ever more numerous journeymen to achieve the status of master, so that the number of so-called "eternal journeymen" continually increased.

· Besides the master craftsmen, who were organized in craft guilds and whose wealthier element constituted the middle stratum, there were also those in other occupations (urban farmers, municipal employees, etc.) who, as owners of property, swelled the numbers of the lower middle classes. They were all of them citizens of inferior status whose rights were considerably curtailed but who were nevertheless better off than the unpropertied disenfranchised populace below them. These included not only journeymen and appren-

tices, but also serving men and women, day labourers, soldiers, seamen and, lastly, the urban poor. Few of them had a home to call their own and, instead, were accommodated in the houses of their lords and masters. As such they were known as *Schutzverwandte*, *Beisitzer* or *Beisassen*, i.e. inhabitants who had no vote but were subject to the control of the municipal authorities. The same applied to the Jews who were obliged to live in certain streets and ghettos.

Full or partial civil rights were enjoyed not only by the population within the town, but also by those living outside the gates in the suburbs, many of which had expanded rapidly from the fourteenth century onwards. Needless to say, virtually none of the patricians and a mere handful from the middle strata lived in these unfortified districts. Those who did so were the lower middle class and the great majority of the urban poor. Others who only enjoyed partial rights were the *Pfahlbürger* who, though not resident within the town limits, stayed there from time to time, the *Gras-* or *Feldbürger*, who lived in villages belonging to the town, and the *Glevenbürger* whose services were called upon only when there was a threat of war. Also accounted citizens of a town, although not, or only conditionally subject to its jurisdiction, were many members of the aristocracy, as well as large numbers of the clergy ranging from bishops to the monks and nuns of the numerous land-owning convents. In view of the very stratified structure of the urban bourgeoisie in the Early and High Middle Ages, which has been no more than touched on here, an investigation of the typology of the middle class town house presents a very complex problem. Nevertheless a few basic types may be defined.

The Middle Class Town House—
Origins and Types

Before the middle class house came into being with the rise of the towns, a highly developed urban culture had already existed among the slave owning societies. There, too, trade and manufacturing had been the life blood of the cities of the Near East, India, Greece and the Roman Empire. Tempting though it may be to compare the house as it evolved over those five millennia and over the bare eight centuries of the period under review, such an idea must be reserved for a separate study. No more need be said save that much of what would seem to have evolved for the first time in the middle class town house had already existed previously, since in each case similar ways of life and modes of production called for similar solutions. In that earlier period, too, the multi-functional, multi-storeyed house with its court-yard took shape. The wealthy merchant's Graeco-Roman peristyle house with its inner courtyard surrounded by columns and, not infrequently, two-storeyed arcades was, like the villa outside the big cities, a direct forerunner of the *palazzi* and *ville* of the Renaissance. The larger towns could already boast apartment houses of between five and seven storeys standing in streets which were laid out in a regular pattern of rectangles; markets and streets were provided with shopping precincts above which were balconied apartments; the houses which accommodated one or more families, were of wood, timber frame or stone construction—magnificent premises for the rich, vast slums for the poor.

By the ninth century, however, virtually nothing but a huge expanse of ruins was left of the wealth of the former cities of Antiquity —wealth such as can only be a matter of surmise today. At least five hundred years separate the fall of the Western Roman Empire (476) from the rise of the towns in central and western Europe. Though their founders generally chose to make use of what remained of the *oppides*, the old colonial towns, which were sited advantageously both strategically and from the point of view of communications, they set their sights a great deal lower. The social structure and the relations of production were too dissimilar, the requirements and way of life of most of the fledgling nations with their agricultural background were too different to permit the general adoption of the developed Roman style. Not until much later, in the fifteenth century, following a process of independent maturation on the part of the Italian communes, was there to be a comprehensive reappraisal of the legacy left by Antiquity. Traces of its later influence are, of course, to be found everywhere, above all on native Roman territory and also—no doubt because their occupants had an eye on the imperial succession—in the palaces, churches and monasteries of the temporal and spiritual leaders of the aristocracy.

. However, the imposing architecture of the feudal period played little or no part in the genesis of the middle class town house. Such relics as the *Kemenate*, or King John type house, an often free-standing, stone strong room next to the main building, were not generally adopted. The fortified tower-house alone succeeded in making any appreciable mark on the early townscape, especially in Italy where it may still be seen today in the small Tuscan hill town of San Gimigniano. Although tower-houses of this type generally served as the town seats of the nobility, they were also sometimes incorporated in the middle class town house. In Florence, when more than a hundred such towers threatened to overwhelm the life of the town, the patriciate ordered that their height be reduced to fifty ells. In so far as the middle classes built towers, these usually formed part of a public building.

, There can be no disputing that the real origins of the middle class homestead lay in the farmsteads of the peasantry from whom the founders of the new towns were drawn. By gradual stages many of the villages grew into towns and, for a long time thereafter, part of the labour process in the new fondations continued to be dictated by the needs of agriculture. Animal husbandry, especially pig-keeping, was a common practice in many middle class houses throughout the whole of the Middle Ages. The transition from the multi-functional organism of the peasant house to its urban successor with its new demands extended over a long period. Normally the principle adopted was that of the farmstead which combined within its precincts the functions of a dwelling for the various generations of a family and its servants, a storage-place for produce and a repository for tools and vehicles. But, apart from the lingering tradition of animal husbandry, the labour process was no longer centred upon the open fields but rather upon the house or its immediate surroundings where the handicraftsman plied his trade and regularly sold his wares. Since limitations of space within the town precluded any enlargement of the courtyard, the constraints imposed by the long, elongated plots urgently called for spatial organization of a new and more diversified kind and it was this that provided the decisive impulse towards changes in architectural design. Nothing indicates these changes more clearly than the narrow, multi-storeyed, middle class town house as distinct from the low, horizontally disposed farmstead, a further development being the introduction between the thirteenth and fourteenth centuries of one or even two storeys below ground level. As to the interior, the single room was subdivided into several rooms which served

an increasing variety of functions, while out-buildings began to fill the yard. Eventually many other factors contributed to the configuration of the middle class town house, such as the development of timber frame construction and, after the twelfth century, advances in building technology and the widespread adoption of stone and brick. One must also take account not only of new domestic requirements—particularly the advance from the open hearth to the stove with its flue and chimney—but also of a natural predilection for display and a firm resolve to erect both a lasting structure and a monument to oneself and to one's town. All these contributed to the configuration of the middle class town house. Only the *Ackerbürgerhaus*, or urban farmstead, with its various regional characteristics, presents a compromise in which scant progress has been made. Up till the nineteenth century its occupants lived mainly in small country towns or agricultural settlements and were directly involved in various branches of agrarian production. To trace the stages in this long process of change would be to exceed the limitations of our study. We have insufficient evidence to go on and, because of regional variations in the types of European farmhouse, there is still a lack of specialized studies in this field. In the German-speaking area it is possible to identify with a certain degree of accuracy three large geographical zones in which transitions from one tradition to another took place. The North German type of middle class town house borrowed from the North German and Lower Saxon hall-type farmhouse the large single unit of the hall and *1, 4, 5* the massive show gable. The South German farmhouse, consisting of several rooms and often more than one floor, influenced South German building styles with its structurally lucid development of rooms and storeys, which also frequently involved the presentation of

21

the long side to the street. Ultimately both *31*
concepts merged in an intermediate zone in
central Germany where a large proportion
of the buildings were of timber frame construction. The more detailed aspects will be discussed later on when we come to the examples.
So enduring was the influence subsequently
exerted by the farmhouse upon each change
of style from Romanesque to Baroque, that it
was only with the advent of Classicism that
territorial distinctions ultimately disappeared.
Regional and traditional characteristics such
as these were strong enough to overlay the
considerable variations which were dictated
by sociological factors, in the types of middle
class town house in any one town. Whereas
the regional aspects are manifold, the traditional ones are similar in all European towns.
These basic, overlapping types are therefore
of crucial importance and their essential
character at the time of their heyday must be
briefly touched upon. The most significant
type is the patrician or upper middle class house.
As the home of the richest and highest stratum
of the urban bourgeoisie, it was the realization
at its most impressive of the entire creative
and aesthetic potential of the middle classes.
In terms of its economic function, it was first
and foremost the imposing abode of the big
merchants and international traders. As befit-
ted their exclusive character, patrician houses
tended to be grouped on the commune's choic-
est sites, either in the market place or in the
main streets. They surpassed all other private
houses in height, size and richness of decoration and, together with the public and communal buildings, demonstrated to the outside
world the might of the town and, to the town's
own inhabitants, the power of its leading citizens. Height and size were, of course, governed by functional considerations. The stock-
ing of large quantities of merchandise in a
limited space frequently necessitated the addi-

ROSTOCK. *Street frontage with gable-fronted houses of the
North German type of middle class town house, thirteenth to
fifteenth century (redrawn from Vicke Schorler, circa 1580).*

Their derivation from the Lower Saxon peasant farmhouse, a long hall-
house with a show- and entrance-front crowned by a lofty gable, is still
plainly discernible. The narrow urban sites, however, precluded side
aisles, while the need for additional space called for the horizontal
division of the lofty hall, the introduction of separate living-quarters at
the rear, and the splitting up of the gable into storeys.

NUREMBERG. *East frontage on the Rathausplatz, with
middle class town houses of the South German type, circa 1614
(redrawn from an engraving).*

The multi-roomed and, even at this time, multi-storeyed, character of
the South German peasant farmhouse (stabling below, living-quarters
above reached by stair and landing and/or an outside stair and gallery)
was adopted by the middle class town house of this type (business
premises below, kitchen and living-quarters with two hearths above),
with the result that greater emphasis was placed on the height and
rectangularity of the main block, and on the additive growth in the
shape of outshots, while less emphasis was accorded to the gable.
Indeed that feature sometimes disappears altogether, as in our
example, owing to the presentation of the long side to the street. For
climatic reasons the windows are often smaller, while their irregular
arrangement betrays a similarly diversified spatial structure within.
The façade of plastered, dressed stone predominates, in many cases
enlivened by the addition of balconies, oriels (residual galleries) and
frescos.

tion of a number of storage floors over the 5, 10 residential floor, the partitioning-off of chambers next to the porte-cochère at ground level, and the construction of multi-storeyed buildings in the courtyard which also had to accommodate vehicles and stables and afford storage space for provisions. Patrician houses of this kind were provided with extensive vaulted cellars for the storage of wine and beer, a circumstance frequently connected with the privilege of a brewing and liquor retailing concession. The ground floor, too, was primarily used for commercial purposes. Here, either indoors or under a projecting arcade, goods were placed on display and incoming or outgoing deliveries checked, while business transactions were concluded in the counting-house. The living quarters of the master of the house and his family were generally situated on the first floor, or *bel étage*, where the need felt by the bourgeoisie for imposing interiors first manifested itself in grand saloons that filled the whole width of the house, state rooms, guest-chambers and oriel windows. The army of servants, on the other hand, was accommodated in closets on the ground floor, under stairways, in the attic or else in the courtyard. The patriciate's love of display is at its most apparent on the side facing the street or market place. Here, by contrast with the courtyard side, the sheer richness of the architectural decoration stands revealed as a token of wealth and culture and as the expression of rivalry between patrons, whether between those of equal standing or those still striving for recognition. Their notions of rank and station are plainly evident from the decoration, whether sculptures, carvings or frescos. Doorways take on the appearance of triumphal arches. Here we have not merely embellishment but a clear symbolism that permeates many of the individual motifs. For all their feeling for tradition and sense of personal

worth, their adaptation of feudal or existing stylistic forms betrays, not only a desire for equality, but also a striving after cosmopolitanism and contemporaneity. How nearly the tastes of the patrician patrons coincided in this respect with those of their aristocratic counterparts is demonstrated in a particularly illuminating fashion by the evolution of the palazzo and the villa in Italy, as well as the Baroque urban palace.

The wealth of the patrons, their pragmatic approach and their desire for greater comfort were also largely responsible for the fact that the patrician house was the first beneficiary of technical innovation, better construction and materials, and improved domestic amenities.

However, it should further be noted that, for the big patrician merchant in particular, a house also represented an object of speculation and a sound capital investment. This was borne out by the frequent changes in ownership and the growing practice of buying numbers of houses, either for resale at a profit or for rent, though it was not, of course, customary for a patrician to admit tenants to his own private house. Before the apartment house evolved as a distinct type at the end of the Middle Ages (e.g. the "terrace" houses and the warehouse-cum-tenement of the Baltic region, and the lodging-houses in Munich) the numerous unpropertied members of the lower strata usually found shelter in the cramped houses of the middle and lower middle classes.

In contrast with the patrician house, the artisan's house was, as a type, a much more modest affair. However, in the matter of architectural lavishness, it varied enormously, and as such reflected the considerable differences within the guilds and between the masters. The home of a rich master may well have vied with many a patrician mansion, but most of these houses (which do not admit of rigid

23

classification and will therefore simply be referred to as middle or lower middle class) betray neither the will nor the ability of their owners to compete with the patrician houses in any of the foregoing respects. They constituted the majority of the houses in a town, were situated in narrow side streets and winding alleyways away from the few, wide main thoroughfares and tended to be grouped according to trade. In central and southern Europe, on the other hand, it was not unusual for slums to grow up in the heart of a town. The houses of the lower middle class were lower (one or two storeys) and narrower (between three and six metres) than the houses of the patricians. For what was involved here was not so much the storage of vast quantities of merchandise as the manufacture by specific groups of articles for sale and for day to day requirements. The work of the various tradesmen obviously called for very different solutions to the disposition of space. Weavers, tailors and goldsmiths, for example, worked indoors, while the rougher, dirtier occupations were necessarily pursued in the courtyard or outbuildings. Again, dyers and tanners needed a ready supply of water. (Initially the ranges of houses were divided by open passageways which led to the buildings, courtyards, wells and privies at the back and also acted as drains to carry away the water from roofs and interiors). But all in all the differences were very slight. The two- or three-celled type predominated with a workshop at the front of the ground floor. This meant that goods could be exhibited and sold next to the street. Livingroom and kitchen were generally on the courtyard side, but might also be above the workshop. Lodgers were frequently accommodated in such houses where, in place of grand portals and entrance halls, a modest doorway led into the front room. Such architectural decoration as existed—chiefly in buildings of timber frame construction—was frequently of an earthy, popular nature not found in the more pretentious style of the patriciate. Later, too, use was made of new techniques and materials that were conducive to greater comfort. However the craftsmen did seek to emulate the pomp of the patricians by giving expression to their pride through the medium of the communal buildings of their guilds, which were also situated in the centre of the town—a sign that they had no intention whatever of treading humbly as inferior citizens.

As the discussion above suggests, the majority of the lesser traders, small craftsmen (including also artists) and other householders whose livelihood depended on manual work or the services they rendered, showed a tendency, dictated by their way of life and social status, towards a reduction in architectural scale. In many centres, where powerful guilds contended successfully with the patriciate, as well as in manufacturing towns, the existence of lavish artisans' houses testifies to a situation which transcends all forms of classification.

Numerous small and medium-sized towns owed their appearance exclusively to the presence of these middle class and lower middle class buildings. Until well into the sixteenth century, many of the big cities of today, such as Munich, for example, or Stuttgart, consisted largely of "artless" urban farmsteads. But, as may be seen from the large number of examples in the plates that follow, the fascination and charm of these houses is no less great and their power of expression no less original than those of their grandiose rivals which overshadowed them.

7

34

33

Early Configurations in the Romanesque Era

In the Romanesque period we encounter the first mature stylistic epoch of medieval art in Europe. Its patrons belonged almost exclusively to the spiritual and the temporal aristocracy. Thus it was not by chance that Romanesque found its purest embodiment in ecclesiastical and monastic architecture. The Church provided the most favourable material preconditions and also gave expression, in a society still in a state of ferment, to concepts of an immutable, divinely ordered scheme of things. A markedly monumental world view permeates the massive religious buildings with their many towers in which block is placed on block to form a lucid, coherent whole. Built in stone, they seem to be constructed for all eternity. With the coming of Late Romanesque the comparative lack of ornamentation gave way to rich articulation and colonnades which, by eliminating the walls, lent animation to the exterior surfaces. Friezes of infinite variety, imaginatively designed capitals, lavishly sculpted doorways and, finally, interior wall paintings also contributed to an architectural decoration that was filled with profound symbolic meaning. From Spain to Russia, from Italy to England, national idioms came into being which were further enriched by the idiosyncratic building methods of the new monastic orders. However, the tendencies towards rigorous organization and monumentality, which determined the style of religious architecture, exerted little influence on secular buildings in the feudal era. These tendencies cannot be seen in the castles of this period, although they are faintly discernible in the growing towns and in the middle class houses of the time. For the most part, these towns still continued to grow amorphously. There was no progress made in communal organization until houses began to be built close together along what were often tortuous streets and alleyways, and not, as before, in haphazard fashion. In the northern latitudes houses were usually "gable-fronted", with the ridge at right angles to the street; in the South, most were "eaves-fronted" with the ridge parallel to the street. The vast majority were built of daub and wattle and roofed with straw, rushes or shingles, which thus betrayed their rural origins. The absence of surviving examples is largely attributable to the impermanent nature of the building materials and to the many fires that ravaged the towns. Nevertheless, if we speak of the middle class town house of the Romanesque era, this is because the twelfth century saw the emergence, in a few centres of industry and trade, of a small upper class, or patriciate that already possessed the wealth and confidence to build houses of stone and brick which also incorporated some of the structural and decorative elements of aristocratic architecture. In the town these decorative elements were everywhere in evidence, in the shape of churches, convents and the private strongholds of feudal lords and ministerials. True, towards the end of this phase and in the wake of urban emancipation, the citizens themselves had already begun to build large churches and town halls. Thus, the incidence of vaults and columns, windows with semi-circular heads, decorated capitals, friezes and other Romanesque forms of ornamentation must be seen, not simply as extraneous borrowings, but rather as adoptions from the monumental architecture predominant at the time. In the Latin countries, where the ruins of Greek and Roman towns were frequently used as quarries, building in stone was commoner than in other parts of Europe.

In the late twelfth and early thirteenth centuries courtly and chivalrous culture was in its heyday and was to exert some influence on the style of life of the patriciate. Though the patriciate's domestic arrangements were still fairly primitive—they continued to live and sleep (without undressing) in one sparsely furnished room—conditions in the houses of wealthier citizens were already improving. Their walls were decked with tapestries, the inclusion of fire-places meant that more than one room was habitable, and people even began to enjoy the luxury of small glass windows.

Less has survived from this early and interesting stylistic period than from any other, which is why the ensuing chapter, devoted to examples of stone buildings, must of necessity be short.

The First Employment of Stone

Prague was accounted one of the most important medieval cities and was, indeed, described as an international trading place by the Arab traveller, Ibrahim Ibn Jakub, as early as 965 A.D. The Prague market settlement grew up at one of Czechoslovakia's earliest settlements whose history goes back to the Stone Age. Situated in what was later to be the Old Town, it possessed stone houses as far back as the ninth century. Its early prosperity was due to the ford in the Vltava valley where important trade routes crossed the river. A market town existed under the protection of the two Slavic castles, Hradčany and Vyšehrad. With the rise of the state of Bohemia from the tenth century onwards, this settlement attained considerable proportions and, by the end of the twelfth century, Prague boasted numerous colonies of foreign merchants, as well as noble households, churches and a stone bridge.

. Here, in the second half of the twelfth century, there arose, on the ground now occupied by the market square and its adjoining alleyways, the Old Town with its many one- and two-storeyed houses with their varying ground plans. Up to now systematic archaeological research has uncovered the remains of no

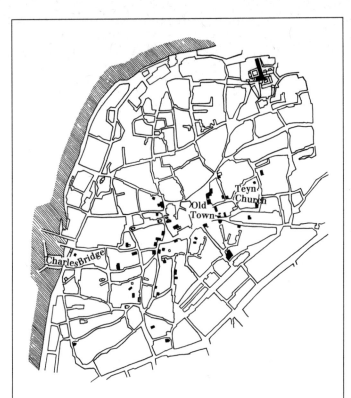

PRAGUE. *Old Town.*

Plan showing the position of Romanesque dwelling-houses (from V. Mencl.

fewer than seventy Romanesque stone houses. A schematic plan enables us to see at a glance their location on the main streets and squares, many of which evolved from the ancient highways and their points of intersection. A considerable part of the Romanesque fabric has been preserved up to ground floor level, because what had previously been ground floor rooms had been converted in the thirteenth and fourteenth centuries into the undercrofts of surviving Gothic, Renaissance and Baroque houses. Repeated floods had forced the inhabitants to raise the ground level of the town by two to four metres. In the Romanesque era Prague, like other European cities, had plenty of space within the precinct and thus the configuration of the town was determined by the random erection of individual detached houses, mostly of wood, along narrow, winding streets and alleyways. Streets with compact ranges of buildings were rare and were at the outset usually some four and a half metres wide, in accordance with what was known as the *Stangenrecht*, or "yard-measure law". Most houses had a ground floor and first floor. Very few had undercrofts or additional upper storeys. The surviving stone houses of merchants and traders have two rooms on the ground floor. A well-known example of this type of ground plan is found in the Old Town House in Prague 2 (No. 16/I), which has a barrel-vaulted unheated room and a larger, cross-vaulted room with a fireplace. In the rooms on the ground floor, stone window embrasures sometimes served as seats. The upper floors were reached either by a timber stair inside the principal room or by an outside stair.

Like Prague, Cologne was an important centre of trade in the Middle Ages. A Roman colonial town as early as A.D. 50 and archiepiscopal see since Carolingian times, it soon came to be the principal city of Germany. It was one of the first to be surrounded by a fortified stone wall, built in the tenth century; a hundred years later, and despite the failure of a popular uprising in 1074, its citizens were able to extort a number of privileges from their powerful rulers. In the Late Romanesque era it had thirty thousand inhabitants and was thus the most populous city in Germany and one of the great cities of Europe. It owed its strength to its highly specialized industry and its extensive foreign trade. Because of this it soon became the inland administrative centre of the Hanseatic League. Largely owing to the havoc wrought by the Second World War, only a few of the numerous houses built of stone by a self-confident patriciate have remained intact, among them the so-called Overstolzen- *3* haus, the finest of all, which dates back to the year 1225. Peculiar to this, as to many other buildings in Cologne, is the position it occupies between the North and South German types of house. On the street side of the high ground floor the house had a wide, hall-like forebuilding on top of which was a low mezzanine with small windows. Above this again rose a high, multi-storeyed stepped gable with several flights of windows in an exceedingly rich composition of applied decoration. It is no accident that the imposing effect of the latter should recall the patrician buildings of the Hansa in North Germany, while the adoption of many Late Renaissance decorative elements—e.g. wall paintings, some actually depicting jousting scenes—, the introduction of a great banqueting hall on the first floor and the use of highly durable dressed stone, inevitably invites comparison with noble residences. The appointments, however, tended to be simple in the extreme, since more importance was attached to amassing stocks of silver an linen; walls were commonly whitewashed and adorned with tapestries only on feast-days.

This fully evolved type of middle class town house, as exemplified in the Overstolzenhaus,

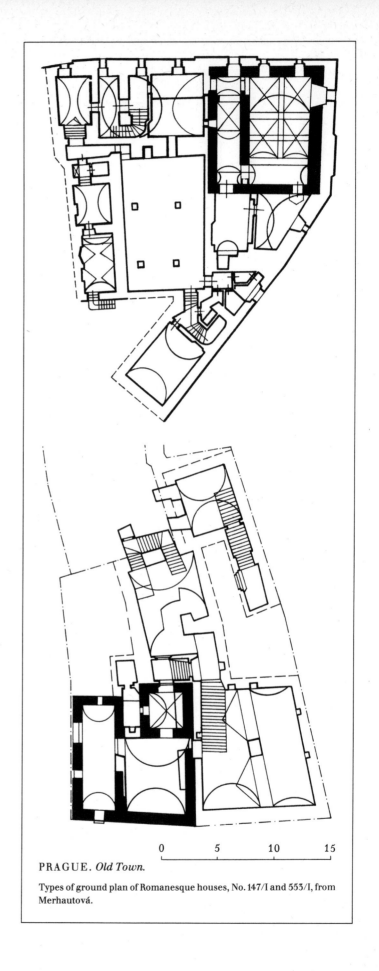

PRAGUE. *Old Town.*

Types of ground plan of Romanesque houses, No. 147/I and 553/I, from Merhautová.

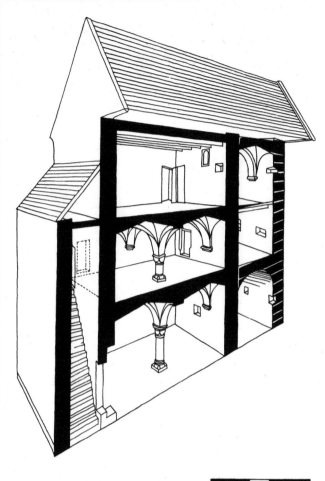

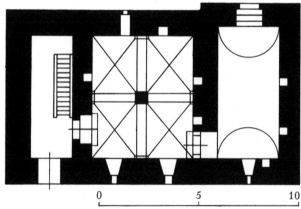

PRAGUE. *Old Town, New Town Hall, house C., No. 16/I (Ill. 2).*

Isometric reconstruction, from Mencl, and ground plan from Merhautová.

cannot be compared fruitfully with North and South German examples of the same date. And whereas the former is indicative of a long, independent process of development, certain of the Romanesque *Kemenaten* or King John type houses, such as those in Lower Saxony, are reversions to one type of feudal private stronghold. The *Kemenate* beside the Grosse Heilige Kreuz in Goslar is an instance of the adoption of the stone chamber with hearth previously found in castles. At a time when fortified and domestic buildings were still often constructed of timber, these chambers served to protect valuables as well as human lives against fire. Though later on they were sometimes an integral part of the main house, most were free-standing, two-storeyed, cellared buildings of rubble construction with small windows and tiled roofs. An external wooden stair led to the upper floor, which was rather less shut off from the outside in that it had a two or three-bayed gallery of round-headed arches supported by twin columns. As a rule there was only one room to each storey, their ceilings consisting of oak beams and a layer of sand and daub or plaster. However there was little scope for variation in the disposition of the rooms and, with the appearance, within the protective walls of the city; of other types of stone-built private houses, the role of the *Kemenate* in urban architecture came to an end.

Again, few examples of Romanesque architecture have come down to us from the early period of urban growth in France where, allied to the monarchy, towns developed at a great pace. As early as 1200 Paris could, by contemporary standards, be deemed a metropolis. In no other country is domestic architecture so illustrative of this phase in which the middle class town house evolved in all its essentials. These were narrow, gable-fronted houses of one, two or, in the bigger centres, even three

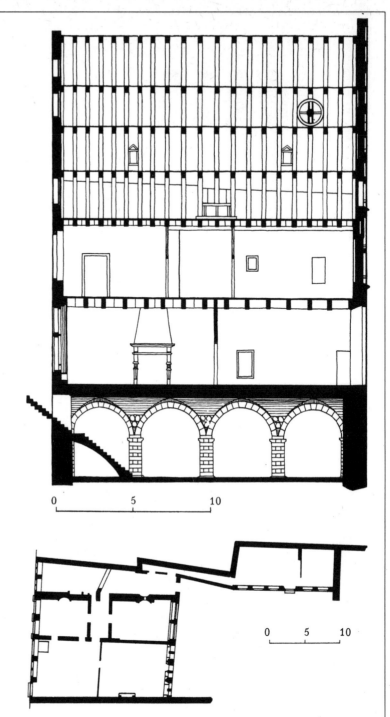

COLOGNE. *Haus zur Rheingassen or Haus zur Scheuer,*
No. 8, Rheingasse (now an exhibition building for the museums
of Cologne). Built between 1225 and 1230 for the patrician,
Werner Overstolz. Rebuilt after its destruction in the Second
World War (Ill. 3).

The patron, Overstolz, was the head of an international trading family,
which had made its way into the class of large property owners. The
front, measuring 14.5 metres across, consists of two storeys each of five
bays and a wide stepped gable of four storeys. The sub-structure
displays more opulent forms than does the gable, the most prominent
being the pairs of lofty two-light windows on the upper floor, with
unarticulated circular openings, encompassing trefoil arches and
delicate capitals, formerly gilded; within the splays are slender corner
and central columns of grey-blue slate. The wealth of forms of the
imposing and stately façade in the so-called Rhenish transitional style
are borrowed from the buildings of the feudal aristocracy, as is the
arrangement of the principal rooms, including the grand state-room
on the upper floor. The architecture of the interior, with its blind
arches, corresponds to the church architecture of the city.

COLOGNE. *Haus zur Rheingassen. View and plan of the*
ground floor (after H. Vogts).

Sale room, on the left the counting-house, ante-room and kitchen. On
the courtyard side, a grand living-room with window embrasures. On
the street side of the upper floor the large state-room, with bedchambers at the back. The section shows the basement, a room of two aisles,
with round arched barrel vaults and an arcade of four freestone piers;
also an adjoining barrel-vaulted room containing the well.

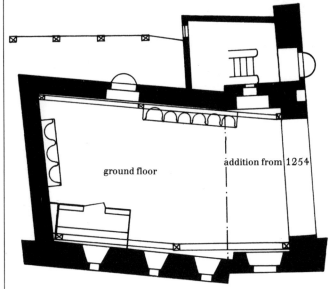

ground floor

addition from 1254

GOSLAR. *Elevation and ground plan of the Kemenate (King John type house) in the Grosses Heiliges Kreuz. From H. G. Griep, circa 1225.*

Rectangular massive stone building consisting of cellar, ground and upper floors with hearth, each consisting of one room. Window openings with sandstone surrounds. In the fourteenth century the building, a borrowing from castle architecture and originally designed for the preservation of life and property, was combined with living-quarters by the addition of a wing in the form of a timber-framed hall-house with kitchen below and parlour above.

storeys, built of timber, stone or brick, with a courtyard and, in many cases, a cellar. The ground floor, usually spacious, contained not only the workplace, but also a living-room, kitchen, dining-room and guest chamber. Above were smaller living-rooms and bedrooms giving on to an open gallery or corridor. Authentic examples of twelfth century Romanesque town houses that belonged to merchants and craftsmen may still be found in, among 8 other places, Périgueux, Saint-Gilles and Cluny. The town of Cluny owes its existence to the foundation in 910 of the Benedictine Abbey which, shortly afterwards, was to produce the influential Cluniac Order and its innovative ideas of architecture. While these innovations were mainly concentrated on the Abbey Church (which was rebuilt for the third time, starting in 1088), they also effected the building of houses near-by. When, in the last century, the French architect, Viollet-le-Duc, was investigating the architectural school of Cluny, he listed a number of Romanesque houses, most of which had been built after the fire of 1159. These two-storeyed houses already had cellars. On the ground floor there was usually a large, arched doorway leading into the main room which served as a shop, workshop or storehouse. Next to this entrance was a stair leading to the sleeping and living quarters on the upper floor. An arcade in the courtyard led from the house to the kitchen, above which there was a heated bedchamber. Some of the Romanesque houses in Cluny had two upper storeys. Indeed several narrow-fronted houses were originally built in a row and formed a compact group. The openings on the upper floor took the form of columned arcades. In the museum at Cluny there is a console depicting a shoemaker talking to a customer while seated at a counter, formed by the lowered shutter of his shop. This method of conducting day-to-day business, whereby goods were sold through the artisan's or tradesman's window, went back to Carolingian times and persisted until the use of the market was made compulsory. To facilitate official supervision it was even laid down that the merchant's counter or the artisan's workshop should give on to the street so that sales might be made through the ground floor windows. For this reason houses were built immediately abutting on the street or square. When the weather permitted, the artisan would ply his trade on the part of the street outside the house.

Despite the remarkably early development of towns in Italy, notably in the North, the birth-place of the first city republics in Europe, the middle class town house did not engender as many independent architectural types. In the towns of the old Roman Empire repopulation took place slowly. For a long time the relationship between the now urbanized aristocracy and the people remained that of lords and vassals. The rise of the towns, however, did not go hand in hand with the rise of an especially strong middle class; rather their trade with the East created a small class of patrician merchants who, with the help of their humbler neighbours, were soon powerful enough to challenge the feudal lords from the private strongholds they occupied within the walls of many of these towns. True, the craftsman was also increasing his output, but this could be of little importance unless he also had recourse to out-workers or manufactories, in which case the enterprise soon came under the control of the patricians. Moreover, it was not long before the patricians allied themselves with their erstwhile opponents, thus forming a new aristocracy of middle class origin.

The *casa* of these great patrician families, or *gentes*, did not long remain a house within the commune of burghers, or at any rate men of similar stamp, as it did, say, north of the

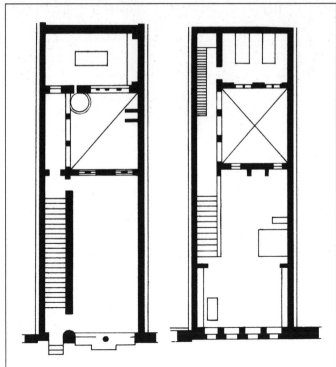

CLUNY. *Merchant's house, second half of the twelfth century (Ill. 8).*

Plan of the ground and upper floors (redrawn after Viollet-le-Duc, 1863).

PARIS. *Panoramic view, copper engraving from Johannes Janssonius, "Illustriorum Regni Galliae civitatum tabulae", Amsterdam, 1657.*

As a town, Paris has grown organically and by fits and starts. Its nucleus was the largest of its islands, in the middle of the Seine, the Île de la Cité, at the junction of the old North-South trade routes, which was already a walled settlement in Celtic times. In 987 it became the capital of the kingdom of France and is said to have had 100,000 inhabitants as early as the eleventh century. It grew, as it were, concentrically on either bank of the Seine and, in the thirteenth century, covered an area of 283 hectares, identifiable on the plan by the inner ring of fortifications. In about 1370, when the population had grown to 280,000, the northern ring wall, seen here on the left, was built; it ran between the Louvre, the Porte St Denis and the Bastille and was to determine the size of the town for the next three hundred years.

Alps, rapidly developed into a defensive palazzo; a change due, not so much to the threat posed by their remaining feudal opponents, as to the struggle for ascendancy between one clan or city and another, and the necessity of keeping the lower classes at bay. Nor did the resulting buildings differ materially from the urban strongholds of the nobility. In the examples we cite of thirteenth century buildings in Viterbo and Bologna, which illustrate the start of this process, a considerable measure of restraint is still discernible, but it is already qualified by a tendency towards the monumental. Apart from this, however, they also bear witness to a national idiom rooted in tradition and climate and determined by a lucid view of space and substance. Thus on aesthetic, no less than on climatic grounds, the high-pitched roof is not used. The houses stand sideways on to the street, their marked flatness and horizontality punctuated only by small windows designed to keep out the heat, ranges of windows set high up and—though these did not come until a somewhat later date—loggias and airy balconies affording shade. Only with the Quattrocento was the patrician mansion embellished with monumental Renaissance ornamentation which was combined with an altogether new approach to the articulation of space. The special developments in Venice will be discussed in the chapter on Gothic.

Compared with the large houses of the *gentes*, each in its own grounds, the undifferentiated mass of small traders' dwellings is of little architectural relevance. Wealthier, non-patrician citizens copied the palazzo on a smaller scale. In Florence the dwellings of the common people were known as *laboreria* or "ground-level houses". Generally speaking, the simplicity of their functional design echoes that of small town houses north of the Alps. They were low, with one or two storeys, while the lay-out of their rooms hardly varied at all.

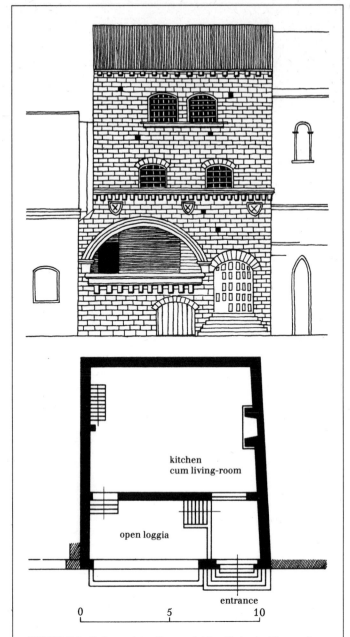

VITERBO. *Palace of the Alessandri family in the Piazza San Pellegrino, thirteenth century.*

Elevation (after Camesasca), and plan (reconstructed from Veltheim-Lottum). A sober Italian patrician house of the early period with a raised cellar and large, arched loggia on the ground storey, which was also used as a storeroom. Two halls on each of the upper floors.

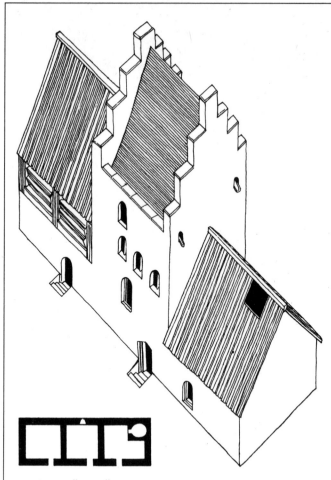

STORA HÄSTNÄS *near Visby. Dwelling-house (Ill. 9).*

Reconstruction of view and plan by Iwar Anderson. All that survives is
the central part of the building which has been altered.

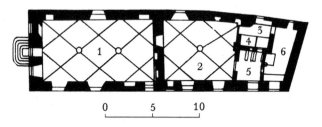

VISBY. *Gamla Apoteket, No. 36, Strandgatan (Ill. 10).*

Plan of the ground floor (from Lundberg). 1. Great dining-room,
2. Small dining-room, 3. Service passage, 4. Privies, 5. Vestibule,
6. Kitchen.

The shop or workshop was invariably situated
on the ground floor (in many cases, too, goods
were manufactured or sold in the street, under
the shelter of a small projecting roof). Alongside or behind the shop or workshop lay the
storehouse. On the upper floor, besides one
or more bed chambers, which also accommodated apprentices and servants, there was
a larger living-room where the cooking was
done and meals were taken. As a rule, warmth
was provided by a hearth. Social standing
depended among other things upon the number of fire-hearths.

Other centres of early urban development
were Flanders and Brabant. Here the cloth
trade (also with its outworker system) and
international commerce had given rise in
towns such as Ghent, Bruges, Brussels and
Tournai, to communes as large as those in
Italy which possessed ample funds for building middle class town houses. These took their
cue from the "hall-house" of Northwest Europe
with its tall, handsome gable and roomy hall.
In the case of these patrician patrons, however,
the building material was no longer timber
but stone or brick. Tournai, which had already
acquired importance as the Merovingian capital and had been politically autonomous since
1187, was exceptionally well-situated in this
respect. For here, hard but easily worked
bluestone had been available as a building
material since Roman times and was, indeed,
used for the three-storeyed, Romanesque,
double-fronted house. The influence of vernacular architecture is particularly in evidence in the horizontal string courses in the
region of the windows, which recall the rails
found in timber-framed gables. In individual
carved features, such as the basket capitals of
the slender columns between the lights, we
may discern a connection with noble residences in the same locality—for instance, the
archiepiscopal palace. The facade of a con-

6

temporaneous house in the Borluutstraat in *11* Ghent is of similar construction save that here, for the first time, we find the stepped gable which, from the thirteenth century onwards, was to play a role of paramount importance on houses throughout large areas of northern Europe.

Since the tenth century Gotland had been the most important nodal point of Baltic trade and the centre of the Gotland Association, one of the German merchants' Hansas. Before the founding of the Hanseatic League, its capital, Visby, had come to be one of Europe's wealthiest centres of trade and culture. It had its own school of architecture and sculpture which executed important sculptural works and church furnishings, some of them for export to the countries of western Europe. As early as the thirteenth century, houses in Gotland were being built of limestone and sandstone, and in Visby alone the existence of *9* some hundred and seventy-five thirteenth and fourteenth century stone houses has been authenticated. A typical two- or three-storeyed, galleried house, most of which would be devoted to storing goods, would have projecting from its lateral wall a narrow forebuilding consisting of a vaulted passageway or corridor on the ground floor and, on the first, a gallery with two-light windows, the two floors being linked by a staircase. This feature, the vaulted passage, was widely used in the domestic architecture of feudal times, from the ninth to the thirteenth century. Moreover, some connection with the *Kemenaten*, or King John type houses, and the so-called *Steinwerke*, or "stone works", of Lower Saxony might also be posited in view of the strong economic and cultural ties that existed between the two areas at this time.

The vernacular tradition and, in particular, the galleried house, set its mark on the type of house then prevalent in Gotland. This was

LINCOLN. *Jew's House, No. 15, The Strait, circa 1170/80. Reconstructed view and ground plan from M. Wood.*

An eaves-fronted house of rubble and dressed stone construction, probably built by a well-to-do Jewish merchant. On the ground floor are a store and sales room, while the upper storey, which was open to the rafters, consisted of a large living hall with hearth. The string courses still recall timber framing. In due course the lofty hall with its hearth was to become the focal point of the household and to become a typical feature of the English middle class town house.

divided into three sections, first, a central structure that had a cellar, a ground floor with passageway, and a first floor with gallery, each consisting of a single room and the whole surmounted by a storage loft; secondly, the principal living-room (left), with a hearth, stove and separate entrance and, thirdly, a wing (right) whose purpose has yet to be ascertained.

Here separate provision was already being made for various domestic functions, a process that will be discussed in detail in the next chapter.

For the time being we shall do no more than touch on it in connection with the Gamla Apoteket, one of Visby's most imposing secular *10* stone buildings which dates back to the middle of the thirteenth century. With its stepped gable, this five-storeyed patrician house would seem to derive from the galleried house, a type more widely distributed in rural areas, and from the "hall-house" of the Baltic coast; the tall, narrow structure has an almost defensive air, reminiscent of a tower.

Towards the end of the thirteenth century Lübeck was gaining pre-eminence in the Hansa and, with the conquest of Gotland by the Danes in the years 1360–61, Visby's career as a centre of commerce finally came to an end.

In England, following the Norman conquest in 1066, the towns allied themselves with their new rulers and became, on the basis of a substantial output of goods (especially in the wool trade), a power to be reckoned with.

Yet virtually nothing has survived to indicate what the middle class town houses (which were for the most part timber-framed) were like at this time.

They were either single-storeyed, with one large and one small room or else two-storeyed, in which case the upper floor would be canti-levered. The shop or workshop, as the case might be, was on street level here. The Jew's House in Lincoln (second half of the twelfth century) is one of the few stone, middle class houses of that date to have survived in England, a country whose insular position to a high degree favoured the search for independent solutions.

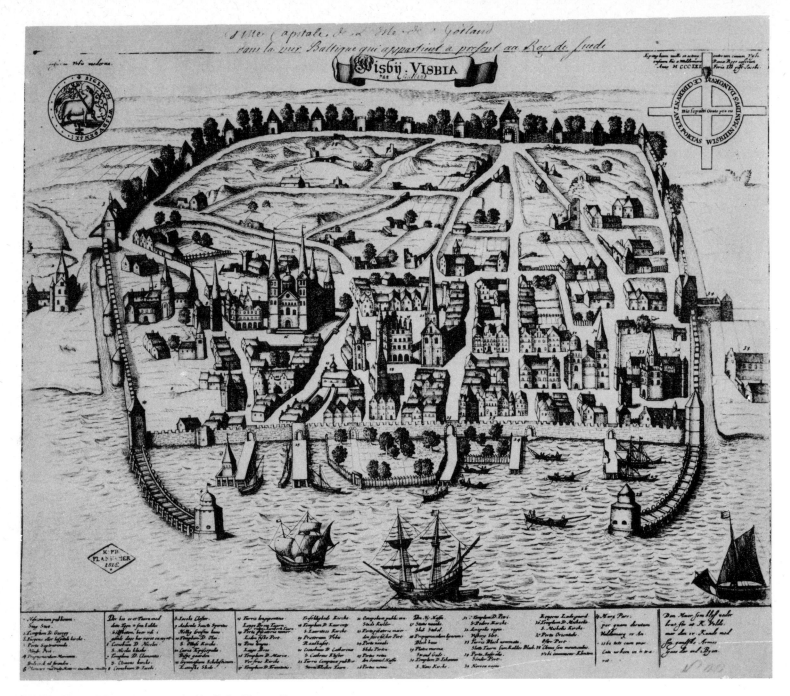

VISBY. *View of the town, engraving by Peder Hansen Resen
from the "Atlas Danicus", Copenhagen, 1677.*

This document came into being several hundred years after the heyday
of Gotland's trading metropolis, the ample precinct of which
accommodated up to 20,000 inhabitants. The stock of buildings dating
from the thirteenth and fourteenth centuries has survived almost
unaltered, as has the empty waste land, which was left undeveloped
for several centuries after the destruction of Visby by King Waldemar IV
of Denmark. Not until the latter part of the nineteenth century did the
number of inhabitants again pass the seven thousand mark, and it was
only recently that its population reached the same figure as in the
Middle Ages.

An Outline of Gothic Types

Throughout large areas of Europe the Gothic era, which lasted for some two hundred and fifty years from the beginning of the thirteenth to the end of the fifteenth century, more or less coincides with the rise of the towns.

The productive forces, now largely freed from feudal tutelage, proceeded to expand in unexpected ways, thanks to increased specialization in manufacturing, numerous inventions and a commodity economy. Within the town walls the stratification of society began to take on a set pattern. Out of the general melting pot there arose an ideology of rationalism, of a realistic world view enhanced by subjectivity, and symbolic of the growing self-confidence of the urban middle classes. True, medieval concepts of a terrestrial hierarchy—which corresponded to the celestial hierarchy—had not yet been left behind; rather they were being subverted by new ideas about the rights of man and the secularization of religion. The result of this development was the onset, towards the end of the period, of a social and ideological crisis of vast dimensions, a crisis that might be described as the early middle class revolution. The peasants rose against their feudal lords; in the towns the craft guilds' struggle for supremacy against the patriciate tended increasingly to take the form of a social struggle by the plebeian masses; the heretical movement against the institutionalized church finally led to the victory of the Reformation. With the dawn of the Renaissance and of Humanism, Gothic and the Middle Ages came to an end.

Until then, however, the bourgeoisie had felt Gothic to be their medium of expression. Having originally evolved in the field of religious architecture, where the style may be seen in its purest form, it was quickly adopted by the towns which in turn supplied it with many fresh stimuli. The forms of German Late Gothic are the clearest possible proof of its specifically middle class provenance. Elsewhere, too, many national variants may be observed, though it should be borne in mind that in Italy, especially, a burgeoning national consciousness and the influence of the legacy left by Antiquity never really permitted Gothic to be absorbed into the vernacular.

Whereas nothing now remains to show what a town of the Romanesque period looked like, Gothic has for centuries dictated the skyline of a large number of towns. In the typically upward thrust of that skyline, with its multiplicity of towers and spires, the increasing vitality of the inhabitants found expression. Nowhere is this more apparent than in the city churches, which still remained the noblest of all architectural undertakings. Never before had towers and spires attained such heights, although they were built at a cost that often exceeded the real resources of a town. After the collapse in 1573 of the cathedral tower at Beauvais (up till then the highest steeple in Europe at 153 metres), Strasbourg Cathedral held the record with 142 metres until displaced by Ulm Cathedral, whose spire (161 metres) was completed in 1890 in accordance with the original plans. With their air of filigree weightlessness, their structural features such as the rib and the pointed arch, their infinite variety of decorative elements—tracery, pinnacles, canopies, crockets and architectural sculpture—these churches with their spires crowned by a cross bear miraculous witness to what was now possible in the field of construction.

In the case of important communal buildings such as town halls and guild halls, towers and rich decoration were introduced as evidence of the prosperity and the power of the towns and corporations. Less attention and money went to other types of contemporary buildings such as schools, universities, hospitals, warehouses, mills and the like. In the most vital field of communal activity during

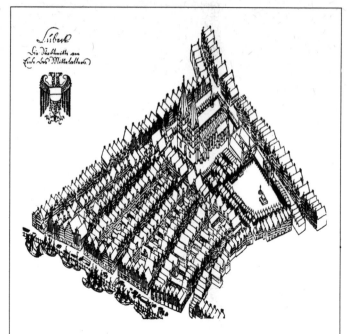

LÜBECK. *Bird's eye view of the centre of the town towards the end of the Middle Ages. Reconstruction after K. Gruber.*

The principal town of the Hanseatic League, situated on a lancet-shaped island between Trave and Wackenitz, Lübeck was laid out to a regular plan as early as 1143, the time of its founding. Shortly afterwards the merchants (whose precedence over artisans was absolute) were allocated plots of a specific size, and this circumstance, combined with building regulations and the persistence of the basic type of brick gable-fronted house, accounts for the homogeneous appearance assumed by the city in the Gothic era. Our reconstruction shows only the market place and town centre immediately to the south of it. Behind the middle class town houses are cramped courtyards, for the most part bordered by single-storeyed, eaves-fronted houses—an early variant of the later social division between the occupants of front houses and back houses.

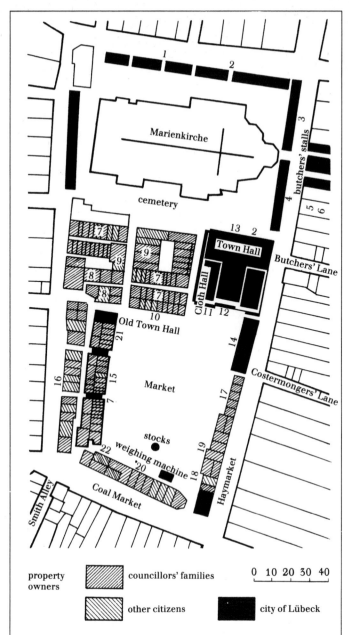

LÜBECK. *Market Place at the beginning of the fourteenth century (from Roerig/Steinmetz).*

1. Gardeners, 2. Bakers, 3. Skinners, 4. Tailors, cutters, 5. Minters, 6. Herringmongers, 7. Cobblers, 8. Small shopkeepers, 9. Spicers, 10. Money changers, 11. Woollen drapers, 12. Pin makers, 13. Cooked meat vendors, 14. Goldsmiths, 15. Hatters, 16. Old stalls, 17. Chandlers, 18. Armourers, 19. Saddlers, 20. Smiths, 21. Tanners, 22. Harness makers.

A typical example of a market area, planned and organized along socio-economic lines, in a strictly administered patrician town of the Gothic era, where market regulations and marketing constraints were already being imposed on a variety of trades purveying articles of everyday use. In the market place proper are the stalls, shops and low, cramped houses of some 250 local artisans and retailers, grouped together according to trade in small areas resembling courtyards.

those strife-ridden days, namely the fortification of the towns—an occupation that virtually monopolized the labour power of entire generations—the municipal love of display found expression in the ornamentation of gate houses. For two centuries the secular architecture of the aristocracy, which was largely confined to the enlargement of castles, became less exciting and less innovative than the architecture of the middle class. The rich vocabulary of the Gothic style and its structural innovations were chiefly realized in large communal buildings. The lesser place allotted to the individual in the community and the rigid division of classes meant that the private middle class town house was relegated to a comparatively subordinate position. Indeed, the desire for order felt by these stabilized communities with their corporate spheres of interest created a new urban structure that tended towards order and unity. New towns were laid out according to an orderly plan that showed the precise location both of public buildings and of the streets and districts specifically reserved for different trades. The plots were all of equal size. In Lübeck, for example, they measured 25 ft by 100 ft and, in Freiburg in Breisgau, 50 ft by 100 ft. Similar measures had already been taken in the past in isolated cases, but the practice now became general and was also extended to older towns which had suffered fire or destruction. Henceforth the streets would be lined with compact rows of houses in accordance with a clearly defined social topography dictated by expediency and the claims of inidvidual social groups. The plans of Lübeck illustrated here give a good impression of this clear and mature inner-urban structure. One source, writing of Lübeck in 1533, shows how receptive people were to the new quality of orderliness displayed by the Gothic town. "And since the splendour of its houses contributes greatly to the fame of a town," he tells us, "it may be said of Lübeck that it consists wholly of stone houses whose gables soar upwards like towers, and so orderly and symmetrical is the manner of its building that it would seem as if the houses had all been constructed at the same time in accordance with one harmonious plan." The drawings clearly indicate how closely the individual citizen's existence was bound up with the community and its social groupings. The contrast between the tall, spacious houses of the patricians and the low, narrow dwellings of the artisans—not to mention the one-storeyed hovels (not visible in the picture) that stood in the rear of houses and were occupied by the lowliest castes—plainly testify to the town's social hierarchy. Nevertheless the overriding impression conveyed by our aerial photograph of the well preserved centre of Nördlingen, a former Imperial Free City, is *13* one of organic, architectural harmony, innocent as yet of the planner's drawing-board. True, there were numerous regulations at that time concerning precautions against fire —spacing, shape of roof, siting of buildings, the use of stone—which, while they did not impose uniformity, were conducive to a measure of similarity amongst middle class town houses. Typically, the streets are more or less tortuous, a fact not solely attributable to economic or military necessity or, for that matter, to incompetence; rather it would seem to have been partly the result of the artistic desire to create an animated effect.

Finally, Gothic middle class town architecture as such affords the most convincing proof of the dialectic of multiplicity in unity. Only now did these types whose origins we discussed in a previous chapter, find expression in all their rich variety. Indeed, so sound were the fundamental principles that, despite later stylistic changes, construction and spatial organization remained virtually unaltered.

Houses were for the most part no longer built of wood or clay with a straw, reed or shingle roof. Instead they were stone or timber frame constructions and roofed with tiles or slates. Stone, which was expensive, was first used only by the well-to-do. In the South, rubble and dressed stone predominated, while in the large central belt the art of timber frame building was entering its finest phase. In the North, however, the preeminent building material was brick in a wealth of forms that was never again to be attained.

Gothic stylistic principles were, of course, adopted in the middle class town house, though with certain limitations. In private buildings intended for business and domestic purposes there was no room for major structural features such as massive vaults, towers and diaphanous walls. At most, cellar, ground floor and porte-cochère were vaulted—a practice later extended to other areas for purposes of decorative display—while towers were largely confined to civic buildings. But in the northern part of central Europe many of the houses have a towerlike air. This is especially true of the tall, narrow buildings whose precipitous façades culminate in pinnacled gables. The outside walls never disappeared, in spite of the fact that the number and the size of windows in regular rows increased, thanks to a more general use of glass. And henceforth a large part of the wall surface was masked by applied embellishment in the Gothic style. In the widespread and varied use it made of Gothic decorative elements, the middle class town house was a true child of its time. Those elements also made their way into the interior of the house and its furnishings. Out of early medieval simplicity there grew a new, intimate, if not gracious, style of living, a subject which we shall discuss at the end of this chapter.

The Gable-Fronted Hall-House
of the Hansa

The Hanseatic patrician house is probably the most characteristic manifestation of Gothic domestic architecture. Here we find a consistent type, the gable-fronted hall-house in which marked verticality and rich architectural decoration are combined with the forms peculiar to North German brick Gothic. Its sphere of influence extends as far as did the commercial operations of that most powerful of all medieval civic alliances between cities, the *Hansa Teutonica.*

The Hansa was originally no more than a federation formed by German merchants for mutual assistance and for protection against the hazards of foreign trade. The Hanseatic League grew in stages. Strengthened by alliances between merchants and cities, and by the foundation of trading settlements, it was a loose but enduring federation of some two hundred towns by the fourteenth century. Its settlements ranged from London to Bergen and Novgorod and its member towns lay not only along the northern coasts of the Low Countries and the Baltic, but also in the heart of Europe. Its power was based mainly on its monopoly of the entrepôt trade in articles for mass consumption—wool, cloth, furs, herrings, grain, minerals, salt—between the Northeast and Southwest of Europe. However, the protection of its commercial interests, and the consequent need to command the waters of the North Sea and the Baltic, soon turned it into a politico-military force as well as one with which even monarchs had to reckon. In the fifteenth century its position began to deteriorate as a result of competition from rivals, the growing strength of neighbouring countries and, in the towns themselves, strife between the patriciate and the lower classes, but not until the sixteenth century did its decline become inevitable.

Lübeck owed its ascendancy over the other Hanseatic towns to the important position it had gained as an intermediary between East and West in the Hansa's trade. The forming of economic, cultural and legal ties between the Hanse towns of the Baltic led to the rapid and widespread adoption throughout that area of the gable-fronted type of house whose basic characteristics—high pitched roof, gable-end facing over the street, hall, storage lofts in the roof-space, and accommodation within the house for trade and industry—were taken over virtually unchanged. Between the thirteenth and fifteenth centuries, however, certain regional peculiarities in the design of the house (principally different forms of gable) were to reach Visby, Riga, Tallinn and Dorpat by way of the trade routes.

The design of the Lübeck house was essentially that of the West European hall type house, which originally consisted of only one principal room on the ground floor, namely the lofty, spacious hall. This was where people lived and carried on their business (the merchant's counting-house, the craftsman's workshop or store). Here, too, was the only fireplace, a hearth which was a source of light as well as heat. The posts at the centre and at the sides of the hall supported the floor beams of the storage lofts above. A trap-door in the floor above the hall enabled goods to be conveyed from the cellar to the various storage lofts by means of a hoist mounted in the top floor.

From the mid-thirteenth century onwards Lübeck wholesalers began to build houses whose gabled fronts and external walls were executed in brick. The fact that those merchants were now stationary—a trend which had begun in 1300 or thereabouts—influenced the disposition of rooms on the ground floor. In 1350 Johann Wittenborg, a merchant of

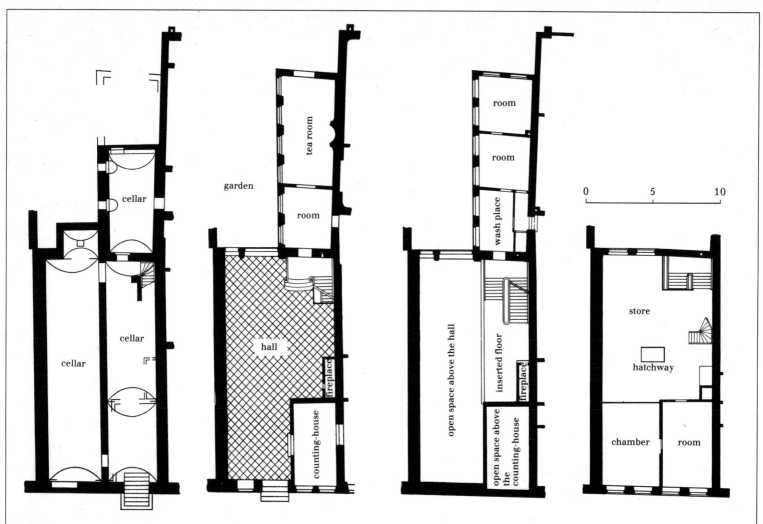

cellar

cellar

cellar

garden

tea room

room

hall

counting-house

fireplace

room

room

wash place

open space above the hall

inserted floor

open space above the counting-house

fireplace

0   5   10

store

hatchway

chamber

room

LÜBECK. *Merchant's house, No. 50, Mengstrasse, plans of the basement, ground, mezzanine and upper storeys (from H. Hübler).*

Taken together, the plans of the different storeys in a Hanseatic patrician house show that the type already possessed a number of rooms serving specialized functions. The barrel-vaulted basement rooms, accessible either from the street or from the hall, emphasize the depth and narrowness of the site. Above them rises the usual lofty hall, with windows both on the courtyard and the street side. This already has a partitioned-off counting-house, as well as a fireplace and, at the upper end, a stair next to which there is also an entrance to the rooms in the courtyard wing. The area of the mezzanine floor (upper end, right) is only a third of that of the hall and counting-house, both of which elsewhere rise to their full height. Here, in place of the inserted or suspended floor, there might also have been typical "suspended chambers" for the servants. However, access could also be had from the inserted floor to the small low rooms (including the wash place) in the courtyard wing. Above the hall, with its four windows giving on to the street and two on to the courtyard, is the first of the storage floors, though here there are still two rooms on the street side. Through the hatchway in this upper storey merchandise could be drawn up by a hoist directly from the hall into the lofts above, which might also be reached by a stair.

The development of the gable in the North German Gothic middle class town house from the the thirteenth to the fifteenth century, from P. Suhr.

Left, triangular gable (with steps at ridge and eaves, and small columns and pinnacles); centre, stepped gable (with crenellations); right, pilastered gable.

Lübeck, reports that he has a *skrive-kamere* (a writing-chamber, office, or counting-house) in which to conduct his correspondence. On the courtyard side buildings were erected for domestic purposes, sometimes to house servants, and later on to serve as banqueting halls, guest-chambers and warehouses. The hall was on average five metres high and in some Lübeck houses, after the turn of the century, so-called "hanging chambers" were inserted to accommodate the servants at night. Suspended from the ceiling beams on the street side of the house, or attached to the lateral walls, these chambers could be reached by a corner stair at the back of the hall and thence by a gallery. This type of mezzanine floor was not an unusual feature even as late as the eighteenth century.

From the fifteenth century onwards many of the Gothic gable-fronted houses received an addition in the shape of a *Dörnse*, or parlour, a ground-floor room next to the entrance, heated by a stove. The problem of introducing more light into the front rooms of the hall and the mezzanine floor was solved by piercing the gable front with a number of large windows. Another approach to the organization of the façade was the articulation of both gables—on both the street and the courtyard side—by means of superimposed vertical panels framing the regular rows of apertures which enabled air and light to penetrate into the storage lofts in the roof space. The fact that Lübeck was an emporium for large quantities of dried cod from Norway, herrings from Schonen, grain from central Europe, cloth from Flanders and England, furs from Russia, and copper and iron from Sweden, necessitated a great deal of storage space. This demand was met by the vast lofts beneath the high-pitched roofs. The resulting expanse of gable offered ample opportunity for rich ornamentation. Inspired by the decorated gable ends of churches, monasteries and town halls, the Gothic style of embellishment displayed an increasing tendency to animate external surfaces with relievo features, and to disguise the straight verges with stepped and pilastered gables (until their complete obliteration in the shaped gable). Our illustration, showing the progressive development of the gable from the thirteenth to the fifteenth century, amply demonstrates the inherent logic and fertile inventiveness of that style. To the wealth of forms the charm of brickwork was added which, from the thirteenth century onwards, had begun to take the place of timber framing in the flat lands of the North Sea and Baltic coasts, at least so far as patrician domestic architecture was concerned. Though fired brick was first used in the middle class town houses of northern Italy, it was only in northerly countries that it came into full flower as an artistically treated building material. In that region, it was the Romanesque churches, monasteries and castles which pointed the way to the art of brickwork, particularly the use of ornamental cut brick and the exploitation of the contrast between dark red brickwork and light expanses of plaster. But the flat surface had not been transcended. Not until the Gothic era, and with the introduction of brickwork of French and Flemish origin did craftsmen, employing a highly developed cut brick technique, venture to break up surfaces with strong relief work and the free application of decorative compositions. Plastered panels were added to the grid of large bricks that was typical of monastic architecture, and vitreous bricks ranging in colour from dark green to dark brown and black were used to offset the overall contrast of red and white.

About the middle of the fourteenth century builders first began to enhance the show gable of patrician houses with this wealth of ornamentation.

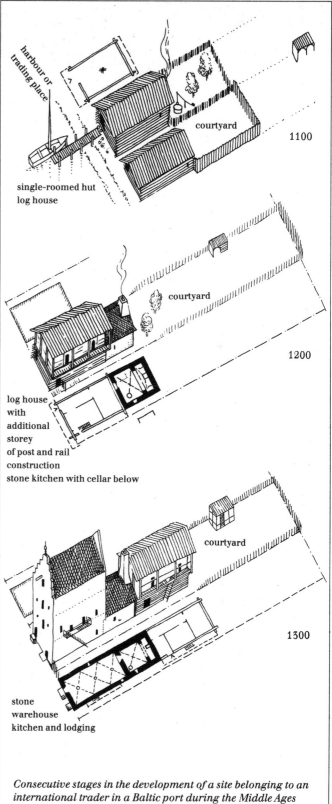

Consecutive stages in the development of a site belonging to an international trader in a Baltic port during the Middle Ages (from H. G. Griep).

The drawings show typical forms of construction from the twelfth to the seventeenth centuries and, by inference, the steadily growing prosperity of the owners.

46

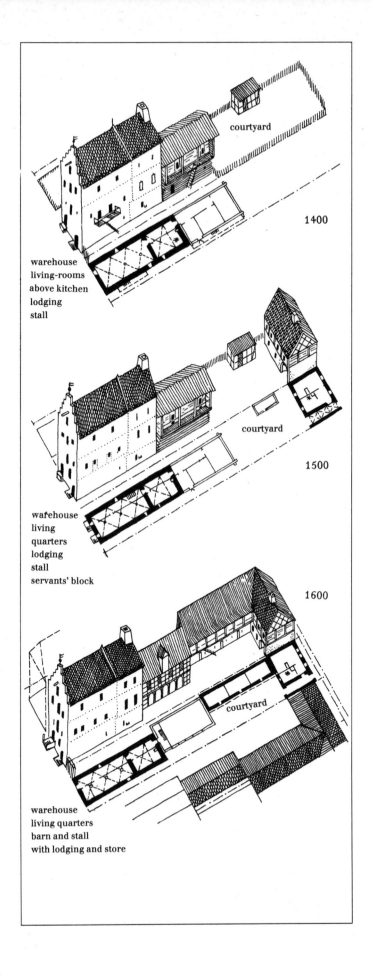

courtyard

1400

warehouse
living-rooms
above kitchen
lodging
stall

courtyard

1500

warehouse
living
quarters
lodging
stall
servants' block

1600

courtyard

warehouse
living quarters
barn and stall
with lodging and store

It was not long before this type of Hanseatic merchant's house spread to other Baltic cities, some of which had been recently founded in the course of expansion to the East. These houses, the first private buildings there not to be constucted of timber, were on average eight to ten metres wide, and the oldest of them, the *12* Alter Schwede, built in about 1380 in the nearby town of Wismar, already shows all the characteristics of brick Gothic in its developed form. Vicke Schorler's "True and Faithful Counterfeit" (see frontispiece), dating from the sixteenth century, testifies to the diversity and architectural cohesiveness of a Gothic centre of commerce such as the Hanseatic headquarters of the Wendish Group, Rostock, which, in the thirteenth century, had grown out of three towns and could boast the oldest university in northern Europe (1419). The flat timber-framed buildings of the artisans and lower middle class are here clearly distinguishable from the lofty patrician houses with their stepped gables. Nor, for some centuries, were the latter to depart radically from their original form, and so the streets present a relatively homogeneous appearance. Houses of similar design were also built in Stralsund which, together with Lübeck, was to become one of the leading ports in the Baltic in the fourteenth century. How long this style persisted may be seen from the patrician gable- *1* fronted houses in the Old Market Place in Stralsund. The illustration shows not only the Gothic Wulflamhaus, but also the Baroque variant of the gable-fronted house.

In the Baltic region the growing need for living accommodation (and also for separate rooms) gave rise in the fourteenth century to a special kind of building, the warehouse-cum-dwelling. One of the finest examples of *19* this type may be seen in the market place of the Hanseatic town of Greifswald. Here the ground floor has been kept relatively low.

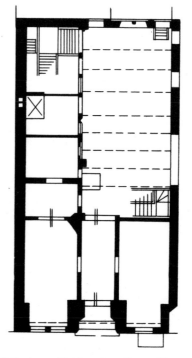

ROSTOCK. *Brick house, No. 40, Wokrenter Strasse, section and plan (reconstruction of the building in its original condition, after Ohle/Lorenz).*

The plan and disposition of rooms is typical. The façade of the stepped gable, largely articulated by means of three bays, is given a rhythmically enhanced verticality by the crenellation and the slender pointed blind arches. The lofty ground storey comprises only the hall which initially extended over the whole width of the house, but was later considerably reduced in size by the introduction of three rooms at the front and as many again at the sides. Roughly at the centre of the house there was a hatchway on each floor, from the hall and/or cellar to the last loft but one, for the conveyance of merchandise. The weight of the internal timber structure with its close-set joists rests on the outside walls and on the braced centre post, which rises from the cellar to the roof of the hall. Only the hall has a fire-proof plaster floor. On the courtyard side it is lit by a large, oblong window known as a *Lucht*, a borrowing from local vernacular architecture.

Preceding page

1 STRALSUND. *Bertram-Wulflam House in the Old Market Place.*

Number 5, house of the Burgomaster Bertram Wulflam. The magnificent Gothic pilastered gable, dating from the second half of the fourteenth century (sub-structure altered in 1927/28; the fifteenth century gable-fronted house on its left has been remodelled in the Baroque style). These are typical patrician houses with the following characteristics: vertical development, thereby permitting several storeys for the storage of merchandise; centrally placed doorways; a choice site in the market place; symmetrical treatment of the façade; sumptuous architectural decoration in the contemporary manner; expensive, durable building materials (in this case brick).

2 PRAGUE. *Chamber on the ground floor of house C, No. 16/I (now the basement of the New Town Hall in the Old Town), circa 1160.*

Vestibule with steps, rooms with ribbed and barrel vaulting. In all probability the house belonged to a well-to-do merchant. This room, heated by a fireplace and with a roof of powerful ribbed vaulting, probably served as accommodation. The massive proportions of the chamber, like the fine finish of the central column with its cubical capital, are a response to demands of a more exacting nature. Vaulted chambers in the residences of noblemen and ministerials would merely have been larger and had several columns or pillars.

3 COLOGNE. *House at No. 8, Zur Rheingassen (Overstolzenhaus)*

Remains of wall-painting, depicting jousting scenes, in an arched recess in the chamber on the ground floor, executed after 1337 when the house was acquired by Everhard Hardefust and combined with the building next door. A rare example of early secular wall-painting which is clearly derived from feudal antecedents. Jousting was the prerogative of knights; the legal validity of single combat was not recognized by the bourgeoisie as an expression of "divine judgment". In a patrician house chivalrous motifs such as these clearly demonstrate the dependence, at this early period, of the citizen upon the culture of the Court.

2

3

4 TORUŃ. *House where Copernicus was born (ul. M. Kopernika 17), fifteenth century, restored in 1972/73.*

The lofty gable of this very narrow house and hall called for a steeply pitched roof. Nevertheless the composition of the late fifteenth century façade decorated with rich tracery work achieves an exceptionally well-balanced effect, thanks to the horizontal articulation of the storeys by means of ornamental friezes and string courses.
On the courtyard side, the building originally terminated in another steep gable enriched with blank pointed arches.

5 LÜBECK. *Houses in the Mengstrasse.*

All three houses have the typical stepped gable; the building at the centre also has blank pointed arches of which the rhythm corresponds to the bays and the steps of the gable. Each places the accent on imposing symmetry, and in each the first string course above the hall-storey provides an indication of the latter's considerable height (approximately 5 metres), though the hall of the central house has already been divided into two floors. The hall-storey of the house on the left, number 27, is fenestrated from floor to ceiling. This treatment already betokens the Renaissance, as does the terracotta frieze produced in the workshop of Master Statius of Düren and consisting of portrait medallions and antique motifs (circa 1550–1570).

4

5

6 TOURNAI. *Twin Romanesque houses at Nos. 10–12, Rue Barre St Brice, circa 1175 (front restored after wartime damage), ground floor largely altered.*

The clear articulation by means of triangular gables and string courses—a derivative of timber framing—characterizes the early period of the Flemish patrician house. The idiosyncratic fenestration with relieving arches above lintels supported by slender shafts became the Tournai type of window. The ground storey of each house formerly contained a hall-like room (either store or workshop) with a wide opening onto the street.

7 CANTERBURY. *Weavers' cottages in the High Street (circa 1500).*

Two-storeyed timber-framed house with typically projecting upper floor and gable (ground storey altered). Characteristics of these artisans' houses are: modest height, workshop on the ground storey and living quarters on the first floor (the space above was little used); situated in side streets; employment of traditional, inexpensive timber frame construction; little architectural decoration, marked similarity between the houses and timeless functional character.

6

8 CLUNY. *Romanesque middle class town house, No. 25, Rue de la République. Second half of the twelfth century.*

In this two-storeyed building there is a rigid demarcation between the business sphere (ground floor) and the domestic sphere (upper floor, with access via a separate door). Architectural embellishment is confined to the relatively small area surrounding the first floor windows, which have twin lights with very finely executed ornamental bands, the whole being surmounted by a round arched frieze. The decoration is restrained and, especially in the forms of the capitals, betrays the enduring influence of the local mason's lodge. In other more southerly, French towns, Italo-Lombardic influences may also be discerned (e.g. in St. Gilles-du-Gard).

9 STORA HÄSTNÄS. *House near Visby. This form predominated during the thirteenth and early fourteenth century and reveals the influence of the "gallery house", a type which took shape in Gotland. The ruins of one of these houses, thought to date from the twelfth or thirteenth century, may be seen near Bringes, Norrlanda.*

It is now believed that the function of the "gallery house" was not primarily domestic. On the Scandinavian mainland, however, it persisted until quite recently in a form in which the ground storey was used as a warehouse, while the upper floor was reserved for sleeping quarters.

8

9

10 VISBY. *Gamla Apoteket, No. 36, Strand-gatan, mid-thirteenth century.*

Most of these tall towerlike structures built of local limestone are to be found in the Strandgatan, with their gabled main fronts facing towards the harbour. The type was certainly not reserved solely for use as a counting-house and store, as the hoist openings at the centre of each floor give reason to suppose, but was also the merchant's home, a fact borne out by the window architraves and privies on the first floor.

11 GHENT. *Borluut House, circa 1175 (ground storey altered).*

Four-storeyed house with markedly horizontal articulation. This is the first instance of the corbie-stepped gable, but as yet it has not really come into its own. Later it was to be typical of the vertical thrust of the Gothic gabled house.

10

11

12 WISMAR. *Alter Schwede, Nos. 20 and 21, Market Place, circa 1380, restored in 1971.*

The oldest dwelling-house in this Hanseatic town. The front, measuring 12.5 metres, is divided into a relatively low hall-storey and a pilastered gable of three steps after the manner of the old warehouse-cum-dwelling-house. What strikes one is the rich use of vitrified moulded brick in the canopies above the windows and the polygonal pilasters and in the broad ornamental frieze above the main doorway. The warm red of the brick, the chalky white of the plaster in the upper, blank windows, and the shiny dark green of the lead-glazed brick together produce an harmonious polychrome composition typical of the Gothic patrician house.

13 NÖRDLINGEN. *Aerial photograph of a well-preserved medieval town.*

The majority of the houses and the city wall with its eighteen towers date from the period between the fourteenth and sixteenth centuries, when the town, with its cloth and allied trades (linen and woollen weaving, dyeing and finishing) was in its heyday.

13

14 TALLINN *(Reval). No. 17, Vene Street, now the municipal museum, fifteenth century.*

Nothing is left of the former patrician house save in part of the façade on the right-hand side of the long, low corner building which at one time was undoubtedly crowned by a gable. The imposing, deeply recessed doorway of receding "orders"—a rarity in Tallinn—the numerous, lofty windows in the hall and the use of limestone masonry throughout are witnesses to the prosperity of the patron.

15 HILDESHEIM. *Tempelhaus, in the Market Place, owned by the patrician family von Harlessem, built in 1457 and the oriel added in 1591.*

The high pitched roof is totally concealed by the towering, aggressively ostentatious, rubble façade. The proportions of its articulation by means of two- and three-light windows are borrowed from timber frame construction. The asymmetrically placed dressed stone oriel, on the other hand—an architectural detail frequently met with in the North German type of house— displays a rich Renaissance decoration of the kind found in other oriels and façades after 1580, when Hildesheim entered a new period of prosperity.

16 TALLINN. *Merchants' houses, Die Drei Schwestern (Three Sisters), No. 71, Pikk Street, fifteenth century. (The long side of the first house and the gables of both the houses beyond it have been altered.)*

The hall and ground floor served as living accommodation. The upper floors were used as store-rooms into which light and air could penetrate through apertures in the wall, the one immediately beneath the ridge being equipped with a beam and pulley for hoisting merchandise. Save for the pointed arches, and the articulation by means of sparingly applied decoration, Gothic stylistic features are hardly in evidence. From this, as from the less steeply pitched gables and the borders of dressed stone round the door, it is evident that what we have here is a regional variant of the Hanseatic type of house.

17 RIGA. *A group of houses, Die Drei Brüder (Three Brothers), Nos. 17, 19/21 and 23, Mazā-Pils- iela. The house on the right, No. 17, is fifteenth century, the gabled houses next to it are seventeenth century, partly reconstructed, and betray the influence of the Netherlands and North Germany.*

The Late Gothic stepped gable of the earliest house is decorated with recessed pointed arch panels. In later buildings this basic form of gable is retained with only slight Baroque modifications in the shape of a more animated outline and a lessening of vertical emphasis. These houses were primarily homes and, by reason of the symmetry of their composition, appear more grandiose than does the Gothic house with small apertures for ventilation purposes and the main entrance placed on one side. Here, as in Tallinn, the highly complex architectural decoration of Late Gothic has been applied far more sparingly than in Hanseatic towns less remote from the centre. Nor is brick used to such striking effect.

18 RIGA. *Hall in the earliest of the Drei Brüder houses (No. 17, Mazā-Pils-iela). Reconstructed in 1955 by the architect F. Saulitisa.*

An impression of spaciousness is created in this imposing hall by the massive beams, the open hearth and the position of the stairway at the upper end. Near the fireplace is an alcove seat in which the brickwork, elsewhere largely hidden under plaster and whitewash, is exposed to view.

18

19 GREIFSWALD. *Patrician house, No. 11, Platz der Freundschaft, early fifteenth century, restored in 1855/56 and 1957.*

After the end of the thirteenth century Greifswald became one of the leading Hanseatic towns of the Wendish Quarter. That the patron of this house was a well-to-do wholesale merchant may be deduced from the opulent decoration of this building with its very long frontage, and from its prominent site in the former market place. The magnificent show façade conceals an earlier two-storeyed, timber-framed building and is characteristic of the type of warehouse-cum-dwelling. A noteworthy feature is the gable articulated by means of eight pilasters. Almost unequalled in its alternation of colours and wealth of ornamental detail, it betrays the influence of Hinrich Brunsberg. The projecting shafts terminating in small turrets are embellished with inlaid traceried rosettes and canopied niches framed by narrow strips of alternating red and dark green vitrified brick. They flank seven no less elaborate window surrounds with traceried rosettes under blank arches spanning both lights and adorned with crockets. All the features consist, or are composed, of specially moulded bricks. What was an initially clear vertical thrust is interrupted by a profusion of picturesque decoration marking both the culmination and the decline of North German Late Gothic brick architecture.

20 LÜNEBURG. *Ensemble of gabled houses Am Sande. The third house from the left, No. 53, dates from the beginning of the fifteenth century (altered in the sixteenth century), the second from the left was built in 1500.*

So strongly have the nineteenth and twentieth centuries impinged upon this range of gable-fronted houses that the Late Gothic gables seem almost intrusive. The organic, crafts nature of the brickwork and the marked relief of the applied pilasters testify to building techniques and theories that differ fundamentally from the drawing-board aesthetics of today.

21 LÜNEBURG. *Gable of No. 46, Am Sande (circa 1500).*

A seven-bayed pilastered gable of alternating vitrified and unvitrified green brick. Above the apertures (subsequently windows) are circular panels. From the top aperture protrudes a beam for hoisting merchandise with, beneath it, the larger openings of the former storage lofts. No. 8, Am Sande possesses a similar gable.

19

20

22 ERFURT. *Zum roten (güldenen) Stern (The Red [Golden] Star), No. 11, Allerheiligenstrasse, probably built in 1459, the date on the oriel. Windows subsequently altered in 1544.*

The highly decorated oriel window on richly moulded corbelling is asymmetrically placed immediately beneath the eaves on the plastered façade of rubble and dressed stone of which it hardly seems to form an organic part. Above and below the window are bands of relief work, the lower of which recalls traceried rosettes.

23 BERNE. *Mayhaus, No. 32, Kesslergasse.*

Here two earlier middle class town houses have been converted into one, the work being carried out in 1515, for a patrician patron, Bartholome May. The ground floor has slightly projecting, bracing members, and ties the house in with the arcade of the neighbouring houses. The landings of the various floors are connected by a spiral stair. The salient feature of what is otherwise a fairly plain, flat, dressed stone façade, with strictly symmetrical two-light windows, is the three-storeyed, asymmetrically placed oriel window. This is echoed on the courtyard side by a stair tower. The polygonal oriel is supported by an Atlas and, with its slender helm roof, rises turret-like above the eaves. The unusual treatment of the interior as a rib-vaulted chamber matches the opulence of the exterior.

23

FRITZLAR. *Market Place with fifteenth and sixteenth century timber-framed buildings.*

In the foreground is the market fountain surmounted by a statue of Roland, the work of Johann Ingebrandt and, at the centre, a former warehouse dating from the end of the fifteenth century. The ground storey has been altered. The market place, surrounded by compact ranges of timber-framed buildings, presents an impressive picture of German middle class architecture. The timber-framed houses are lent particular charm by the wealth of structural members in the walls, the contrast of colours and materials, and the animated plasticity of the projecting upper storeys. In the case of the two buildings on the left, the timber framing of South German provenance is given especial emphasis by the braces which form curvilinear triangles in the panels below the windows—the cusps are reminiscent of pointed arches.

25 TÁBOR. *No. 22, Market Place, built after 1532.*

The Late Gothic decoration applied to the tympanum has lost the characteristically Gothic tendency towards verticality as a result of the ranging of the ogee arches at three horizontally accentuated levels, and this, despite the multitude of small pinnacles. The overwhelming impression is one of a balance between vertical and horizontal forces. What is foreshadowed here is a characteristic typical of Renaissance composition. Nothing more was needed save a change of decorative detail. This gable was the progenitor of numerous Renaissance gables in Tábor.

Following page

26 KUTNÁ HORA. *Stone House (Kamenný dům), now a museum.*

A magnificent Gothic patrician house which, before the days of the Hussites, belonged to the Pöttinger family. Between 1487 and 1515 it was converted in the Late Gothic style by the Court Steward Prokop Kroupa of Chocenice. The sculptural decoration of the gable was executed after 1490 by Master Brikcí. During reconstruction in 1901/02, the original sculptures were transferred to the museum. They portray, amongst other subjects, Adam and Eve, the Virgin and Child under the Tree of Heaven and, above the three windows, the coats of arms of the Czech provinces. On the cornice are the municipal coat of arms and the insignia of the miners' guild, consisting of hammer and mallet. Other details include charming vine-decorated friezes, figures of dogs, and consoles in the form of heads.

27 STEYR. *Bummerlhaus,*
No. 32, Stadtplatz, circa 1490.

The finest Late Gothic middle class
town house in this Upper Austrian
town. Its large oriel, embellished with
a frieze of applied tracery, takes in the
whole front of the house. Together with
the dormer window in the hipped roof,
this goes to make up a structure of
exceptional tectonic animation in
which vertical and horizontal forces
achieve a perfect balance.

28 BUDAPEST. *Nos. 18–20,*
Országház utca.

No. 18 on the left, with a fifteenth
century oriel window, was converted
in the Baroque style at the beginning
of the eighteenth century. When
restored in 1950, however, it was again
given a Gothic front. No. 20 dates from
the end of the fourteenth century, while
the Baroque articulation of the façade
was effected in 1771. The four niches
with pointed arches in the entrance
passage are typical of the period in
which this house was built.

29 BUDAPEST. *Alcove seats in*
the entrance passage of a middle
class town house in the Úri utca.

Alcove seats of this kind occur frequently in Hungarian middle class
town houses (i.e. in Nos. 2 and 9,
Országház, in Nos. 34, 36, 38 and 48,
Úri utca and Nos. 4/5 Dísz tér). The
frequency of their occurrence is
unusual, as is their opulent design.

30 SOPRON. *No. 3, Pozsonyi*
utca, a Gothic middle class town
house with later alterations.

A fortified town on the western border
of Hungary, it was much fought-over
and, after its destruction by King
Ottokar II of Bohemia in the thirteenth
century, was rebuilt by German and
Austrian immigrants. The massive,
two-storeyed, eaves-fronted house,
with its irregular façade dates back to
the same period.

31 MILTENBERG AM MAIN.
Market Place leading up to the Mildenburg, with a picturesque ensemble of middle class timber-framed houses.

The last building in the range of gable-fronted houses, in which the gate-keeper used to live, is linked to No. 185, "Schnatterloch" (centre) by an archway. This was built in about 1530 with a polygonal, two-storeyed oriel and curved saltires in the panels beneath the windows. The living-quarters were originally confined to the first and second floors, the former comprising a large, imposing room; the hall in the basement storey, the cellars and the three lofts were devoted to storage (possibly connected with the salt trade). In this gable-fronted house, with its close, inventively variegated framing, we may discern the increasing tendency in the six-teenth century towards picturesque enrichment and decorative elaboration (using the forms of both the Renais-sance and the Late Middle Ages). The house on the right of the picture, also erected round about 1530, has a flight of windows set close together and long rows of brackets of Hessian prove-nance.

32 QUEDLINBURG. *No. 3, Word. The oldest surviving German timber-framed house. Late fourteenth, early fifteenth century. Stud construction. After being rebuilt in 1974, it was turned into a museum of timber framing and local history.*

As compared with the example in Marburg, the timber frame construction of this house seems a good deal more straightforward (for instance there are few girding beams and no arch and tension braces) and hence more archaic. The comparative paucity of structural elements is attributable to, amongst other things, the more modest requirements of the patron, as well as to the fact that the house is not as high, i.e. the load to be borne by the skeleton is appreciably less. As far as building techniques are concerned, however, the house in Quedlinburg is more advanced than the one in Marburg, in as much as its posts are tenoned into the sill beams, which rest on rubble foundations. Previously the posts rested immediately on the foundations or on console-like projections, when they would, at most, be tied together at the base by sections of rail known as interrupted sills, thus completing the frame. Plainly in evidence is the distortion of the structure due to the aging of the timber in the course of more than five centuries.

33 NAESTVED *(Island of Zealand). Apostel-huset, No. 5, Riddergade, circa 1500.*

This Late Gothic, timber-framed house takes its name from the figures of Christ and the Twelve Apostles carved on the posts at window level. Numerous carvings, together with the herring-bone brick infilling beneath the windows, heighten the decorative effect.

34 CHIPPING CAMPDEN *(Gloucestershire). Artisans' houses, late fourteenth century.*

The view through the arcade reveals, on the opposite side of the street, two plain artisans' houses, each of identical construction, with stone-built ground storey, and oversailing upper storey of simple timber framing. These gable-fronted houses are unornamented and altogether functional buildings. Typical features are the wide windows divided by slender mullions to ensure good lighting within.

33

34

35 BOURGES. *Hôtel de Jacques Cœur, courtyard front with octagonal stair tower.*

The courtyard contains two further towers with spiral stairs, like the one in our picture. They open up the whole complex of two- and three-storeyed buildings within which the problem of the organization of space is brilliantly solved by a system of corridors giving access to the owner's private apartments, the visitors' rooms and the servants' quarters, each of these being separate from the others. There is a large *salon* on each floor of the three-storeyed *corps-de-logis.* The kitchen and base-

court are accommodated on the ground floor. Remarkably enough, the courtyard façade is more richly decorated than the street front.

36 BOURGES. *Hôtel de Jacques Cœur in the Place Jacques Cœur, built between 1443 and 1453 by Jacques Cœur, a wealthy merchant who was Minister of Finance to Charles VII. Restored between 1928 and 1938.*

This building, reminiscent of a château, includes two round towers and part of the old town ramparts, the

result being that the axis of the ground plan of the main block is out of line. Despite its asymmetry, the latter with its magnificent traceried balustrade, is impressively accentuated by means of a three-storeyed, towerlike central pavilion. Behind the large window is a private chapel, as in a noble mansion, its existence is further emphasized by the polygonal bell and stair tower on the left with its opulently decorated heim roof.

37, 38 BOURGES. *Hôtel de Jacques Cœur. Busts in front of blank windows above the main entrance.*

They represent a man servant and a maid servant who, leaning on the window-sill, are watching for the return of their master. In the traceried panels below are allegorical representations of the owner's names, a scallop shell *(coquille Saint-Jacques)* and a heart *(cœur)*. The Late Gothic naturalism of the figures and the trompe-l'œil effect of a door standing ajar are truly remarkable. Egocentric, secular motifs such as these are seldom found in middle class architecture and testify to a high degree of pride on the part of the patron.

39 LEUVEN. *Huis van 't Sestich, No. 69, Naamse Straat, circa 1450.*

The fenestration was altered in the nineteenth century, the upper windows with semi-circular heads, for instance, being new. The two-storeyed brick building belongs to the very widely distributed type of gable-fronted hall-house. A particularly remarkable feature is the balanced and very delicate decorative composition beneath the simple corbie stepped gable. The four, narrow, sword-like panels, terminating in pointed arches, which frame the flights of windows are themselves comprised within a large, slightly recessed, arched panel which forms part of the tympanum of the gable. In the spandrels of varying sizes thus created, circular panels have been inserted which are symmetrically disposed and increase in size as they approach the apex. These circular panels are richly decorated with filigree-like crosses, hexagrams and trefoil. The articulation of the façade, whereby each individual feature has been incorporated harmoniously into the whole, displays a degree of inventiveness and delicacy which enables us to experience Late Gothic architectural decoration in its most consummate form.

37

38

40 *ROBERT CAMPIN (Master of Flémalle), central panel of the Mérode altar piece: "The Annunciation", circa 1428. New York, Metropolitan Museum of Art.*

It is no coincidence that it should be the Netherlands, a centre of early middle class art and industry in Europe, to which we are indebted for our first pictorial records of the middle class style of life. True, this reference to reality could not as yet dispense with religious themes. In no way awed by the Angel of the Annunciation, Mary sits on the foot rest of a long seat, reading a book. An interesting feature is the window with heraldic glass paintings in the upper lights and, below, a system of wooden shutters which open into the room and outer ones, some of them perforated and divided into several flaps, with a massive, inner shutter to close off the whole.

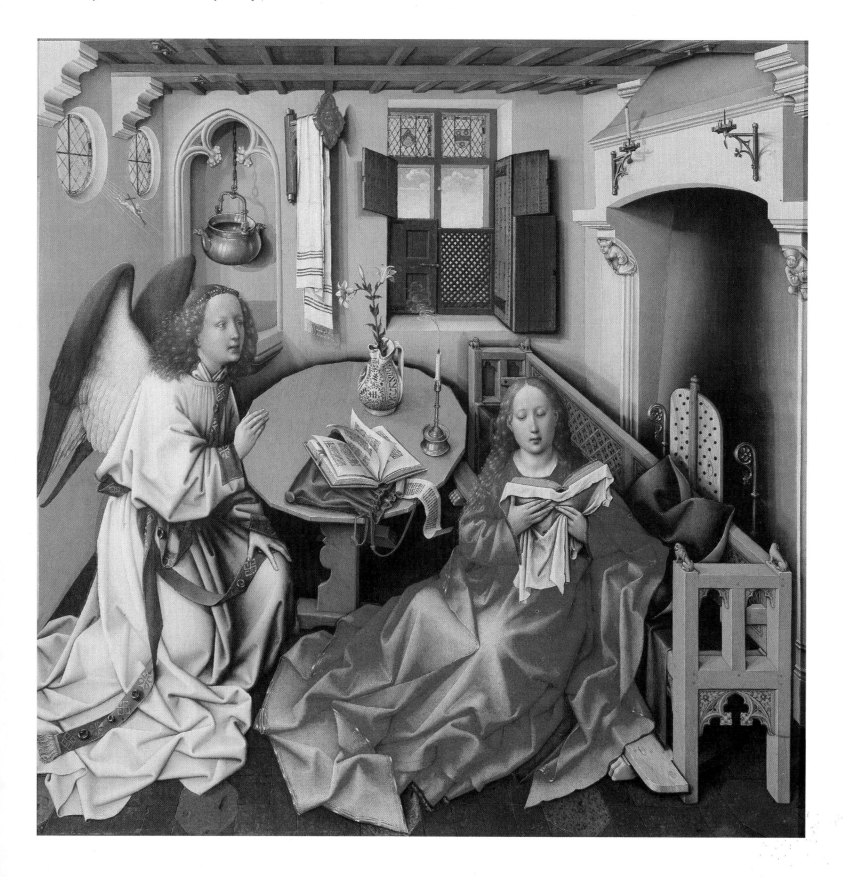

41 CHILDREN'S ROOM IN A MIDDLE CLASS TOWN HOUSE. *Miniature from a fifteenth century Splendor-Solis MS, Nuremberg, Germanisches Nationalmuseum.*

This is a "children's" room in appearance only, for the nursery is not commonly found before the eighteenth century. Prior to this, the same living-room was used by young and old alike. In the daytime the large room in the picture may well have been the sole preserve of the housewife and her usually numerous offspring. It has a deal floor, wainscotted or white-washed walls, and is shielded from the outside by bull's eye window panes; the furnishings consist of a long seat and a large tiled stove. Not only the intimate rendering of the interior, but also the portrayal, for its own sake, of children at play, is indicative of the new middle class feeling for naturalism.

42 NORWICH *(Norfolk). Houses in Tombland Alley, fifteenth and sixteenth century.*

Here, too, timber-framed, close-studded upper floors, which have been almost completely plastered over, project beyond a brick and stone sub-structure. The passage of time has invested these buildings with an animation that is almost organic.

43, 44 NUREMBERG. *Dürer's House. Ground floor hall and Dürer's study dating back to the time of building in the second half of the fifteenth century.*

Thick octagonal wooden posts set in massive bases support the ceiling of the second storey where Dürer had his study and living-room. Because well-proportioned, the Late Gothic room, immortalized by the master in his engraving *St Jerome in his Study*, has a pleasing and comfortable air, despite its size and relative absence of furniture. The stone walls, wooden ceilings and windows with bull's eye panes, accord with one another in their simplicity and distinctive clarity. A similar room in a patrician house would be given over to a display of wealth. Here everything is subordinated to work and translated into a solid, uncluttered functionalism. Meaningful use was also made of the many other rooms in this four-storeyed building. Accommodation had to be provided, not only for the family and domestic servants but also for a business primarily concerned with engraving and wood-cutting, which demanded comprehensive workshops, including rooms for production and for the storage of drawings.

Following page

45 NUREMBERG. *Albrecht Dürer's House (No. 39, Dürerstrasse), second half of the fifteenth century.*

Dormer window added in 1898. The house was acquired by the municipality in 1826 and turned into a museum. After its destruction in the war it was reconstructed in 1949 and refurnished in accordance with its original condition in 1970/71. In June 1509 Dürer bought this dignified, four-storeyed house by the Tiergärtner Tor from the executors of the mathematician, Bernhard Walther, for the price of 275 Rhenish gulden. In the same year he was elected a member of the Greater Town Council. This consolidation of his social standing and the purchase of a larger house were closely linked and lend credence to the assumption that his house must have served as a voucher for his social position. The property, a timber-framed building of a kind typical in Nuremberg, with a two-storeyed stone sub-structure, was sufficiently grand and practical for the purposes of the esteemed master. In 1512 Dürer also acquired from Jakob Bauer a garden outside the Tiergärtner Tor.

43

44

This permitted the building of another storey with living accommodation. Such floors were not—as the description might suggest—merely intended for domestic purposes, but also for the storage of goods. Plainly visible in this Greifswald house which, with its wealth of ornamentation, must be accounted one of the finest examples of brick Gothic in existence, is the influence of one of the most outstanding master builders of his day, Hinrich Brunsberg, a citizen first of Danzig and, subsequently, of Stettin. In the decades preceding and following the turn of the fourteenth century he received commissions from cities in Brandenburg, Mecklenburg and Pomerania for impressive buildings which marked the apogee of Late Gothic brick architecture, characterized as this was by a love of ornamentation. Two buildings attributed to Brunsberg are St Catherine's Church in Brandenburg and the town hall in Tangermünde. Indeed, the fact that master builders' names were beginning to be mentioned in connection with private building is proof that the centuries-old anonymity of the craftsmen was almost a thing of the past.

The Baltic ports of Riga and Reval (Tallinn) which, since the thirteenth century, had been the most northeasterly members of the Hanseatic League, were situated on the Lübeck-Novgorod trade route. Reval's favourable position with a secure, rock-girt harbour giving onto the open sea, attracted Lübeck merchants and craftsmen who settled in the Lower Town. Already under Danish suzerainty since 1238, the city adopted the Statutes of Lübeck ten years later and, from 1346 to 1561, was to be ruled by the Order of Teutonic Knights. The Old City, whose appearance even today is still dictated by buildings erected in the thirteenth, fourteenth and fifteenth centuries, has been subjected since 1975 to a programme of reorganization and reconstruction intended to turn it into an administrative and business centre with many amenities both for gastronomes and for tourists.

The group of gable-fronted houses, Die drei
16 Schwestern (Three Sisters), was erected by wealthy merchants in the fifteenth century. Though certain alterations have been made to the façades, these houses are still characteristically sited with their gable ends facing the street. Built on a long, narrow strip of land, the Tallinn hall-house is basically the same as its Hanseatic counterpart, with hall and hearth on the ground floor, living accommodation on the first and perhaps even the second floor and, above that, storage space beneath a pitched roof covered with red pantiles. After fire had ravaged the town in 1433, builders began to use fireproof materials such as brick and also limestone of which there was an ample supply. Some of the grand houses boast gables adorned with blank niches and many have doorways which are embellished with heavy stone mouldings not customarily found in the Hanseatic towns of North Germany. At one time the doorways gave on to terraces (raised platforms with seats) flanked by *Wangelsteine* or stone slabs. On the courtyard side there would be annexes for servants as well as offices, though by a gradual process of agglomeration, the front and rear blocks (the *Dörnse*, or parlour, being a separate structure) would often merge to form a single domestic complex. The hall extended right across the house with, behind it, the kitchen and a large living-room, the parlour, which could be heated by means of a stove in the cellar or basement. A stair at the back of the hall led to two or three small living-rooms in the upper storey. Some idea of what domestic conditions were like in the house of a Tallinn merchant may be gained
14 from the building at No. 17, Vene Street, which has been turned into a municipal museum. Craftsmen, however, lived and worked in

small simple timber-framed dwellings of a far more modest kind.

In the Late Middle Ages Riga enjoyed considerable importance as a Hanseatic port and commercial centre, and middle class town houses still exist which recall its heyday. The closeness of its ties with the Hanseatic League meant that its architecture was influenced by the art of western and central Europe (particularly that of the Rhineland, Westphalia and Gotland). The group of gable-fronted houses, the *Drei Brüder* (Three Brothers) is the counterpart of the group in Tallinn mentioned above. The fifteenth century Late Gothic house on the right, No. 17, is a typical Hanseatic merchant's house. Its design betrays the rural origins of the hall-house, while the treatment of the façade is reminiscent of that of a patrician residence. The building is set back from the street, for at one time there was a terrace in front of the entrance flanked by stone slabs which have since been restored. Thus the space immediately in front of their houses was used by the middle classes as an extension of their living quarters, while the handicraftsmen could, in fine weather, ply their trade in the street outside their workshops. Here, too, goods were sold, thus facilitating official inspection. Later on, with the decline of Riga's commercial activity, many of the houses were taken over by the landed aristocracy, their storage space being converted into living-rooms. Hence few, if any, remain to show, like the restored hall, how the rooms had originally been disposed.

For a variety of reasons—ethnic, traditional, material and technical—the Northwest European hall-house in the peripheral towns of the Hanseatic League were less grandiose than in those nearer its centre. Largely owing to the havoc wrought by the Second World War, few early examples survive of Danzig's (Gdańsk) once considerable stock of middle class houses

17

which, with their lofty halls, great diversity of rooms and large terraces, marked the transition to a very grandiose type of patrician house. Here the influence of Lübeck may be seen at work, as well as at Thorn (Toruń) where a bourgeoisie of almost exclusively German origin left its stamp upon the Gothic face of the city. In terms of architectural quality the gable-fronted houses of Toruń are in no way inferior to similar buildings in the capital cities of northern Germany, whence the impulse spread as far as the flourishing Polish metropolises of Cracow and Warsaw. Thus the market square in Warsaw's Old Town was originally surrounded by the stone houses of wealthy merchant-princes. These were later replaced by Baroque buildings which, however, retained the long, narrow ground plans. The earlier houses were divided into a front section between twelve and fifteen metres deep, which consisted of the hall, the stair and one or more separate chambers, and a contiguous rear section with a living-room and a through-passage to the yard. The rooms on the ground floor were sometimes vaulted, while many of the upstairs rooms had painted ceilings and walls. In Cracow, the seat of the Polish kings, member of the Hanseatic League since 1430, and one of the most important centres of commerce and industry, the Old Market Place (Rynek Główny) likewise owes its character to similar buildings. Some of these houses may still be seen today. Owing to taxation and building regulations, they were for the most part very narrow and, on the ground floor, sometimes had large vaulted halls. However the traces of Hanseatic influence have largely been overlaid by local idioms. Not every Hanseatic town, however far back its membership went, was to adopt the North German style; virtually all the places further inland, such as Cologne, Münster, Frankfurt-am-Main, Brunswick and Magdeburg, continued to de-

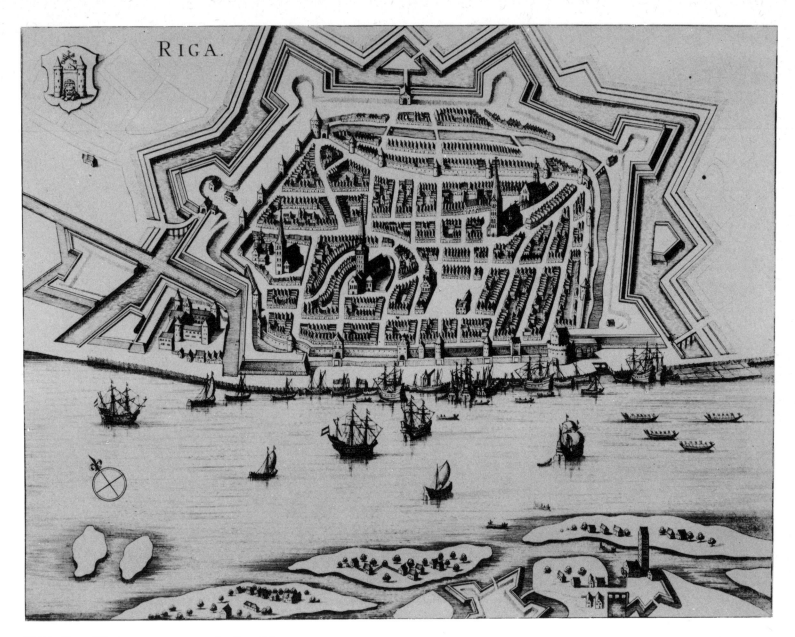

RIGA. *View of the town, copper engraving from Johannes Janssonius, "Illustriorum principiumque urbium septentrionalium Europae tabulae", Amsterdam, 1657.*

Though the town was conquered in 1621 by the Swedish king, Gustavus Adolphus, who surrounded it with mighty Baroque bastions, the medieval precinct with its typical ranges of Hanseatic gable-fronted houses dating back to that time, subsequently remained intact. Even today the city, founded in 1201, retains what is an essentially Gothic structure.

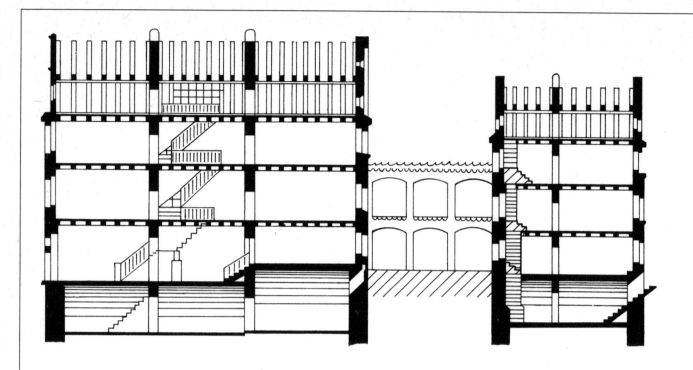

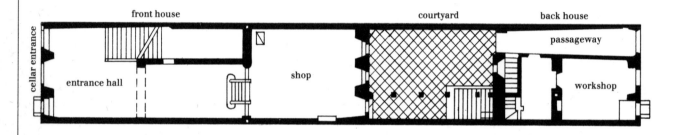

front house   courtyard   back house

cellar entrance

entrance hall   shop   passageway   workshop

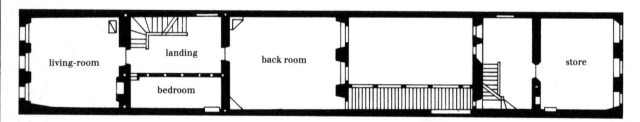

living-room   landing   back room   store

bedroom

POZNAŃ. *Reconstruction of a typical medieval dwelling-house in the Market Place.*

Section of the dwelling-house, courtyard and back premises, plans of the ground floor and first floor, from Henryk Kondziela. The ground floor of this merchant's house comprises a shop on the courtyard side. On the first floor there is a front and back room on either side of the stair. The upper floors at the back of the house were used for storage.

velop their own style of building, a style deeply rooted in tradition. But where assimilation was favoured by the available material (e.g. brick as in Lüneburg), we again find ourselves presented with the ostentatious, richly ornamented façade of the gable-fronted house. Thanks to its rich deposits of salt, that city enjoyed particularly close ties with Lübeck. With its fifty-four saltworks it was, between the fourteenth and sixteenth centuries, a town of importance. Round about 1400 there evolved a type of house peculiar to Lüneburg. A stepped gable surmounted a façade eight to ten metres wide, while the ground floor consisted of a hall used both for business and for domestic purposes. The first floor, three metres in height, rested on a beam supported by two posts. First used as a storehouse, it was also to serve as living quarters from the sixteenth century onwards. Later the hall was subdivided into smaller rooms, while additional blocks were added to the sides or rear of the house. In a number of cases the entrance would be flanked by stone slabs. There are many interesting middle class houses in this well preserved town which largely owes its appearance to the brick buildings of the fourteenth and fifteenth centuries.

The local form of houses in Hildesheim evolved out of the Lower German urban farmstead. Characteristic of this type are a lofty porte-cochère which widens into a hall, on either side a parlour and bedchambers and, on the courtyard side, a kitchen and further rooms. On the mezzanine floor above were rooms for the domestics and, above that again, storage space for goods and provisions. The magnificent patrician house was probably built already between 1320 and 1330, but has undergone numerous alterations in later years. In its heyday, the Hanseatic town had a population of some 12,000, that was in the early fifteenth century. During the Thirty Years' War the town lost more than two hundred of its houses and, during the Second World War, nearly all the timber-framed houses which had won it universal renown. At one time the monumental stone façade of the Tempelhaus, the adjoining timber-framed houses, the Knochenhaueramtshaus (Butchers' Guild House) and the town hall, had gone to make up one of the most beautiful ensembles to be found in any square. However, the flat, unadorned stone façade of the Tempelhaus and the half-timbered buildings with their jettied storeys are so untypical of the brick middle class town house in the Hanseatic towns that their discussion must be left to another chapter.

Organic Stone and Brick Architecture in Central Europe

The year is fifteen hundred or thereabouts. To the sound of fife and drum the colourful spectacle of a tournament unfolds in the market place of a South German town. In his copper engraving, Master MZ (Matthäus Zasinger) has depicted with a naïve delight in narrative detail the stirring sight of a pugnacious group of knights to whom the peaceable town is playing host. Like the burghers on the far side of the square, he would appear to have observed all this from the safe vantage point of the balcony or upper floor window of a South German middle class town house. In clumsy perspective, though again with considerable charm, he portrays such houses in all their rich variety. These buildings are three or four storeys high, with a corresponding number of bays. All have large doorways and shop entrances on the ground floor and small windows in the compact structure above, which, however, is in some cases punctuated by oriels, balconies and loggias. Thus they present a picture that is very different from that of their more northerly neighbours. Here, too, while the houses are tall and narrow and, because of the restricted space within the town walls, crowded together into compact street frontages, they lack the close "family likeness" to be found among the brick and stone gable-fronted hall-houses. They stand alternately end-on, and long side-on to the street, with plaster or "grid-pattern" dressed stone surfaces unrelieved by any system of applied decoration, and were further distinguished one from the other by what appear to be haphazard additions.

Thus the diversity of designs in Master Zasinger's engraving indicates that this is the final phase of the development of the Gothic middle class town house in southern Germany. Its internal construction permitted a number of different structural solutions to the division of space. For example, the houses at either corner, where streets open onto the square, each have a large shop window on two sides of the ground floor, while in between there is a pair of grander houses, one of which has an imposing balcony and the other a kind of loggia. Both have dressed stone façades and large doorways. Commerce would seem to have played little part in the appearance of either. Behind each may be surmised the existence of a stateroom typical of a gentleman's residence, a feature unlikely to be found in the more simple dwellings in the background of the picture. Here, because of the density of the housing, the shop or workshop has to give directly onto the street, as does the passage-way, in some cases resembling a porte-cochère, which leads to the yard. In the houses of more than one storey the ground floor is invariably devoted to the trade of the occupants, while most of the upper storeys are given over to apartments each having a kitchen and several other rooms. Provision for the storage of goods, which manifests itself so impressively in the multi-storeyed gables of the Hanseatic international trader's house, is architecturally far less in evidence here. Both cellar and upper storeys were reached from the single room on the ground floor or from the yard by a spiral or ladder-like stair. The living-rooms situated on the street side on each floor are clearly distinct from the kitchen or "house place" which had also taken over the function of a landing. As the South German town house increased in height, so this stair and landing system came to acquire ever greater importance. Besides the addition of storeys, increasing use was made of the courtyard for the erection of extensions of more than one storey which were in many cases linked to the house by means of galleries or intermediate buildings. These courtyard ranges with their tiers of galleries became a feature of some consequence in the fifteenth, and more especially the sixteenth century, when they assumed the form of arcaded courtyards designed as a unified whole (for example the Pellerhaus in Nuremberg).

87–89

Towards the end of the Middle Ages, the oriel window and the external pulpit—a relic of the upper gallery surrounding the South German farm house—are the focal point of decorative composition. This small feature, which projected to a greater or lesser extent, was primarily intended to give the owner a wider field of vision, but sometimes also served as a private chapel. Against the flat, unadorned wall of a house in Erfurt, it stands out like an architecturally embellished jewel. In Austria and Switzerland the oriel window was often of particularly lavish design; it would sometimes be carried up through each of the upper floors to project like a tower above the cornice, or again it might extend across the full width of one storey. This decorative element of middle class town houses can be seen on numerous façades in the town of Linz on the Danube. The

MASTER M Z (Matthäus Zasinger), jousting scene, copper engraving, circa 1500. Staatliche Kunstsammlungen, Dresden, Kupferstichkabinett.

View of Late Gothic middle class town houses in a South German town, in which a tournament of knights is taking place.

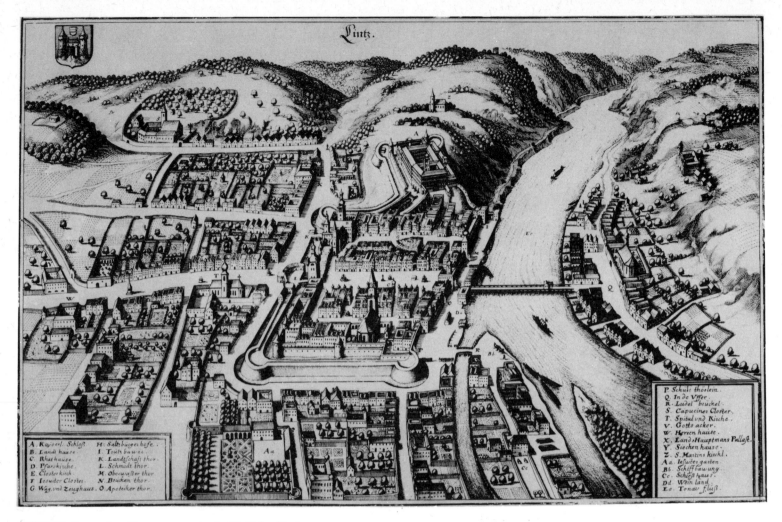

LINZ. *Bird's eye view. Copper engraving by Matthäus Merian,*
"Topographie Österreich", 1649.

By reason of its favourable position at the junction of the Danube and
the Salt Road leading from the Salzkammergut in the South to Bohemia
in the North, the town had already attained a position of importance as
a centre of trade and fairs as early as the middle of the thirteenth century. During the fifteenth and sixteenth centuries in particular, the
show fronts of the middle class town houses were enlivened not only
with oriels, but also by the addition of projecting storeys or bays (a
development not unconnected with the town's expansion as a seat of
the Habsburgs in the second half of the fifteenth century). Also clearly
in evidence are numerous stereometrically plain dwelling-houses.
Devoid of tectonic articulation, these have simple openings and valley
roofs, while to the rear and in the courtyards they are furnished with
arcades. The interiors on all floors were served by wide landings and
continuous central corridors. Outside the fortifications, parks and
gardens adjoined the houses.

Merian prospect shows polygonic corner oriels and corner roundels, which came up in the sixteenth century on houses lining the main square, the Old Town and the highways.

The most beautiful adornment of the Late Gothic Göglhaus at Krems on the Danube is the external pulpit with its richly traceried windows between pinnacled corner canopies. Inside this small private chapel dedicated to St Martin is a latticed vault. The Untere Landstrasse contains several fine middle class town houses built between the sixteenth and eighteenth centuries which are embellished with oriels and reliefs or sgraffiti, and possess courtyards surrounded by arcaded buildings of several storeys. These bear witness to the wealth of the town whose trade in wine, grain, salt and iron had been steadily growing since the fourteenth century.

Steyr, as a commercial and iron working centre, was the wealthiest and most powerful town of Upper Austria in the Middle Ages. The Late Gothic Bummerlhaus, virtually unaltered *27* since its building in about 1490, has a projecting upper storey with five windows between which are blind arcades beneath a broad band of tracery. Above the gable, with its panels of blind arches, there rises a hipped roof. The presence, not only here in the main square, but also in the Grünmarkt, the Enge Gasse, and the Kleinkehrgasse, of numerous Late Gothic and Renaissance houses, has helped to preserve the original aspect of the streets.

In Switzerland the earliest middle class town houses date back to the fourteenth century. The Confederation's largely successful struggle for independence from Hapsburg domination, as well as its favourable position on important trade routes, had fostered the rise, in Berne, Zurich, Basle and elsewhere, of a strong bourgeoisie. In Berne, which had joined the Confederation in 1353, there still remain a few streets lined with Late Gothic

houses which display such characteristic features as a continuous arcade at ground floor level and two or three upper storeys with windows arranged either singly or in groups of three. In other towns, houses might only have a side entrance on the ground floor. Master builders showed a special predilection for articulating façades by means of applied tracery and for piercing house fronts with tripartite windows. A particularly lavish example is the Mayhaus in Berne which was *23* converted in 1515 by Bartholome May, a wealthy merchant and diplomat, from two earlier Gothic houses. The forms used in the richly embellished oriel of several storeys are those of the last stages of Gothic and betray the influence of the Münster masons' lodge. It was not long before the decorative elements of the Renaissance were to gain acceptance in the areas on either side of the trade routes to and from Italy.

That tendency also took hold in the Kingdom of Bohemia, economically and culturally one of the leading countries of Europe. Even before that time, courtly art had flourished under Charles IV, while the works of Peter Parler, in particular, testify to the emergence of a strong middle class element. By the thirteenth century, the Old Town of Prague had assumed its final shape. The first university in central Europe was founded in 1348, and the New Town was laid out methodically as a segmented circle bounded by a wall and having a radiating network of streets, seven churches, seven monasteries, and three large market places disposed round the Old Town. In 1360 the town was again enlarged, this time on the left bank of the Vltava and to the south and west of the Small Side, so that in the fourteenth century Prague, covering an area of 534 hectares, became the largest city in Europe. Its prosperity was reflected in the widespread use of stone and brick as building materials. Large numbers of rubble or brick built houses set their stamp on the face of the town, half timbering being now employed only occasionally for upper floors. True, most of the façades today are Baroque in character, yet the architectural alterations are so organically integrated with the original Gothic structure that here, as nowhere else, the essential characteristics of two epochs combine to form a single whole. Thus, during the building of the Old Town under Weneeslas, the arcades on the east side of the Market Place were already being given Early Gothic ribbed vaulting. These link the ground floor façades of the middle class town houses, the disposition of whose fourteenth century ground plans is astonishingly diverse, and makes the best possible use of the limited space available. Smaller houses consist of one or two blocks, while larger ones are often of the three-block type, having a passage, a parlour, and a rear chamber with, in many cases, the stairway in between. Some rooms have ribbed vaulting and many others barrel and cross vaulting. The surviving Gothic nucleus is still more or less clearly discernible today.

Further interesting solutions, which also indicate a connection between the size of a town and the individual plot, are presented by the ground plans of the two-storeyed middle class town houses in Žatec (Saaz) in northern Bohemia. Each site facing the square measured 17 metres and provided for a range of six or seven windows. This permitted a concept of space that emphasized breadth, whereas the narrower sites in the streets and alleyways were conducive to development in depth.

Kutná Hora (Kuttenberg) was, after Prague, the most important town in Bohemia. The region's silver mines were the main source of wealth for the last of the Přemysls and the rulers of the House of Luxembourg. In about 1300 King Wenceslas had decreed that the

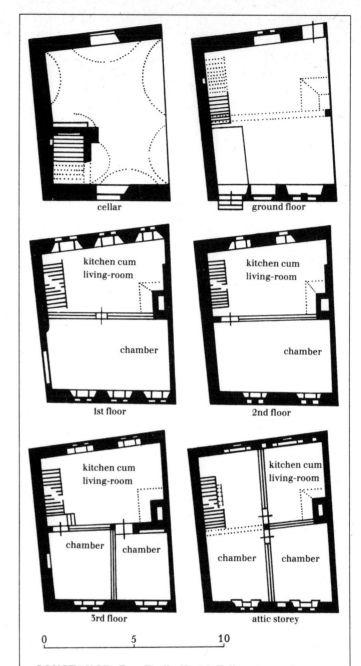

CONSTANCE. *Zum Kindle, No. 35, Zollernstrasse, fourteenth/fifteenth century, plans of original storeys.*

An example of the clearly additive spatial structure of a multi-storeyed house of the South German middle class type. The single-roomed cellar is vaulted. Close to the entrance there are steps down to the cellar and a system of stairs leading up to the attic floor. Each of the floors has, one above the other, living-quarters and kitchen, all of similar dimensions. In each case the kitchen is at the back, adjoining the chimney which is carried up through the house. Only on the attic floor has the landing been properly partitioned off from the living-quarters. A striking feature, by comparison with the Northwest European hall-house, is the stacking of self-contained and almost identical storeys of which the number is limited only by considerations of stability.

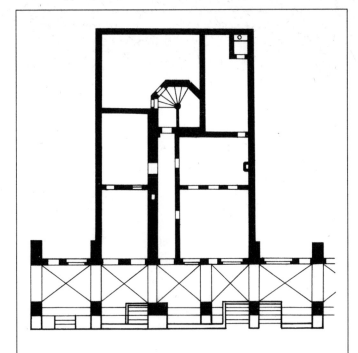

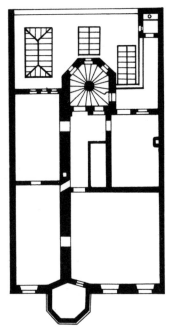

BERNE. *Mayhaus, No. 32, Kesslergasse (Ill. 23).*

Plans of the ground and first floors.

minting of all coinage for Bohemia and Moravia should be concentrated in this town which, by the fifteenth century, was able to boast a total of no less than six hundred houses.

At the time of its heyday, a patrician patron built the magnificent Steinernes Haus. This exceptionally tall, gable-fronted house has a richly decorated façade by Master Brikcí. The oriel in the centre is adorned with sculptures depicting the Virgin, flanked by two horsemen, beneath the Tree of Paradise.

The remarkable wealth of ornamentation on the tympanum of the Late Gothic gable persisted into the ensuing period, more especially in the towns of Bohemia. Half a century later an example drawn from Tábor shows that all title to structure has been abolished in the curvilinear decoration of blank ogee arches. The verges of the gable also begin to curve and thus are already a premonition of the stepped, segmented gable of the Renaissance, which was to play such a considerable role in this area.

In Hungary, as in many other countries of Europe, the centralized power of the monarchy played a vital role in the rise of the towns from the thirteenth and fourteenth centuries onwards. At about the turn of the fourteenth century there arose in Buda, at the foot of the Königsburg and close to the Aquincum of Roman times, a flourishing centre of industry and of the international entrepôt trade. In addition its citizens engaged in wine growing and a profitable trade in fruit. Buda consists of a Hungarian settlement to the north of the castle hill and a German one (Ofen) to the south of it. In 1437 these two settlements possessed a total of 322 houses and several stables. Thus the town was not particularly large but, because most of its inhabitants were urban farmers, it contained substantial farmsteads. The streets were wide and lined on either side with compact ranges of two- and three-sto-

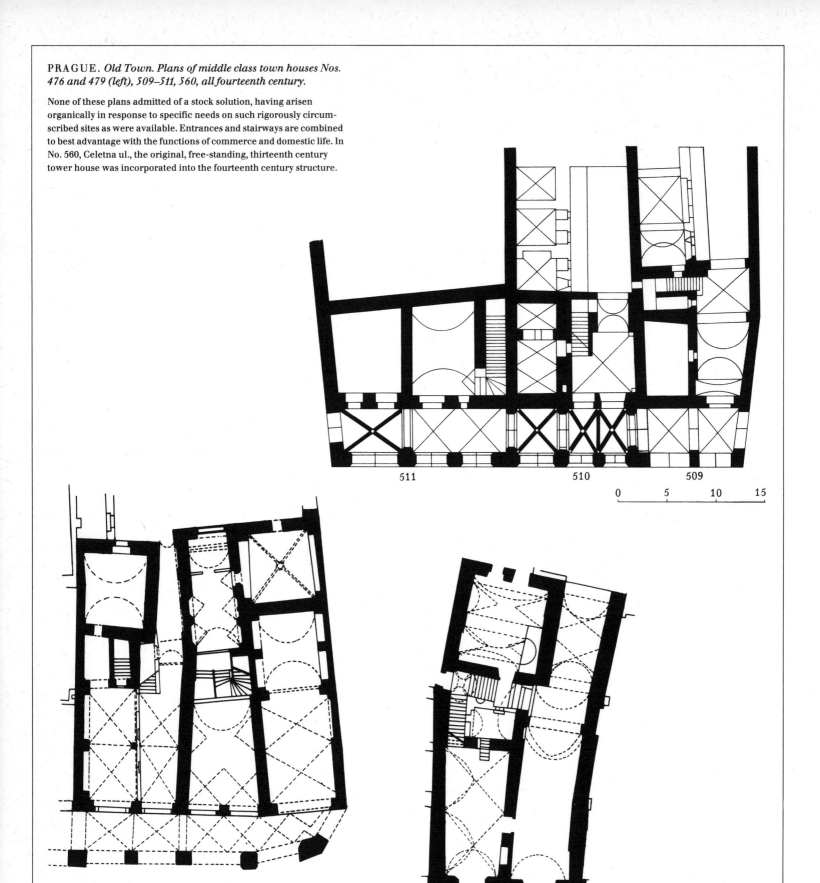

PRAGUE. *Old Town. Plans of middle class town houses Nos. 476 and 479 (left), 509–511, 560, all fourteenth century.*

None of these plans admitted of a stock solution, having arisen organically in response to specific needs on such rigorously circum-scribed sites as were available. Entrances and stairways are combined to best advantage with the functions of commerce and domestic life. In No. 560, Celetna ul., the original, free-standing, thirteenth century tower house was incorporated into the fourteenth century structure.

511   510   509

0   5   10   15

0   5   10

560

92

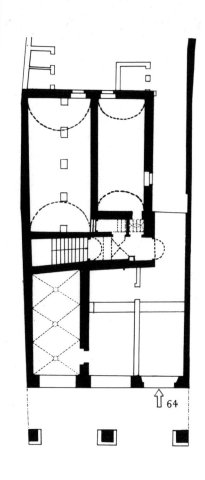

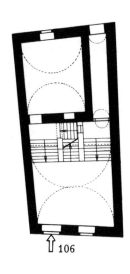

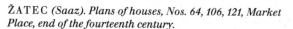

ŽATEC *(Saaz). Plans of houses, Nos. 64, 106, 121, Market Place, end of the fourteenth century.*

Although the articulation of the single-storeyed houses in this small town is in principle not unlike that of similar houses in the metropolis of Prague, the disposition of rooms is less complex. Moreover the technically more exacting cross vault is less often in evidence.

⇧ 64

⇧ 106

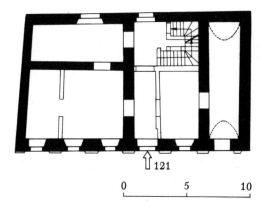

⇧ 121

| 0 | 5 | 10 |

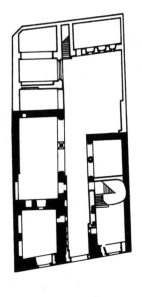

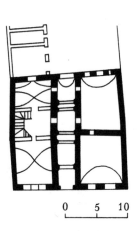

| 0 | 5 | 10 |

BUDAPEST. *Nos. 2 and 9, Országház utca. Ground floor plans of two Gothic middle class town houses.*

What is striking about this building with its wide, centrally-placed porte-cochère, is its relative spaciousness and the considerable diversity of its rooms. The stair has been relegated to one side of the building; some of the rooms are vaulted while others have beamed ceilings supported on stone consoles. The courtyard of No. 2 displays what was later to be the typical L-shaped wing. This plan is so devised as to cater for the requirements, not only of sophisticated commercial and industrial activities, but also for those of agriculture, which continued to play an important role.

93

reyed houses. The façades of the eaves-fronted stone buildings, which were up to eighteen metres wide, were pierced either in the centre or at one side by portes-cochères. On either side of these there would as a rule be one or two rooms. The yard, which was very spacious, contained stables, barns and storehouses which, later on, frequently took the form of an L-shaped wing. In recent decades the investigation and reconstruction of many war damaged buildings has brought to light the Gothic fabric in many cases still concealed behind the Baroque plasterwork. The finest examples of restored middle class town houses dating back to the late fourteenth and early fifteenth centuries are to be seen in the Úri utca, the Országhás *28* utca and the Tárnok utca. In the decorative motifs on the stone houses we may detect the hand of the workmen of the Buda masons' lodge who had also worked on the Königsburg and St Mary's Church (St Matthew's Church). The impression conveyed is that of a self-confident middle class, existing in this Southeast European kingdom that had the Ottoman Empire as its immediate neighbour. As a precaution against fire, houses were already provided with barrel vaults. On the upper floor there would often be a dining-hall (*palatium*) decorated with wall paintings on themes borrowed from courtly prototypes. Other features were arcades, projecting upper storeys supported by consoles, and oriels and doorways with segmentaled and round-headed arches. Two- or three-light windows with a horizontal lintel and moulded architraves were also favoured. A popular, national element is evident in the preference shown for façades painted in strong colours and geometrical patterns. Again, there was a predilection for the alcove seat, borrowed from the ecclesiastical sedilia, on one or both sides of an entrance gate, a feature found not only in Buda but also in Székesféhérvár, Sopron and Pécs. These

"sedilia" assumed many forms, being embellished with round-headed and pointed arches as well as tracery.

Origins of the Timber-Framed Town House

Our picture of the Gothic middle class town house in Central Europe, a district between the Alpine and Danubian area on the one hand and the North Sea and Baltic coasts on the other, would be incomplete were we to leave timber frame construction. In this section we intend to consider its general aspects, with especial reference to its development in the heartland of Germany. Examples from other areas in northern France, the Netherlands, England and Scandinavia, where timber framing commonly occurred, will be considered in the next chapter.

The history of timber frame construction goes back to Stone Age post construction. Even in the twelfth century, when the process began which was ultimately to lead to its structural perfection, it remained closely akin to the farmhouse, so that the distinction between the farmhouse and the town house long remained blurred. In the towns of the Romanesque era virtually all buildings were still either constructed wholly of timber or else were timber-framed with posts embedded in the ground and joined to each other by rails and, at the top, by a wall plate. Because of the impermanent nature of the material and the frequency of fires, few examples have come down to us either from this or from the ensuing Gothic period when, for safety reasons, brick and natural stone came increasingly to be used in the middle class town house. Even in regions favouring the use of stone, timber framing was still preferred by less well-to-do citizens as the far cheaper method, and therefore tended to predominate, particularly in side streets and suburbs. Some idea of this may be gained from Vicke Schorler's view of Rostock (frontispiece), which shows zones of brick patrician houses at the centre, and low, half-timbered buildings on the periphery. However, many districts of Germany as, for instance, Lower Saxony, Franconia and Swabia, where the history of timber framing went back to Teutonic times, possessed distinct traditions and constructional principles of their own. Here the carpenter's art as applied to house-building was to reach its apogee in the fifteenth century. Largely concentrated in the thickly wooded areas of the Rhineland, Hesse, Franconia, the Harz and Thuringia, it was also common in Lower Saxony, while its influence penetrated even as far as the Vistula and Transylvania. Timber frame architecture lent a remarkable consistency to the general appearance of many towns such as Brunswick, Goslar, Halberstadt, Quedlinburg, Wernigerode, Strasbourg and—up till the Second World War—also Hildesheim. However, owing to rebuilding in subsequent centuries, the picture they present today is, for the most part, very different. Some smaller towns, such as Fritzlar, Hesse or Miltenberg in Lower Franconia, still retain idiosyncratic, Late Gothic ensembles which, as architectural achievements, are in no way inferior to similar buildings in stone or brick. Nor is the timber-framed town house materially different from these as far as height or the arrangement of the ground plan is concerned; rather, it is distinguished by the structure, plainly exposed to view, of the external walls which, in its organic harmony, exerts a peculiar fascination. As may be seen from our two examples *24, 31* which show the art of German timber framing at the height of its development, each individual building has a different structural skeleton which, besides meeting the technical requirement of stability, possesses an intrinsic

decorative quality of its own. This derives largely from the variability of the panels and their symmetrical arrangement, as well as from the contrast in colour and texture between the white plaster infilling and the dark, linear timber. The construction consists of vertical timbers or posts, one floor in height, framed into a horizontal sill beam and, at the top, into a wall plate. The posts are joined to each other by rails and are strengthened by diagonal tension braces and arch braces which assume an extraordinary diversity of forms; straight or curved, single or cusped, they lend stability to the frame or are disposed as saltires within the panels. This self-supporting skeleton which, despite the fact that all members were jointed together, was intrinsically rigid —distortion being due only to subsidence, or to the ageing of the timber— permitted of a great deal of flexibility in the building of walls. In the attempt to enlarge the upper storeys on what was usually a restricted site, it became the custom early on to extend the joists beyond the wall, and support them on brackets, thereby enabling them to carry a jettied storey. Such jetties, each of them projecting beyond the one below, would not have been possible in brick or stone but, in the case of a timber-framed structure, they actually made for greater stability. However, this practice also meant that, in many cases, the already narrow streets and alleyways were almost completely overhung, a circumstance that often led to building regulations that limited the projection. According to a late thirteenth century inscription, chiselled on the east buttress of Strasbourg Cathedral, the maximum overhang permitted there was 1.12 metres beyond the foundations. However, with the coming of the Renaissance, overhangs fell out of favour.

Similarly, the introduction of oriels presented few structural problems. In this as in many other details, Early Gothic timber fram-

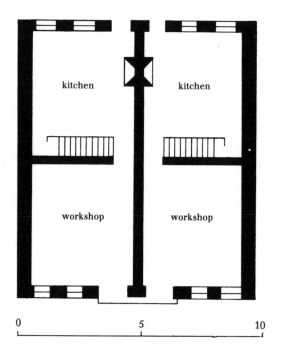

kitchen   kitchen

workshop   workshop

0   5   10

MARBURG. *View of gable and plan of a timber-framed house (from Schäfer/Stiehl) built in about 1320, demolished in 1875.*

Pair of symmetrically disposed, semi-detached artisans' houses, sharing a common roof and with an overall width of nine metres. Though of post construction, the building did not yet have a sill beam but rested on a ground storey of masonry. Each storey on either side of the party wall contained two rooms. Downstairs, there was a workshop on the street side and a kitchen with hearth facing the courtyard. Between these a stair led to the upper floors in which were the living rooms, bedrooms, apprentices' chambers, lofts and store-rooms.

ing was not without influence upon stone and brick construction, in the same way as the latter was subsequently to make its mark on the timber-framed house, particularly in the field of decoration. However, a growing richness of ornamentation from the sixteenth century onwards generally went hand in hand with a decline in the independent structural clarity.

In the towns of Germany there remain only a few timber-framed middle class houses which might testify to the rapid advances in structural design made between the thirteenth and fifteenth centuries. One of the oldest, an artisan's house built in Marburg in about 1320, of which an accurate drawing was made before its demolition towards the end of the nineteenth century, provides a certain amount of information about Early Gothic post construction. However, in this case the posts still rest directly upon the walls, being joined to each other by a rail on each floor and a wall plate at the top. In addition, one row of posts has also been strengthened by arch braces and tension braces. The panels, in so far as they are not reserved for windows, are filled in with plastered stone or brick. In ealier times they were frequently infilled with wattle or laths and then daubed with clay. A slightly later and important innovation was the replacement of the lower rails by the sill beam, into which the posts could be tenoned; together with the wall plate at the top, this produced a self-supporting frame. An example of this new stage in post construction is presented by No. 3, Word *32* in Quedlinburg, a house dating back to about 1400. The house has little artistic merit but is of interest to the architectural historian. The posts are inserted into the sill beams and are carried up through both floors to the wall plate. In between, besides a few cross rails, there are also ceiling beams whose ends are tenoned into the posts. In the fifteenth century

the most important development was the use of single braces to strengthen studs or posts, and of long, continuous braces to tauten whole sections of wall. By this time the territorial fragmentation of Germany had already led to the emergence of regional and local peculiarities in matters of stuctural detail. Thus, in the North, the ranging of uniform, rectangular panels was the norm, while the timber frame architecture of the central and southern regions, with its widely spaced studs, engendered a system of bracing which admitted of considerable variety, the panels being often decoratively enriched with saltires, lozenges, curved or arched bands, and other such motifs.

43–45 Albrecht Dürer's house in Nuremberg represents the quintessential German middle class town house at a time when the Middle Ages were giving way to the Renaissance. The artist had acquired the four-storeyed house near the Tiergärtner Tor in 1509. Built by an unknown master mason in the second half of the fifteenth century for Bernhard Walther, the mathematician, it is a typical example of the timber frame architecture found in Nuremberg. The upper timber-framed storeys have an air of almost playful lightness, and rest, as was customary throughout Franconia, upon a solid sandstone base. The building consists of, amongst other things, a hall on the ground floor with, above it, the great master's living-room-cum-study, which is still in its original condition. The view of the ground floor hall reveals the existence, within the stone exterior, not only of an impressively beamed ceiling, but also of stud walls used for screening off rooms. The study, on the other hand, which in size is reminiscent of a hall, has thick walls pierced by alcove-like window embrasures, and this, together with the massive boarded ceiling, combines to create an impression of a synthesis of stone and timber that is typical of timber frame architecture. Dürer himself has depicted this room in his masterly engraving, *St Jerome in his Study*, as the embodiment of both intimate domesticity and contemplative absorption. It is an expression of the prevailing mood of a new age which, in its endeavour to make man the measure of all things, achieved a closer relationship with its immediate surroundings.

Contrasts in Western and Northern Europe

In France, the *fons et origo* of Gothic, the evolution of style was closely bound up with the rise of the towns at a time when the centralized power of the Crown was steadily increasing. Not even the Hundred Years' War (1347–1453) between the kingdoms of France and England was able to inhibit materially the emergence of the urban bourgeoisie. In the course of the struggle between the two countries, many towns achieved a large measure of independence. In the second half of the fifteenth century centralized government by the States General gave way to an absolute monarchy; at the same time the out-worker and industrial system rapidly expanded to include the production of silk, linen, cloth and metal and luxury goods of all descriptions. Nevertheless, the stock of middle class town houses that has come down to us from that period is neither large nor particularly comprehensive. This is mainly attributable to the fact that, between the twelfth and sixteenth centuries, the bulk of such houses adhered with few if any changes to simple, vernacular types which were ultimately to prove inadequate. These were typically very narrow, gable-fronted houses of brick, stone or timber frame construction with a cellar and two or more storeys like the examples in Tours. Similar buildings in Paris are Nos. 11 and 13, Rue François Miron dating from the fourteenth century, No. 3, Rue Volta, probably built in about 1300 (timber frame rail-and-post construction with a masonry ground floor containing two shops whose window sills do duty as counters), and No. 51, Rue de Montmorency, the house of Nicolas Flamel, Scrivener to the University, built in 1407. The ground floor usually consisted of a hall-like, well-lit room—used as a warehouse or as a combined dining-, living- and reception room—and sometimes also of smaller ancillary rooms. The upstairs rooms were linked by side passages, while the courtyard wing containing the living quarters was generally reached by way of open galleries. There is little evidence here of the development of a patrician domestic architecture with marked local characteristics, such as is found throughout the Hanseatic area. After the victorious conclusion of the war, however, there was clearly a need for solutions offering better amenities and a greater opportunity for display, and here Italian influences are already discernible, notably in the field of internal appointments. At the forefront of this trend were houses that belonged mainly to a small class of educated and financially powerful burgesses who, as servants of the Crown, also wielded great political influence. Their *hôtels*, which were evidently inspired to a very large extent by the town mansions of the aristocracy, are a token of their claim to social equality. One of the finest examples is the Hôtel de Jacques Coeur at Bourges dating from the middle of the fifteenth century. In Charles VII's reign, Coeur was one of a group of royal counsellors of middle class origin and, for a decade or more, occupied a leading position in the financial administration of the country. He enjoyed, not only political power, but also enormous wealth, possessing as he did three hundred depots and manufactories, thirty châteaux and hôtels and seven ships—hence the opulence of the build-

35–38

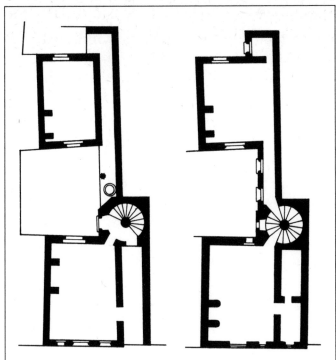

TOURS. *Gothic house "de Tristan", plans of the ground floor and upper story (from Vitry).*

On the street side of both floors is a large, well-lit living-room or workshop. A spiral stair leads to the upper floor; the garde-robe and closet are situated above the entrance hall.

ing. However, in the very same year that this palatial residence was completed, its proud patron fell victim to the intrigues of aristocratic courtiers and political bureaucrats; in 1453 his property was confiscated by the King.

Coeur's hôtel has nothing whatever in common with the traditional middle class town house, in which domestic and business functions were organically combined. It is the ostentatious seat of an early capitalist entrepreneur which, as a type, may be placed somewhere between castle and château. The former is suggested in particular by the wealth of towers, two of which form part of the town's fortifications. In addition, three staircase turrets are situated in the courtyard while, to one side of the private chapel in the turriform central block, there is a stair bell tower. Its affinity to a château, on the other hand, finds expression in the large rectangular windows, in the multiplicity of living-rooms, guest rooms and banqueting rooms linked by halls, and in the extraordinary richness of the architectural decoration. The asymmetry, both of the layout and of the ornamental forms, are wholly the product of French Late Gothic.

The material employed in this pretentious building is, of course, dressed stone. Timberframing remained the province of the middle class town house and of the peasant farmhouse especially in Northwest France, Normandy and Alsace where, in about 1500, it displayed an interesting multiplicity of regional forms. (In the South of France, on the other hand, brick or stone generally predominated.) A fine example, the Maison d'Adam, has survived in Angers, the capital of the old French Duchy of Anjou (Département de Maine et Loire). Here the posts are carved in imitation of the columns of stone architecture, while the panels are adorned with a lozenge pattern formed by the closely intersecting braces. The Franconian motif, the saltire, is still retained for the struts in the panels of the oriel and also beneath the windows, being used, so to speak, as an all-over design.

Timber, along with brick and stone, also played an important role as a building material in the middle class town house further north, in the immediately adjacent coastal areas of Flanders and Brabant where, despite the annexationist proclivities of the kings of France and England, economically powerful towns (e.g. Ghent, Bruges, Lille, Arras, Ypres and Douai) had grown up on the basis of cloth manufacture. However, virtually no wood or timber-framed buildings of that period have survived. Their construction was closely related to that found in Lower Saxony and, being light, was much favoured in Holland because of the soft nature of the ground. In the fourteenth century, the risk of fire gave rise to strict regulations whereby roofs had to be tiled and certain parts of the external walls and gables built of brick. The loadbearing members, the dividing walls and, in many cases, also the front and rear walls of the narrow, gable-fronted houses were of timber. The ground floor contained a large hall, the *voorhuis*, or front block, used as shop, workshop or living-room, which was separated from the *hang-kamer*, or smaller rooms, occupied by the family in the rear block. Like everywhere else where brick predominated, many of the gables were corbie stepped and, from the fifteenth century onwards, came increasingly to be decorated with blank tracery, while a feature peculiar to the Low Countries were quoins of alternating brick and stone. The miniature in Brunetto Latini's manuscript depicts artisans' dwellings of this period whose uniformity recalls that of terrace houses. The ground floor of these two-storeyed buildings whose interiors were all disposed in much the same way, contained the artisan's shop and workshop with a shutter that could be lowered for use as a counter, while the first floor, which in some cases projected by some twenty or thirty centimetres, contained the living-rooms.

In the wealthy trading and cloth manufacturing centres of Flanders, the upper middle class town house evolved at an earlier date than in Holland and on a considerably more lavish scale. Cloth halls, magnificent town halls with lofty belfries, and the richly decorated buildings of guilds and craft fraternities set the standard for numerous patrician town houses whose structure (narrow façades with tall, corbie stepped gables and large windows flanked by long, vertical strips of applied decoration) in turn exerted an influence on the form assumed by public buildings. The Huis van't Sestich in Louvain, a prosperous cloth manufacturing town whose Late Gothic town hall is one of the finest of its kind, is a good example of this highly developed style of domestic architecture. As in the Hanseatic patrician houses of North Germany, imaginative tracery work is used to embellish the medallions between the blind pointed arches on the gable, but in this case is even more delicate and filigree-like. This proud middle class culture provided the soil from which there grew, not only a splendid secular architecture, but also the new realism of the Early Flemish school of painting. It is no mere chance that many of its pictures should have, for their background, scenes of urban life.

Things took an altogether different course in England where a great many populous towns were already in existence in the Romanesque era. Yet if the ensuing phase did not see the emergence of, say grander type of patrician house, this was due to a number of inhibiting factors, among them the feuds between powerful nobles and the Hundred Years' War with France which brought about the impoverishment, if not the actual ruin, of certain towns. The only cities that prospered were London and those ports which served the profitable trade in wool and cloth.

The interests of a small class of merchant princes and industrialists were closely bound up with those of the lesser aristocracy in as much as the latter were the land-owners who supplied the wool. Not infrequently members of the former class would also acquire real estate. Thus, as in France, the picture presented by the Gothic middle class town house is one of contrast between the vast mass of relatively unassuming dwellings and a few opulent residences, the property of well-to-do citizens who borrowed freely from the castle and country house architecture of the aristocracy. The mansion of the London woollen merchant, Sir John Crosby, is a typical example of this trend. Like the seats of the aristocracy, it is a self-contained structure of dressed stone and has a large hall, rows of Gothic windows, and turriform features on the courtyard side, but its roof is not pitched, nor does the house proclaim its middle class function.

On the other hand, the more modest type of merchant's or craftsman's house of the Gothic era, commonly referred to as *Bude* in the Hanseatic towns, frequently took the form of a two-storeyed, gable-fronted structure with a ground storey of brick or dressed stone and a projecting upper storey of timber frame or daub and wattle construction. The ground floor contained a spacious workroom giving onto the street. Mullioned windows with two or more narrow lights and, in some cases, several transoms, were typical of the English house in Tudor times.

In the once powerful kingdom of Denmark, the building material which determined the early development of the middle class town house was timber which soon was used also in conjunction with brick for timber frame construction. From the twelfth century onwards, it is true, dressed stone and brick

played their part in shaping the religious and secular architecture of Scandinavia, as did the influence of Central European Romanesque and Gothic, yet the middle class town house was long dominated by a strong rustic tradition. One of the few houses of this kind to have survived is the single-storeyed Apostelhuset in Naestved which, with its long, low façade, is still strongly reminiscent of a peasant farmhouse and is noteworthy on account of its richly carved posts. The symmetrically disposed rectangular panels betray Lower Saxon influence, while the skilful decoration would seem to be a legacy of the highly developed Scandinavian art of wood carving.

33

In eastern, as in northern Europe, the rustic log house long remained the standard type in what were, for the most part, sparsely inhabited urban settlements. In Russian towns, for instance, the one- or two-storeyed log house with an outside stair, overhanging eaves and rich vernacular decoration was to predominate for several centuries. Brick was not introduced there until the fifteenth century. Almost two hundred and fifty years of Mongol oppression and the persistence of a barter economy were crucial factors in inhibiting the development of a self-confident urban bourgeoisie.

From Casa to Palazzo

In Italy, where powerful middle class city republics – the first of their kind in Europe – had already come into being in the Romanesque period, conditions were altogether different from those obtaining in the areas we have considered up till now. In northern Italy, the centre of early capitalist growth, the big guilds and patrician families had, in the course of the thirteenth century, all but broken the resistance of the aristocracy. The castles and town

LONDON. *Plan and view of the courtyard front of Crosby Place, a house built in Bishopsgate for Sir John Crosby between 1466 and 1475 and demolished in 1908.*

After two fires in 1666 and 1672 all that remained of this house was the great hall (Crosby Hall) with its magnificent pendant roof of oak, and a vaulted oriel window of stone (E and D), restored between 1836 and 1842. From 1860 to 1907 it was used as a restaurant and in 1910 was removed to Chelsea where it became part of London University. This, incidentally, was the first important achievement in the field of conservation at a time when many of London's historic buildings were being demolished. In its grandiosity the plan (from Norman/Veltheim-Lottum) resembles those of the great country houses then being built by the aristocracy. (A = gatehouse, B = courtyard, C = screens passage, D = hall, E = hall, F–H = private apartments, I = private chapel, K = stair, L and M = domestic offices and kitchen). Like their French opposite numbers (for instance, Hôtel de Jacques Cœur) the more eminent English citizens (in this case a knight) sought to advertise their status through the medium of château-like mansions. The house was lived in by, amongst others, the philosopher Thomas More, and there are several allusions to Crosby Place in Shakespeare's play, *Richard III.*

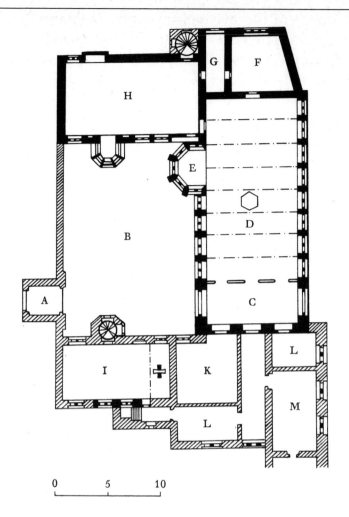

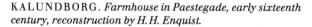

KALUNDBORG. *Farmhouse in Paestegade, early sixteenth century, reconstruction by H. H. Enquist.*

Two-storeyed stone dwelling-house with pointed arched windows and corbie stepped gable. Adjoining is a half-timbered building which also presents its long side to the street.

residences of the aristocracy were, in many cases, either razed to the ground or seized, while in numerous localities serfdom was abolished. However, it was not long before the new rulers themselves became an élitist class of merchant princes, bankers, owners of manufactories, employers of out-workers, and big landowners. As such, they wielded not only economic but also political power. By degrees they abandoned the republican form of government and set up despotic régimes, in many cases with the support of the *condottieri*, to subdue the populace and put down the latter's frequent rebellions (e.g. the Ciompi uprising in Florence in 1378). This new, upper middle class urban élite combined in itself wealth, power and cultural awareness of an order that was certainly comparable with, if not indeed, superior to, that of the aristocracy in other countries. Thus, towards the end of the Trecento and long before the Transalpine aristocracy had solved their own particular architectural problem by building castles, the patriciate of northern Italy had, for their part, found an answer in the grandiose palazzo. At the same time, however, the new type of upper middle class town palace was defined by the need for greater domestic comfort, by economic and administrative functions and by the desire for opulent display. It can no longer, of course, strictly be described as a *casa borghese* or middle class town house whose form is dictated by the combined functions of a home and a business, yet its social basis still remains unmistakably middle class. Hence, to exclude it from this study would be to disregard an important bourgeois contribution to domestic architecture.

In Tuscany, as in many of the towns of northern Italy, these early palaces were all of much the same type—namely an austere, towering pile with between two and four upper storeys and, on the ground floor, a central doorway or several large openings used for commercial purposes. As a rule, the markedly symmetrical articulation of the plain façade was achieved solely by means of the round-headed openings of the windows and/or the ground floor entrances. At most the horizontality would be further accentuated by narrow string courses under the window sills and a crowning cornice. A typical example is the 53, 54, Palazzo Davanzati, built in the second half of 57 the fourteenth century in Florence. The rustic appearance of the ground floor lends an almost defensive air to this merchant's house, in spite of the fact that it is pierced by three large round-headed entrances leading to the store rooms. Also on the ground floor were a large hall and a counting-house. All the upper floors were devoted to living accommodation. The first floor, or *piano nobile*, comprised a state room with a chimney and the apartments of the head of the family; the next floor was reserved for the other members of the family, while the top floor, with its low rooms immediately beneath the roof with its abrupt changes in temperature, was occupied by the army of servants. Although the loggia had already been a favourite family haunt in the fourteenth century, that of the Palazzo Davanzati was not erected until the fifteenth century. In Florence, the centre of this type of development, such loggias might only be built by a select circle of families.

By now the Florentine Signoria was intervening in private building to an even greater extent than the authorities of other North Italian towns who, in the thirteenth century, had already sought to minimize the risk of fire by means of stringent building regulations (e.g. a ban on timber buildings and thatched roofs, and ordinances governing the construction of chimneys). By its directives relating to the building of houses, the Signoria also exerted an influence on town planning. When,

103

in 1390, a new square was proposed the size and design of the houses that were to abut on it were laid down by the supervisory authority concerned. Florence was also the first town in Europe to have a system of paved streets. A further noteworthy circumstance, both reminiscent of Antiquity and extremely modern in flavour, was the tendency of many of its citizens to escape from the hurly-burly and the intolerable stench of the thirteenth century town, and build themselves villas outside its walls. Giovanni Bocaccio, a friend of Petrarch's, depicts a situation of this kind in his *Decameron*, written between 1348 and 1353. These stories plainly demonstrate how much headway had already been made by the worldly, hedonistic Renaissance mentality, as well as by a cultural awareness that was bound up with the Classical tradition and inevitably found expression in the domestic architecture of the ruling élite. This, together with a burgeoning national consciousness in an as yet fragmented Italy, prevented what was felt to be an alien Gothic style from ever really taking root there. However, certain elements were adopted that had been the hall-mark of Romanesque— namely, the cubiform house, flat walls and symmetrically disposed, round-headed window and door openings. Now, however, buildings became larger, more comfortable and more imposing and, notably in the case of the palazzi, were increasingly pervaded by a sense of beauty and monumentality.

Needless to say, the typology of the medieval Italian middle class town house cannot be understood solely in terms of the town palace of the new, middle class élite. Virtually nothing has survived that might show the many intermediate stages between this and the dwellings of the artisan or day labourer. An approximate picture of their diversity may be gained from the painstakingly detailed fresco by Ambrogio Lorenzetti in the Public Palace at Siena. His

48, 49

mural, painted between 1335 and 1340 and entitled *Effects of Good Government*, depicts a section of this important Tuscan town which, having been engaged since the thirteenth century in cut-throat competition with Florence, had become, by European standards, a leading manufacturing, industrial, and banking centre. Lovingly and minutely, the painter depicts the everyday life of the town—merchants returning from their travels laden with goods, tradesmen selling their wares under projecting eaves and arcades, craftsmen tiling a roof. The narrow streets are lined with stone houses of many kinds. Next to the earlier towers of the patriciate stand palazzi, tower-houses and simpler buildings as well, some with wide, some with very narrow façades. The number of storeys varies, while some houses have flat roofs and others low-pitched, or pentice roofs covered with tiles. There are also projecting storeys and oriels, in some cases strengthened with wooden struts, but no timber, or timber-framed, buildings. Communal life takes place out of doors, here and there invading the ground floors of houses which are wide open to the street. The upper storeys, with their loggias and ranges of windows are devoted solely to living accommodation. Many of the windows are equipped with a transom reminiscent of a guard rail to which waxed linen can be attached for protection against the sun and the vagaries of the weather. In the houses of prosperous citizens some windows might already be glazed. The entrances and many of the windows could be secured by means of strong wooden doors and shutters.

Only a few of the architectural elements, notably the pointed arch, recall the fact that, at this time, High Gothic was in its heyday. Certain typical characteristics of the transalpine middle class town house are lacking— the high pitched gabled roof, for instance, unnecessary in this climate, and the verticality of the articulation of the façade. On the contrary, its horizontality is accentuated by narrow, moulded string courses on a level with the window sills or with the springers. Most of the round-headed windows cut cleanly into the surface of the walls, only a few of the more opulent buildings having two-light windows with small mullions, while tracery is confined to one window in the house on the extreme right of the picture. Another characteristic is the great diversity of colouring displayed by the plastered surfaces; only here and there is the masonry-work left uncovered. Thus, despite a "family likeness" between individual houses, the panorama of a North Italian town presented an extraordinary wealth of individual forms that corresponded to the many gradations on the social scale. In so far as their means and social position permitted, and within the limits laid down by the building regulations, the non-patrician classes endeavoured to imitate the more grandiose buildings. But this had little or no effect on the traditionally simple lay-out of the small artisan's or tradesman's house with its shop, workshop and store room on the ground floor and, on the next, anything up to three bedchambers, in addition to a room which served as a combined kitchen, living- and dining-room. It is a type that has hardly changed at all, as may be seen from the small shops on the Ponte Vecchio in Florence.

In Venice, however, the development of the middle class town house displays characteristics of a markedly regional nature. The city, founded in the fifth century in the shelter of a lagoon, grew during the ninth into an important centre of the Eastern trade while, from the thirteenth century onwards, she could be styled "mistress of the Mediterranean". At about the same time, she came under the control of an aristocratic oligarchy and, as such, defeated the rival city of Genoa in 1379, annexed many of the towns in the Po Valley and extended her possessions along the Dalmatian coast as far as the island of Corfu. Life in the city republic revolved solely round its sea-borne trade. Every citizen was obliged to serve at sea and all warships and merchantmen were owned by the state. Venetian galleys, which took about one hundred days to build by the assembly line method, were to prove invincible up till the end of the fourteenth century. The city was a centre of international commerce, and possessed trading posts in Zara (Zadar) and Ragusa (Dubrovnik), as well as in Crete and in the Aegean Islands. Venetian vessels plied across the Black Sea and the Adriatic, and there were firm trading links with Isfahan, Cairo, Ceylon and Sumatra. Venice enjoyed a monopoly in the manufacture of glass. Among the most important goods traded were hides and tin from England, cloth from Flanders, silver ore from Bohemia, copper and iron from Germany, and spices, gold, silver, glass, silks, damasks, jewellery and slaves from Turkey. The spatial organization and design of the façade typical of the Venetian palazzi and dwelling-houses was determined, not only by climatic and social factors, but also by the peculiar geographical situation of Venice as an island city enjoying the secure, natural protection of a lagoon. The fact that the houses were built alongside the canals on wooden piles meant that strict account had to be taken of such matters as town-planning and commerce . The republic's exceptional prosperity and its internal unity were extraordinarily favourable to its cultural development. From the second half of the thirteenth century onwards, dwelling-houses in the form of massive blocks with L-, C- and U-shaped ground plans, and variants of the latter, were built on the original deep, rectangular plots. The C-shaped design with central courtyard set the pattern for the further development of the dwelling-

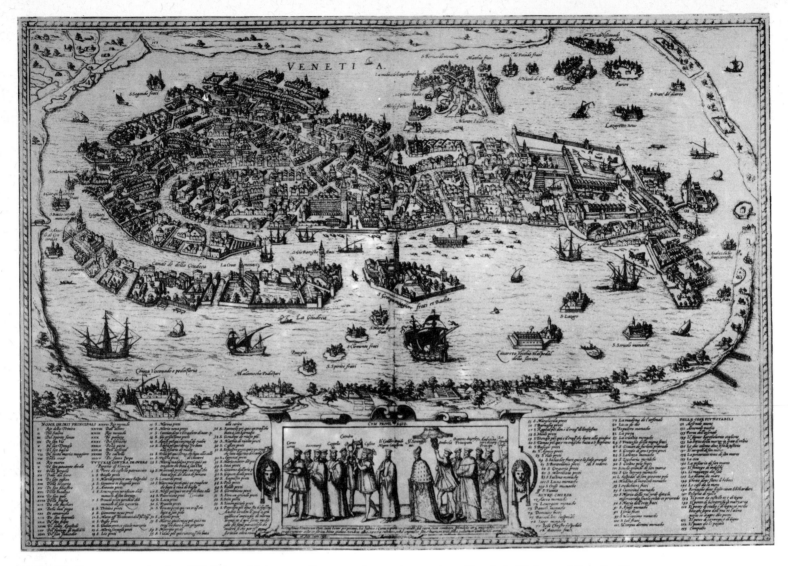

VENICE. *Copper engraving from "Civitates orbis terrarum", vol. 1, by Georg Braun and Frans Hogenberg, Cologne, 1588.*

The siting and lay-out of many European towns were largely determined by features such as mountains and water which afforded them natural protection. Of these, Venice is the most famous. Situated on 118 small islands in the middle of a lagoon, the city covers a triangular area of 7.5 square kilometres and, even without expensive fortifications, was readily defensible, the more so in that it was heavily built-up, as our illustration shows, and possessed, as early as the Middle Ages, a population already well in excess of 100,000 (attaining 190,000 in its heyday). Venice boasts 160 canals, including the Canale della Giudecca, over 300 metres wide, which separates the long, narrow, southern portion from the main body of the city, and also the sinuous, S-shaped Grand Canal, 3.8 kilometres long and anything between 40 and 70 metres wide; it is these canals, together with the narrow alley-ways, or *calli*, which go to make up the "communications network". To enable gondolas to pass, there were bridges spanning the canals which were equipped with steps and built in the form of a segmental arch. Owing to shortage of space there could be only two large piazzas, namely that of San Marco and the adjoining piazetta beside the entrance to the Grand Canal. It was here that the finest and most grandiose public and private buildings were erected. On the right, at the southeastern extremity,

may be seen the extensive and heavily fortified arsenal, the pride of the Republic, with its shipyards, armouries, supply depots, gun foundries, and workshops of all descriptions. In the course of more than 1,300 years this powerful city (founded in 452 by Illyrian Venetians fleeing before the Barbarian invasion of the Huns), survived many vicissitudes, including investment by the French in 1797 and the fall of the Doges.

106

house. The use of waterways for commercial traffic called for a type of house whose front entrance gave onto the water. Moreover, in those days of communal enterprise, the natural protection afforded by water was an additional safeguard against foreign intervention. The ground floor comprised the business premises, warehouses and store-rooms. A large, imposing vestibule ran through the whole building from canal to courtyard with, on either side of it, smaller rooms that served as offices and stores. From the courtyard, in which there was a draw-well, an outside stair led to the upper floors. The entrance facing the water originally took the form of a grand gateway though it was later to assume somewhat more modest proportions. The doorway on the landward side led to a small, unostentatious courtyard. Some buildings were only accessible by water. On the upper floor, where the family lived, were arcades looking over the canal. Since little space was available for sizable courtyards, let alone gardens, there were numerous open loggias and balconies where the occupants could take the air and watch the comings and goings on the water as well as participate in the gorgeous political and religious ceremonies that took place on the Grand Canal. Here, too, next to the city's principal artery, stood the finest palaces, belonging to the wealthiest families from which were drawn not only the Doge, but also the members of the all-powerful Great Council and Council of Ten. After 1297 this group had closed its ranks and thus inhibited the rise of new families.

Their power, their immense wealth and the international nature of their connections were manifested on the canal side of their palaces in extravagantly embellished show fronts in which the formal elements of Gothic and Lombard art are fused with those of Arab and Byzantine origin, a notable example being the Palazzo Sagredo. Here, the patron was concerned not so much with harmony of proportion as with the proliferation of decorative motifs and the costliness of the materials on the show front—the rear elevations are relatively unadorned, their only feature being an outside stair. The columned arcades and extensive groups of windows which open up the façade often bear little organic relation to the main structure. The blithe, animated impression conveyed by the filigree-like tracery of the walls is further reinforced by the richness of their colouring. To the warm red of the brickwork and the colour-washed, plastered surfaces were added carvings on the marble string courses and window frames, parts of which were also painted and gilded. And this sensuous abundance was magically enhanced by being reflected in the water. The interior appointments, in the shape of textiles and works of art of many kinds, were equally costly, while fountains and small parterres betray the influence of an advanced Moorish style of life. In many of these palazzi, the first floor, whose plan was a repetition of that of the floor below, centred round a large hall, or *portego*, on to which the adjoining rooms opened and which served in summer as a refuge from the warm, humid climate of the lagoon. In Vicenza, which had been under Venetian rule since 1404, the same arrangement of rooms was adopted and, indeed, was made use of by Palladio when he built the Villa Rotonda in 1550.

46 With the Ca' d'Oro on the Grand Canal palace architecture of the Venetian fifteenth century reached its zenith. In this "House of Gold", the property of the rich patrician, Marino Contarini, the façade of coloured Istrian marble is a triumph of kinematic transparency. No less delightful is the organic effect created by the contrast between the apparent weightlessness of the much perforated façade on the

left and the flatness and compactness of the right wing, a principle of design repeated in the horizontal articulation that recalls the Doge's Palace from which the loggia motif on the upper floor also derives. At a time when the Renaissance was already under way in Tuscany and central Italy, Venice experienced a late flowering of Gothic ornamental and tracery work that was specifically regional. The stimulus came not least from the Ca' d'Oro, because the latter's wealth of lively motifs was singularly suited to the purpose of producing an artistically complex perforation of the wall.

Compared with the palaces of the merchant princes with their magnificent façades and multifarious solutions to the disposition of space, the houses of the small artisans, labourers and seamen were, as a type, all of very simple design. Flanking narrow canals and alleyways, they stood huddled together in order to occupy the smallest possible amount of space; indeed, even at this early date land was so valuable as to necessitate the building of large, multi-storeyed, communal dwellings. As a rule, a dwelling in one of these blocks had its own street entrance and stairway. Many of the dwellings were two-storeyed, with a kitchen-cum-living-room and a store room on the ground floor, and bedchambers above. The loggia, if any, was reached by an outside stair. Blocks such as these, built as a continuous range, would not, of course, have courtyards. There was also a different type of house with a shop on the ground floor.

In Spain the design of the middle class town house varied considerably from region to region. Similarly, the country itself was divided between two mutually antagonistic cultures. In the course of the successful campaign against the Moors in the thirteenth century the greater part of Spain was reconquered. The year 1492 saw the fall of Granada, the last

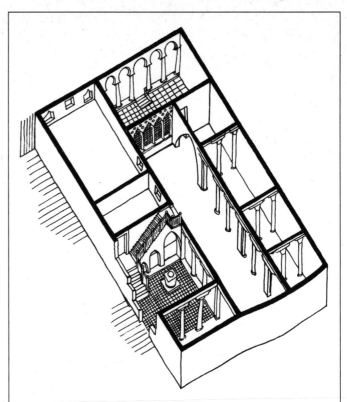

VENICE. *Ca' d'Oro (House of Gold) on the Grand Canal. Isometric projection of the ground storey, from Lundberg (Ill. 46).*

A glance at the projection of the ground storey reveals, beside the water, the columned arcade of the ante-chamber, one side of which opens into the business offices consisting of a long, columnar hall. The left wing comprises separate store-rooms and a miniature *cortile* with a dog-legged stair. The rooms on the upper floors were similarly disposed, save that the loggias were open to the central hall, or *portego*, whereas the rooms at the side were partitioned off.

of the Moorish strongholds. The towns had become strategically and economically important centres, many of them having attained a large measure of communal autonomy. However, their fortified walls harboured numerous aristocratic residences alongside densely built-up areas of small middle class houses. There was no really powerful patriciate as in Italy. The design of these markedly block-like brick or stone houses was determined, as in Italy, not only by the climate, but also by the still active legacy of Roman domestic architecture. Small, shady courtyards, with wells and outside stairs leading to a gallery on the upper floor, served as a refuge from the heat, while the flat, overhanging roofs were often used as a terrace. As a rule the narrow plots also contained a small garden. As everywhere else in Europe the ground floor was devoted primarily to trade, though it also contained a kitchen and servant's rooms, while the upper floor was given over to living-rooms and a saloon. The existence of gardens and airy inner courtyards, as well as privies and drainage, betray the influence of an advanced Moorish style of life. A combination of Moorish and Gothic decorative elements went to make up the delightful style known as Mudéjar which was particularly prevalent in central and southern Spain. Whereas the houses of Catalonia were thoroughly modest in design, those of Salamanca, Toledo (lofty gables and large, arcaded courtyards) and Seville were of appreciably more opulent construction and much more richly decorated. Here, too, the rise of Spain to the status of great colonial power was accompanied by the development of a palatial type of house with a large doorway, a courtyard, several staterooms and many other rooms, including a bathroom.

Inside the Gothic Town House— the Middle Class Style of Life

At the end of the Romanesque era the development of the private house was still defined by a courtly and feudal way of life which the patriciate sought to emulate. In other types of middle class town house, however, the functions of the rooms, like the furniture and equipment, remained relatively undiversified, being as practical and simple as the unsophisticated requirements of the occupants; amenities were non-existent, as were artistic pretensions. Not until the Gothic era—by which time the middle class town house was fully evolved—did the new requirements and the new potential of the productive forces create an independent middle class style of life. From rudimentary beginnings, it quietly matured so organically and in such multifarious ways as to be able to satisfy all the essential needs of society as a whole and to continue to do so, at least in part, up till the present day. We propose to do justice to this pioneering achievement, but only in broad outline and without entering either into the wealth of interesting detail or into regional differences.

Needless to say, there are no longer any authentic interiors of so early a date—reconstructions in museums being no more than an approximation—and thus we must fall back on material that has been drawn for the most part from pictorial documents of middle class realistic art which was then in its infancy. One need only consider the difference between Dürer's study as actually reconstructed and the incomparably livelier depiction of the interior of that same room in his masterly engraving, *St Jerome in his Study*. The multiplicity of objects (as opposed to furniture) here recorded, namely books, cushions, utensils, candlesticks, lamps, shelves, and so on, is alone capable of conveying a true idea of the intimate, homely atmosphere of the middle class town house.

It was in the fourteenth century that the outlines of that middle class style of life first became plainly apparent. In effect, it sprang from the constant endeavour to improve the practical conditions and efficiency of life and labour within the small, circumscribed world of the house. Many important, if apparently humdrum, innovations and inventions in the sphere of lighting, heating, the disposition of space, and improved industrial and domestic equipment, marked the long road which led to a greater measure of fulfilment of the desire for improved amenities and artistic design. New specialized tradesmen appeared on the scene, e.g. joiners and cabinet makers (as distinct from carpenters), and potters for the manufacture of stoves, etc., while the invention of the sawmill (first recorded in 1322) now rendered feasible the production of furniture and wainscotting on a considerable scale.

We have already had occasion to discuss the increasing subdivision of the interior according to various functions and activities and the decisive advance this represented. In so far as social status allowed, completely separate zones were now set aside for business, household management and living. As a rule, the whole of the ground floor was devoted to industry and commerce as were to some extent the attic floors and the cellar for the storage of goods. These rooms were usually large and allowed free passage, though in many the counting-house was partitioned off. For the purpose of street trading, use was already being made of stalls and of shutters which could be lowered to form a counter on which merchandise was displayed. The domestic sphere included not only the stables and the provision stores in courtyard and cellar, but also and above all the kitchen, which was

ALBRECHT DÜRER, "St Jerome in his Study", copper engraving of 1514.

St Jerome, a Father of the Roman Church and translator of the Bible, together with his attributes—lion, human skull and crucifix—is portrayed in the setting of the artist's Late Gothic study as the embodiment of the new, humanist ideal of scholarship. In this way the mythological scene becomes a realistic genre painting whose every detail expresses the citizen's inward relationship to the spatial environment he himself has created, and does so more convincingly than any other contemporary representation. The foreground almost seems part of the frame, thereby reinforcing still further the impression that this is a calm, sheltered place of meditation.

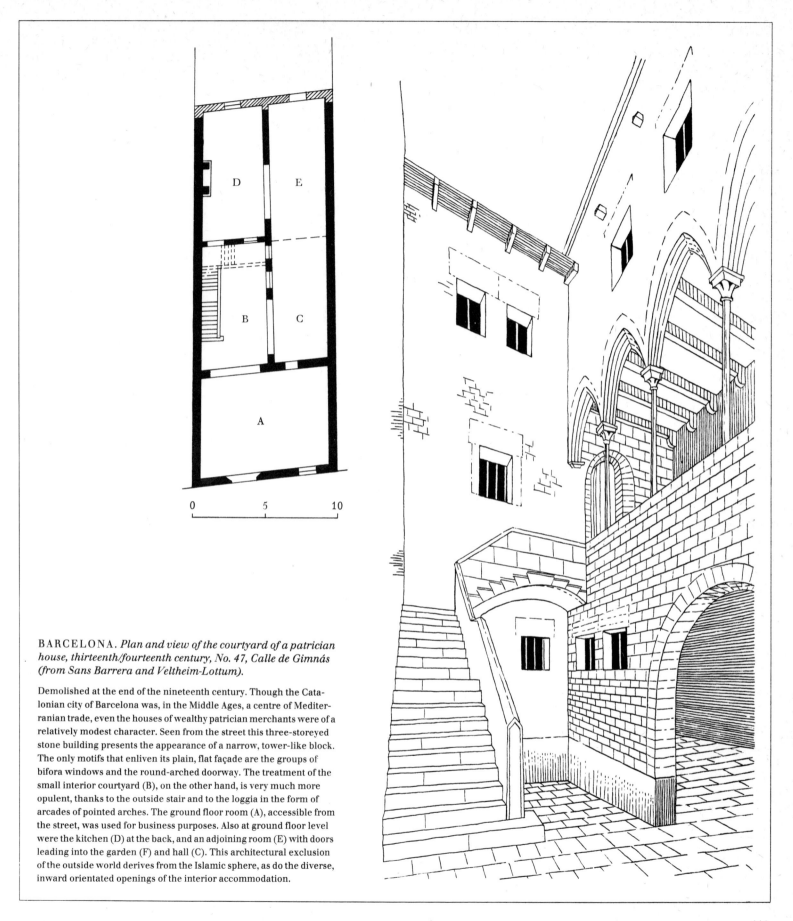

BARCELONA. *Plan and view of the courtyard of a patrician house, thirteenth/fourteenth century, No. 47, Calle de Gimnás (from Sans Barrera and Veltheim-Lottum).*

Demolished at the end of the nineteenth century. Though the Catalonian city of Barcelona was, in the Middle Ages, a centre of Mediterranean trade, even the houses of wealthy patrician merchants were of a relatively modest character. Seen from the street this three-storeyed stone building presents the appearance of a narrow, tower-like block. The only motifs that enliven its plain, flat façade are the groups of bifora windows and the round-arched doorway. The treatment of the small interior courtyard (B), on the other hand, is very much more opulent, thanks to the outside stair and to the loggia in the form of arcades of pointed arches. The ground floor room (A), accessible from the street, was used for business purposes. Also at ground floor level were the kitchen (D) at the back, and an adjoining room (E) with doors leading into the garden (F) and hall (C). This architectural exclusion of the outside world derives from the Islamic sphere, as do the diverse, inward orientated openings of the interior accommodation.

often on the ground floor. Its isolation from the living quarters was an important advance as far as hygiene and fire precautions were concerned. By this time the kitchen occupied a considerable amount of space in the houses of the more well-to-do citizens. Amongst its fittings were the open hearth with chimney hood and a gutter to carry away waste water. In addition to these there were dressers, tables, racks for the crockery and, even at this early stage, small food cupboards; also tripods, chains on which to hang ladles and cooking pots, fire irons and other such items. Most striking of all, however, was the subdivision of the private living quarters on the upper floors. The servants' accommodation consisted of cubicles and closets (e.g. under the stairs, in "suspended chambers" or attics), divided off from the apartments occupied by the family. The family now began to make use of separate rooms for such basic functions as living, eating and sleeping, though a strong sense of community continued to unite all members of the family, young and old alike. Thus it was customary for everyone to live and sleep in one room and for children to share their parents' bed. The staterooms of the patricians and the oratories they used for their private devotions represent this separation of functions in its most exquisite form. This development was made possible only because advances in the fields of lighting and heating permitted the constant use of such rooms irrespective of the vagaries of the weather. Hitherto, windows had afforded little or no protection against the elements, so that the life of the entire household had revolved around the hearth as the only source of warmth, if not of light. Now, however, windows could not only be closed but could also be made translucent, while the development of fireplaces and stoves, as well as improvements in oil lamps, lanterns and candles (hanging lamps, sconces, candle sticks,

chandeliers and candelabra) meant that a large number of rooms was now habitable. They were also more agreeable, being partially wainscotted and, above all, furnished in a more comfortable and, in due course, more luxurious manner.

Some interesting information on the subject of bedchambers and living-rooms in central Europe may be gleaned from the paintings of Late Gothic artists. Thus the Annunciation is depicted by Robert Campin as taking place in a typical living-room of a well-to-do Flemish citizen's middle class town house during the first half of the fifteenth century. Though the room is small, its appointments are solid and pretentious. The main architectural feature is the large fire-place with a projecting metal hood and two sconces for candles. The alcove, which could be used to accommodate items such as jugs, books, etc., is also characteristic of such rooms. The bench and table are among the more important items of joined furniture. They appear in a remarkable variety of forms, as do chairs and footstools. In Dürer's study, for instance, there is an advanced form of trestle table, as well as X-shaped armchairs. Practically all the items, especially the larger pieces of furniture, are decorated with tracery work, carving and other types of Gothic embellishment. Another picture, *Arnolfini and his Wife* by Jan van Eyck, depicts a parlour-cum-bedchamber of the same period. The chest, armchair and looking glass beneath the magnificent Flemish chandelier are eclipsed by the mighty cabinet bed and tester, a piece of furniture much prized by the citizen of medieval times, especially in the colder parts of the Continent. Protected on all sides by curtains, and equipped with a mountainous feather quilt (then used for sleeping on, rather than under), it was frequently big enough to accommodate an entire family. In the South beds were, of course, less cumbersome, while

Windows in medieval middle class town houses.

The Gothic era saw a very significant technical advance in the shape of windows which, when closed, continued to admit the light. Hitherto darkness had set in with the closing of the appreciably smaller windows of the Romanesque era (A) by means of removable shutters secured by a sliding wooden bar. At most, a certain amount of light might percolate through small barred embrasures or openings covered with waxed and stretched linen or parchment. As the production of glass increased during the Gothic era, this expensive material, which had primarily been used in painted form to embellish the enormous windows of churches, gradually invaded the sphere of secular architecture, being at first confined to the houses of the more well-to-do citizens. Drawing B shows a window the upper part of which is covered with material, while the lower half consists of a sliding section glazed with small, square quarries. In drawing C there are diamond-shaped panes at the top of the window, the lower part being equipped with wooden shutters that open inwards. In the fifteenth century, the parts of the windows that were glazed, usually with leaded, bull's-eye panes, grew steadily larger and, in many cases, came to occupy the entire opening. The apertures in storage lofts could be closed by means of wooden shutters.

Forms of heating in Gothic middle class town houses.

It goes without saying that, in central and northern Europe, the solution of the heating problem in a middle class town house of several storeys was of paramount importance. The farmhouse hearth was no longer adequate while the hypocaust method, namely the under-floor heating of air as found in castles and monasteries, was too expensive. Hence the advance represented by the fireproof extraction system of flue and smoke chamber went hand in hand with the introduction into the middle class town house of the fire-place which had been a feature of castle architecture since the eleventh century. (A = thirteenth century fire-place, B = fifteenth century fire-place). In France, England and Italy, in particular, it developed, in the shape of the chimney-piece, into a sumptuous interior appointment. However, it threw out relatively little heat as compared with the brick and tiled stove (also made of iron after about 1500) which, deriving from the farmhouse bread oven, assumed an opulent form (C) from the fourteenth century onwards when it became a feature of the middle class town house. Partial heating was also provided by portable foot-warmers, warming-pans and braziers.

in France the alcove eventually developed into a separate room. However, poorer citizens slept on truckle beds, plank beds or simply on the benches surrounding the stove. In his painting, *The Birth of the Virgin Mary*, the *51* anonymous master of the Life of the Virgin (Cologne School) depicts a lying-in room in a grand patrician house on the Lower Rhine at the end of the fifteenth century. Here we can see every detail of the big, double four poster which, since the thirteenth century, had become the norm; a typical feature of this was the unusual height of the head end which necessitated a semi-recumbent position. Next to it are two richly decorated examples of what was by far the most common piece of cabinet furniture in the Middle Ages, namely the chest. Originally a receptacle hewn out of a single tree trunk, and subsequently made of stout timbers clamped together with iron bands, it now assumed a number of different forms, aided by advances in joinery. The low, narrow chest on the left was used for the storage of linen, while the one in the background on the right, with tall legs and decorated with typical German linenfold panelling, could serve both as a dressing table and as a receptacle. By the middle of the fifteenth century, the chest had evolved into the cupboard, one of the largest pieces of furniture in the middle class town house. At first this took the form of a wardrobe, a chest standing on four tall legs with cupboard doors at the front and drawers beneath. This was used primarily for the storage of clothing, which was to become increasingly sumptuous. Clothing had previously been hung on racks or placed in chests especially reserved for the purpose.

As our previous illustration shows, the walls of the rooms were often hung with patterned materials or pictorial tapestries—the forerunners of the carpet. Otherwise, the walls would be whitewashed, wainscotted and, in the more grandiose rooms, also painted. The walls were seldom if ever adorned with framed pictures because secular painting of this kind were as yet largely unknown. The floors of living-rooms were mostly boarded, though by now carpets and decorative, multi-coloured floor tiles were also coming into use in middle class houses. In the picture by van Eyck the wooden pattens standing on the floor and the dusting brush hanging on the wall show the growing desire for cleanliness.

A general survey of the way the average citizen lived in the Late Middle Ages, however, must take account of the widening gap between central and southern Europe. As compared with the very private, intimate, homely atmosphere of Transalpine domestic architecture, the patrician houses and palaces in the North of Italy have an aura of formal, aristocratic aloofness. A good idea of this may be gained from the Palazzo Davanzati which has been turned into a museum of early Florentine *53, 54* domestic life. Not only the dining-room, but even the bedchamber, are lofty, saloon-like rooms in which the few pieces of furniture are all but lost. In the architecture of the interior, the warmth of wood is confined to the ceiling; what mainly strikes the eye, however, is the smooth plaster of the walls, in some cases richly painted, and the marble and stone flagging on the floors, though even then some were already laid with parquet. The superb appointments include objets d'art, chests, or *cassoni*, embellished with painting and intarsia work. Thus, as the Middle Ages drew to a close, the general style of life of the middle classes was determined, not so much by the natural availability of space, as by a culture oriented towards the display of wealth and already imbued with the spirit of the Renaissance; confined to the most civilized region of Europe, it was not to cross the Alps for another hundred years or so.

VITTORE CARPACCIO, "St Jerome in his Study", oil,
1502–1505. Venice, Scuola di S. Georgio degli Schiavoni.

A contemporary pictorial record is better able to conjure up the spirit of
an epoch than the partial reconstruction of reality. This is because, as
here, it faithfully reproduces, not only the man, but also the many small
objects that have not survived, and the manner in which these are
disposed about the room. Moreover, in the figure of the saintly Father
of the Church, the Venetian artist conveys a lively impression of an
existence such as any scholar might have led at that time. Little heed
is paid to grandiose trappings, while art is thrust aside in favour of a
host of books, writing materials and measuring and experimental
instruments, lying ready to hand and by no means all having to do with
the translation of the Bible. Imperceptibly, the thirst for research is
opening up new fields of inquiry. Here we have early intimations of the
library and the laboratory.

Stylistic Reform— the Renaissance

No previous epoch can really be said to have wrought such far-reaching changes in the *Weltanschauung* of society as did the Renaissance. In all spheres of life the dogmas of the Middle Ages were demolished in the name of Humanism and the search for knowledge. Both the spiritual and the temporal systems, theology and the social hierarchy, were undergoing a profound crisis. The oppressed used rebellion as a means of expressing their claims; discoveries and scientific inventions widened men's horizons, opened up undreamed of possibilities and radically changed the face of the world. In all spheres of art, man and the real world took pride of place. In accordance with the model of Antiquity, man became the measure of all things and the search began for aesthetic ideals which could be seen to conform to the laws of logic and reason. It was the beginning of the modern era.

The leaders of this tremendous, progressive revolution, which had already begun in Italy in the fourteenth century and was to spread to many other countries in the sixteenth, were the urban middle classes. As the unquestioned controllers of the productive forces, they made a determined attempt to overcome the anachronisms by which central Europe was bedevilled. But the force of the early days spent itself in a series of pitiable compromises with the resurgent forces of feudalism. Only in the Netherlands was the early middle class revolution victorious; in other countries such as France, England, Spain, Poland and Hungary, the task of shaping the nation was, it is true, carried out by the crown in alliance with the towns, though at the cost of the latter's subjection to absolutist monarchical rule. Italy, fragmented as she was, became dependent, save for a few enclaves, on foreign dynasties. In Germany, the rise of the regional princes meant that even the imperial cities were in many cases reduced to impotence. Centuries were to go by before a second attempt at revolution on the part of the middle classes was to meet with better success.

Nevertheless, the victory of political reaction did not succeed in preventing either the triumphant emergence of the new cosmography or the further development of the productive forces. So strong were the inhibiting factors, however, that the now dependent middle classes could not in any real sense become patrons of architecture in an imposing form until the end of the eighteenth century. Though splendid council chambers and guild halls were, in fact, built in the towns, they were still outshone by the castles and palaces, the churches and monasteries of the temporal and spiritual princes. And, in essence, the middle class town house, still confined within the city walls, retained the organic structure it had assumed in the Gothic era. For despite the advances made by new modes of production, namely the out-worker system and manufactories, the combination, under a single roof, of the functions of a home and a place of work continued to be a crucial factor in middle class existence. Similarly, the social stratification of the bourgeoisie still persisted and, indeed, became increasingly polarized while experiencing a number of new accretions. To the ranks of the mercantile patriciate and the wealthy masters of guilds were added entrepreneurs, bankers and landowners; the middle stratum of independent artisans and traders absorbed most of the officials and scholars as well as many artists; finally, the plebeian masses grew rapidly as a result of an influx of out-workers and factory workers, not to mention impoverished artisans and other victims of the harsh struggle for existence. The life of the urban farmer, however, remained relatively unaffected by these changes. Generally speaking, then, the basic conditions of middle class life in the towns did not change either rapidly or drastically enough to render obsolete those types of middle class town house which had stood the test of time. As a result of the growth of the unpropertied plebeian strata, however, and the growth of capital speculation, the apartment house assumed greater prominence as a type in its own right. Nevertheless, by comparison with the Gothic era, the number of towns, as of their inhabitants, no longer grew at such a dynamic rate.

Hence, in spite of the many remarkable innovations in building technology—in the field of household amenities, for instance—the history of the middle class town house from the Renaissance up till the beginning of the nineteenth century is the history of the stylistic changes that affected its external appearance. Here, the well-to-do citizen was influenced to a greater extent than hitherto by a desire, first to parade his culture and status and, secondly, to follow the fashion by plagiarizing the new architectural forms adopted by the nobility. And whereas the first still indicates a high degree of self-confidence, the second betrays a certain loss of independence which, in the newly founded princely towns of the Baroque era, was to lead to the total subordination of the middle class house to a pattern prescribed by the local ruler.

Nevertheless, as far as this type of house was concerned, the great revolution of the Renaissance was by no means of such crucial importance as it was in the case of other kinds of building type—the palace, say, or the castle. Many of the essential features of the comfortable town house had already been engendered in the course of the fifteenth century by the Early Renaissance in Italy and, elsewhere, by Late Gothic. Thus in Italy the transition to High Renaissance at the turn of the fifteenth century took place without a break, whereas further north the influx of new forms and ideas could do no more than clothe anew, by way of many transitions, those types of house already in existence. The Gothic decorative system with its animated interplay of pointed and ogee arches, canopies and pinnacles, mouldings and tracery, intricate foliated motifs, and rib vaulting, gave way to a clear tectonic structure with semi-circular arches and shallow pediments, porticos and aediculae, the classical orders, pilasters and architraves, balustrades and attic screens, arabesques, grotesques, medallions and a wealth of figurative ornamentation—usually of a secular nature—as well as barrel vaults and coffered ceilings. Those responsible for importing these ideas from the South were mainly the princes and the cultivated mercantile patriciate who had business connections with Italy. In this way, Renaissance forms gradually became part of the general tradition, being also transmitted by itinerant Italian artists as well as by decorative engravings, the dissemination of which was becoming more widespread. However, the new principles of composition—balanced proportion with emphasis on seriality and symmetry and likewise on horizontal development—were unable, in the case of the middle class town house north of the Alps, wholly to suppress the deep-rooted predilection for exuberant abundance, asymmetry and verticality. Such a rigidly standardized form of articulation presented complications enough, even in regard to the design of the façade behind which was concealed a variety of rooms serving different functions, but when it came to the preparation of the ground plan, those difficulties were compounded. The ideal of a plan conceived along strictly logical and geometrical lines could only be realized in major architectural projects such as castles and palaces, villas and churches. In the case of the simple middle class town house, domestic and oc-

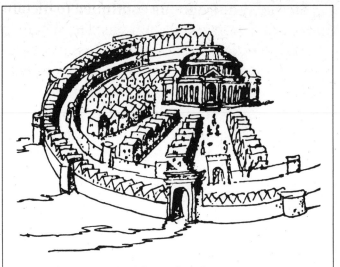

JACQUES ANDROUET DU CERCEAU, drawing of an ideal town (probably after a drawing by Fra Giovanni Giocondo, fifteenth century), middle of the sixteenth century.

The lay-out is wholly subordinated to the concept of the geometrical construction of a circle, with a dominant centre in the form of a domed building from which the streets radiate. True, important elements of the late medieval town are retained, as for instance the encompassing walls with their towers and gateways, the main central square, and streets lined with rows of gable-fronted houses. However, no account is taken in practice of the complex mechanism of life (for instance, all the houses are of uniform design without courtyards, those in the outer precinct are cut off from the centre and, by reason of the radial lay-out, the streets grow progressively wider after the manner of a trapezium). In order to build a town in which all the streets were of even width and the houses and courtyards disposed in squares, it would, in fact, be necessary to have recourse to well-tried, rectangular lay-outs, as found in La Valetta (1608), Zamość (1581) and Freudenstadt (1599), or to compromise with a polygonal solution such as Palmanova, near Udine (1593).

cupational requirements continued to dictate an organic arrangement of rooms. The schemes and theories of interest to the art historian and produced by the new class of artist-architects schooled in Antiquity, were concerned almost solely with large, rewarding subjects or future-orientated Utopias. The middle class town house, still largely the province of the master builder and carpenter, had to make do with embellishment. Rarely does one come across reflections of as fundamental a kind on the subject of this type of house, as propounded by one of the great pioneers and all-round personalities of the Renaissance, Leone Battista Alberti. Inspired by the classical example of Vitruvius, he calls in his book, *De re aedificatoria*, for a private house—as opposed to a princely residence—for the citizen, a house in whose interior (centred round a courtyard) domestic life is so organized as best to comply with the needs of all its occupants, each of whom must have his own room.

As a project, town-planning offered a far greater incentive to the high-flown fantasies of the Renaissance artist than did the modest middle class town house. The concept of an ideal city as a monumental radial lay-out first took shape in the mind of the Italian Filarete (or rather, Antonio di Pietro Averlino), and was subsequently modified by numerous other architects. At the same time his Sforzinda scheme symbolizes the Utopian notion of harmonious social co-existence. The drawing of a similar ideal city, supposedly made by Fra Giovanni Giocondo towards the end of the fifteenth century, and copied, at a later date, by the French architectural theorist, J.A. du Cerceau, not only conveys some idea of what this and other such projects were like, but also demonstrates just why nearly all of them were fated to remain on paper. Life is made to conform too forcibly to a contrived pattern. Radiating like the spokes of a wheel, with a vast

domed building for hub, are rows of identical houses without courtyards, occupied by a citizenry amongst whom all distinctions have been eliminated. The few towns built at this time in accordance with these or similar ideas, as for instance Palmanova, La Valette, Livorno, Zamość or Freudenstadt, are to some extent a compromise. Moreover, they were not the spontaneous creation of the citizens themselves, but rather—like their successors in the Baroque era—the creations of princes and local rulers. A system which reduced everyone to the same level was at variance both with the social structure and with the individualism of the citizen. Hence, right up to the nineteenth century, the forms that continued to predominate in the majority of cities were those which had acquired their definitive stamp in the Gothic era.

Italy as Exemplar—Palazzo and Villa

It is one of the apparent illogicalities of art history that, in the cities of northern Italy, centre of middle class economic power and illustrious birthplace of the Renaissance, the spirit of the new age is best documented, not by the vast mass of middle class town houses, but rather by their aristocratic neighbours—the palazzo inside, and the villa outside, the city. These cannot, strictly speaking, be accounted middle class houses, nor were they of middle class origin, save in a limited, sociological sense, and this only at the outset. Nevertheless, they deserve a brief mention because of the multi-faceted influences they eventually exerted on secular architecture in the towns.

At about the turn of the thirteenth century, long before the beginning of the Early Renaissance—and this applies especially to Tuscany, Lombardy and Venetia—there had already been indications of the development which was to culminate in the élitist isolation of the *popolo grasso*'s town and country seats from the houses of the rest of the citizenry. At the outset the relationship of the medieval patrician *palazzo* to the *casa di borghese* was still plainly discernible, the only distinction between the two being that the former was larger and more impressive in appearance; like the latter, however, it usually had an open arcade for trading purposes on the ground floor and seldom possessed an inner courtyard. Except in Venice, the façades were still relatively plain. Indeed, during the first flowering of the Renaissance, the majority of middle class town houses was to remain fairly unpretentious, artistically speaking, and hence an impression of their anonymous simplicity is obtainable only from pictorial evidence. In the city republics the moving spirits were the exclusive patrician families, the most powerful of whom, as despotic rulers, came increasingly to determine the fate of these towns. In terms of power, splendour and patronage, such banking and mercantile families as the Medici, the Strozzi, the Pitti or the Albizi, in a Florence that was still nominally republican, were in no way inferior to the nobility, whether old or new—the Visconti, the Sforza, the Gonzaga or the d'Este families—who had again seized the reins of government in Milan, Mantua, Modena and Ferrara. The castelli, palazzi and ville were the family seats and residences of a new aristocratic, if not actually ducal, caste of middle class origin who combined sober business sense, overweening ambition and élitist cultural awareness to an extent unequalled anywhere else in Europe.

In the fifteenth century the palazzi of this group retained few of the characteristics of the merchant's house. For the most part a defensive, rusticated wall took the place of the open arcades on the ground floor. All that remained of the arcades were a doorway and a range of small, elevated windows. This completely enclosed, quadrangular complex, with its planimetric, spatial system has ousted all its immediate neighbours in order to make room for a garden and a large cortile surrounded by graceful arcades. The ground floor counting-houses, business apartments and store rooms, like the stables and domestic offices, become of almost secondary importance in a private residence which henceforward would be primarily dedicated to high living and social interaction.

62–65   The Pazzi and Medici-Riccardi palaces in the Tuscan metropolis of Florence are prototypes of the new "private residence" born of the Renaissance mentality. Both were built for old-established patrician families either shortly before or around the middle of the Quattrocento. The former building probably owed its harmoniously balanced façade to one of the pioneers of the Early Renaissance, Filippo Brunelleschi, while the latter is the work of Michelozzo. His patron was the unavowed ruler of the city republic, Cosimo di Medici, under whom the town experienced its finest flowering. Though it never fulfilled an official function, this palazzo nevertheless proclaims Cosimo's ambition that it should be *primus inter pares* among patrician buildings. Like a fortress, the ground floor shuts itself off from the outside world with its heavy, rusticated masonry, while the upper floors, each lower than the last, with their comparatively smooth masonry and their flights of round-headed twin-light windows, appear less ponderous, without detracting from the deliberately monumental effect. As a novelty in a palazzo the wall is crowned by a roof cornice of classical design, whose massiveness and wealth of forms seem to proclaim a schematic intention. Another innovation, this time in the interior, the coffered ceiling, was borrowed from the

FLORENCE. *Palazzo Medici-Riccardi. Plans of the original building before it was enlarged in the Baroque era. Ground, first and second floors (Ill. 63–65).*

Round the square, arcaded *cortile* at the centre, the four wings of the building and the open courtyard to the rear exhibit a spatial sequence which, despite some attempt at axial regularity, is still organic in conception. At ground floor level, behind the small, highly placed windows, are the domestic offices, store-rooms and stables. Only the *cortile* with its arcade and the family loggia in the left-hand corner were used for social intercourse and display. Several stairs (some of them subsequently altered; the main staircase is on the left-hand side) led up from the *cortile* to the first floor, which contained the private saloons, bedchambers and chapel. At one time there was a gallery, but this was later enclosed to form a corridor. Apart from the upper saloon on the street side, the rooms on the less lofty, brick-built second floor were used to accommodate the servants. These in their turn were grouped round a columnar loggia.

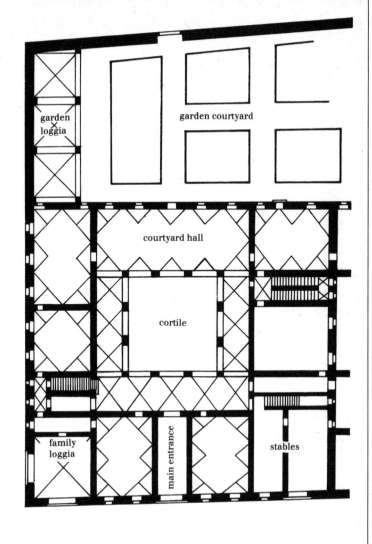

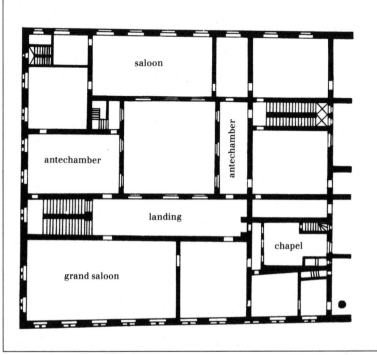

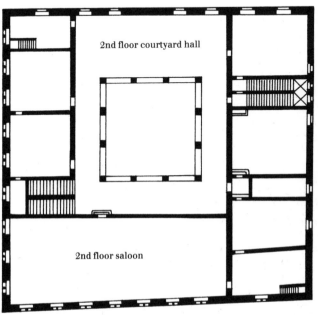

buildings of Rome, and is a manifestation of the desire to document accession to a great legacy. Nor has the arcaded cortile characteristic of the ancient Roman peristyle house been forgotten. The inner courtyard as the centre of a complex comprising four wings is here fully realized for the first time. That courtyard no longer has any domestic function; rather it is the focal point of family and social life and, with its ordered rectangularity and the buoyancy of its airy arcades, perfectly reflects the *joie de vivre* of Renaissance man. Originally a fountain stood here which, together with many works of art, was taken to the Palazzo Vecchio when Lorenzo moved there. In the private chapel on the first floor, however, one valuable decorative piece remains. This is Benozzo Gozzoli's fresco, *The Adoration of the Magi*, in which he portrays the most eminent members of the family—an example of the secularization of religious themes in the Renaissance.

At about the same time the Palazzo Rucellai 58 was built in Florence to the designs of Leone Battista Alberti, the leading architectural theorist of the Quattrocento. While all the elements of the grand residence—symmetrical, monumental lay-out, rusticated masonry, stylobate, twin windows and crenellations— are retained, there is also an innovative concept, namely the vertical articulation of storeys by means of pilasters. Together with the wide architraves of classical section, they lend a stronger rhythm to the façade and make it appear less fortress-like. Here we find applied for the first time the Renaissance principle of the equilibrium between loads and load carriers, and of the seriality of plainly distinct architectural members. So novel was this concept that it evoked severe criticism at the time and, indeed, several decades were to elapse before it found general acceptance. With the Palazzo Piccolomini in Pienza, built immed-

iately afterwards, between 1460 and 1464, the same architect, Bernardo Rosselino, went a step further in his strictly symmetrical arrangement of the whole complex along either side of the central axis (from the main entrance through the cortile to the garden).

Neither before nor since has the spririt of competition engendered in the field of private middle class architecture results as grandiose or as generally stimulating as the Palazzi of the fifteenth century. If a citizen sought high office, his motive might well be the construction of a yet more beautiful palace; indeed, the authority responsible for preserving the beauty of the city of Florence received numerous applications for the reconstruction of façades. In 1458 the powerful patrician Pitti family embarked upon a scheme more ambitious, perhaps, than any other, involving as it did a truly monumental residence intended to surpass even the palazzo of the Medici. The win- 61 dows of the Pitti palace were to be as big as, if not bigger than, the portals of the latter. In imitation of Early Roman rusticated architecture, and of aqueducts in particular, the massive pile on seven axes and with storeys each eleven metres high, was built of gigantic stone blocks, the largest to be used since classical times. However, a few years later the Pitti family was forced to suspend operations because of the vast building costs and also because its fortune had been depleted by fierce competition. The vast building was left incomplete and unoccupied until acquired by the Grand Duke of Tuscany about a hundred years later, when it attained its present dimensions.

Everything that had hitherto conspired to make the Tuscan palazzo what it was, is com- 56 bined in the Palazzo Strozzi, which was begun in 1489 and was not to receive its projecting cornice until after 1536. This building, with its splendid monumentality and strict regard for

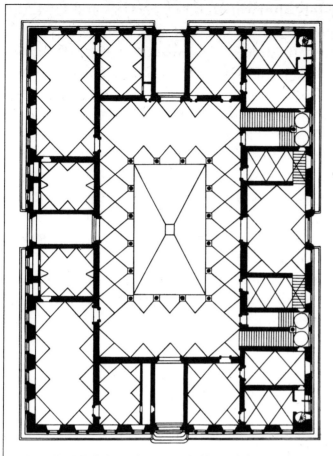

FLORENCE. *Palazzo Strozzi in the Via degli Strozzi. Plan of the ground story (Ill. 56).*

What is remarkable about this plan is the rigorous symmetry upon which the concept of the whole lay-out is based.

composition, is the epitome of High Renaissance palace architecture. As may be seen from the ground plan, all the rooms are disposed with complete symmetry about the central axis. Here, then, a tendency that had long been apparent has finally prevailed, namely, the carrying through to the internal spatial structure of the regularity of the façade and inner courtyard. As far as its elements are concerned, the simple, rusticated façade does not surpass that of the Palazzo Pitti, yet by constituting a focal point, not only in its right, but also within the context of town-planning, it bears witness to what was then a new aspiration. For the piazza in front of this building is completely dominated by the powerful façade. Here we see first indications of an authoritarian claim to pride of place within the city such as had never before been put forward by the middle class town house.

Our excursion into the specialized field of the palazzo cannot, of course, cover the great diversity of regional types. For instance, the Roman palace may be distinguished from the Tuscan primarily by the predilection for majestic effect and a strongly plastic treatment of the walls. The presence of the classical architecture of Imperial Rome undoubtedly encouraged this tendency towards the monumental. The very opposite is true of the third main type, the Venetian palace of the Renaissance, whose show front overlooking the water displayed what was already, by tradition, an uninhibited wealth of decoration. Late Gothic with oriental overtones was to predominate here until after the middle of the fifteenth century, and it was not until the end of the fifteenth century that Renaissance forms asserted themselves, albeit with backward glances at their precursors. Gothic tracery is still in evidence in the treatment of the windows of the Palazzo Vendramin-Calergi which dates from the end of the Quattrocento. The wall is so pierced by

67

123

openings as to be almost invalidated and, with its three-quarter columns—here appearing for the first time—and its cornices, forms a framework that is strongly sculptural in conception. Although Venice entered into a political and economic decline in the sixteenth century, there still persisted, in the centuries that followed, the regional peculiarity of an opulently decorated and uninhibitedly light-hearted palace architecture – but an architecture that was feudal and directed rather towards public display.

Just as the Venetian palace was formed by its situation on a waterway, so the ground, rising steeply like an amphitheatre, on which the rival seaport of Genoa lay, contributed to the development of a local type of palace. This was ingeniously adapted to the terrain by being built on terraced sites on a longitudinal axis. Austere and lucid, though spatially of remarkably versatile conception, the Genoese palace is the consummation of the High Renaissance. Our example, the Palazzo Podesta, built after the middle of the sixteenth century with an oval vestibule that already presages the Baroque, has been specially selected to give an idea of the richness of the highly developed architectural ornamentation of the Renaissance. The wall is articulated by means of a decorative composition in which delicately worked forms—festoons, masks, caryatids, trophies, medallions, cartouches, volutes and flat bands—are combined, and which exceeds in richness anything that has gone before. At this time, town palaces in Italy were, it is true, commissioned mainly by the resurgent nobility and by the patriciate who had now become their peers.

Another building type, the villa, rapidly adapted itself to the changing social circumstances of the day. Ancient Rome had already seen the emergence of various types – the often luxuriously appointed urban or suburban villa (*villa urbana* and *villa suburbana*), as well as the rural *villa rustica*, which is a kind of farm with a house and ancillary buildings. In the fourteenth century, a little less than a thousand years later, when the rich merchant princes in the Italian towns had acquired vast estates and thereby became big land-owners and heirs to that aristocratic legacy, they, too, built houses of much the same type. In addition to the palace, the villa now became a favourite resort in which the citizen might lead a sociable life outside the town, and take a rest from the world of business. Surrounded by walls and fences, the Renaissance villa consisted of more or less extensive gardens in which there were geometrically laid out paths, flower beds, lawns, pools, fountains, pavilions and pergolas. This close, harmonious association of internal and external spaces manifests Renaissance man's new relationship to nature which had to subordinate itself to him. Many great architects of the day dedicated themselves to that fascinating form which demanded more charm and fantasy than solemnity and grandeur. Probably the best known example—and also the most important from the point of view of the history of architecture—is the Villa Capra (Rotonda) just outside Vicenza, a structure with a central dome, designed by Andrea Palladio. With its imposing porticos and broad flights of steps, the building is open on all four sides. A lively impression of a villa of this type may be gained from a contemporary picture of the residence 69 of the Maggi family. Like many other prominent Venetian merchants, the latter had planned to build a handsome villa on the mainland (*terra ferma*) in the valley of the River Brenta. The main building has several storeys, but is not otherwise particularly large and serves as the focal point of the symmetrically laid out gardens in which to stroll. There is also a pavilion for banquets and more intimate repasts

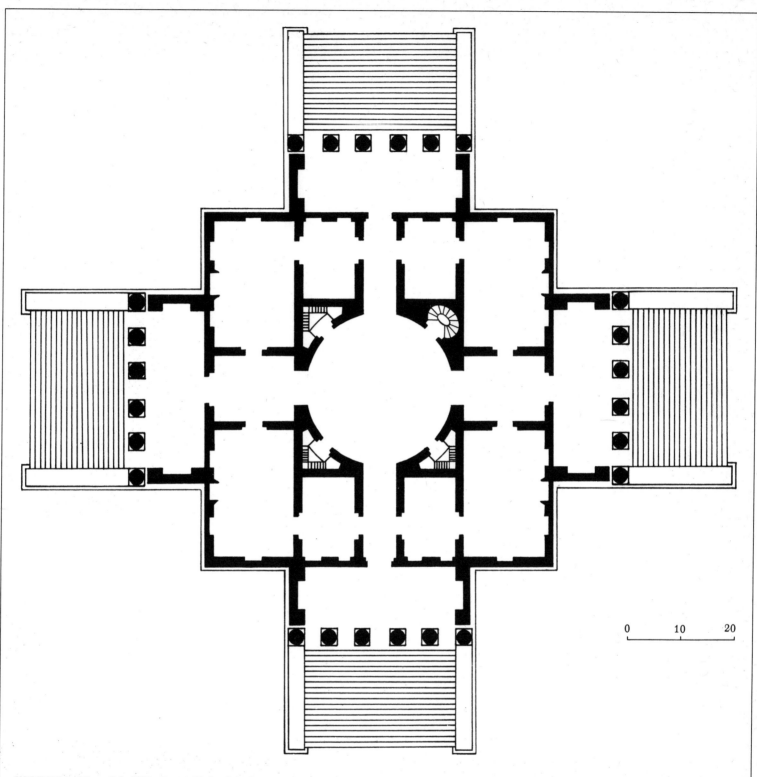

VICENZA. *Plan of the Villa Capra (Rotonda), designed by Andrea Palladio in 1550/51, and largely completed by 1553. The mezzanine floor is a later addition.*

Palladio, one of the pioneers of the classical school of thought, built some thirty villas in and around Vicenza. In this building he adopted the schema, normally restricted to church architecture, of a cruciform structure with a central dome. The geometrical regularity of the plan is wholly in keeping with the spirit of the Renaissance. The building's character as a villa manifests itself chiefly in the fact that, on every side, it affords free access to the surrounding countryside.

0   10   20

125

and, for occasional diversion, a maze. Despite its many connections with middle class patrons the villa, no less than the palace, was first and foremost an aristocratic form. Not until the nineteenth century was it adopted by the well-to-do middle classes, a development which owed its origin to the desire to withdraw from the rapidly growing towns to the peace of the suburbs, away from industrial districts and the houses of the proletariat.

The Synthesis with Tradition
North of the Alps

In the countries of the "Holy Roman Empire of the German Nation", the now considerable economic power of the towns went hand in hand with the political impotence of the Crown and the consolidation of regional particularism. This peculiar combination of historical circumstances conferred on the middle class town house of the Renaissance a richness and multiplicity of forms virtually without parallel anywhere else in Europe. Whereas in many parts of the Continent nations evolved as a result of the alliance between an absolutist monarchy and the urban bourgeoisie, so that castle, palace and church architecture predominated, there was no such guiding influence in Germany. Yet the system of small states was exceptionally favourable to the development of regional peculiarities in the field of middle class architecture. Thanks to the economic prosperity of the towns, the latter—along with castle architecture—was to play an outstanding role in the German Renaissance. For in spite of the growing dependence of the towns on their princely rulers, especially after the failure of the early bourgeois revolution at the beginning of the sixteenth century, those princes encouraged the business activities of their middle class subjects in so far as they

seemed conducive to the consolidation of their own dynastic power. Towards the end of the fourteenth century, the German economy had been pre-eminent in Europe thanks to numerous improvements in productive methods and equipment, increased specialization in the crafts' trades, the extension of early capitalist relations of production in the outworker system and in manufacturing and, last but not least, the continuing prosperity of foreign trade. This flourishing state of affairs was to persist right into the second half of the sixteenth century when stagnation set in under the rule of the princes. In the industrial and commercial regions of southwestern, central and northern Germany, there was a vast accumulation of wealth in the hands of a small patrician upper class or of powerful business concerns such as those of the Fuggers and Welsers. But since there was at this time little call for the founding of new towns or for any material enlargement of existing ones, that wealth evoked a wave of rebuilding, old traditional middle class town houses and communal or corporative buildings such as town halls, guild halls, arsenals and weigh houses, being remodelled in accordance with the new style of the Renaissance. Here it was not so much a question of practical or technical improvements in the domestic and occupational fields, as a desire to display power and wealth in the forms assumed by a culture then at its zenith and intimately associated with Humanism. An Italian, Giorgio Vasari, known as "the father of the history of art" had stigmatized Gothic as being of "barbarian" origin.

Obviously this "aesthetic anathema" from Italy could not effect an immediate revolution north of the Alps. The roots of Gothic had struck too deep and had survived too long for that style to be rejected by the vast mass of traditionally minded citizens. Despite the spread of education in the towns, a genuinely comprehensive appreciation of the Renaissance nevertheless still remained confined to a small circle of artists. At first it was in paintings and drawings that the latter—foremost among them Albrecht Dürer—depicted the new world of forms. Next, the architectural style of the Renaissance was systematically adopted, for reasons of prestige, by princely rulers, some of them also influenced by courtly art in France, and by wealthy patricians in the centres of Italian trade. The larger public, on the other hand, adopted it only with reluctance, usually changing it in the process and confining their borrowings to decorative motifs. The new world of forms largely owed its dissemination to a stream of manuals and decorative engravings by painters, draughtsmen, architects and artist craftsmen, chiefly from the Southwest of Germany. Needless to say, much of the original clarity and logic was lost in the course of this didactic exposition, which was all too seldom based on first-hand knowledge. What was gained, on the other hand, was the freedom to transform the foreign motifs organically and imaginatively in accordance with an outlook in Gothic and a predilection for abundance and exuberance.

Contradictory factors accompanied the influence on Transalpine architecture by the Renaissance. By the end of the fourteenth century it was already beginning to find acceptance in the ruling houses of France, Bohemia, Poland and Hungary, thus acquiring what was at first a notably aristocratic character which the leaders of the patriciate sought to emulate. Especially after Europe had been split in two by religious controversy, non-artistic motives also played some part in the acceptance or rejection of the Humanism of the Renaissance. This style did not become representative until the middle of the sixteenth century.

As far as the countries of Germany are concerned, it is interesting to note that it was in Augsburg, a centre for Italian trade, that use was first made of Renaissance forms by leading patrician families. Speculation, exchange and loan transactions, the exploitation of mines in the Tyrol, Styria and Hungary, and foreign trade that extended as far as the East Indies, had made the Fuggers the richest mercantile family in Germany. Ennobled by their debtor, the Emperor Maximilian, they recorded their social elevation and cosmopolitan outlook in grandiose Renaissance buildings. In Babenhausen, Kirchheim and Oberkirchberg they built castles and, some time after 1509, a burial chapel in Augsburg which was indeed the very first example of Renaissance architecture in Germany. They drew on the Italian palazzi for their town palace erected between 1512 and 1515 in the Maximilianstrasse. Nothing now remains but written accounts of the frescos on Hans Burgkmair's façades, of the art treasures in his gorgeously appointed saloons or, for that matter, of his other Renaissance buildings in Augsburg. Worthy of mention is the design for a house whose ground plan is that of a typical middle class town house, executed by the architectural theorist Josef Furttenbach the Elder. The plans and elevations have come down to us in his *Architectura privata* published in Augsburg in 1662, a book that was not without influence on the subsequent development of the type of domestic architecture with which we are here concerned.

However, such early, consistent and supranational borrowings in the field of architecture were the exception rather than the rule for the majority of citizens. Only with reluctance did they adopt the details of the new style, applying them to the doorways, windows, oriels and gables of the existing fabric which were traditionally the features upon which embellishment was lavished; at most a partial reconstruction of the façade, interior or courtyard might be undertaken in deference to this or

127

that requirement. The narrow streets lined with houses remained unchanged, as did the cramped plots, save when these were enlarged by the purchase of additional land. There was little or no increase in the number of storeys and the basic differences between the South and North German type of house continued to persist. In the case of the latter, however, numerous alterations were demanded to make it conform to the markedly sculptural articulation of the walls characteristic of Renaissance architecture. Moreover, it was not easy to base the North German gable-fronted hall-house on a principle of composition based on lateral expansion. The South German type, on the other hand, which was often eaves-fronted and clearly divided into rooms and storeys, was better suited to such adaptation. Hence it is here, and in the vernacular of the timber-framed house, that the development of the German middle class town house of the Renaissance attains its apogee. Even centres of Renaissance culture such as Augsburg and Nuremberg exhibit examples typical of this slow transition during which the basic medieval structures were preserved.

Together with its two great sons, Albrecht Dürer and Hans Sachs, the imperial city of Nuremberg was the embodiment of the new artistic outlook in Germany and, as the repository of the crown jewels, the town occupied a pre-eminent position. Its flourishing foreign trade, notably in cloth, and numerous craft trades, especially in the field of metal-working (armourers, goldsmiths and silversmiths), had produced a prosperous and numerically strong middle class who confidently opened their minds to what was new without rejecting the old-fashioned ways of their forebears. Builders adapted their designs to the narrow, irregular sites in an extraordinarily ingenious and rational manner, the typical lay-out being front block, courtyard and rear block, with a small

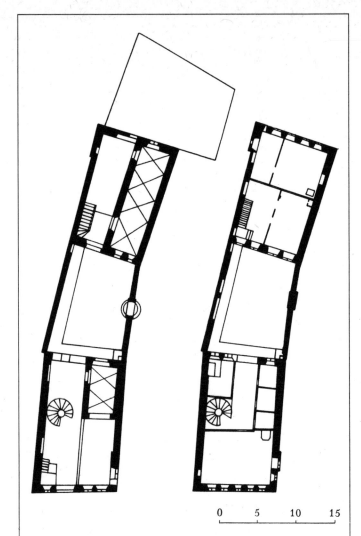

0   5   10   15

NUREMBERG. *No. 7, Bergstrasse, plans of the ground and first floors of a merchant's house at the turn of the fifteenth century.*

Oblivious of Renaissance symmetry, the German middle class town house of the sixteenth century remained an organism moulded by tradition. The irregular parcels of land, some ten metres wide by forty metres or more deep, permitted neither lateral expansion on a horizontal plane nor the symmetrical development of the whole along an axis. The South German type of house, with its varied system of stairs and landings, enabled each story to be subdivided without rigidity and in accordance with requirements. Only in specific zones, such as the compact façade, the state-rooms overlooking the street and the inner courtyard surrounded by arcades on several storeys, could the new decorative forms be employed in a grander setting.

128

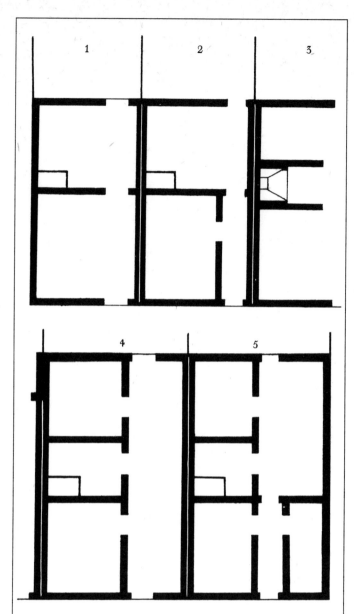

Phases in the development of the ground plan of the lower middle class town house.

This schematized presentation of ground plans exemplifies the spatial diversification that took place in two and three cell types, between the Middle Ages and the Renaissance, as a result of growing needs and technical innovations. 1 = direct access from street to shop/workshop and rear living-room with hearth; 2 = introduction of the vestibule as a separate place of entry; 3 = partitioning-off of kitchen; 4 = addition of outshot, the vestibule being enlarged to hall-like proportions; 5 = vestibule subdivided into hall-living-room, additional chamber and narrow entrance passage. In the sixteenth century spatial diversification went hand in hand with improvements in lighting (glass) and heating (fireplaces, tiled and cast iron stoves in addition to the hearth).

adjoining garden. The ground floor rooms were still devoted exclusively to the owner's occupation—a shop or workshop with storage vaults in the front building and stables at the back. Newel, geometrical or straight stairs connected the landings of the upper storeys which contained numerous heated rooms and chambers—an indication of the wide variety of their uses—as well as one or two large staterooms at the front. These, like the façade and the typical inner courtyards with their arcades on one or more sides connecting the front and back ranges, afforded free play to the traditional love of ornamentation. Until well into the sixteenth century, however, Gothic tracery was still used in the parapets of the courtyard galleries, while houses still had gables facing the street. Since soft, coarse-grained nagelfluh was still the most usual building material, the ornamentation of façades by means of carvings was largely ruled out, though the smooth, compact surface served *73–77* as a good base for fresco painting. In the hands of masters such as Hans Burgkmair, Mathias Kager, Hans Bocksberger, Christoph Amberger, and Guilio Licinio, this medium was to attain its greatest flowering, not only in some of the other towns of South Germany—Regensburg, Ingolstadt, Passau, Landshut, and Wasserburg—as well as in Switzerland and in Austria.

There are few surviving examples in Nuremberg, a city which suffered particularly severe damage during the Second World War. Indeed, its most important Renaissance middle class *87–89* town house, the Pellerhaus, was destroyed during an air raid. True, this building erected between 1602 and 1605, with what was probably the finest arcaded courtyard in Germany, was an exception so far as Nuremberg was concerned because of the strongly sculptural treatment of the façade as well as the emphasis on symmetry which is the conscious expression of

129

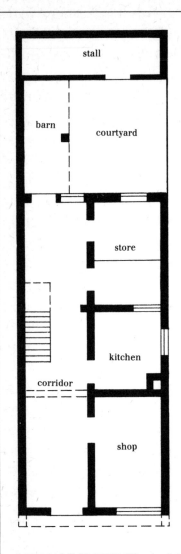

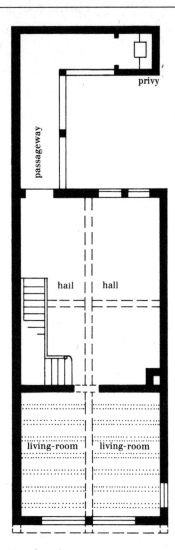

stall

barn

courtyard

store

kitchen

corridor

shop

privy

passageway

hall | hall

living-room | living-room

0 1 2 3 4

SCHMALKALDEN *(Thuringia). Plans and street elevation of an artisan's timber-framed house, circa 1500.*

On a site no more than five metres wide all the multifarious domestic and business functions are combined in remarkably organic fashion by making use of the courtyard, too. The focal point of domestic life and commerical intercourse is situated on the well-lit street side, while the centre is mainly taken up with living-rooms, domestic offices and storage and communication areas, lit either from the side or from the courtyard.

the Renaissance mentality. Yet the national idiom is also discernible in the lively, if sometimes cluttered, decoration, as well as in the oriel windows and in a dormer gable so lofty that it almost concealed the fact that this is an eaves-fronted house.

But before we turn our attention to the artistically important houses built by the patriciate, and to the multiplicity of their regional types, we must accord a brief mention to the usually unadorned domestic architecture of the lower middle class. The lower middle class had remained outside the mainstream of ideas, while its social standing had, if anything, deteriorated. Everywhere there still persisted the simple, well-tried lay-out of the two or three celled type. Barely distinguishable one from the other, tucked away in narrow streets and alleyways near or outside the perimeter of the town, and exemplifying the solidarity of the craft trades, these houses are interesting, if artistically anonymous, witnesses to the history of our civilization. For they, too, reflect the progress made in the practical subdivision of rooms. Originally, there had been a back room with a hearth and a front workshop directly accessible from the street; this workshop was then partitioned off by means of a side corridor, while the insertion of a kitchen became the norm. Finally, extra bedchambers and other rooms, such as a hall and a separate privy, were created by adding further storeys, outshots or other buildings in the courtyard. Not infrequently these houses, with frontages between three and six metres, were lived in, not just by one family, but by a growing number of lodgers and tenants; citizens without property of their own who needed cheap accommodation. With the exception of servants, members of these plebeian strata rarely found shelter in the town houses of the patricians.

Nevertheless, some of the better-off members of the middle classes, notably the patri-cians, were now increasingly interested in the growing need for additional rented accommodation. There was a very good reason for this interest: they could use the middle class town house as a profitable capital investment, a circumstance consistent with the general tendency of merchant's capital to develop into usurer's capital. Without lowering his social status a landlord could accommodate a large number of tenants in a small space by renting his surplus back rooms and ancillary buildings, or else by building or acquiring houses specially for that purpose. Profitability apart, there were other attendant reasons that were not to be sneezed at—the elimination of a potential cause of unrest, for instance, or the possibility of enhancing one's prestige by endowing "pious" foundations under the guise of humanitarianism. The process whereby the tenement evolved as an independent type entirely devoted to the accommodation of a number of different parties, was, of course, a gradual one, and initially involved the use of existing buildings. Nor did it require any revolutionary innovations, for the self-contained domestic unit, which consisted of living-rooms, bedrooms, kitchen and landing, and sharing the same roof with similar units, one to each floor, had already existed in principle as far back as the Middle Ages. However, co-existence with other apartment dwellers who were not members of the same family called for more positive delimitations, as also a private entrance for each tenant. Not only the renting, but also the purchase, of apartments became customary, as for example in the Munich *Herbergen*, where up to seven owners of apartments might live in one house, or the so-called *Kanzelhäuser* in Danzig which already consisted of one-roomed apartments with kitchen.

The clearest manifestation, however, of the extent to which the system was gaining ground lies in the rows of very simple, rationally planned, one-or two-storeyed houses put up at this time near or outside the town perimeter which were usually for renting to the less well-to-do classes. Here, too, one can see the origins dating back to the late Middle Ages of charitable foundations, as in Cologne in the thirteenth century, or the fourteenth century Béguinages in Ghent. Examples that survive from the fifteenth century are the group of six single-storeyed *Seelenhäuser* in Nördlingen and the Sieben Zeiten built in Nuremberg for homeless weavers in 1488. Good works of this kind being then the rule, it was no coincidence that a new standard should have been set with the founding of the Fuggerei in Augsburg by *85* the Fuggers, not only the richest patrician family in Germany, but also the most receptive to the influence of the Renaissance. With an eye to his own renown and (as the deed of the foundation has it) "to the Glory of Almighty God . . . and to the furtherance of Eternal Bliss and in order that certain poor needy citizens and inhabitants of Augsburg . . . should not thus publicly solicit alms . . . from artisans, day labourers and others", Jakob Fugger purchased seven parcels of land in the Jakobervorstadt upon which, between the years 1516 and 1525, he built fifty-two houses numbering a hundred and six dwellings in all. Each of the two-or three-roomed dwellings in the rows of two-storeyed houses had its own street door, kitchen and hall or stair. The ground plan and domestic arrangements (fireplace, stove, bread oven, cold storage pit and store room, either under the stairs or in the attic) was simple and well thought-out, if standardized. No less logically conceived was the gridiron lay-out of the six streets. Most of the houses presented their long sides to the street, while the ends of the rows were lent rhythmic animation by the gable fronts. With its communal institutions—chapel, pest house, hospital, school and ad-

ministrative buildings—this area, surrounded by a wall with three gates, constituted an urban organism in its own right. Though the principle of a standardized residential district with philanthropic institutions was far ahead of its time, it nevertheless smacked of a ghetto for the indigent. What was new was its rationality, a product of the spirit of the times.

The love of embellishment that characterized the upper middle class houses increased. Thus, the houses of the patricians in, for example, the imperial city of Frankfurt, an international banking and commercial centre, are picturesque if unpretentious and, with their oriels, high pitched gables and timber frames, remain firmly rooted in the Gothic. The strikingly large, arched openings for trading purposes on the ground floor point to a middle class attitude that is pragmatic rather than vainglorious. An exception to this was the Salzhaus, nearly completely destroyed in the *72* Second World War, or again, the Laderam House on the Römer, dating from 1627, at the back of which was a gorgeously embellished stair tower. In this narrow, gable-fronted house, with its superabundance of Renaissance carving on the timber framing of the upper storeys, and its frescos on the side elevation, foreign and native elements are combined in exceptionally happy partnership.

In Alsace the middle class town house presents a similarly organic picture. In this well wooded region, timber frame architecture in the Franconian idiom had long played a dominant role. Its development into a richly decorative style inspired by the ornamental work of the Renaissance as found in stone and brick architecture, reached a high-water mark with *70* the building of what is known as Kammerzell's House in Strasbourg. When the three upper storeys were reconstructed in 1589 a cheesemonger, one Martin Braun, ensured that the surfaces of posts, braces and rails were em-

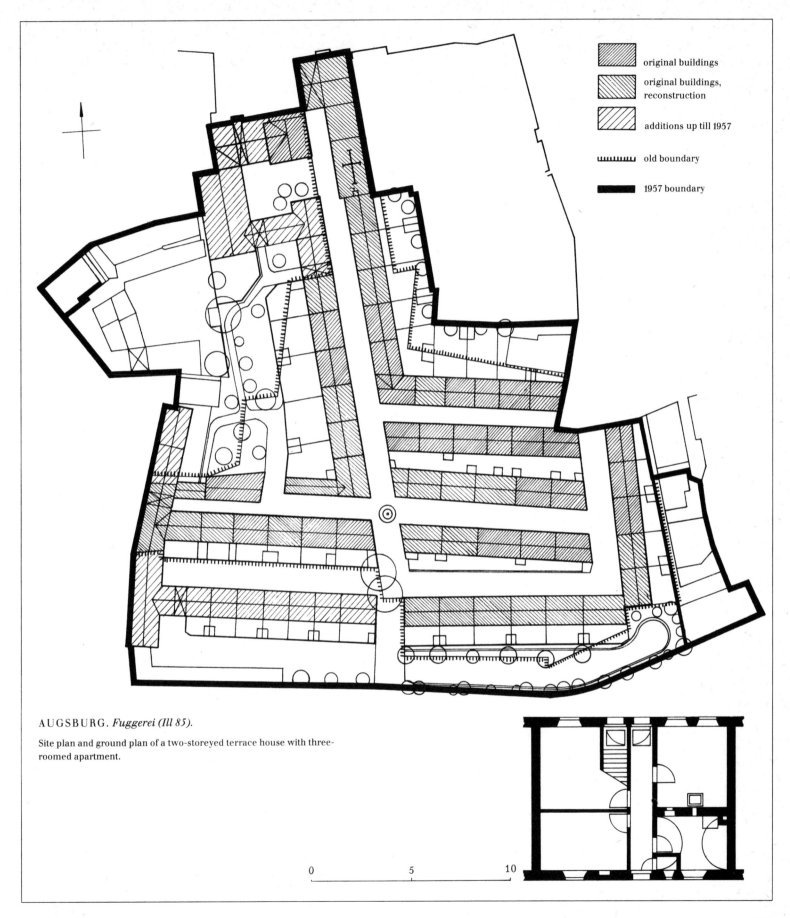

original buildings

original buildings, reconstruction

additions up till 1957

old boundary

1957 boundary

AUGSBURG. *Fuggerei (Ill 85).*

Site plan and ground plan of a two-storeyed terrace house with three-roomed apartment.

0   5   10

bellished with an abundance of finely carved ornaments, emblems and other figurative motifs. Compared to a home such as this that proclaims the wealth, culture and virtues of the client, the artisans' houses in the tannery 71 district have an almost poverty-stricken air. The timber framing above the stone built ground floor is devoid of all decoration. And whereas the individual storeys are still jettied —though less boldly than heretofore, in accordance with current practice—those of Kammerzell's House are on one plane as in stone or brick architecture. In Colmar, too, there, still survive numerous timber-framed buildings which show a similar, sociologically induced disparity of treatment. The houses in the tannery district on the Logelbach, which originally had open floors with racks for drying hides, are without embellishment, unlike the Pfisterhaus where the new forms have been lavishly applied. Here, however, they are completely integrated into a structure which, with its corner oriel, wooden gallery and stair tower, is still in the medieval Gothic style.

There is also a relatively large stock of middle class town houses in the Swiss Confederation where, after its de facto secession from the German Empire following the Peace of Basle in 1499, the urban bourgeoisie grew quickly in the cantonal capitals along the north-south trade routes. They determined policy and for this reason there is an absence of large, impressive buildings. Rather, the houses, built of stone or brick, are of the traditional South German type, solid but unassuming, in which all the various impulses from the countries round about combine to create a national idiom. To the oriels and arcades inherited from the Late Gothic period was added, in the sixteenth century, the extensive painting of façades, a characteristic also common in Southwest Germany. The smooth plaster surfaces of what were often eaves-fronted houses af-

forded a first-class base for frescos and sgraffiti with their wealth of illusionist architectural designs and portrayals of secular themes. One of the first examples of Early Renaissance wall painting, dating from between 1520 and 1525, 75 may be seen on the Weisser Adler (White Eagle) in Stein am Rhein. The relationship of the painting to the architecture is exceedingly free and by no means strictly logical; indeed, it reveals not so much a monumental frame of mind as delight in a multiplicity of decorative motifs. Fitted into the spaces available with great versatility, and framed by architectural elements treated in a perspectival manner and by decorative borders reminiscent of contemporary book ornamentation, are noteworthy representations of scenes from Roman history, Boccacio's *Decameron* and the classical Pantheon. The fact that many of the Late Gothic patrician houses in the market square at Stein am Rhein were embellished with wall-paintings of a similar nature shows how strong was the desire for representational art at this time. Hans Holbein's magnificent design for the painted decoration of the Haus zum Tanz in Basle (1530/31) can almost certainly be said to have set the standard for this medium.

The most important wall-painting in Switzer- 76 land may be seen on Das Haus "Zum Ritter" in Schaffhausen. It was executed for a goldsmith by Tobias Stimmer between 1567 and 1570 and extols the middle class virtues in the guise of classical mythology. Even the idea of sacrificial death was allegorized, as an expression of the deep-rooted libertarianism of the Confederates and their militant humanism which was closely bound up with Calvinism. Another 73, 74 martial theme appears on the Goldener Ochse (Golden Ox), namely the Trojan War, this time actually accompanied by explanatory texts. Here an obvious parallel presents itself, for just as in the past, the walls of churches were adorned with paintings of stories from the

Gospel as a means of conveying their teaching to a congregation that was largely illiterate, so now, on the façades of middle class town houses, recourse was had to secular and classical mythology through which were represented a spirit of worldliness and the new virtues that went with it. The last-named example is also noteworthy on account of the magnificent surface sculpture on the oriel windows and the main entrance. Despite the fact that the house was rebuilt towards the end of the Renaissance period, the oriels, like the asymmetrical treatment, are still Gothic in conception.

Rarely have the forms of the Italian Renaissance been applied in such consummate form and with such purity as in the Ritterscher 84 Palast in Lucerne. Until well into the sixteenth century the façades, doorways and windows of most of the city's middle class town houses still continued to display a combination of Gothic elements and Renaissance decorative detail; Schultheiss Lux Ritter, on the other hand, as *primus inter pares*, brought in master builders from Italy and the Ticino to build a patrician palace that was stylistically orthodox. Its finest feature is the gracious courtyard with its three tiered arcade which looks as if it had been transported direct from Florence to Switzerland. It was also to serve as the model for the pillared courtyard of the Göldlinhaus in Lucerne, built in 1600.

In the heartlands of Austria, as in Switzerland, Italian influence was to play a decisive role, though here, in the hereditary territory of the Habsburgs, it was the noble patrons who took the lead. As far as the middle class town house was concerned, however, we may observe the characteristic pattern of gradual transition from Gothic to Renaissance or, alternatively, the juxtaposition of the forms of both styles especially in the mining towns. A typical example is the Gemaltes Haus (painted house) 77

in Eggenburg. The oriels, doorways and window surrounds of this building, erected after 1525, are evidence of the above-mentioned transition, whereas the sgraffito paintings with their illusionist architecture (rustication, round-headed arches, pilasters and architraves) and scenes from both classical mythology and the Old Testament point to the new era. Other important painted façades may still be seen in Retz and on the Trautson Haus in Innsbruck (No. 22 Herzog-Friedrich-Strasse, with its fifteenth century nucleus, and Late Gothic coats of arms, tracery and reliefs on the oriels) which dates from about 1541 and is the work of the 106 painter Gregor Türing. The castello-like design of our example in Retz clearly betrays the predilection for castle architecture of its patron, a leading merchant by the name of Firenz. Similarly, the finest Late Renaissance arcaded court-83 yard in Vienna (No. 7 Bäckerstrasse) could hardly be conceived of without the monumental castle courtyard of the same period, although it probably had other roots in the typical treatment of that feature in the South German plateau.

Regional Multiplicity in Germany

In the parts of Europe we have so far considered, the proximity of Italy and the pre-eminence of stone and brick architecture meant that the middle class town house, while still retaining many Gothic traces, was to a greater or lesser extent influenced by the Renaissance. Timber framing, a traditional form of construction firmly rooted in Alsace, Swabia and southern Germany, was far more ready to adopt, and at the same time adapt, the decorative elements of the new style which were already well established in brick and stone architecture, than was its counterpart further to the north, in the hilly, well-wooded districts of Central Germany. Here, especially in the country round about the Harz Mountains, timber framing had been common ever since Germanic times as a highly developed form of the traditional carpenter's art. The influx of Renaissance forms did nothing to change what were well-tried constructional principles, but simply provided the impulse for the further enrichment of the surface decoration of all wooden parts which were transformed by the imaginative application of folk art and enhanced by the use of colour. A fine example of this, as well as of the harmonious interplay of periods, is the Brusttuch in Goslar, an imposing house built between 1521 and 1523 for Master Johannes Thilling (Tillig), a mining and iron-smelting entrepreneur. The lofty stone ground floor of the almost triangular house has crocketed pinnacles and "pelmet arched" windows which still derive from Late Gothic. Though the timber framing of the upper storeys was invested only three years later with High Renaissance decoration, probably by the wood carver Simon Stappen, there are no glaring stylistic anomalies. As an integral part of the grid pattern formed by the timber framing and the oriel window, the Renaissance surface decoration with its lively colouring runs round the house like an ornamental frieze. Traditional features that have been carried over into the new period are the lofty North German type hall in the front part of the ground floor and the steeply pitched roof containing several storage lofts. Here, as elsewhere in the North, magnificent halls and high pitched roofs were still a badge of middle class prosperity, as were richly embellished doorways, windows and façades generally. At the same time the mingling of the new decorative motifs and the old fantastic figures inherited from pagan times (such as may be seen, for example, in the doorway of the Mönchehaus), shows how foreign to the mind of the average citizen was the "orthodox" application of Renaissance principles.

78, 79

90, 94

The customary wall-paintings with their bright colours which were often translated into a robust popular idiom, went a long way towards bringing about the full integration of the Renaissance into the traditional middle class sphere of existence.

Franconia and Lower Saxony could boast many fine timber-framed buildings, notably in Hildesheim (largely destroyed in the Second World War), Goslar, Brunswick, Quedlinburg, Wernigerode and many other places between the Rhine and the Oder, with isolated instances as far afield as the Vistula and Transylvania. Here we need only cite two typical examples. The Huneborstelsche Haus in Brunswick, with its rich carvings by Simon Stappen (1536), displays on the one hand that positively picturesque abundance of decoration which, in timber-framed architecture, reached an apogee in the Renaissance and, on the other, a loss of structural clarity. Since plasticity in the articulation of the façade was not feasible (nor was the jettying of the upper floors any substitute for this), the desire for ornamentation could find expression only in the low relief work on the wooden portions where it was literally allowed to run riot. A glance at the detail of the upper storeys reveals that, in the region below the windows, the studs, rails and braces are barely in evidence as discrete structural parts; rather, as a decoration, they increase in size and their surfaces merge until they almost obliterate the panels. It is here, as on the posts between the windows and on the brackets that were now reshaped to form consoles, that the carvings are mainly concentrated, either in the form of symbolic figures or of ornamental plants. The more geometrical motifs, such as, for example, strap and fretwork, guilloches, cable and bead mouldings, rosettes, palmettes (or sunbursts) and shellwork were used for preference on the sill beams.

Preceding page

46· VENICE. *Ca' d'Oro (House of Gold) on the Grand Canal.*

Built between 1424 and about 1440 for the patrician, Marino Contarini, by Giovanni and Bartolomeo Bon, in place of the old Palazzo Zen; the columned hall and loggia on the first floor, together with the windows (later balconies) on either side, are attributed to the Lombard sculptor Matteo de'Raverti. The house owed its name to the rich gilding on its façade, though nothing now remains either of the gold or of the other pigments, ultra-marine and red. The charm of the show front of Istrian marble (the other fronts are of brick) stems from the imaginative decoration of Late Gothic open tracery, incomparable in its lightness and delicacy.

47 VENICE. *Palazzo Manolesso-Ferro (centre), to its right the Palazzo Contarini-Fasan on the Grand Canal, mid-fifteenth century.*

Both these palaces exemplify the increasing tendency to open up walls by means of serried ranges of arcaded windows. By this time the picturesque Late Gothic decorative forms had largely been superseded by a clear Renaissance articulation (horizontality accentuated by details such as cornices and continuous, balustraded balconies, pilaster strips and windows that are either arcuated or trabeated).

48, 49 *AMBROGIO LORENZETTI, fresco, "Effects of Good Government", in Siena Town Hall, painted between 1335 and 1340. Detail of left-hand side and general impression.*

Ambrogio Lorenzetti, a leading exponent of the Sienese school of the Trecento, was the first European painter to portray, in his magnificent series of wall-painting, *Good and Bad Government*, an almost topographically accurate picture of a town, namely Siena. Hence this work is of incalculable documentary value. All the details are lovingly depicted, even down to the nail head mouldings on the wooden oriel (right). As next compared to that great innovator, Giotto, Lorenzetti here shows himself to be a naturalistic, homespun artist. He makes skilful use of perspective in portraying many different types of house whose like might also have been found in other North Italian towns. Again, this work is of historical significance in that it provides an accurate account of contemporary life. People of all classes may be seen going about their many and various occasions, both outside the houses and indoors, the ground storeys being wide open to the street.

47

VOLGIETE GLIOCCHI A RIMIRAR COSTEI VOI CHE RAGGIETE CHE QUI FIGURATA 7 PSVE CIELLEGIA CORO

50 *JAN VAN EYCK, "The Marriage of Giovanni Arnolfini and Giovanna Cenami", oil on oak, 1434, National Gallery, London.*

This astonishingly early and lifelike double portrait of Arnolfini, a merchant of Lucca living in Bruges, and of Giovanna Cenami, the daughter of another Italian merchant who had settled in Paris depicts their wedding ceremony in a patrician bedchamber of Flemish stamp. The magnificent convex looking-glass, whose frame contains scenes from the Passion done in enamel, not only reflects part of the room, but also two witnesses to the marriage, one of whom is the artist. Another miraculous piece of painting is the sumptuous Late Gothic brass chandelier, in which there symbolically burns a candle at the couple's feet.

51 *MASTER OF THE LIFE OF THE VIRGIN, "The Birth of the Virgin Mary", oil on oak, second half of the fifteenth century, Alte Pinakothek, Munich.*

The picture of this bedchamber, done by an anonymous painter of the Cologne School, might have had for model a real room in a patrician house in that town. It is particularly illuminating because it faithfully renders the large double bed, the chests of various shapes and sizes and the treatment of walls and floor. The height of the wooden headboard is dictated by the raised position of the head of the bed. During the daytime the movable curtains of the tester were drawn back and/or gathered up into bags. At night, however, the "inner chamber" was entirely screened off from the rest of the room by cloth hangings to protect the sleeper—at a time when people went to bed naked—against draughts and prying eyes. Save for the gold-painted wall at the back, there is nothing to indicate that this is a religious painting. In other respects it is a naturalistic rendering of the activities surrounding a confinement in what was, to judge from the wall hangings and tiled floor, an elegant middle class town house.

51

52 *MASTER OF THE LOWER RHINE, "Der Liebeszauber" ("The Love Charm"), oil on wood, circa 1470 or 1480. Museum der Bildenden Künste, Leipzig.*

This miniature-like portrayal of a nude in a small but well-appointed, wainscotted living-room, bears eloquent testimony to the newly-awakened self-awareness and sense of reality of the middle classes. However, the motif may also have an underlying magic meaning stemming from medieval popular superstitions. Ribbons inscribed with magic spells surround the girl who, with sponge and flint, seeks to kindle sparks of love in a wax effigy of the heart of her betrothed; he may be seen, already lurking in the background.

53 *FLORENCE. Palazzo Davanzati, No. 13, Via Porta Rossa (since 1950 Museum of the Early Florentine House), dining-room on the second floor with fourteenth and fifteenth century appointments.*

With their large and sumptuously if sparsely furnished rooms, the palazzi of the aristocratic patricians in nothern Italy bear witness to a style of life which, while centred on display and ordered beauty, was nevertheless not devoid of comfort. The impression created by these interiors is one of harmony, clarity and distinction, an impression in keeping with the new, freer, but at the same time urbane and cultivated, manners and mode of existence of this élite. The long, lofty chamber with its whitewashed walls is given a character all its own by the impressive beamed ceiling (the beamed structe of the floor is concealed beneath a typical covering of tiles). In the background, beyond the table and chairs, are two *cassone*, decorated with fine intarsia work, which were also used as seats. In the right foreground is an armoire. The niches, which are equipped with doors, contain statuettes and, more notably, magnificent majolica and faience vases.

53

54

Preceding page

54 FLORENCE. *Palazzo Davanzati, bedchamber on the second floor, with a mural dating from 1395 and furniture of the fourteenth to sixteenth centuries.*

If proof be needed of the difference between the domestic atmosphere of North and South, cosy and private on the one hand, grandiloquent and extravert on the other, it is to be found here, in this Italian patrician's bedchamber decked out like a state-room. Beneath the richly decorated wooden ceiling, and behind rows of airy arcades, may be seen a paradisal landscape enlivened by human figures, beasts, flowers and trees. The walls below are adorned with magnificent poly-chrome decoration reminiscent of tapestry and of the Pompeian incrustation style. A cradle stands at the foot of a bed which, though wide, is far less ponderous than those of central Europe.

55 CAREGGI *(near Florence). Villa Medicea di Careggi, medieval fortified seat of the Lippi, acquired in 1417 by the Medici, reconstructed in 1457 by Michelozzo at the behest of Cosimo il Vecchio.*

This, Cosimo's favourite place of residence, became, under his son Lorenzo the Magnificent, a famous gathering-point for artists, philosophers and men of letters. Gutted by fire after the expulsion of the Medici, the villa was restored in the sixteenth century by Alessandro. In the course of rebuilding, Michelozzo retained the castello-like character in the projecting gallery crowned by battlements, the massive shell and the irregular treatment of the façade, ground plan and courtyard. But whereas the street elevation is still expressive of the spirit of an earlier time, the side facing the courtyard and garden, with its elegant loggias and decorative details in the Renaissance style, heralds the arrival of a new era of humanist aspirations.

56 FLORENCE. *Palazzo Strozzi in the Via degli Strozzi.*

Begun in 1489 by Benedetto da Maiano from a model by Giuliano da Sangallo and completed by Simone del Pollaiuolo Cronaca. When work was interrupted in 1536, the cornice was still unfinished. The severely conser-vative façade, derived from the Palazzo Medici, is a witness of conscious traditionalism. The patron achieved his ends by stealth and in defiance of the ruling Medici family. Originally it was to have been a simple house without rusticated masonry, and was to have had shops on the ground floor. Not until later did the Medici give their assent to its being executed in magnificent bossed masonry.

57 FLORENCE. *Palazzo Davanzati, No. 13, Via di Porta Rossa, second half of the fourteenth century. The loggia at the top is a later fifteenth century addition.*

The façade of dressed stone and brick is virtually unadorned and of puritanically austere design, though the effect is decidedly monumental owing to the marked symmetry and the clear, block-like articulation. The cultivated Florentine was already showing a tendency towards Classicism and the Antique which repudiated the Gothic decorative forms prevalent at that time. Though still in the thrall of the austerity of Romanesque, it nevertheless presages the Renaissance which, in the Quattrocento, was already manifesting itself in the palazzi of Florence.

58 FLORENCE. *Palazzo Rucellai, No. 18, Via della Vigna Nuova. Built by Bernardo Rossellino between 1446 and 1451 from designs by Leone Battista Alberti. Restored in 1931.*

The patron of this forward-looking piece of domestic architecture was Giovanni di Paolo Rucellai, a man who had risen from humble origins to the status of merchant prince. This, the first instance of a clearly thought-out Renaissance façade, should obviously have been extended further to the right. It testifies to Alberti's profound knowledge of antique architectural forms, of which he was then the leading connoisseur and theorist. The rustication gives the impression of panels within what appears to be a load-bearing framework of pilasters and entablatures. The pilasters consist of superimposed Doric, Ionic and Corinthian orders. Those on the ground floor rest on a plinth, the joints of which form a mesh pattern as in the Roman *opus reticulatum*. Unlike the lintels, the tympana of the doorways and windows are recessed. As in the case of so many far-reaching advances, the bold innovations made by Alberti in the shape of logically thought-out and more opulent architectural decoration at first gave rise to considerable controversy.

57

58

59, 60 ERFURT. *Zum Breiten Herd (The Wide Hearth) No. 13, Fischmarkt, circa 1584.*

This Late Renaissance patrician house with its exceptionally rich decoration is typical of the modification undergone by the ideas of the Renaissance north of the Alps. Notwithstanding the wholesale adoption of what were then new, "modern" decorative elements (pilasters, herms, architraves, trabeated windows with straight pediments, arabesques and scroll- and strapwork, not to mention an abundance of busts, reliefs and other forms of figurative architectural sculpture) and principles of articulation (seriality, symmetry and horizontality), it was unable to renounce the other traditional national idiom. Similarly, the effect of the over-opulent, indeed almost luxuriant, architectural ornamentation in the Netherlandish "Floris style", is utterly "un-Renaissance-like" by comparison with the Italian principle of restrained clarity. Its organic liveliness at one and the same time recalls Late Gothic and points the way to the Baroque. The land on which patrician houses stood was not infrequently extended by the purchase of adjacent buildings.

61

62

61 FLORENCE. *Palazzo Pitti in the Piazza dei Pitti. What is today the central block of seven bays was begun sometime between 1448 and 1466 by Luca Fancelli on the orders of Luca Pitti.*

It was sold in 1549 while still unfinished (only the façade and the rooms lying immediately behind it having been completed) to Eleonora of Toledo, the spouse of Cosimo I, Grand Duke of Florence. As the grand ducal palace it was given a *cortile* some time after 1560 by Bartolomeo Ammanati and, in the seventeenth century, two projecting wings by Giulio and Alfonso Parigi, thus acquiring a frontage of over two hundred metres. The history of the enlargement of the original nucleus into a princely residence is in itself a proof that all the elements necessary to such "promotion" were already inherent in what was probably the most monumental middle class private house then in existence. (It also served as model for the castle built by King Louis I of Bavaria in the nineteenth century.) The effect aimed at was one of eloquent, monumental simplicity such as is found, for instance, in the Roman aqueduct. On all storeys, each of which is of equal height and slightly set back from the one below, the powerful rustication is given similar treatment and acquires rhythm from the vigorous modelling of the voussoirs in the heads of the arcade-like ranges of windows and doors. Three cornices with balustrades of small Ionic columns form unequivocal divisions between the straight strips of the storeys. According to a drawing made by Bernardo Buontalenti at the end of the sixteenth century, the second storey was formerly crowned by a loggia.

62 FLORENCE. *Palazzo Medici-Riccardi, detail of the cornice.*

In this cornice Michelozzo, who owed an especial debt to the Antique, has virtually copied models found in the buildings of Imperial Rome.
The rich mouldings include dentils, egg and dart, modillions, metope-like panels and Doric cymatium and cornice. True, there is neither architrave nor frieze, which goes to show that acceptance of the Antique did not involve the sacrifice of native genius.

63 FLORENCE. *Palazzo Medici-Riccadi at the corner of the Via Cavour and the Via dei Gori. Built by Michelozzo di Bartolommeo between circa 1444 and 1454.*

Subsequent to 1670 the building was altered and enlarged by its new owners, the Riccardi family, who added seven more bays. It was restored in 1911. The majestic façade of this palazzo, which was to be the prototype of many others, is a proclamation, not only of the leading Florentine patrician family's power and grandeur, but also of their claim to the legacy of Ancient Rome. The composition adheres to a strict logical system comprising only a few elements—graduated rustication, doorways and windows with semi-circular heads, also small, rectangular windows on the ground floor (placed high up for reasons of security), and a massive cornice. The underlying principle is symmetry and the ordered sequence of like forms such as windows, for which blank windows were substituted where necessary—i.e. if they did not relate to any particular room. The elegant twin-light windows, with quasi-traceried decorative rosettes in the tympana, are a last reminiscence of the Gothic. The attempt to achieve an harmonious balance between all parts of the façade has not, however, been entirely successful, for the somewhat lower first and second floors, the former of ashlar, the latter of brick, seem as though compressed between the rugged, bossed rustication of the ground floor and the excessively ponderous cornice. Moreover, the original palazzo comprised only that part of the building at the far end, with the three gate-like openings. Initially these were, in fact, doorways, the one on the right leading to the stables, that in the centre to the *cortile*, and that on the left to an open loggia on the corner where, within sight of all, the family conducted their festivities. In 1517, by which time this custom had lapsed, three of the four doorways were walled up and replaced by rectangular windows crowned by straight pediments. When the Riccardi enlarged the building, they made use of all the already extant forms.

63

64

65

64, 65 FLORENCE. *Palazzo Medici-Riccardi, garden and inner cortile.*

More than any other part of the building, this cheerful, festive-looking *cortile* exerted an influence not only on the architecture of its own day, but also on that of the future. Originally the first floor (the openings of which now consist only of twin-light windows), also possessed an airy gallery so that the contrast between the compactness of the exterior and the light, animated rhythm of the courtyard must have struck the beholder with even greater force. It would seem improbable that any direct connection exists between this and the arcaded courtyard of the villas of Ancient Rome; rather, the monastic cloister suggests itself as the point of departure. Once a place of pious meditation, this architectural feature became a place of intellectual and social intercourse between the standard-bearers of the Renaissance. The coat of arms of the Medici, marble *tondi* with relief carvings of classical subjects, and columns with intricately worked composite capitals, are the outward and visible signs of a new, traditionally-minded worldliness.

66 *MASOLINO DA PANICALES and MASACCIO, detail from the "Awakening of Tabita", fresco in the Brancacci Chapel of Sta. Maria del Carmine in Florence, probably 1424/25.*

This detail, with its lifelike portrayal of an urban scene that is typically middle class rather than stylishly patrician, is probably the work of Masaccio, a pupil of Masolino and a pioneer of the new naturalistic and monumental painting of the Renaissance. Varying considerably in height, the narrow, unadorned houses, depicted in convincing perspective, stand cheek by jowl. The majority of citizens lived in houses such as these which, unlike the palazzi of the patricians, were not considered worthy of preservation. Their lack of uniformity recalls the smoothly plastered buildings of a nineteenth century street.

67 VENICE. *Palazzo Vendramin-Calergi on the Grand Canal, begun in 1481 by Mauro Coducci, and completed in 1509 by Pietro Lombardi.*

Even in the Renaissance Venetian palazzi continued to uphold the tradition of façades articulated by means of luxuriant decoration and the strongly accentuated invalidation of walls. From the canal one enters a large, imposing vestibule. On both upper floors are state-rooms, each of them lit by three large windows with semi-circular heads and flanked by smaller living-rooms. The ground floor is articulated by means of pilasters, a function performed on the two upper floors by three-quarter columns. Architrave-like cornices accentuate the horizontal element which blends harmoniously with the vertical features, although the crowning cornice with its heraldic reliefs appears somewhat ponderous.

68 GENOA. *Palazzo Raggio-Podesta, No. 7, Via Garibaldi, begun in 1563 to a design of G. B. Castello, known as il Bergamo.*

Renaissance principles have been applied with far greater rigour to this town palace in Genoa than to the palazzo in Venice. The wall appears compact, yet the then prevalent trend towards sumptuous architectural decoration is no less in evidence. The detail of the façade reveals not only greater refinement and diversity in methods of decoration, but also a new wealth of motifs derived from a study of Antiquity and consisting prim-arily of figurative, foliate and naturalisic elements.

69 *View of the Maggi family's villa near Venice, attributed to the workshop of Veronese. From "Voyages et Adventures", 1578, Bibliothèque Nationale, Paris, Cabinet des Estampes.*

Set in the open countryside the villa, along with its elaborately laid-out grounds, constitutes a private enclave devoted solely to recreational conviviality and the pleasures of life. Not one workaday building is to be seen, nor is there yet evidence of any romantic feeling for nature as in the eighteenth century English garden; rather, nature is subordinated to the desire for a mathematically harmonious plan.

69

70 STRASBOURG. *Kammerzell's House, No. 16, Place de la Cathédrale.*

The stone ground floor dates from 1467, while the upper storeys were rebuilt by Martin Braun, a cheesemonger, in 1589. Of all the many timber-framed buildings to have survived in the town, this is the finest. The stock of Renaissance motifs, which had evolved exclusively in the fields of stone and brick architecture, has been here adapted in a manner appropriate to half-timbering. The restrictions imposed by the structural skeleton meant that decorative elements were confined to relief work on the straight wooden members. While the bressumers are carved in imitation of vigorously moulded stone cornices, the posts, in particular, are given over to symbolic representations of the ages of man, the Virtues and the senses, as well as to scenes from Christian and classical mythology. Distributed over the whole surface of the building, this conceptual world is an expression of the cultural pretensions of the Renaissance citizen.

71 STRASBOURG. *Rue du Bain-aux-Plantes, Quartier des Tanneurs (tanners' district), seventeenth century.*

The principles of Franconian timber-framed architecture, which evolved towards the end of the Middle Ages, have been adhered to throughout the centuries, virtually untouched by stylistic and decorative innovations.

72 FRANKFURT-AM-MAIN. *Stair tower of 1627 to the rear of the Laderam House in the inner courtyard of the Römer, No. 19, Römerberg (in the foreground, the Hercules fountain by J. Kowarzik, 1904).*

Despite the Late Renaissance detail, the stair tower does not repudiate its Gothic origins.

70

71

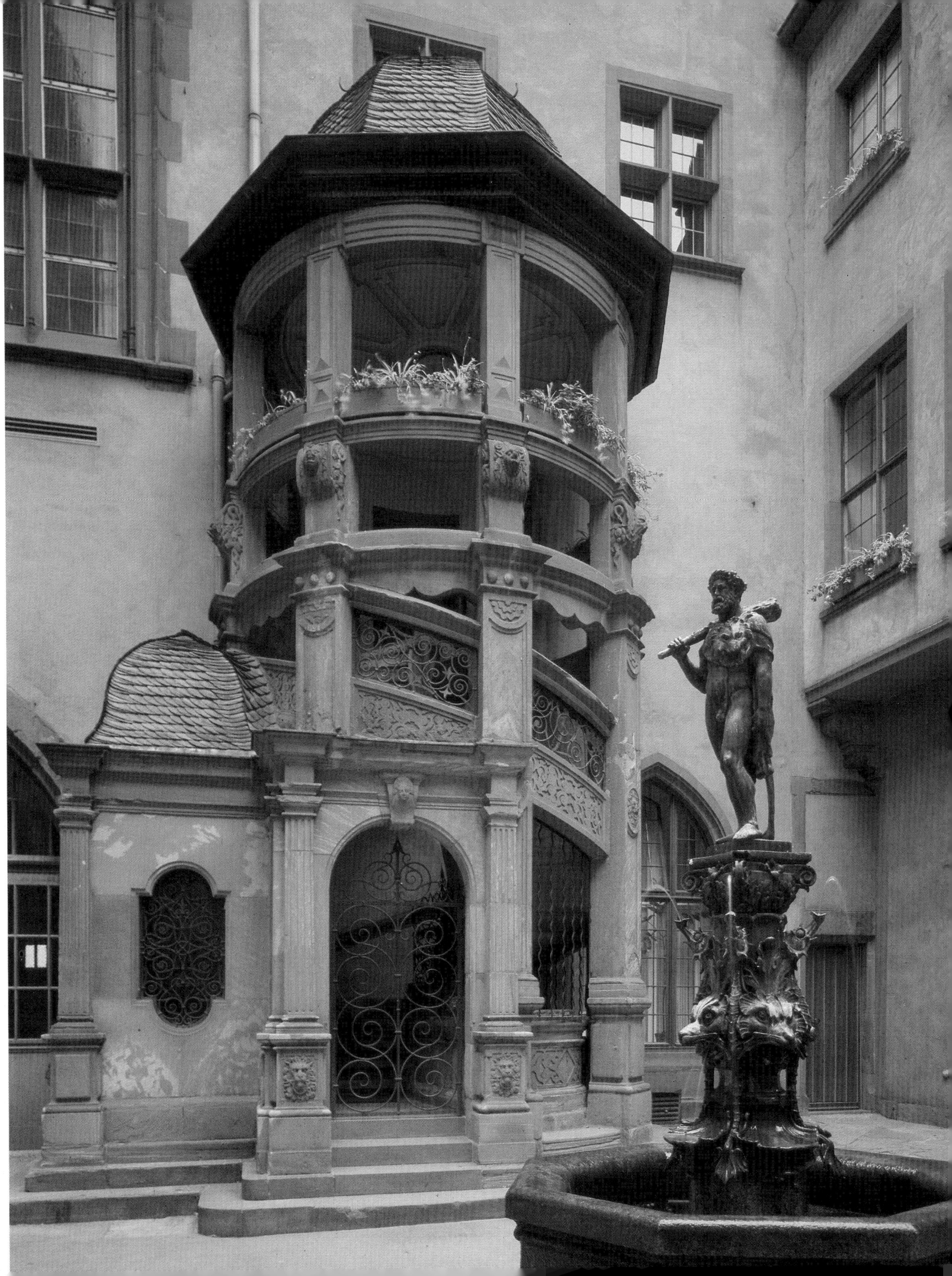

73,74 SCHAFFHAUSEN.
Goldener Ochse (Golden Ox), No. 17, Vorstadt, Late Gothic house, altered in 1608 and decorated by an unknown master circa 1610 with wall paintings on the theme of the Trojan War.

The theme is illustrated, not with battle scenes, but with individual characters—Dido, Regina, Aeneas, Menelaus, Helen and Paris. As in many other examples, the name of the house is also indicated. (The ox as a house sign may also be seen on the Roter Ochse at Stein am Rhein; executed by Andreas Schmucker in 1615, it is in the manner of the one in Schaffhausen.) The richly fashioned doorway with its semi-circular arch (dating from the end of the sixteenth century), the work of the masons Martin Müller and Hans Windler, bears the portraits and hatchments of the two founders, Hageloch and Seiler. Together with the oriel of 1609 whose lavish decoration includes a courting couple, herms, a satyr and, on the aprons, the allegories of the five senses, it represents one of the great achievements of architectural sculpture in Swiss middle class building.

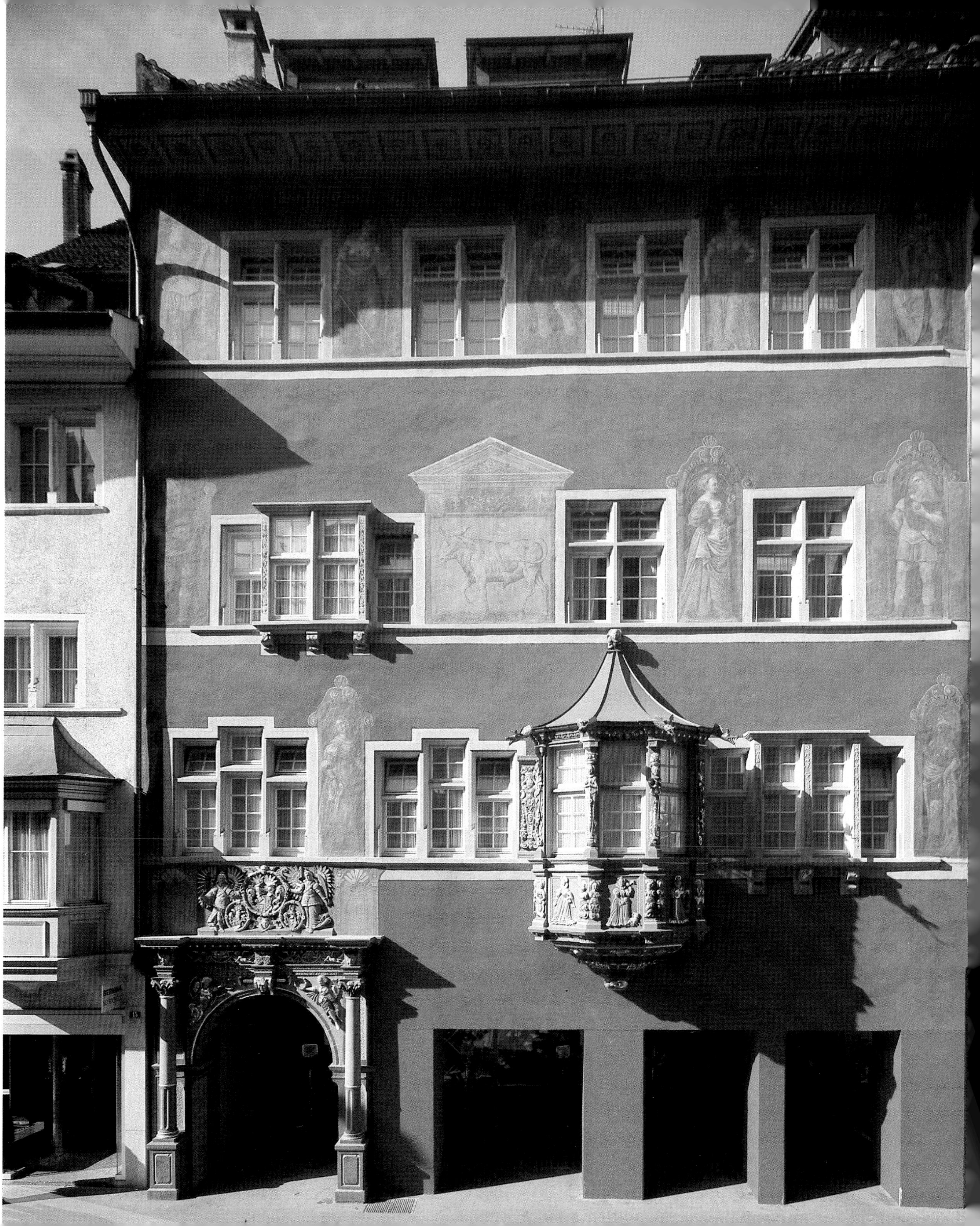

75 STEIN AM RHEIN. *Weisser Adler (White Eagle), No. 14, Hauptstrasse, ground floor modernized.*

Sigmund Flaar was a wealthy merchant and erstwhile burgomaster of Constance whose Confederate sympathies had caused him to flee in 1510. Between 1520 and 1525 these, the earliest Renaissance wall-paintings to have survived on a Swiss middle class town house (four frescos, painted over in 1780 and several times restored), were executed to his order, supposedly by the local master, Thomas Schmid. The façade, though tending towards symmetry, is nevertheless irregular. Across it, between painted illusionist architecture, window frames and decorative borders reminiscent of book ornamentation, is spread a series of iconographic pictures largely inspired by panel paintings and the graphic arts. The predominant shades are yellow, green and white. On one side of the first floor are pictures, after the manner of Urs Graf, of lust and of a mercenary with a prostitute. Immediately above are two scenes from the *Decameron*, the heraldically painted house sign of an eagle and illustrations of the Roman legend. On the top floor, next to two scenes from the parables, are the figures of Venus, Justice, Fortune and Cupid. Here we see revealed a conceptual world situated between coarse sensuality on the one hand and high moral aspirations on the other—a realistic adaptation of Antiquity.

75

76 SCHAFFHAUSEN. *Zum Ritter (The Knight), No. 65, Vordergasse, built in 1492.*

Altered in 1566 and decorated with wall paintings by Tobias Stimmer between 1567 and 1570 to the order of the goldsmith, Hans von Waldkirch. These frescos, some of the most important in Switzerland, were replaced in 1935 by a copy; the remnants of the originals may still be seen in Schaffhausen Museum. The proto-type of this building was the Hartensteinhaus in Lucerne with paintings by Hans Holbein. One of the scenes depicted is the sacrificial death of Marcus Curtius, a youth who, to save his country in the year 302 B.C., is said to have leapt into a deep chasm which suddenly opened in the Forum, whereupon it closed over his head.

77 EGGENBURG *(Lower Austria). The so-called Gemaltes Haus (Painted House), No. 1, Hauptplatz, built after 1525.*

The sgraffito paintings, some taken from Hans Burgk-mair's woodcuts, were done in 1547. The house is of picturesque design with an asymmetrical façade and oriel windows deriving from the Gothic period. Though the painted decoration is in the Renaissance style, the irregularity of the pictorial panels is entirely in keeping with that of the main structure. Only on the front with its hipped gable do we find the Renaissance principle of the additive use of ranges of similar architectural elements—in this case, illusionist arcades.

76

77

78, 79 GOSLAR. *Brusttuch, No. 1, Hoher Weg.* The house was built between 1521 and 1523 to the order of Johannes Thilling, a magistrate and mine and ironworks owner.

There is some doubt as to whether the timber-framed upper storey, with the oriel at the gable end, was built in 1526 or whether this was simply the year in which it was decorated with carvings (ascribed to Simon Stappen). The house is a prime example of the wilful synthesis of divers influences and periods in Central Germany. In one and the same structure we find stone and brickwork, timber framing, Late Gothic window surrounds (the work of the Master of the Goslar Jacobi-Vorhalle, 1516), and Renaissance sculptural decoration translated into carved and painted reliefs. In addition, North German building conventions (oriel, subdivision of rear ground floor into kitchen, living and bedrooms) are combined and made to harmonize with South German influences (lofty hall on the ground floor front, steeply pitched roof with slate hung gable). The oriel, with "pelmet" arched windows, is lent considerable charm by the imaginative use of ornamental and pictorial Renaissance motifs. The surfaces to which these are applied are brackets, posts and rails and wooden infill panels. Comical monkeys cavort amidst candelabra, vases, bead mouldings, dolphins, tritons, putti and acanthus leaves, while fabulous beasts and grimacing countenances are indicative of deeply ingrained popular beliefs.

80 PÜNDERICH/MOSELLE. *Timber-framed house, No. 163, (former ferryman's house).*

This house is decorated with vernacular carvings done in 1562, amongst them masks of bearded men and rosettes so large as almost to fill the panels.

81 GOSLAR. *Doorway of the Mönchehaus, No. 3, Mönchestrasse,* with carvings of 1528 (date above the door).

Alongside Gothic forms (foliate work and pointed and ogee arches), Renaissance elements (candelabra surmounted by trees of life and a man, woman and child) are strongly in evidence. Here we find evidence—in the "wild men" standing in niches, for instance, or the masks with dragons' tails gripped in their jaws—of the continuing influence, not only of a lively popular imagination that is rooted in tradition, but also of the

belief that symbolic representation will help to guard the house against evil.

Preceding page

82 FREIBERG *(Saxony).* *Doorway, created in 1530 by the sculptor Paul Speck, of a patrician house at No. 17, Obermarkt, once the property of Hans Weller von Molsdorf.*

The doorway, with its clear Renaissance forms (aedicula motifs with typological reversion to the Late Gothic, central German doorway equipped with alcove seats), has been turned into a grandiloquent triumphal arch celebrating a middle class citizen. The patron and his wife are immortalized in medallions in the spandrels. Instead of classical symbolic figures, the bas-relief in the gable lunette points to the contemporary reality of extracting and working silver ore—the source of the family's wealth. The work may be compared to the portrayals to be seen on the celebrated "mining" altar of 1521 at Annaberg and the illustrations in contemporary booklets on art, assaying and mining, one such being the well-known treatise *De re metallica libri XII* by Georgius Agricola, Basle, 1556.

83 VIENNA. *No. 7, Bäckerstrasse, I. Bezirk. The most important arcaded courtyard in the city, late sixteenth century.*

The clear articulation of the four-storeyed courtyard, with its once open, elliptically arched arcades and encircling balustrades, recalls Italian prototypes. The two wings without arcades were not added until the eighteenth century. Similar arcaded courtyards, typical of the Early Renaissance in the Alpine region, may still be found at No. 9, Fleischmarkt in Vienna and in the so-called Krebsenkeller (Crabs' Cellar) of 1538/39 in Graz.

84 LUCERNE. *Interior courtyard of the Ritterscher Palast (now the Cantonal Government Office), built between 1557 and 1564 for the Schultheiss, Lux Ritter, to the design of the Italian master builder Domenico Solbiolo de Ponte, and completed by J. P. del Grilio.*

Such direct borrowings from the Italian Renaissance—the derivation from Florentine prototypes is obvious—were rare as far as middle class town houses north of the Alps were concerned. In a foreign country this purity of style could only have been achieved by Italian artists. But what had been the organic product of Italian life was here no more than a borrowing from an alien culture, since the aristocratic social intercourse, for which these courtyards were intended, was foreign to puritanical Switzerland. The fountain in the middle of the yard was begun by Konrad Lux in 1481 and originally stood in the Weinmarkt.

85 AUGSBURG. *Fuggerei, view of the Herrengasse and chapel.*

Almshouses for impoverished artisans and day labourers. Built between 1516 and 1525 by the master mason, Thomas Krebs, to the order of Jakob Fugger. Partially destroyed in 1944, but subsequently rebuilt and enlarged. The small settlement, covering an area of 9914 square metres, contains six streets of 52 two-storeyed tenement houses built in rows and comprising 106 two-or three-roomed apartments. The technical excellence and functional exemplariness of their design, as also the practical and harmonious lay-out of the whole, represents a truly remarkable achievement, for which medieval antecedents in Holland (Béguinages) and Germany (Nördlingen and Stuttgart) served as a basis. The majority of the houses are eaves-fronted, but at the junctions and ends of streets some animation is introduced by gently stepped gables, which thus offset the lack of diversity between the three standard types with their virtually uniform measurements. On each floor,

84

with its own access from the street,
there is an apartment of exceptionally
rational design. Each of the two rooms
covers 14.50 square metres (in a three-
roomed unit, the third covers 12.80
square metres). The area of the vaulted
and flagged kitchen, invariably
situated at the back of the house on the
left, is 8.50 square metres. It contained
the hearth and from it the stove in the
living-room could also be stoked. Since
the height of the water table precluded
a cellar, a cold storage pit for foodstuffs
was provided outside each front door,
while there was further storage space
under the stairs and in the attic. The
rooms, between 2.20 and 2.40 metres
high, originally had exposed wooden
ceilings, which at a later date were
plastered and white-washed. Each
house had a courtyard and in many
cases a garden. Communal institutions,
such as a hospital and a school, were
available to all—an extraordinarily
advanced concept in those days.

86 BERNE. *View from the
cathedral tower of streets and
middle class town houses, the
character of which bears the stamp
of the Late Middle Ages.*

The radical upheaval wrought by the
Renaissance in so many fields failed to
bring about any material change in
towns and houses with an established
basic structure which had stood the
test of time. Still in evidence are the
ranges of multi-storeyed, arcaded,
eaves-fronted houses, with their
narrow plots. Alteration, modernization, the addition of outshots or extra
storeys, and the incorporation of new
decorative elements ranging from
Renaissance to the classical—all this
had perforce to be done inside the
city walls (not demolished until the
nineteenth century) and within the
context of existing structures.

87, 88, 89 NUREMBERG. *Façade, chimney-piece and courtyard of the former Pellerhaus, as it still existed in 1934. What was left of the building after its destruction in 1944 was preserved and eventually reconstructed as a municipal library and repository for the city archives.*

It was built between 1602 and 1607 to the design of Jacob Wolff the Elder for the patrician, Martin Peller, the sculptural decoration being done by Hans Werner.

Peller had been consul in Venice and the impulse of the Italian Renaissance is apparent both in the strictly symmetrical articulation—then still uncommon—and in the many decorative elements of this building. The large central doorway on the rusticated ground storeys is flanked on either side by a counting-house and leads to an arcaded courtyard of magnificent design which, however, is not co-axial with the house, nor is there any regularity in the organization of the interior space. In this, as in the oriel windows on the façade and above the courtyard, the exaggerated height of the dormer gable

and the picturesquely restless rather than tectonically clear composition, we may discern the typically German character of the Renaissance middle class town house. The same may be said of the interior appointments as, for instance, the chimney-piece on the landing of the second floor. The exuberant decoration, created in 1606 by the sculptor Hans Werner, consists of allegorical figures, foliate ornamentation and scroll- and strapwork.

87

88

90, 94 BRUNSWICK. *No. 2 a, Burgplatz, Guild House (the so-called Huneborstelsches Haus), built circa 1536, originally in the "Sacke", it was re-erected on its present site in 1902. Ill. 94 (left): No. 2, Burgplatz, a former palace of the nobility, now the Chamber of Handicrafts, erected in 1573.*

The carvings on the upper floors are by Simon Stappen, who also worked in Celle, Osterwieck and Goslar. Like many other timber-framed buildings in Brunswick, this magnificent, four-storeyed house of the South German type (it has a lofty hall), presents its long side to the street. The apertures above the large entrance show that the upper floors and loft were used for the storage of goods. Late Gothic and Early Renaissance motifs are merged in the decoration of the timber framing. Here the studs are not yet disguised as pilasters, as might well have been the case. Rather they are embellished with carvings, taken from a wood-carver's pattern book and suggestive of candelabra-like columns of which the surface is covered with fruit and foliage (above the entrance and on the attic storey). The consoles are decorated with symbolic figures from Antiquity and the Middle Ages, if not from real life. The figure of a miner is a direct allusion to the patron who derived his wealth from the silver mines of the Harz.

91 GÖRLITZ. *No. 3, Untermarkt. View of the upper part of the central hall of a mercantile house, with Gothic fan vaulting dating from 1535.*

The plastering of the arcades and the landings, like certain other alterations, are eighteenth century. Since Late Gothic vaulting was considered more attractive than flat modern ceilings, these forms were retained in the interior, whereas the façades of houses such as these were usually decorated in accordance with the taste prevalent at the time.

92, 93 GÖRLITZ. *No. 29, Neissstrasse, Biblisches Haus (Bible House), now a museum, 1570.*

Thanks to its magnificently decorated façade, this is one of the finest German middle class town houses of the second half of the sixteenth century. While Renaissance forms are accurately employed, this three-storeyed house displays neither the classical orders nor the all-important principle of symmetry. The front is articulated exclusively by means of Corinthian pilasters, as also by the Tuscan engaged columns on either side of the doorway (in this it resembles the Silesian Renaissance, e. g., as in the Piastenschloss in Brieg/Brzeg), as also by richly figurative reliefs depicting scenes from the New and Old Testament. The central hall has here already been equipped with a narrow staircase.

95 QUEDLINBURG. *Klopstock's House, No. 12, Schlossplatz, built in about 1560.*

The house in which Friedrich Gottlieb Klopstock was born now does duty as a commemorative museum. The rails and tension braces of the two-storeyed timber-framed building with its two dormer windows are embellished in comparatively restrained fashion with trellis mouldings and sun motifs. The oriel window is supported by two buttresses and a wooden architrave, the effect being to give the entrance the air of a portico. Such borrowings from stone and brick architecture

became increasingly common during the second half of the sixteenth century. This Harz town, steeped in tradition, can also boast other fine timber-framed middle class town houses of the Renaissance period, such as No. 39, Breite Strasse (the Gasthaus zur Rose of 1612), Nos. 5 and 6 Marktplatz dating from 1562, No. 48, Pölle and No. 28, Am Stieg, both second half of the sixteenth century.

96 ERFURT. *Zum Roten Ochsen, No. 7, Fischmarkt, given a new façade in 1562 at the behest of Jacob Naffner, a woad merchant and leader of the council.*

The building, as was usual in Erfurt, presents its long side to the street, but nevertheless possesses a dormer window in the likeness of a gable. The classical orders, reduced to the capitals of the pilasters, appear in superimposed Doric, Ionic and Corinthian form. On the entablature above the ground floor a frieze with figurative metopes depicts the sign of the house, the muses and the personification of the seven planets and days of the week. Themes and figures derive from the Little Masters of Nuremberg. At the same time the doorway (basket arch with faceted masonry and lion's head) and the dormer gable (scroll- and strapwork incorporating winged horses and the figures of devils) point to the rapidly spreading influence of the mannerist Floris style of the Netherlands.

97 LEMGO. *Hexenbürgermeisterhaus (now a folk museum) No. 19, Breite Strasse. Built between 1568 and 1571 and named after the burgomaster and witch-hunter Cothmann. The façade of 1571 is by Hermann Wulff.*

In this masterpiece of the so-called Weser Renaissance, the new forms transmitted by way of the Netherlands were grafted in a highly idiosyncratic manner on to the façade of the traditional, South German, gable-fronted house. Not only is it notably asymmetrical by reason of the juxtaposition of the projecting bay, the off-centre doorway, and the oriel window, but the staggering of the engaged columns which articulate the gable runs contrary to the logic of superimposing load-bearing members in the interests of stability. Typical features of the Weser Renaissance are the pronouncedly structured nature of the division of the façade into panels and the lively outline of the stepped gable, offset by the fan-shaped panels, voluted copings and crowning pinnacles in the form of obelisks. The use of figurative decoration is relatively restrained, being confined to the aprons of the bay and oriel windows and to the spandrels and tympanum above the doorway (aptly depicting the Fall). The interior retains the traditional arrangement of a lofty hall (in this case transverse and longitudinal) on the ground floor, living accommodation on the floor above, and storage lofts in the gable.

96

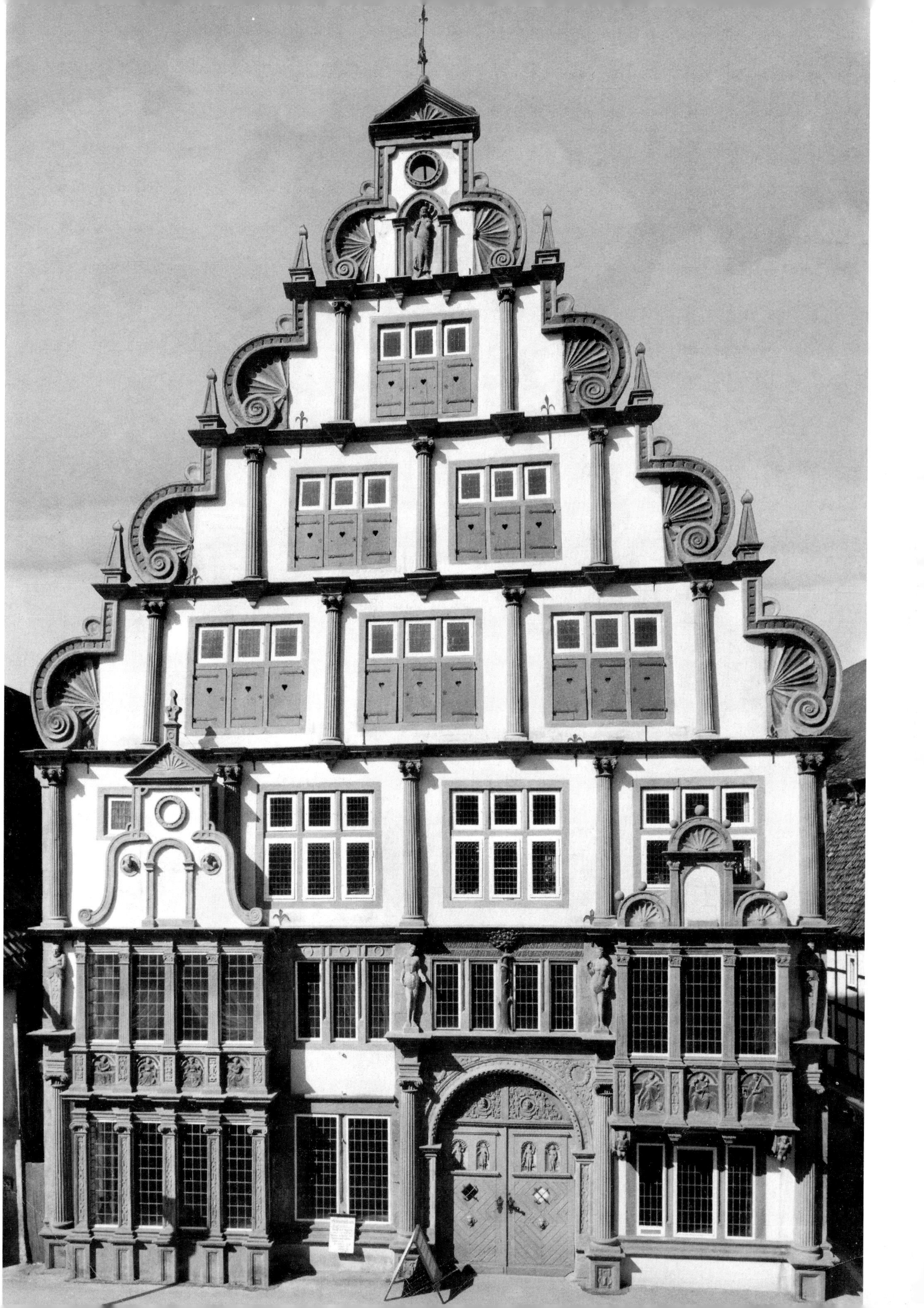

98 WEIMAR. *Cranach's House, Nos. 11 and 12, Markt, built between 1547 and 1549 and lived in by Lucas Cranach the Elder in 1552 and 1553.*

This pair of three-storeyed houses, each with a dormer gable, was erected by the Saxon master builder, Nikolaus Gromann, for Christian Brück, Cranach's son-in-law and chancellor to the Elector and for Court Secretary Pestel. The façade on the ground floor is richly embellished with polychrome sculptural decoration. Both the façade and the interior were restored between 1970 and 1972.

99 ERFURT. *Zur Hohen Lilie (The Tall Lily), No. 31, Domplatz. Masonry gable-fronted house with a transverse wing ("Kemenate", or King John type house), formerly part of the courtyard of a monastery and rebuilt after a general conflagration in 1472.*

In 1538 Johannes Ludolff, a goldsmith, had the interior and the façade altered, presumably in accordance with his own ideas, drawn perhaps from contemporary decorative engravings, Hans Brosamer's pattern book, and the architecture of Augsburg and Nuremberg. The gable was altered once more in 1769. Between 1963 and 1967 the building was restored and its interior enlarged to form what is now a wine restaurant. All that remains within are the vaulted cellars and parts of the beamed ceiling in the hall. In the sixteenth and seventeenth centuries this imposing gable-fronted house served as accommodation for distinguished visitors to the city, including Luther, Melanchthon and, in 1631, King Gustavus Adolphus. In addition, Gerhart Hauptmann's uncompleted work, *Die hohe Lilie* (1937), has assured it of a place in German literature.

100 HAMELN. *Rattenfängerhaus (Pied Piper's House), built at the corner of the Osterstrasse and the Bungelosenstrasse in 1602/03 by an unknown master for Councillor Herrmann Arendes.*

The name of the house goes back to the legend of the Pied Piper who, cheated of his wage, is said to have led almost all the children of the town into the nearby Koppelberg which had opened to receive them. The clear Renaissance articulation of the walls by means of pilasters, entablatures and rustication disappears beneath a plethora of small decorative elements. Masonry bands with incised designs also invest the pilasters, the capitals of which are surmounted by *Bartmannbüsten* (busts of bearded men), a feature of popular art. The doorway and the oriel window are assymmetrically placed in the façade, the restless treatment of which seems to presage the Baroque.

101 ARREAU. *Maison Valencian-Labat, sixteenth century.*

As a traditional form of construction, half-timbering was largely confined to northern France, where typical features were a masonry ground storey and a criss-cross pattern of close-set timbers. In our example the panels thus formed contain cruciform wooden members, decorated with carvings in low relief in the form of lilies, the ancient emblem of the kings of France. In so far as Renaissance forms reached French timber-framed architecture, these were used solely in the decorative treatment of posts, horizontal members and consoles, with a few exceptions—in Carcassonne, Bar-sur-Seine and Rouen—in which the articulation of whole walls might be said to have been imitated.

102 BOURGES. *Hôtel of Jean Lâllemant, a merchant, No. 5, Rue Hôtel Lâllemant, (now a museum), early sixteenth century.*

The buildings round the courtyard, which recalls that of a castle, are characterized by picturesque irregularity and Renaissance features deriving from château architecture. These are particularly apparent round windows and doorways where they take the form of boldly projecting and richly decorated architraves. On the round stair-tower leading to the former warehouse they may be seen in the superimposed aedicular motifs in which Gothic reminiscences are still in evidence (e.g. in the blank ogee arch above the first window). This elegantly decorative and, at the same time, lively and exuberant adaptation of the Renaissance style displays a character that was specifically French, at a time when Gothic was being abandoned in favour of Renaissance. The latter's

100

101

wealth of forms was not to give way to sober Classicism until the end of the sixteenth century, when puritan (i.e. Huguenot) influence began to make itself felt. The view of another corner of the courtyard reveals a typically French motif in the region of the roof, namely a lucarne in the shape of an aedicula resting on the cornice—in other words, a kind of monumental dormer window. Lucarnes had been a common feature in France from the thirteenth century onwards, their purpose being to give adequate light to the lower part of the attic used for living accommodation. A range of such windows often constituted a conspicuous feature of the façade. In the seventeenth century, with the introduction of the mansard roof, they assumed the form of mansard windows.

103 TOULOUSE. *Courtyard of the hôtel belonging to Jean de Bernuy, a merchant of Toledo. Begun in 1505 by the master builders G. and Jean Picart and Aymeric Cayla. Continued after 1535 by Louis Privat, who also designed the inner courtyard.*

The adaptation of château architecture, a common practice amongst the patrician bourgeoisie in France, was productive of buildings of greater magnificence than in Germany. Typical of this trend was the wholesale adoption of the system of articulating façades by means of engaged columns, pilasters, architraves between storeys, and balustrades. In addition, a great wealth of sculptural decorative detail, reflecting the influence of the Spanish Plateresque style, was handled with exceptional skill. Also specifically French is the frequent employment of the depressed basket arch. The French

love of decoration was materially advanced by an ample supply of a fine-grained natural stone which was initially soft and did not harden for some little while. However, this was seldom to be found in the plain where, as in Toulouse, which lies in a river basin, brick assumed importance as a building material, though it was seldom used in moulded form. As a rule it constituted the wall surface or else served as a core to which stone dressings or facings might be added.

102

103

104 LÜNEBURG. *No. 1, Am Sande, double house with two stepped gables, dating from 1548.*

Windows and projecting bays were altered according to modern style. In Lüneburg, still a prosperous town in the sixteenth century thanks to its salt springs and salt trade, the most dignified houses, a peculiar synthesis of Gothic and Renaissance, are to be found in the street known as Am Sande. By comparison with the richly decorated dressed stone and half-timbered façades of the Renaissance, however, these brick buildings seem very restrained, their only direct borrowing being the relief-like, figurative medallions in terracotta. Yet the contemporary approach is evident in the emphasis on horizontal articulation, in the repetition of bold, receding orders in the doorway and windows, and in the generally clear definition of all parts of the façade. This restraint is in turn relieved by the interplay of many natural colours—the red of the brick, the muted white of the plaster, the strips, alternating between green, brown and black, of the vitrified brick, and the gold of the terracottas, many of which have been given a blue ground.

105 ROSTOCK. *Kerkofhaus (now a registry office and municipal archive), No. 5, Hinter dem Rathaus, a Late Gothic structure, to which a show façade of polychrome brick and glazed terracottas was added in the middle of the sixteenth century by the burgomaster, Barthold Kerkof.*

Even as late as this, the stepped gable still displays a composition of slender blank arches that is wholly of Gothic provenance. It rests, above the generally proportioned upper floor, upon a decorative horizontal frieze of polychrome terracotta from the workshop of the Lübeck master Statius von Düren, depicting warriors heads, female figures, dolphins and other ornaments.

106 RETZ *(Lower Austria). The so-called Verderberhaus, No. 15, Hauptplatz, built in about 1580 for Firenz, a wealthy merchant.*

The design of this house with its two projecting pavilions, large central doorway and crowning battlements (as found in castellos or city gates) is unusual in a middle class town house. Inspired by contemporary pictorial representations, the sgraffito decoration contains scenes from Ovid's *Metamorphoses* and other works. (Restored in 1964/65.)

104

105

107 AALBORG. *Jens Bangs Stenhus, No. 9, Østeraagade, 1623–1624.*

A Renaissance feature typical of the Danish middle class town house is the richly decorated dormer gable in many and varied forms, the predilection for which was fostered by a building regulation stipulating that houses present their long sides to the street. It was above all in the squares of mercantile towns that the dormer gables, windows and doorways of patrician houses displayed a wealth of decorative forms executed in low sandstone relief which, together with the scroll- and strapwork motifs, bear the imprint of the Netherlandish Renaissance. The desire for proper display of rank was in no way incompatible with utilitarian considerations, so far as the structure of the house was concerned.

108 GORINCHEM *(Gorkum). Dit is in Bethlehem (now a museum), No. 25, Gasthuisstraat, built in 1566, restored in 1910.*

The name of the house is symbolically depicted in a relief above the lofty ground storey. In the Netherlands, the middle class town house of the Renaissance not only retained the form it had acquired during the Late Middle Ages and the tradition of a picturesque blend of brick and natural stone but also, by imaginatively modifying foreign decorative motifs, rapidly evolved a national idiom, thanks largely to the work of Cornelis Floris, the influence of which was later to extend to other countries.

109 STOCKHOLM. *No. 20, Stortorget (middle house), built in 1650 for Secretary Johan Eberhard Schantz.*

The small gable of this four-storeyed corner house already displays early Baroque forms, while the magnificent limestone doorway is adorned with figures of recumbent Roman warriors, the work of Johan Wendelstam. These, together with the stone dressings round the windows, are evidence of the relatively belated if powerful influence exerted by the Netherlands in Swedish towns.

110 AMSTERDAM. *Rembrandt's house (since 1911 a museum for Rembrandt's drawings), Nos. 4–6, Jodenbreestraat, built in 1606.*

The second floor with its dentilled cornice and straight pediment was added in about 1633. The house with its lofty hall and traditional forms is built of stone and brick. The presentation of the long side to the street is emphasized and made more imposing by Early Baroque alterations in the contemporary mode. The handsome building was bought by Rembrandt in 1639 for the sum of 13,000 gulden and furnished by him with art treasures worth some 30,000 gulden. In 1658, when the Netherlands were in a state of general economic decline, and the artist himself had fallen into debt, the house and entire contents were sold at auction for the paltry sum of 5,000 gulden.

111 HELSINGØR. *View of the Stengade. Beside the Gothic house with the blind gable is one of the earliest Danish middle class town houses of the Renaissance (No. 76) dating from 1579.*

Built by Antonius van Opbergen, a Dutchman born in Mecheln, who had been working near-by at Kronborg Castle since 1577. In northern Europe the characteristic features of the new epoch appeared relatively late and still in close conjunction with traditional domestic architecture, in which much importance continued to be attached to the gable. Initially the impact of the new style was slight, being largely confined to the abandonment of verticality in applied decoration, in which greater emphasis was placed on the horizontal (notably in the form of string courses and regular rows of windows) and to the use in brick architecture of sandstone elements for stretcher courses and also as dressings in doorways, window surrounds, quoins and gable copings.

107

112

112 *JAN VAN CONINXLOO, Picture of a Flemish kitchen with a glimpse of a dining-room in the background, painted on the panel of an altarpiece and depicting the "Miracle of the Broken Sieve", 1522, Musées Royaux des Beaux-Arts, Brussels.*

The lovingly portrayed details of this kitchen and of the man and woman in contemporary costume almost make one lose sight of the religious theme. The same two people reappear outside the window in accordance with the medieval principle of continuous narrative. Though early sixteenth century, this kitchen still smacks of the Late Middle Ages and, but for a few inessentials, was long to retain much the same appearance. With its large fireplace, functional furniture, pewter- and copperware of all kinds, tiled floor and adequate fenestration, this homely kitchen was generally located in a separate compartment at the end of the great hall, next to the family dining-room. If, for lack of space, the latter room had to be on the first floor, it was connected to the kitchen by a spiral wooden stair. Many patrician living-rooms were lined with wainscotting and Delft tiles. In his autobiography written in 1542 the Italian money-lender, Caspar Duitz, describes what he considers to be the most noteworthy features of houses in Antwerp, namely the multiplicity of differently appointed rooms, the harmonizing of colours and sumptuous materials (which already included curtains), the comfortable furniture (almost every room contained a sleeping-chair), and the abundance of musical instruments.

113 *PIETER BRUEGHEL the Elder, "The Battle Between Carnival and Fasting" (detail), oil on wood, 1559. Kunsthistorisches Museum, Vienna.*

This important Flemish painter has minutely rendered every detail of a busy street scene in a lower middle class district—the crumbling patches of plaster, for instance, or the varying colour of the tiles—doing so with an authenticity that could hardly be matched by reality itself. For these simple, functional buildings, unadorned save for an occasional corbie stepped gable, and showing no trace—even as late as the mid-sixteenth century—of Renaissance decoration, were not considered worthy of preservation. And yet the picture is redolent of "history". Only a few years were to elapse before the onset in 1566 of the struggle to cast off the Spanish yoke, yet already the growing tension is apparent in the juxtaposition of a devout procession debouching from an alleyway and the cheerful antics of the carnival—in the background a straw effigy of winter is being burned in accordance with pagan custom. The decrees issued at the time by Philip II to enforce the observance of religious fast days proved incapable of restraining the high spirits of the populace.

114

114 WITTENBERG. *Living-room and study in Melanchthon's house, No. 60, Collegienstrasse, built in 1536. (Now serves as a memorial to Philipp Melanchthon.)*

As compared with the sumptuous patrician room of the Late Renaissance, this combined living-room and study is characterized by an almost spartan simplicity. The scholar and protestant humanist to whom it belonged had no need for outward display. The sturdy trestle cabinet table and chair upholstered in leather, the tiled stove, the wainscotted alcove seats for pupils, a bookcase and a small wash-handstand with cupboard over—such are the functional, solid and, at the same time, beautifully designed appointments of this room.

115 ZURICH. *Living-room of the Zurich silk merchant, Rudolf Werdmüller, fitted out in 1615 for his house, Zum Seidenhofe, erected in 1592.*

On the demolition of the building in 1874, the room was removed to the Swiss Landesmuseum in Zurich. This, the finest Late Renaissance middle class living-room in Switzerland, with its richly carved panelling, coffered ceiling and magnificent polychrome majolica stove, goes to show that the patrician's need to display his wealth also asserted itself in the interior. The wealth of decorative forms which were to serve as model for the *Gründerzeit* style in the late nineteenth century must be accounted an innovatory achievement on the part of a newly self-confident bourgeoisie. Here the Renaissance motifs used in architectural decoration are adapted for application to interior appointments and furniture. Many new specialized occupational groups participated in the middle class contribution, originating in the Gothic era and culminating in the sixteenth century, to a new style of life which, thanks to numerous technical improvements, was not only richer but also more comfortable and functionally diverse. Indeed, that style of life forms the basis of many aspects of our present-day existence.

115

116 OUDEWATER. *Gable-fronted house, No. 64, Donkere Gaard, built in 1611.*

The colourfulness of the façade is picturesquely enhanced by the variegated and rhythmical use on brick surfaces of plastically embellished dressed stone elements. The projecting upper storeys recall one of the principles of timber frame construction, a form of building which still persisted in the Netherlands, especially among the less well-to-do. Noteworthy features are the large windows, each with a mullion and transom and—an innovation at the time, but thereafter common—shutters which open outwards, and were nearly always painted green.

117 DEVENTER. *De Drie Haringen, No. 55, Brink (now the municipal museum), 1575.*

Despite the reticent use of pilasters to articulate the façade, the lofty gable with its *mouvementé* outline constitutes a vital element in the design. The animated sculptural detail and the lively, polychrome effect produced by the different materials combine strangely with the sober clarity characteristic of the outlook of the protestant citizen. Practical common sense is also in evidence here, for in order to provide more space a mezzanine floor has been inserted in the hall and a goods hoist built into the long side of the house.

116

117

118, 119 GREAT COGGESHALL *(Essex), Hall and living-room in Paycocke's House, West Street, built circa 1500 for Thomas Paycocke, a rich clothier.*

As compared with its continental counterpart, the English timber-framed house had continued, ever since the Norman Conquest, to evolve and perfect indigenous forms in the rich tradition of the carpenter's craft. In the interior, too, timber as a material proved no less important. The richly carved wainscotting in the living-room, with its large fireplace, no less than the foliated decoration of the beams in the hall, testify to the refinement of the art of wood carving in England. That art had already received its imprint in the Gothic period and, by 1500, had not as yet advanced beyond the Late Gothic Perpendicular style. Carvings are also to be seen on the façade, in the form of a frieze on the projecting upper storey, and of figurative decoration on either side of the entrance door.

119

120 STRATFORD-ON-AVON *(Warwickshire)*. *The house in which William Shakespeare was born in Henley Street, originally two sixteenth century timber-framed houses.*

Since the building was reconstructed from a drawing in 1858, it cannot, of course, serve as evidence for original detail dating from the period when the great English dramatist lived here as the son of respectable, middle class parents.

121 CHESTER *(Cheshire). The Rows. Sixteenth and seventeenth century.*

These three- and four-storeyed timber-framed houses, of which a considerable number still survive, chiefly in the two main thoroughfares Bridge Street-Northgate Street and Watergate Street-Eastgate Street, have boldly projecting upper floors beneath which—a regional peculiarity, this—there are two storeys of shops. The façades and interior decoration are largely eighteenth century and underwent restoration in the nineteenth. Above the rooms at ground floor level (cellars, trading-vaults) are shopping arcades some four metres wide to which stairs lead up from the pavement. These houses bear witness to the former importance of this city which was founded in Roman times.

122 BRISTOL *(North Somerset). The Llandoger Trow, King Street. Group of three gable-fronted, timber-framed houses with stone ground storeys, 1664.*

This group of houses, almost merging into a unified whole, displays a feature characteristic of the development of the English middle class town house at the end of the sixteenth century, namely, the bay window—here large and polygonal. Throughout northern Europe such windows, also known as oriels, played an important role in providing more light, for which reason they have frequently been retained up till the present day. As may be seen from our example, these bay windows were carried up through two storeys, despite the jetties, and this presupposes technical expertise of a high order. At the same time they constituted a crucial structural element in the façade articulation of the English middle class town house. The latter was not open to outside influences, nor did it adopt the alien decorative forms of the Renaissance, during which period it thus became an outstanding example of organic development and was to serve as a model for the English Domestic Revival in the nineteenth century.

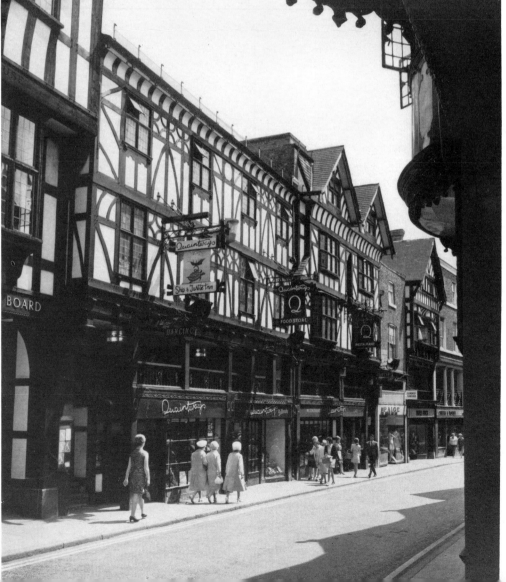

123, 124, 125 KAZIMIERZ DOLNY. *Market Place, At the Sign of St Nicholas, and At the Sign of St Christopher, circa 1615.*

The names refer to the patrons, Mikołaj and Krzysztof Przybyła, patricians of that town. Here, away from the big cities, we find displayed in true vernacular style the small town citizen's need for self-advertisement. Robustly executed by local craftsmen in low relief, the architectural ornamentation, which included certain mannerist forms, overruns the façade after the manner of a textile design. The treatment of the crowning parapet is likewise exceptionally lively and opulent. There can be little doubt that these buildings mark the apogee of the type of middle class town house peculiar to the Polish Renaissance. At ground level, behind the arcades, are halls and rooms decorated with stucco.

124

125

126 WARSAW. *No. 27, Old Town Market Place, Fukier House (residence of the Fuggers), built for Jerzy Korb prior to 1566, above a Gothic cellar. Destroyed in 1944 and rebuilt between 1948 and 1953.*

The façade is decorated with sgraffiti and with Renaissance ornamention. The house, which is noted for its wine cellar, has a small courtyard with balustrades supported by stone consoles.

127 WARSAW. *No. 36, Old Town Market Place, Pod Murzynkiem, (The Moor's House), early seventeenth century.*

Like most houses in the Old Market Place, it is three bays in width with a doorway on one side, a separate room on the ground floor for business transactions and, above the roof proper, a lofty stair-well light. The façade is enriched with decoratively painted masonry in the sgraffito technique of the Late Renaissance, as are those of some of the other buildings.

 126

 127

128 WARSAW. *Old Town Market Place, early seventeenth century with later alterations. After its destruction in 1944, rebuilding was completed in 1953, the façades being renovated between 1970 and 1972.*

The interiors have been largely adapted to meet modern domestic requirements. The narrow-fronted houses, dating from the Gothic period, were given Renaissance façades after Warsaw's promotion to capital city in 1596. However, most of such parapets as had still been retained, fell victim to the next phase of modernization in the nineteenth century, when alterations were made in the Baroque style. The unusually cramped situation of these multi-storeyed buildings called for the construction of a separate, centrally placed stair-well lit by a storey of its own rising above the pitched roof.

128

129 BISTRIŢA *(Bistritz). Dornei Street, Casa argintarului, doorway.*

The sixteenth century house of a goldsmith and silversmith. Its doorway displays simpler forms than do those of the rich international traders. Despite the generally debilitating effect of Turkish military rule in subjugated Hungary, business continued to flourish, especially in the metalworking handicrafts, in Transylvania (Romania), still a relatively autonomous district, as did that country's culture, which bore the imprint of the Renaissance. Its close commercial ties with Italy meant that new decorative forms—which also found application in the highly developed field of handicrafts—were quickly assimilated into middle class architecture, as is apparent from the arched doorway and the motifs in the architraves of doors and windows.

130 ZAMOŚĆ. *Arcaded houses in the Great Market Place, circa 1600.*

This town (one of the few to be founded during the Renaissance) was systematically laid out subsequent to 1581 under the aegis of Jan Zamoyski, the Chancellor and Commander-in-Chief, each citizen being allotted a plot of standard size. True, the treatment of the details of the façades were left to the competitively minded merchants and craftsmen who sought to outdo one another in the decorative richness or flat of frieze-like architectural stucco ornamentation. Many of the houses in the town retained their decoration and opulent parapets— witnesses to a highly idiosyncratic and original view of the Renaissance—until the nineteenth and twentieth centuries when they were unfortunately removed.

131 CRACOW. *Prałatówka House, No. 6, Mikołajska Street, 1618–1625.*

This town, seat of the Polish kings and, in the sixteenth century, a centre of Renaissance culture, possesses a rich stock of middle class town houses dating from that period. The Polish Renaissance, with its love of decoration, rapidly adapted the forms transmitted by Italian artists to its own native genius. Here abundance, vitality and a wealth of forms were of greater account than the logical application of a classical order. The middle class town house acquired a palatial aspect as a result more particularly of the widespread adoption of the lofty parapet concealing the roof. What contributes to the visual enrichment of the building here illustrated is not only the opulently sculptural doorway and the inventive handling of the plastic decoration—chiefly in the upper storeys—but also and especially the painted rustication on the façade.

131

132

133

132, 133 ZAMOŚĆ. *Arcaded house in Ormiánska Street, circa 1600.*

The richly decorated façade is as typical of the architecture of this time in Zamość as are the arcades of the merchants' houses.

134 NOVÉ MĚSTO, NAD METUJI. *Middle class town houses on the west side of the Market Place.*

A compact, homogeneous frontage with an arcaded ground floor and a crowning parapet, begun in 1526. The picture shows the houses as they were after the restoration that was carried out between 1950 and 1953; on the right, the Town Hall with tower.

134

135 TELČ. *Market Place, middle class town houses, ranging from the Renaissance to the classical period, with arcades typical of many Czech towns.*

Despite the subsequent alterations, the face of many small towns was determined by the important changes—no longer detectable in a metropolis such as Prague—that were made during the sixteenth century and involved the application to façades of Renaissance decoration and the general imposition of a new, compact town plan. But since the Czech middle class town house of the Renaissance also retained its Gothic structural nucleus, this frontage on the Market Place is an almost

perfect illustration of the fact that a basic type, once found, will persist throughout the centuries. Between houses with modified, medieval stepped gables there appear, in the middle distance, others which have been given rectangular façades with painted rustication in imitation of Renaissance palaces—a regional peculiarity found more especially in the towns of southern Bohemia (e.g. Třeboň).

136 TELČ. *No. 61, Market Place, 1555. Paintings uncovered and restored in 1952.*

The so-called Maz House has a hall for business purposes and an adjacent stair and chamber, with living-quarters on the floor above. The architectural decoration in sculptural relief consists of a balanced composition of pilasters, architraves and continuous cornices; likewise

a segmented gable (this last, in particular, being typical of Bohemia) with an exceptionally animated outline. The national predilection for polychrome embellishment also finds expression in the form of figurative sgraffito paintings of scenes from the Old Testament in the panels of the gable, while the same technique is used to cover with grotesques and arabesques the other surfaces between the architectural elements which serve to articulate the façade. Indeed, it accentuates those elements by the versatile use of colour, and sometimes actually imitates them (as in the "rustication" of the uppermost panel in the gable).

135

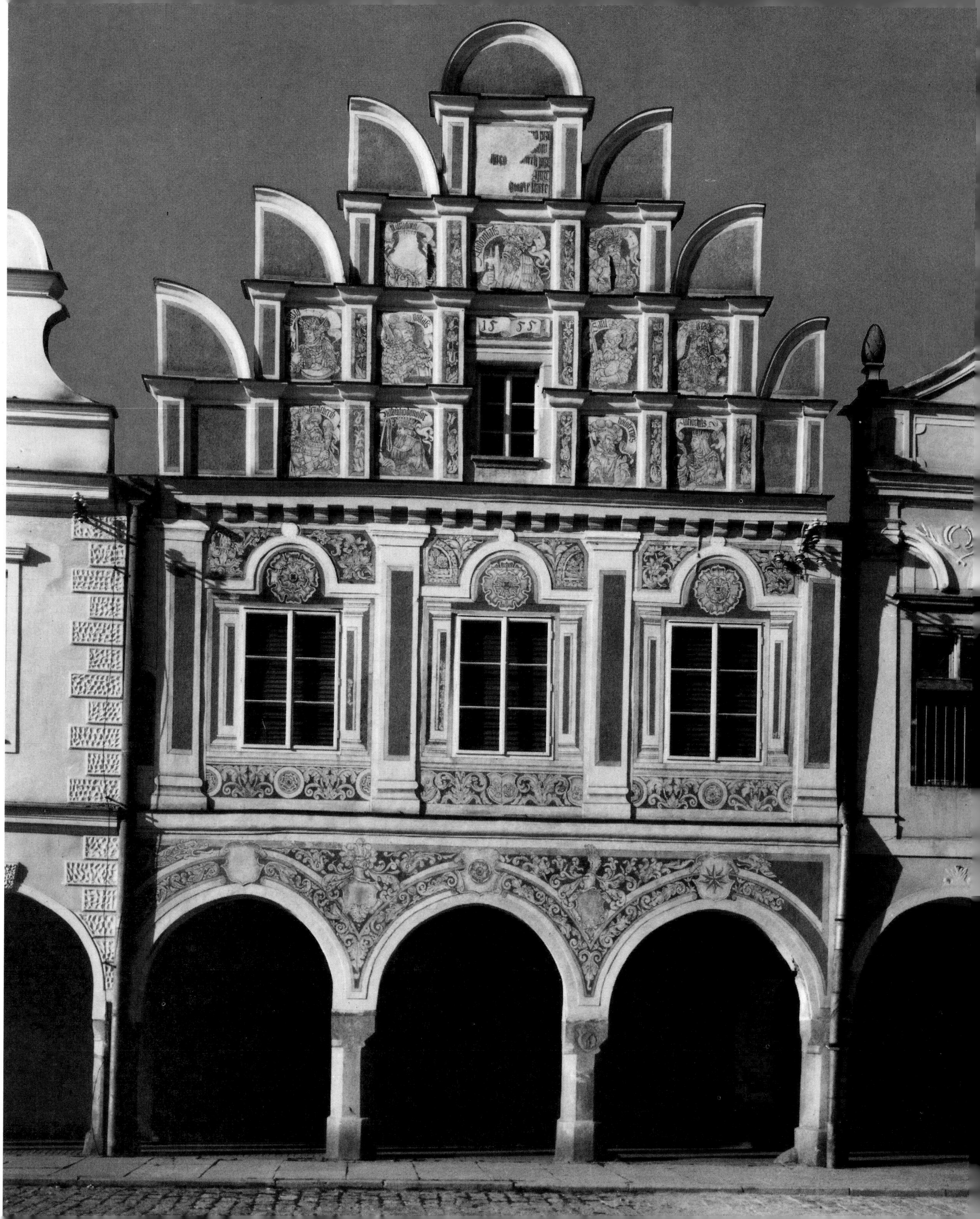

137 SLAVONICE. *Grand saloon in a patrician house (No. 45, Market Place). The wall painting is dated 1549.*

The Market Place in Slavonice, most of which still survives, is an outstanding example of middle class Renaissance building. Wall paintings imitative of architecture are not only to be found in rich profusion on the façades but may also be seen—and were once undoubtedly quite common—in the interiors where, as in our example, they take the form of sumptuous murals.

137

138 CLUJ *(Klausenburg). Entrance to the former Wolphard House, the work of a local master mason, dating from 1579 (now in the Historical Museum).*

The patron of this house (built between 1534 and 1541 and extensively altered between 1576 and 1579, 1590 and 1600, and again in 1894) was Adrianus Wolphard, Vicar General, humanist and Councillor to the Royal Hungarian Court in Buda. During the early stages of construction, Renaissance influences were at work here, transmitted in part by Italian artists of the Tuscan School, and translated into a pungent local idiom.

139 PRAGUE. *Old Town, No. 1/475, Market Place, Kožná ul., The Two Golden Bears. Entrance.*

In the course of conversion between 1567 and 1575 the house received the finest Renaissance doorway in Prague, while its courtyard was extended by the introduction of a vaulted arcade. The building, restored between 1970 and 1978, is today the Municipal Museum. Because the site was small, irregular, and three-sided, the tiny, arcaded courtyard did not, of course, lend itself to remodelling in a monumental Renaissance style. Here "women and maidens hearken to the song of blind Methodius, and between the columns there hang lambrequins". Thus Egon Erwin Kisch, the great Czech man of letters who was born in the house, when describing, in his "Market Place of Sensations" (from the series *Inside Story of S. Kisch & Brother*), his recollections of this charming, dream-like architecture.

Following page

140 PRAGUE. *Old Town, No. 3, Staroměstké námĕsti, At the Sign of the Minute. Originally a Gothic building, embellished between circa 1603 and 1610 with sgraffito paintings of classical and biblical scenes, and with allegories of the Virtues.*

The carving of a lion at the angle dates from the end of the eighteenth century when the house contained an apothecary's shop, The White Lion. From 1889 to 1896 it was the home of the writer, Franz Kafka, then a youth. Little has survived of the rich stock of Renaissance middle class town houses in Prague, largely because of the widespread introduction of the Baroque style during the eighteenth century.

138

139

In the later sixteenth century, as the Renaissance gradually gained a footing, timber-framed building, too, began to take greater account of the elements of stone and brick architecture. Amongst these were the moulding of rails and their continuation around projections and angles, the conversion of posts into pilasters by the application of appropriately carved boards, and the use of columns in the façade as in the Klopstockhaus in Quedlinburg, a town in the Harz boasting numerous timber-framed houses. In this otherwise relatively unadorned building a classical note is struck by the oriel supported by columns and an architrave.   *95*

In the towns of the Harz, in the Mansfeld district and in the Erzgebirge, the rise of the middle class town house was largely attributable to mining. Wealthy citizens and members of the nobility acquired shares in that industry and thus became representatives of early capitalist enterprise. The silver works of the Erzgebirge proved particularly profitable for a great many citizens, not only in Freiberg, Chemnitz and Zwickau but also in Leipzig, Nuremberg, Augsburg, Lübeck and Hamburg. Indeed, so advanced were economic conditions in the Electorate of Saxony that prince and citizen alike soon began to show a desire for a more refined display of wealth and employed the forms of the Renaissance. The magnificent doorway by the sculptor, Paul   *82*
Speck, which was commissioned in 1530 by Hans Weller von Molsdorf for his four-storeyed residence in the Obermarkt in Freiberg, no longer displays any of the robust characteristics of popular art. The round-headed doorway is framed by aedicular architecture of perfect proportions. The patron and his wife are immortalized in medallions, while on the tympanum there is a very realistic portrayal of mining which triumphantly proclaims the source of his wealth. This use of the doorway

as a triumphal arch with its unmistakable references to the person of the patron in the form of portraits, to his family in the form of arms and also to his field of activity, is the clearest evidence of the growing self-confidence of the middle class Renaissance citizen who prided himself on his calling. True, this generalization applies only to the upper stratum of the urban bourgeoisie. In almost every part of what was a much fragmented Germany the urge to build, in combination with other factors – whether traditional, political, social or economic—expressed itself in types of houses that differed widely from one part of the country to the other.

We shall now consider some of the more noteworthy regions. In Görlitz, for instance, there are Late Gothic and Early Renaissance houses which clearly illustrate the contradictory nature of the typical trends peculiar to the "Görlitz school". Of this there is no better example than the patrician cloth hall house, a type which, thanks to the rapid expansion of the cloth trade, had largely been perfected as early as the fifteenth century. Its main characteristics were a hall for the sale of merchandise occupying a transverse position on
91 the ground floor, and a lofty central hall situated above the porte-cochère and between the front and rear blocks. This type of house reached a high-water mark at the beginning of the sixteenth century when the coming of the Renaissance coincided with both the development of the out-worker system in the local textile industry and the acquisition by the bourgeoisie of real property, shares in mines, and privileges such as brewing and liquor retailing concessions. It was then, too—more especially after the great fire of 1525—that the ambitious patrician families of Görlitz built themselves houses with splendidly decorated façades (e.g. No. 8, Brüderstrasse, 1526) and doorways. The moving spirit in all this

was the master builder, Wendel Roskopf the Elder, who had trained in Prague under Benedikt Ried and, in true entrepreneurial fashion, also ran a business employing numerous specialized workmen who supplied architectural components in the new style. Inside the house the central hall was enlarged and given arcades, galleries and a vaulted roof, thereby becoming a richly appointed, imposing room for social interaction, the display of cloth or the retailing of beer. As opposed to the symmetrical cortile of the Italian Renaissance palazzi—also used for social purposes—these picturesque central halls, still vaulted in the Late Gothic style and serving as intermediate areas between the various levels of the front and rear blocks, betray the altogether different, if not actually hidebound, outlook of the German patrician, who confined the use of Renaissance forms solely to the façade.

As these gained currency in the second half of the sixteenth century, however, they were used not only with greater lavishness but also with increasing academic rigour. A typical example is presented by one of the best-known German middle class town houses of the Renaissance, the Biblisches Haus built in Görlitz in 1570. It betrays a strong Renaissance influence that came by way of Breslau. Itinerant Italian artists, who had already been long employed by the ruling houses in Germany and neighbouring countries, rarely had anything to do with middle class architecture which relied on native talent. Nevertheless it is plain that the patricians of Görlitz sought to emulate the aristocrats in this respect. The middle stratum, on the other hand, generally had to make do with a timber-framed building and a much smaller central hall—if any—and the petty bourgeoisie with a small wooden house roofed with thatch.

Like the cloth trade in Görlitz, the woad trade was, in Erfurt, the source of renewed economic prosperity in the sixteenth century, and this enabled many of the bigger merchants to rebuild or convert their houses in the contemporary Renaissance style. Trading links which extended as far afield as Nuremberg, Bremen, Hamburg and the Netherlands brought many impulses to bear. It is even possible to detect the influence of the North German-Franconian farm house. Typically these houses had the ridge parallel to the street, a porte-cochère to one side, vaulted store rooms, woad lofts beneath the high roof, and living accommodation on the upper floor. In Erfurt, too, the patrician houses have a special character of their own that derives not only from the strongly traditional and functional nature of the design, but also from Renaissance forms that had already undergone modification in southern Germany and the Netherlands. Thus, in the house Zur Hohen Lilie of 1538, a building important both from the cultural and the historical point of view, the polychromatic decoration is concentrated on the doorway and the highly original window frames. South German impulses are obviously a determining factor here, whereas in the house Zum Roten Ochsen, one of the most beautiful middle class town houses in Erfurt, they intermingle with those from the Netherlands. The faceted masonry of its doorways and the wholly un-Italian strap- and scrollwork on the dormer gable are particularly indicative of the considerable influence of the Dutchmen, Cornelis Floris and H. V. de Vries who since 1548 had published some series with engravings of ornamentation. The private house of Lucas Cranach, built in Weimar in 1549, is also closely akin to the style found in Erfurt. The personal mark of the foreman mason, which appears on the house Zum Breiten Herd, is identical to that on the door of Cranach's house.

As was only to be expected, the Renaissance, after modification in the Low Countries, ex-

99

92, 95 96

98

59, 60

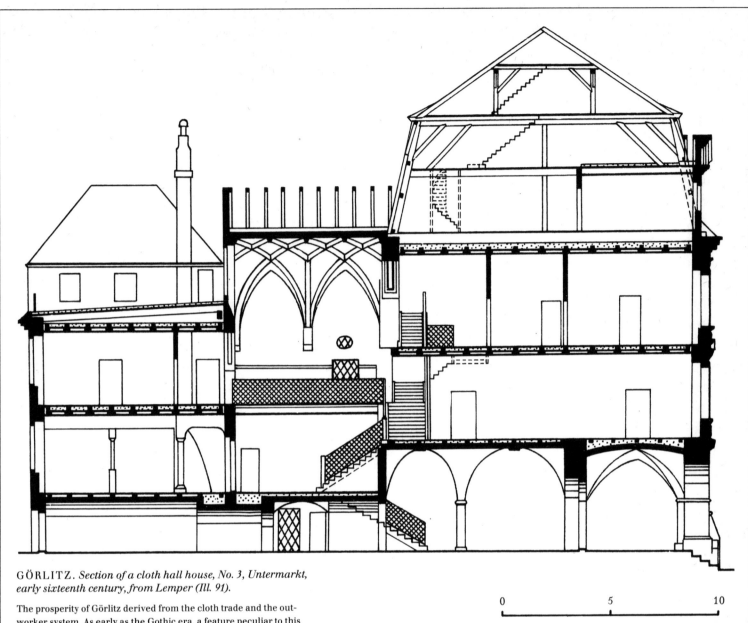

GÖRLITZ. *Section of a cloth hall house, No. 3, Untermarkt, early sixteenth century, from Lemper (Ill. 91).*

The prosperity of Görlitz derived from the cloth trade and the out-worker system. As early as the Gothic era, a feature peculiar to this region emerged in the shape of a central hall interposed between the front and back parts of the house. This covered area, which may be located between the inner courtyard and the staircase, and from which access could be gained to all levels of the house, was considerably enlarged in the early Renaissance when it was used for the sale of goods and for social intercourse. As early as the sixteenth century, however, the central hall again began to dwindle to the size of a narrow stair cage. Our section shows the Late Gothic stone vaulting of the central hall and, in front of the latter, the ground floor hall with the typical arcade giving on to the street.

0   5   10

erted its influence most strongly through the latter's many commercial ties with the neighbouring regions of North Germany and the Lower Rhine, whence it spread as far afield as East Prussia and Westphalia. Castles erected by Dutchmen or Flemings for princely rulers frequently provided the stimulus for regional middle class architecture. In the case of most middle class town houses, brick and timber were the usual building materials, while expensive dressed stone, which was seldom readily available and hence had to be imported, was only employed for the houses of the wealthiest citizens. As one of the above-mentioned localities, each of which had its own peculiar characteristics, we might cite the region along the Weser, progenitor of the so-called Weser Renaissance. Furthered by the trade in grain after 1570, Dutch and Flemish influences penetrated, first to Bremen, and thence to the towns of Minden, Hameln and Lemgo, to name only a few. In this way the North German gable-fronted houses with their asymmetrical arrangements of oriels and bay windows received flat, richly articulated façades and gables of markedly dynamic outline. The finest examples are the Hexenbürger-meisterhaus (Witch-hunting Mayor's House) in Lemgo of 1568–71 and the legendary Ratten-fängerhaus (Pied Piper's House) built in Hameln in 1602/3 by Herrmann Arendes. Here picturesque abundance reaches a high-water mark in the continuous bands of masonry which in turn form a pattern in their own right.

97

100

The situation was materially different in the old Hanseatic towns which, with their mighty gable-fronted hall-houses of brick construction, had made such a decisive contribution to the configuration of the middle class town house in Europe during the Gothic era. The international politico-economic balance of power had already been upset in the fifteenth century, not only by disputes with Holland and England, but also by internal dissension. That process was greatly accelerated in the next century—the century of discovery—when the centres of gravity of world trade shifted to such an extent that, even in Northern Europe, the Hanseatic League lost its leading role. More and more cities defected and submitted to the sovereignty of the local rulers. Just as those that remained clung doggedly to outmoded positions so, in what was the region of brick architecture, men continued to adhere to the forms they had inherited from a more glorious past. Needless to say, the particular technical requirements necessitated by the use of plain and moulded brick militated against the wealth of subtle Renaissance forms, nor did the lofty gabled façade readily lend itself to a clear, horizontally accentuated system of articulation. Yet the adoption of a wealth of new forms in the other German fields of construction would seem to indicate that the comparative inactivity in the old Hanseatic towns in the sixteenth century was not due to technical limitations alone.

Some of the finest examples of middle class buildings of strongly Gothic stamp that survived from the Renaissance may be seen in the still important town of Lübeck, notably in the Mengstrasse, and more especially in Lüneburg, whose continued prosperity derived from its salt springs. In other Baltic ports such as Rostock, the brick-built middle class town house was rather more unassuming. In the case of all these houses the general appearance is determined by the tall, Gothic, corbie stepped gable which in most cases, however, is no longer articulated by a vertical system of applied decoration that is carried up through the whole building, but rather by horizontal string courses and friezes between the individual storeys. Most conspicuous among the new elements were relief-work, strongly

104

105

moulded bricks, and medallions with portraits and figures in polychrome terracotta. That last feature was an art for which Statius von Düren and Gabriel von Aken, master craftsmen of Lübeck, were renowned. The wealth of colour provided by brick, whether plain or vitrified, and strips of plasterwork is, as a rule, retained. Engaged columns of brick around doorways and between windows are less frequently used for purposes of articulation. Windows are seldom ranged as they are in an arcade, though the pointed arch has, for the most part, given way to the flatter, three-centred arch, while the sophisticated fenestration of the hall and adjacent areas provides evidence of a desire for more light. In addition, the frames of most openings display a wide variety of mouldings.

The enlargement of the window openings at this time, however, was not solely the result of the desire, characteristic of the Renaissance, for a better standard of living and greater domestic comfort for the glazing of windows was still a very expensive business. The small Gothic bull's eye panes were superseded by plain diamond-shaped or rectangular quarries, in many cases painted. The household accounts of the Nuremberg patrician, Anton Tucher, for example, contain an entry for the year 1516 relating to the furnishing of the garden front of his house with sixty-two glass panes painted by Veit Hirschvogel. The custom of accepting the present of a window pane from one's guests got so out of hand that in many places the authorities put a stop to the practice. Nor did the interiors of houses go unchanged. High living and joie de vivre, no less than the desire for comfort, domestic refinement and a display of wealth, called for a host of new improvements so far as living accommodation, interior appointments, furniture and articles of household use were concerned. Hence there arose a large number

of new, specialized callings in the fields of cabinet-making and joinery, glass and textile manufacture, ceramics and gold-, silver- and tin-smithing. More often than not, it was the artist craftsmen who, in their pattern books and engravings of ornamental details, were responsible for disseminating the new decorative forms. Within a comparatively short space of time these displaced the Late Gothic ornamentation of interior appointments and articles of household use and introduced into the middle class town house a hitherto unprecedented wealth of finery which incurred the wrath of many moralists, including Hippolytus Guarinonius (1571–1654), author of *Die Grewel der Verwüstung menschlichen Geschlechts (The Abominable Ravages wrought by the Human Race)*, Ingolstadt 1610; also Johannes Geiler, otherwise known as von Kaysersberg (1445–1510), and Cyriacus Spangenberg (1528–1604). Though the latter inveighed against the luxurious life led by the middle classes in the impoverished towns of Thuringia, Saxony and the Mark, he was nevertheless prepared to make concessions in the case of those living in more prosperous centres such as Nuremberg, Augsburg and Venice.

The magnificent saloon of 1615 in the house 115 of the Zurich silk manufacturer, Rudolf Werdmüller, can convey an approximate idea of the more exacting demands then being made by the patrician caste. The whole room, including the floor boards, is embellished with elaborate carvings, as are the wainscotting and the immense coffered ceiling with its intarsia work which was then a new technique. The articulation of the wainscotting by means of columns, entablatures, aediculae, arcades, etc. which was a borrowing from Renaissance architecture, was to persist until the middle of the seventeenth century. Similarly, other pieces of furniture, in particular stoves and cupboards, many of which were as high as the ceiling itself, were designed in accordance with architectonic principles. Thus the faience stove with its polychrome painting, built-in throne-like seats, pictorial panels and superb head-piece, is not only a work of art in its own right, but also a witness to what was a significant advance in the art of living.

The pursuit of greater comfort and beauty in the home, which was confined almost exclusively to the middle classes, had already produced important results as early as the fifteenth century. At the same time, the concept of gracious living had revolutionized the relationship of man to his home. During the Renaissance, this process led to the production of many domestic furnishings and fittings which are still in use today. The splendour of the Late Renaissance went hand in hand with the search for convenient and functional forms. The relatively simple study of the Humanist, *114* Philipp Melanchthon, in his house in Wittenberg, reveals that this great scholar of the Early Renaissance had no need for rich ornamentation with which to boost his personality. The appointments are solid and functional. Sufficient warmth is dispensed by a typical stove which is covered with glazed and moulded tiles, a new design introduced around about the turn of the century, when tiles of this kind were first manufactured. This, along with the iron stove, which began to be produced in quantity towards the end of the sixteenth century, was the main source of heat. On the wall, protective wooden covering is confined to niches fitted with shelves that hold all manner of decorative objects. The former Gothic trestle table has now become a heavy, strongly constructed piece of furniture, a combination of trestle table and cabinet table. In front of it stands a padded, leather-clad arm-chair, heralding the advent of soft upholstery on various types of furniture, including the bed. There are bookshelves between the settles and a

small wash-handstand by the door which serve as an indication, not only of the importance attached to books and the requirements of hygiene, but also of the growing number of different types of cabinet furniture. Cupboards became truly imposing pieces of furniture—almost monumental in the case of the large, carved hall cupboard that was used for the storage of increasingly opulent clothing. They were elegant and richly decorated with intarsia work, metal and semi-precious stones, if they were used to display valuable ornaments and china. The chest was still retained though. As a *cassettone* with several drawers, it presaged the coming of the chest of drawers. The middle classes also continued to use the huge, wooden, box-like four poster bed with tester, while at princely courts the state bed was all the rage. A cosy atmosphere was created by carpets, wall hangings and—now used for the first time—wall paper. What had been created was a small, private world of household possessions calculated to instil a sense of well-being. According to a passage in the *Book of Rhymes* (1544) by Hans Sachs, the master singer of Nuremberg, these included: "Table, arm-chair, chairs, benches, bench cushions and other kinds of cushions, and a sleeping-bed; clock, screen, looking-glass, inkstand, ink, paper, seals, the Bible and other books to while away the time and for moral instruction." Pictures on the walls were, however, comparatively rare, as were window curtains. Painted window panes and the wealth of pictorial and other embellishment were, at the time, enough to satisfy the newly-awakened need for an intimate, imaginatively structured environment.

National Variants in Western and Northern Europe

The wealth of regional types of middle class town house in Germany—as well as the latter's significance as a building type—is not only reflected in the growth of particularism, but also in the economic power and the adaptability of the bourgeoisie. Amongst Germany's northwestern neighbours, on the other hand, the dictates of expediency led monarchy and bourgeoisie to join hands in what was a more unified national development. Any detailed examination would, of course, show that, in the period of upheaval preceding the new era and the emergence of the civic state, numerous, traditionally induced ethnic and regional distinctions continued to exist. But they are less plainly in evidence in the increasingly rapid adaptation of the middle class town house to a contemporary style of which, for another three hundred years or so—from the Renaissance to the Baroque—the nobility were to remain the chief proponents.

France is a notable case in point. When, in 1494, that country embarked on the Italian campaign in order to extend her sphere of influence, the conquerors eagerly seized the opportunity to take back with them to France not only the new, entrancing style from Italy, but also many of its exponents. The arrival of the Renaissance was a courtly occasion marked by the building of imposing châteaux and urban seats (*hôtels*) by the nobility. This development was characterized by two main phases, the first, which lasted until about 1540, was that of a modified form of Palladian Classicism with a continuing bias towards rich and animated embellishment, while the second and later phase was one of rational restraint. Leading architectural theorists such as Philibert Delorme and Jacques Androuet du Cerceau

imposed upon these forms academic rules which took little if any account of the middle class town house. In his *Livre d'architecture* of 1559, du Cerceau recommends, for the middle class citizen, a standardized house without a courtyard, which could hardly serve as a model, the stipulated measurements being a width of some 24 metres, a depth of 11 metres and a height of 5.84 metres. To the best of their ability the bourgeoisie strove to emulate the châteaux and hôtels, and their peers in the rest of Europe soon followed suit. However, most of the simpler middle class town houses of the sixteenth century still retained the forms inherited from the past. In the North of France, the narrow, gable-fronted type of house prevailed alongside timber-framed buildings, often of grid-like construction. Sometimes posts and rails are used in a way that simulates the articulation of stone walls by means of columns and pilasters. As a rule, however, Renaissance forms appear only in certain localities as a decorative adjunct. They were, on the other hand, more readily accepted in the stone and brick architecture which predominated in central and southern France where they acquired a picturesque exuberance in which the influence of Late Gothic forms is still apparent.

102 Thus the *hôtel* of the merchant Jean Lâllemant in Bourges, dating from the beginning of the sixteenth century, is still strongly reminiscent of a castle. Yet all the openings, whether doors or windows, in the otherwise flat, compact surfaces are given projecting, exceptionally plastic, frames, the supporting members, e.g. columns or architraves, being adorned with such a profusion of finely-worked ornamentation that hardly seem to be structural elements. In wealthy mercantile towns such as Dijon, Toulouse and Orléans, there are other magnificent patrician palaces hardly inferior in size to the *hôtels* of the nobility. They, too, adopted the clear articulation of

walls characteristic of the Renaissance and, like the *hôtel* of the merchant Jean de Bernuy 103 in Toulouse, bear witness to the national idiom in their wealth of detail and richness of embellishment. Also at work here were influences emanating from near-by Spain, whose gradual emergence as a great colonial power had set its mark on town palaces that were decorated in the ebullient and fanciful Mudéjar, Plateresque and Desornamentado styles. Since the main emphasis in these sumptuous residences was on the display of wealth and not on any commercial function they contributed nothing to the typology of middle class architecture. Only in Orléans were merchants' houses given wide arches and arcades for the accommodation of shops and thus struck a remarkably modern note and anticipated the shopping areas of our own day. Oriels and dormer gables are seldom used, unlike that peculiarly French phenomenon, the sumptuously embellished lucarne in the form of an aedicule which rises above the cornice on the main façade. Courtly splendour is also reflected in the interior of the house, where the coffered ceiling, the wainscotting and—most important item of all—the mantlepiece, are adorned with delicate motifs which in many cases were painted. A parallel development was the growth of craftsmanship, notably in the Île de France and Burgundy, where furniture making was brought to a fine art. This, along with its early and strongly accentuated Renaissance architecture, made France an important architectural middle man as far as her neighbours to the North and East were concerned.

In the Netherlands, French influence made itself felt, especially in Flanders and to a lesser degree in the North, where a strong, long-established self-confident urban bourgeoisie was increasingly absorbing the local nobility. The country's continuing economic growth as a centre of cloth production and foreign trade militated against the adoption of courtly architectural forms. Slowly but surely, as the sixteenth century wore on, there evolved a national style fostered by a middle class architecture that was to a large extent based on the clear and vigorous forms of Palladio. Whereas the new principles manifested themselves unequivocally in town halls and corporate buildings, they were subordinated, in domestic architecture, to the traditional type of the gable-fronted hall-house. Renaissance forms were incorporated into the façade in an idiom that showed great creative intelligence as well as a certain measure of fantasy. At the same time a typical characteristic of Dutch architecture was retained, namely the combination of brick, which was the chief building material and the more expensive imported limestone and sandstone, which were used to strengthen the angles, the surrounds of all the openings, and the walls. In the interior, too, the cosmopolitan Dutch citizen remained conservative, though the number of rooms continued to multiply. On the ground floor, the part of the lofty hall devoted to business that faced the street, the *voorhuis*, was separated from the familiy parlour and kitchen at the back. Sometimes, if more rooms were required, the *voorhuis* might also be split into two storeys, so that a low entresol was formed. Pale, colour-washed walls, dark ceiling joists, painted furniture, polychrome tiles, and flagged floors, as well as textiles, majolica ware, metal utensils and other household equipment, created a domestic atmosphere that was at once cosy and opulent. This atmosphere was to find expression not long afterwards in what was to be the heyday of Dutch interior painting.

Indeed nowhere, save in this self-confident cultural environment could Cornelis Floris, architect, sculptor and decorative engraver, have created his typically Dutch brand of Renaissance ornamentation. His series, which appeared from 1548 onwards, and in which Roman grotesques are imaginatively blended with arabesques, cartouches, masks, scrolls and many other decorative elements to form the so-called Floris style, acted as a vital stimulus not only in the Netherlands, but also throughout northern and central Europe. For instance, in the gable-fronted house "Dit is in Bethlehem" in Gorinchem (Gorkum) the Floris style comes into its own in peculiar synthesis with the traditional design of the façade. Without adhering to the classical orders, the subtle decoration, consisting of carved limestone is concentrated on the upper parts—on the string courses, the angles and, especially, the curved "Dutch" gable. It is to be seen at its richest between the windows and the relieving arches that are typical of brick-built houses. The gable which had no importance in Italy is here awarded pride of place. In Bruges, gables were provided with niches for the windows, in Ghent the stepped gable with pinnacles predominated, while in the southern part of North Holland gables displayed pointed arches interrupted by horizontal guttering. Like our example in Gorkum, a slightly later house in Deventer, De Drie Haringen consists of a hall with inserted storey and two upper residential floors. Here, however, the national idiom finds expression in a more rational and restrained style of architecture. Many buildings have survived from the town's golden age which lasted until 1650 or thereabouts. These houses, with their less emphatic use of sculptural embellishment, emphasize the picturesque contrast in colour presented by brick and dressed stone.

The consummate beauty of No. 64, Donkere Gaard in Oudewater, a gable-fronted hall-house built in 1611, comes not only from its vivid colouring, but also from the versatile use of sculptural elements in the articulation of the wall surfaces. The upper part of the ground floor façade is pierced by small windows between which strongly moulded consoles support the slightly projecting upper storeys. These upper storeys, with their red brickwork, green painted shutters, white window frames and basket arches combine to produce an extraordinarily colourful spectacle, and it was no coincidence that it should have caught to catch the eye of the Dutch architectural painter. One of these select and traditional middle class town houses, a brick building with stone dressings and strapwork embellishment erected in Amsterdam in 1606, was at one time occupied by Rembrandt. When he bought it in 1639, by which time he had gained general recognition, the house had, in fact, undergone a modishly opulent conversion. A second storey had been added, topped by a classical cornice with dentils and a pediment, which clearly stresses the Baroque concept of presenting the long side of the house to the street. While the two lucarnes show a French influence, the strictly classical treatment of the façade is both Palladian and representative of a typically Dutch approach to the Baroque.

We have already had occasion to note the exemplary influence of Dutch architecture on northern and central Europe. By the second half of the sixteenth century the master builders from the Netherlands were very active in the Scandinavian countries, especially in Denmark, which now controlled the Baltic. Under King Christian IV these influences were to acquire a national accent, not only in middle class, but also in châteaux, architecture. Close trading relations, a similar anti-Catholic attitude, a common architectural frame of reference and the common use of brick were important prerequisites for this interaction.

One of the great master builders of the northern Renaissance was the Dutchman Antonius van Opbergen. In 1577 he was employed on the restoration of Kronborg Castle at Helsingør, where he also built private houses in the new style—the earliest of that type to have survived in Denmark. While the façade and stepped gable of No. 76, Stengade, dating from 1579, still display a close affinity to the brick-built Late Gothic house in the Hanseatic tradition next door, the use of sandstone in the window surrounds, the doorway and the copings on the gable, shows what progress has been made, as does the omission of vertical articulation by means of applied embellishment. Indeed the gable, because of the opportunity it provided for decorative purposes, was to retain its importance albeit in the form of the dormer gable of diverse design. For by a building regulation issued as early as 1520 in Copenhagen, the middle class town house was required to be built of brick and to present its long side to the street, thus diminishing the risk of fire. Hence the predilection for imposing gables could find expression only in the dormer gable, magnificent examples of which, dating from the first half of the seventeenth century, still survive in the Dyveckehus in Copenhagen (later the Royal Porcelain Factory), or in Bangs Stenhus in Aalborg. The impression conveyed by this four-storeyed building, with decorative sandstone elements in the panels of the gable and above the windows, is not in the least provincial, it looks like a palace built of brick. The varying height of the storeys, dictated by practical considerations, did not prove to be an obstacle to the adoption of Renaissance forms; on the contrary, it may be regarded as an indication that an alien style has been deliberately adapted to fit local circumstances. Timber-framed construction, which was another traditional form, was subjected to severe restrictions by the authorities owing to the increasing shortage of timber. Needless to say, the influence of the

Netherlands also spread to Sweden, which was now in competition with Denmark, having gained her independence in 1523. The urban bourgeoisie, however, being still comparatively weak, was incapable of achieving anything noteworthy on its own account. Hence it was the Dutch merchants living in Stockholm who were first to commission brick or stone houses from their countrymen as well as from German and French master builders.

If the middle class town house did not as yet play any substantial role in this northernmost country of Europe, the situation was very different on the other side of the North Sea. For in fifteenth century England, early capitalist relations of production had already begun to take shape in the wool and cloth industry. In alliance with the absolutist Tudor monarchy the propertied middle classes and the new landed gentry with whom they had merged, since the sixteenth century, determined the course by which the country became a colonial power and sovereign of the seas. Her insular position and her long-standing tradition of native Gothic architecture, as well as her early secession from Rome and the establishment of a national church, had placed considerable obstacles in the way of the Renaissance. Moreover, in secular building the elevated social status of the leading bourgeoisie increased the importance of country seats of the manor house type. Here, as in the middle class houses of the older towns, the late Gothic perpendicular style persisted until well into the sixteenth century, both in timber construction and opulent internal appointments, as may be seen, for instance, in Paycocke's House in Great Coggeshall in Essex. The large hall-house of post and rail construction, often with curved braces, still remained typical, as did the wealth of embellishment on the closely spaced joists and the wainscotting where fillet-shaped elements such as mouldings, frames and linenfold, and Late

111

107

118, 119

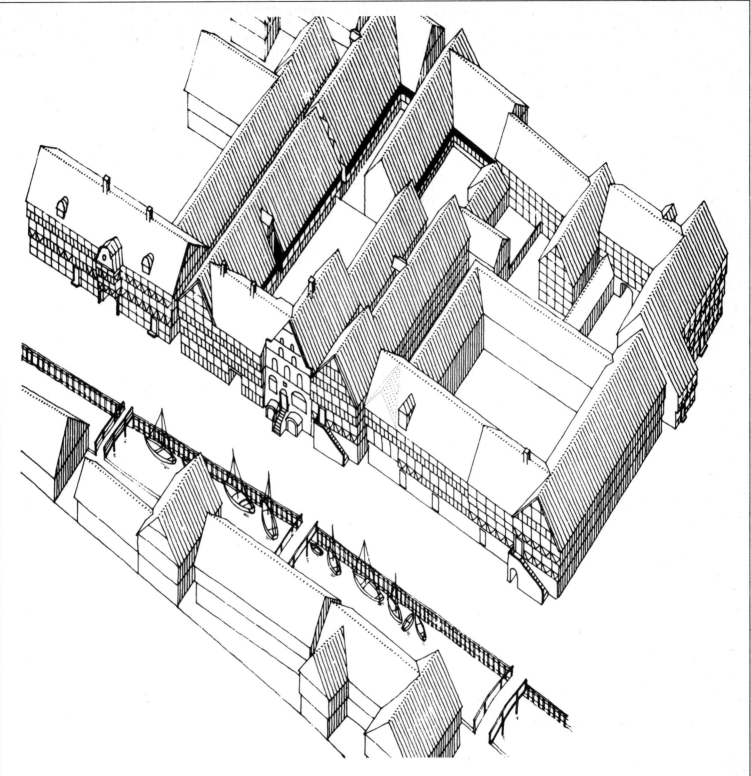

AALBORG. *Part of the town with merchants' yards, beside the Østerå, circa 1600. Reconstruction by H. H. Enquist.*

The three-storeyed gable-fronted houses extended far back into the sites they occupied. In most cases the living-rooms were situated above lofty basement storeys and were reached by an outside stair at the gable end. To that extent the features they share in common with the Hanseatic merchant's house are plainly in evidence. Adjoining the dwelling-house, either immediately behind it or long-side on to the street, were large warehouses or granaries. The siting of the merchants' yards was determined by the waterways in which the vessels could lie alongside.

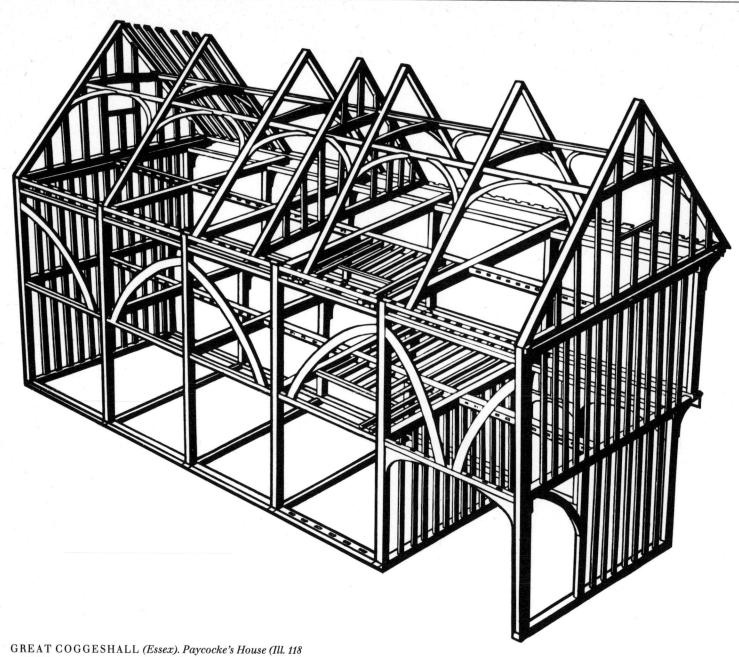

GREAT COGGESHALL *(Essex). Paycocke's House (Ill. 118 and 119).*

The projection shows the large timber frame with close studding between the posts and curving braces reminiscent of cruck construction.

Gothic foliate motifs predominated. In the Tudor period with its predilection for splendour, Renaissance features could make little or no headway; in their Italian, Dutch and German variants they mingled with the native Gothic to form the sumptuous, albeit chaotic, Tudor style, which only came to an end in the seventeenth century with the Classicism of Inigo Jones.

As everywhere else, of course, the form assumed by a client's house was determined by his social and financial position. The house in which Shakespeare was born embodies the *120* type of simple, two-storeyed, timber-framed building with a strongly vernacular stamp of the type that was still lived in by respectable middle class families in the sixteenth century. As a rule these timber-framed houses had projecting upper storeys; on the ground floor there was a front and a back room, each with its own hearth, and also a side passage, while the second floor consisted of the great room equipped with a fireplace. With the constantly growing demand for more rooms in the sixteenth and seventeenth centuries, houses were frequently rebuilt and given extra storeys, and the attics would also be put to use as accommodation. Special regional types came into being, as, for instance, in Chester where business was so brisk that, in the timber-framed houses lining the old thoroughfares, the citizens laid out the two lower floors as commercial premises with shops below and open arcades embellished with carvings above. A typical national characteristic of the middle class town house was the bay window which became increasingly popular in the second half of the sixteenth century. This was a large oriel-type window, either rectangular, polygonal or semi-circular in shape (the latter being known as a bow window), which might also be carried up through several storeys. The relatively large openings were generally divided by wood, stone or brick mullions. They were glazed with small, leaded panes or quarries, sometimes decorated with heraldic paintings and formed a grid-like pattern. Together with the clear, structural skeleton of the imaginatively designed timber framing, and the nogging, which was usually white plaster but sometimes brick laid in herringbone pattern, they bestowed on the English middle class town house a character that expressed domestic ease.

The Melting-Pot—the Vernacular Imagination in Southeastern Europe

The history of the period between the Middle Ages and the Renaissance saw the steady growth of the power of the bourgeoisie in the countries of central and western Europe and this in turn enabled the middle class town house to branch out into a wide number of types and variants. On the other hand, the picture presented by eastern and southern Europe in the sixteenth century is one of far greater contrasts. In the kingdoms of Bohemia, Poland and—at any rate at the outset—Hungary (including Transylvania) there existed an advanced bourgeois culture. But in the last-named country the development was soon brought to a standstill by the inexorably advancing tide of Osmanli conquest. In 1526 the Turks were victorious at Mohacs and in 1541 they captured Buda.

In Russia, this epoch is also characterized by the fight against the Mongol overlords and the struggle for political unity. In these regions on the fringes of the Continent, the bourgeoisie, subject as they were to foreign and native despots, could not as yet be a factor of any moment. What had already been attained in the towns of the Balkans was now lost, while in Muscovy itself the construction of richly ornamented timber buildings still persisted,

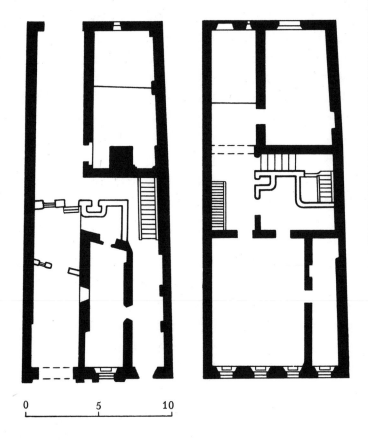

0   5   10

BISTRIŢA *(Bistritz). Dornei Street, Casa argintarului (now the town's historical museum). Plans of the ground and first floors of a house belonging to a silversmith and goldsmith, sixteenth century (Ill. 129).*

Inside this house, at least ten metres wide and some twenty-five metres long, the pragmatic, asymmetrical organization of space, also apparent in the façade, is dictated by the combination under one roof of business and domestic functions. The large porte-cochère gives access to the shop and workshop, as also to the store-room on the ground floor, while the smaller door leads via the vestibule to a centrally placed stair serving the upper floor, with its imposing state-room and other family apartments on the street side, and a kitchen overlooking the courtyard.

although there is evidence of brick-built houses with several rooms as early as the fifteenth century. Compared with the timber houses of the middle classes, however, they were to remain the exception until the middle of the seventeenth century. Renaissance forms, transmitted by Italian master builders and incorporated in the brick residences of the nobility since the sixteenth century, could hardly be expected to have found favour among the middle classes and the peasantry whose timber architecture was of an essentially regional and vernacular character.

Though its progress was soon to be violently interrupted, the Renaissance made a far greater impact upon Hungary where King Matthias I Corvinus had turned Buda into a centre of Renaissance culture. However, it is only in localities which never came under Turkish rule, i.e. Trans-Danubian towns such as Györ and Sopron, that there still survive houses with arcaded courtyards built by citizens engaged in viticulture and trade. Transylvania, occupied by the Turks in 1541, remained an enclave in which an independent economy and culture continued to flourish. Its towns, including the capital Sibiu (Hermannstadt), had been laid out by German settlers on the model of those at home and, as early as the fourteenth century, these could already boast, alongside timber buildings, middle class houses of brick or masonry construction with vaults and stepped Gothic gables. An example of this is the Casa Haller, No. 10, Piaţa Republicii, which was erected in 1470 and subsequently altered. Renaissance forms, transmitted through Italian trade and by Italian artists working in Hungary, were already being adopted in the fifteenth century to merge organically with the vernacular, a process that was to continue unabated. Thus, the façade of a house belonging to a goldsmith or silversmith in Bistriţa 129 (Bistritz), an important centre of that trade,

displays doorways and windows whose details are treated in a style that derives wholly from the Renaissance. Nevertheless, the asymmetrical arrangement of these openings on the ground floor, as well as the disposition of the rooms within, reflect practical needs that were not amenable to any kind of orthodoxy. The house built in Cluj (Klausenburg) by the Hungarian Royal Counsellor, Adrianus Wolphard who also employed Italian masons, has 138 a doorway executed in 1579 by indigenous artists, which demonstrates the vigorously idiosyncratic nature of this regional interpretation. In fact the lintel, with its triglyphs, masks and coat of arms, is far too heavy for the delicate, deeply fluted half-columns.

In the kingdom of Bohemia, since 1493 a largely autonomous part of the multi-national Habsburg Empire, far more witnesses to a rich, historical past have survived than in districts frequently ravaged by war. As far back as the Middle Ages, foreign trade and the mining industry had given rise to a strong self-confident urban bourgeoisie that was quick to open its mind to the spirit of the new age. King Wladyslaw II Jagiello and the aristocracy introduced this bourgeoisie to the Renaissance by constructing imposing new buildings. Without interfering with the basic structure of their inherently Gothic houses, the citizens set about refashioning the fronts of whole streets and squares. Even though they may now be overlaid with later baroque alterations, the market squares of a great many of 135 the smaller towns such as Telč, Slavonice and Litomyšl can still convey a fair idea of the marvellous unity imposed upon a medieval nucleus by the spirit of the Renaissance. The typical Gothic covered passageway, a feature not only practical but effective in terms of town planning, was widened and converted into an arcade with round-headed arches. The façades of individual houses were covered by

PRAGUE. *Old Town, No. 1/475, Kožná ul., The Two Golden Bears (Ill. 139).*

The plan shows the Gothic nucleus of the house (originally two houses).

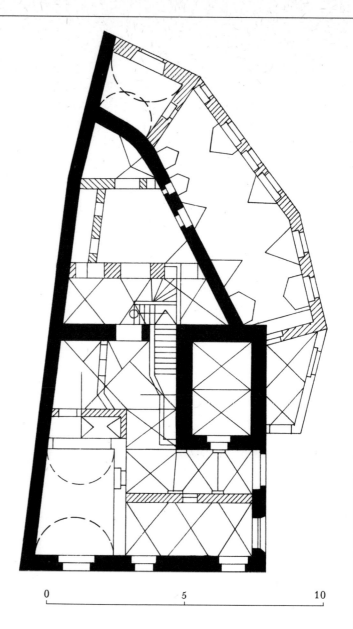

WARSAW. *East (or Barss) side of the Old Market Place.*

In 1944 all that remained of this row were the ruins of the ground floor, here indicated in bold outline. In the course of an admirable rebuilding operation, the façades were faithfully restored down to the smallest historical detail. However, the apartments behind them were redesigned to accord with modern requirements.

0   5   10

pilasters, architraves and string courses in high relief, a system of articulation that laid emphasis on the horizontal. The traditional stepped gable was given a lively, animated outline by the superimposition of semi-circular or quadrantal panels and volutes. Nearly everywhere the love of colour—a basic national trait—finds expression in wall painting and sgraffito. Colour was used to set off projecting structural elements, to cover wall surfaces with lively decorative motifs, mythological figures or pictorial friezes, or again, by employing the technique of sgraffito, to simulate those decorative architectural features such as rustication, pilasters, window frames, etc., commonly found on palace façades. When, in certain regions, it became customary to restyle the gable—again after the manner of the palazzo—by concealing it behind a rectangular wall surmounted by a parapet, the surface was embellished for preference with a sgraffito simulation of facetted masonry. The patricians were also given to adorning their staterooms with murals which articulated the walls in the manner of architecture, even to the point of producing a three-dimensional effect. However, the main entrance still remained the focal point of purely sculptural figurative and ornamental decoration, a personal, richly symbolic triumphal arch for the client.

After the turn of the sixteenth century the towns of Poland showed themselves no less eager to adopt Renaissance forms, though this was modified to fit in with their own concepts. Their geographical remoteness from Italy was offset by the many Italian artists who were summoned to the country by the king and the nobility and who, together with master builders from Germany and the Netherlands, furnished the principal cities, notably Cracow and Warsaw, with sumptuous residences. Renaissance culture reached Poland in successive waves, its splendour being, of course, reflected first

and foremost in the houses of the patrician class. Like almost everywhere else where the original structure was retained, remodelling was confined very largely to the façade, the magnificent doorways, the painted, sculpturally articulated walls and the inventively conceived roofs and gables. Local traditions, nurtured by indigenous craftsmen, quickly set their own stamp on the impulses from abroad. A house in Cracow, the Prałatówka, with its combination of painted diamond-pointed masonry and imaginatively designed parapet which conceals the low roof, is a typical example. Thanks to the exemplary work of the Polish authorities responsible for the preservation and restoration of ancient buildings, many other fine examples of the middle class town house, including their valuable interior decorations, may now be seen in their original condition in the ancient royal city of Cracow.

Needless to say, the widespread enthusiasm for building at the time of the Renaissance was stimulated by the growing need for more and better rooms. Thus ground floor business premises were extended, separate shops introduced and the number of living-rooms increased by the addition of extra storeys or by expansion in depth where many courtyards were given arcaded passageways.

Warsaw's promotion to capital city in 1596 led to a busy phase of building activity at the beginning of the seventeenth century, and this radically altered a picture in which Hanseatic influences had hitherto been predominant. The Old Market Place, restored down to the smallest detail following its total destruction in the Second World War, provides an excellent record of the organic metamorphosis from medieval patrician house to Renaissance residence. Since there was no possibility of increasing the width of the existing sites, which usually accommodated no more than three bays, houses where extra storeys had

128

been added were given their own central stair-well that was illuminated by a sky-light rising above the pitched roof. Originally some of the roofs were concealed behind parapets and hence the imposing square illustrated here, with its decorated façades, must have seemed to consist of a collection of small, disproportionately lofty palazzi. In Zamość we have a rare example of a Polish town that came into being during the Renaissance. It was commissioned by the chancellor and royal hetman Jan Zamoyski as his residence, and built between 1581 and 1585 to the design of Bernardo Morando of Padua, with streets laid out in a grid and a large central market place. The plots were all of uniform size save for the sociologically significant difference that those of artisans were twenty metres in depth and those of merchants forty metres, a circumstance which allowed the latter to build more commodious dwellings, as well as warehouses with readier access to the main thoroughfare. In the market place and adjoining streets, houses were built with arcades and rich stucco decoration of which the picturesque abundance and rustic character ought not simply to be dismissed as provincial, but rather should be seen as the expression of a vigorous, deeply-rooted love of ornamentation. Heedless of logic and proportion or, indeed, of anything but its own concept of beauty, it clothed façades with a truly cornucopian wealth of exuberant ornamentation. Similar examples are also to be found in the little town of Kazimierz Dolny.

132, 133

123–125

In the rooms, whose disposition was dictated by practical considerations—hence the irregularity of the fenestration—the popular imagination has seized on Renaissance elements and combined them, in robust artisan fashion, with its own meaningful figurative motifs. Again, the interior often contained stucco decorations and painted rooms. Wide parapets of lively design, which concealed the roofs,

WROCŁAW *(Breslau). Market Place. The so-called Greifen-haus (Griffin House) has a multi-storeyed gable of which the verges are adorned with heraldic animals. Built between 1587 and 1592 by Friedrich Gross.*

In Wrocław, which at that time was still under Bohemian, or rather Austrian, suzerainty, the development of the middle class town house was determined to a very large extent by the German patrician caste. When carrying out their Renaissance and, at a later date, Baroque, alterations, they retained the traditional type of gable-frounted house.

were a favourite feature in the Polish middle class town house of the Renaissance. Not only were they useful in case of fire, but also lent these buildings the much sought-after appearance of palaces. Houses such as these in the smaller towns are an example of Polish domestic architecture in its most personal form.

In the rich Silesian and Hanseatic towns, largely shaped by their German citizens, the traditional type of gable-fronted hall-house still persisted, if in Renaissance and, later, Baroque attire. Though severely damaged in the Second World War, Wrocław (Breslau) which, as far as the Renaissance was concerned, occupied a kind of intermediate position between Prague and Cracow, possesses in the market place a row of proud patrician houses, now restored, with opulently designed doorways and verges, and clearly articulated symmetrically composed façades. The character of the houses belonging to the leading Danzig merchants, on the other hand, was defined by a circumstance that had persisted ever since the Middle Ages, namely the existence of deep, narrow plots, which in turn called for gable-fronted houses of corresponding depth, with a terrace on the street side. The pressing need for more rooms could only be met by the addition of extra storeys, thus giving rise to soaring, towerlike façades, gorgeously embellished with fine Renaissance masonry work of Dutch, German, Bohemian and Silesian origin. In addition, the tall windows, closely ranged between slender pilasters, and the narrow aprons decorated with reliefs, gave the buildings a character of airiness and translucency. Their height, already a dominant feature, was accentuated by the figures that crowned them. The interior appointments in a Danzig patrician's house had an air of solid luxury. Large halls on the ground floor were once used as reception rooms, while the saloon on the street side of the first floor served as an imposing state-room. Adjoining this was a landing lit only by a sky-light, beyond which were living-rooms facing over the courtyard.

141 Our example, the Goldenes Haus (Golden House), in what used to be the Long Market Place (Dlugi Targ) is the product, like many of the other middle class town houses in Gdansk, of painstaking restoration carried out by the Poles. Thus a townscape of great character, apparently destroyed beyond repair in the Second World War, has been recreated—at least in outward appearance—, for the interiors of the houses have been designed in accordance with modern needs.

In the Steps of Courtly Baroque

The history of the middle class town house in the Baroque era must be seen in the context of an enriching metamorphosis that reflects the peculiar, prolonged, albeit unequal and hence conflict-ridden, interdependence of nobility and bourgeoisie. The optimistic bid for freedom made by the middle classes in the early bourgeois revolutions of the sixteenth century met with success only in the northern part of the Netherlands and, to some extent, in England. Over large areas of Europe, absolutism again reduced the citizens to political impotence, while the Counter-Reformation sought to extinguish the spirit of *humanitas* by means of the inquisition and of a pageantry calculated to bemuse the senses. In the heart of Europe the struggle for hegemony between powers and faiths gave rise to the Thirty Years' War, a conflict of unprecedented barbarity which set Germany back by several centuries. The peasant again relapsed into serfdom.

Courtly splendour, standing armies, the apparatus of law-enforcement and of bureaucracy, to name only a few types of governmental expenditure, called for an increasingly abundant source of finance, in other words a strong economy upheld first and foremost by the bourgeoisie. That economy is manifested above all in the steady expansion of mercantilism and manufacturing industry. Its organizers were the merchant princes, its parasitical beneficiaries the local rulers, while its chief opponents were primarily members of craft guilds engaged in small scale production and bound hand and foot by rulers and regulations. Hence, in this interplay of opposing forces, the patriciate, which held the reins of government in many of the towns, and the absolutist provincial or central authority, allied themselves from time to time with the hierarchically constituted nobility in consolidating the nation, extending markets and maintaining internal law and order against the rapidly growing and often rebellious plebeian classes. As a class, the bourgeoisie was, it is true, not regarded as socially acceptable, though the extremely rich were able to buy their way into the élite by purchasing patents of nobility. On the other hand, many of the princes also had recourse to capitalist methods when, for example, they set up manufactories. And when, with the coming of rationalism and the Enlightenment in the eighteenth century, the middle classes confidently proclaimed their ideas for the first time, the enlightened despots adapted themselves as often as not to the changed circumstances. Yet the inevitable clash could at best only be postponed and in France, the one country in which absolutism had seemed irremovable, the rotten régime was swept away in 1789.

Nevertheless, our short survey reveals that, over a large area of Europe, the middle classes long remained in a state of dependency which scarcely permitted their having an architecture peculiar to themselves. Few of the towns had expanded to such an extent as to have outgrown the traditional structures. As often as not the old nucleus was now surrounded, not by walls, but by extensive bastions, the better to protect it against modern artillery. Nor did the bourgeoisie inspire any of the attempts, such as are observable in many countries, at grandiose town planning which adheres to the absolutist, Baroque principle of a centre to which all else is subordinated. The increasing desire of princes to proclaim their greatness and absolutist power found its most obvious expression at this time in the founding of new residences. Following the unique example set by the Roi Soleil in the planning of Versailles, even the pettiest potentates sought to demonstrate the principle "l'État, c'est moi" in radial plans whose hub was their palace. A typical example is Karlsruhe, laid out between 1715 and 1717 by the Margrave of Baden-Durlach, one of many in an impoverished Germany that was split up into more than three hundred petty principalities. Thirty-two streets, intersected by a concentric network, radiate from the palace at the centre, nine of these constituting the town proper, while the rest sub-divide the park. Nature, like the Grand Duke's subjects, was expected to subordinate itself completely to the divine will of the ruler. The method used to incorporate the citizen into the system is revealing. He was banished from the immediate vicinity of the Grand Duke who surrounded himself with his household in the palace. In front of this were the inner "defences" in the shape of two-storeyed buildings occupied by the nobility and officials and forming an arc round a segment of the Great Circle. Only beyond that arc were ordinary citizens allowed to settle in one-storeyed houses of prescribed design. Servants were accommodated on the south-eastern perimeter of the town. Originally there was not even a market place, but merely the Great Circle and parade ground—an interesting indication of the insignificance of the role played in this instance by the market that was once the origin of the European town and served as both centre of trade and communications and as a collective manifestation of middle class prosperity.

However, such radical demonstrations of absolute power were not feasible in the many towns of Europe which had grown up over the centuries. If the Baroque nevertheless contrived to play an important role in the middle class town house, this was chiefly because of the singularly unliberated position of the middle classes whose predilection for display and for the amenities of life was dominated by the influence of the splendid architecture of the nobility. Never before had architecture been dubbed the "mother of the arts" with greater truth than now. Both on the outside and in the

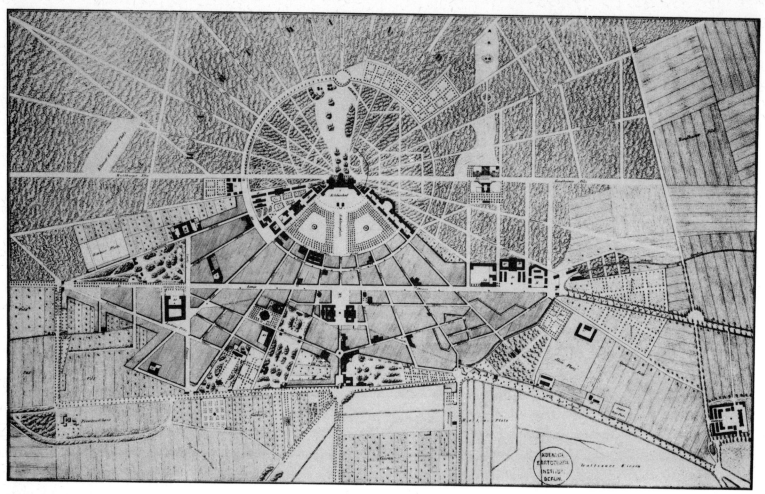

KARLSRUHE. *Town plan, published in 1830 by J. Velten. First laid out in 1715 by the army engineer, Jacob Friedrich von Betzendorf, and enlarged between 1800 and 1825 by Friedrich Weinbrenner.*

Of all the cities founded in the Baroque era, Karlsruhe—the concept of the Margrave Karl Wilhelm of Baden-Durlach—is the most logical expression of the principle of absolutism as applied to society and the State. Like a sun, the princely palace, with its free-standing Bleiturm or Octagon Tower, stands at the centre of a geometrically clear, circular lay-out of thirty-two radial streets. In its somewhat elevated position it is visible from all sides as a symbol of authority to which everything else must conform—the large park, the palace gardens and the buildings of the ordinary citizens. Forming part of the actual princely environment are the blocks adjoining the palace and containing kitchens, mews and orangeries, likewise the sector immediately to the south of the palace gardens, with its two-storeyed buildings for the aristocracy and Court officials. All these lay within the circle. Outside it, and extending as far as the straight east-west axis, though still rigorously integrated into the radial system, were the areas allocated to the citizens and servants, who were only permitted to build single-storeyed houses and this, moreover, to a prescribed design. There was no market place to serve them as a social and commercial centre. The citizens had been attracted to the town by the lure of tax and building concessions and the possibility of earning money in manufactories (porcelain and tobacco), as also by purveying luxury goods (jewellery, timepieces, carriages) to what was a considerable princely household.

Nevertheless they were robbed of self-respect to an extent never before experienced, even in the early days of the European town when, at the very least, idiosyncratic building and a central market place were regarded as inalienable rights. However, this historical anachronism was eliminated barely a hundred years later by Weinbrenner's additions in the classical manner, when the citizens acquired a town centre of their own with a market place, town hall and church.

interior of a building painting and sculpture were so combined as to give the illusion of a marvellous and transcendent unity. Castles and palaces, churches and monasteries, became leaders in an orchestra whose intoxicating polyphony brought out the leitmotiv all the more brilliantly by intensifying the individual parts, each of which depended on and combined with the rest in fluent motion. Like the earlier principles of seriality—horizontal accentuation and the clear delimitation of each independent part—all the decorative elements engendered by the Renaissance underwent this change, as may be seen if only from the detail on the window frames. The ever-growing wealth of forms and the proliferation and abundance of detail are complemented by the imposing effect of the symmetrical ordering of masses with a dominant centre and subordinate parts that tend less to height than to lateral expansion. Plans and elevations begin to acquire sinuous curves and playfully call in question the tectonics of building in general. In secular architecture the château, usually situated outside the town and consisting of many parts, with central and side pavilions, or with projecting wings forming a cour d'honneur, set the standard for a luxurious, ceremonial existence. This ambiance was heightened by great staircases, saloons and an enormous number of sumptuous rooms (the palace of Versailles was capable of accommodating ten thousand people), amongst which the bedchamber of the potentate played an important role.

Needless to say, the middle class citizen had neither the means nor the power to emulate the architecture of the monarch. Most country mansions were never more than a pale reflection of their courtly counterparts. Yet in the type of the town palace, the château-like successor to the palazzo, the middle class citizen was presented with an aristocratic form of architecture that could be more readily copied. Like the middle class town house, the multi-storeyed town palace stood alongside others in the square or street, yet presented an entirely new picture of grandiloquent urban domestic architecture in that it was eaves-fronted and latitudinally extensive, with tall storeys and a decorative composition to which the bays lent a strict rhythm. The evident contrast between this and many of the traditional features of the habitually gable-fronted middle class town house—the asymmetrical articulation of the façades by means of oriels, the jettied upper storeys of timber-framed buildings, the conventional decorative elements and, finally, the cramped appearance of such structures, both within and without—was inevitably felt to be a stigma. Thus the middle classes also succumbed to a building craze which was to change the face of whole cities to an even greater extent than the Renaissance had done. According to his wealth or station, a man would seek to enlarge his plot and would demolish the old building, or at least do his best to alter it by giving it a more imposing and modish façade and a more commodious interior. Economic factors had little to do with the alteration of the façade. Rather, it was the narrowing of the gap between himself and the nobility, competition with his peers, proof that he was keeping abreast of the times and possessed a natural aesthetic feeling for architectural effect, that made modernization of this kind a point of honour with him and others of his class. This generally involved positioning the ridge parallel to the street and also, because of the narrowness of the plots, combining several houses under one roof, at the same time destroying their gables. Architectural elements of the middle class town house which had long been retained (such as oriel windows, dormer gables and projecting upper storeys) were superseded because they

223

were incompatible with the articulation of the wall by means of a decorative composition that consisted of a rusticated ground floor, a central pavilion and classical orders of pilasters.

These innovations, which called for a number of compromises in the case of existing structures, could, of course, be realized to most striking effect in the middle class town palace. In the Baroque era this represented domestic architecture at its most opulent, whether in the form of a private house occupied by one family, or of an apartment house whose various floors would be let or sold to persons of wealth and distinction. There was no sharp dividing line between the nobleman's town palace and the middle class variant, since the latter's commercial function could be largely thrust into the background. An example—in many ways an illuminating one—is provided by the Romanushaus in Leipzig. It was commissioned by Franz Conrad Romanus, a Doctor of Law and favourite of Augustus the Strong who forced the town to accept his protégé as mayor. Found guilty of embezzling communal funds in 1705, Romanus had to spend the rest of his life in prison. The builder of the palace, which even in those days created a considerable stir, was Johann Gregor Fuchs. He had been appointed master mason to the city in opposition to the wishes of the craft guild, a fact which casts an interesting sociological light on the background of despotic behaviour in the commercial metropolis—a background without which the radical departure from tradition in domestic architecture would assuredly not have been possible. The only reminders of that tradition are the two-storeyed oriel at the angle, forming a pendant to the oriel on Lotter's Renaissance building opposite, and the gables over the central pavilions. For the rest, the unwonted grandiosity of concept is apparent from the Brühl frontage that ex-

153

Forms of window in the Baroque era, from the late seventeenth to the mid-eighteenth century.

The changing forms of the window may be regarded as representative of other architectural details in illustrating the characteristic tendency of the Baroque towards exuberance and vitality. There was a gradual departure from the tectonic lucidity and separation of all elements characteristic of the Renaissance, e. g. tall, rectangular openings, either arcuated or trabeated. Their sills and reveals surrounded by a carved, projecting frame and the whole crowned by a shallow triangular pediment, as in an aedicula. The plasticity of the frame becomes more strongly accentuated, every effort being made to avoid the strictly rectilinear in decorative work. Not only the broken outlines of the external reveals, but also and above all the decorative head-pieces, undergo organic enrichment; triangular and segmental pediments are broken by vases and figures. Subsequently the verges become sinuous, curve outwards, are frequently interrupted and, eventually, in Rococo, are abandoned in favour of playful, somewhat asymmetrical ornamental work. The design of the openings becomes equally fanciful, the rectangle being joined by a large variety of curvilinear forms in response to the dictates of ornamentation—fiddle-shaped apertures and horizontal and vertical ellipses (in the form of oeils-de-boeuf in dormer gables). The window itself, now without internal subdivisions, is absorbed as a member of the whole into the general composition of the façade.

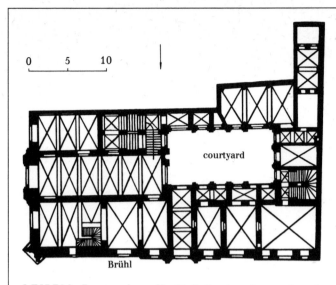

LEIPZIG. *Romanushaus, No. 23, Katharinenstrasse, plan of ground floor (Ill. 153).*

The often necessary compromise between the desire for display and the demands of commerce is clearly in evidence in the plan which does not reflect the powerful grandeur and lucid symmetry of the façade. Rather, its chief concern is with the irregular nature of the site and the diverse functions of the building. The intimate courtyard is not co-axial and the various staircases, landings and different types of room are combined within a restricted area in accordance with the principle of maximum functional efficiency.

tends to thirteen bays, from the articulation on the main block by means of the slightly projecting central and side pavilions, and from the use of a giant order of pilasters and the rich, sculptural decoration on doorways, windows and gables. The three-storeyed building, with a typical mezzanine floor for the household officials and a baroque-style mansard roof, was originally crowned by a belvedere. Also designed in accordance with contemporary architectural taste were the intimate inner courtyard, which had virtually ceased to perform any commercial function, the interior of the house with single flights of stone stairs, and the rooms on the first and second floors which were sumptuously decorated with stucco and paintings. The façade of regular design gives no intimation of the ground plan with its complex of staircases and rooms and its asymmetrically disposed courtyard. Soon after the building of the Romanushaus had been completed, many other patricians in Leipzig felt compelled to convert their houses into palaces.

The spread of the building craze cannot, of course, be attributed solely to a love of display. Many alterations were carried out as a result of more stringent municipal building regulations, especially those concerned with the treatment of façades (overhangs, for example, were not permitted), and with the prevention of fire (the carrying of fire-resistant party-walls up to the roof, the covering of the latter with slaters or tiles, the construction of fire-places, etc.). Other factors were improvements in building techniques and domestic amenities. Thus, the roof frame was places directly on the walls, which did away with the supporting arcade posts and made possible a more varied disposition of rooms. Additional space was gained by means of mansard roofs and by the building of wings in the courtyard. Further developments in heating and also in lighting, the introduction of large panes of transparent glass, the replacement of narrow spiral and other kinds of stair with wide staircases and landings, and the enormous advances made in the furnishings of the by now larger rooms—all this ushered in a new phase of civilized living which was compatible with the practical outlook of the middle classes and was not primarily intended to impress. No less a man than Goethe, writing in *Dichtung und Wahrheit (Poetry and Truth)* of his paternal home in Frankfurt-am-Main, gives what he 177 describes as an "artful" instance of such rebuilding. Because of recent regulations, their old house "full of nooks and crannies, much of it dark", could no longer be replaced by a new building equipped with several projecting upper storeys. "My father," he goes on, "not wishing to forfeit the space afforded by the overhang on the second floor, and concerned not so much with an architecturally pleasing exterior as with a good and comfortably appointed interior, had recourse, like a number of others before him, to the subterfuge of propping up the upper parts of the house, removing each storey in turn from below and, as it were, inserting new ones, so that, although little or nothing ultimately remained of the old, the whole of the new building could nevertheless be accounted a restoration."

It is to the robust self-confidence of the middle classes, which enabled them to preserve what was old in the new, or even to leave the old unchanged, that we are indebted for the many examples of the middle class town house which still bear witness to past epochs, in spite of the all-pervasive influence exerted by the Baroque upon the development of that type. Again, the new high standards set by the aristocracy called for substantial means, and hence the great majority of houses belonging to the lower middle and middle classes took little account of fashion. The building of unadorned, one-storeyed houses to a prescribed design for

the citizens of the grandducal seat of Karlsruhe is indicative of increasing social polarization within the bourgeoisie; thus the hands of the lower middle classes were tied, while the upper middle classes were left completely free to develop an individual style of their own. In areas where a plan was imposed, the perpetuation of the nondescript, functional, lower middle class type of house was ensured by the disenfranchisement and lack of rights of the occupants, whereas the patricians, in their town houses, or rather palaces, did their utmost to emulate the spirit of courtly Baroque. However, there were certain parts of Europe in which, for one reason or another, a countercurrent of Classicism prevailed throughout the whole period. It was no coincidence that this tendency, which was also concerned with the preservation of traditional house forms, should have manifested itself in countries such as England and the Netherlands where absolutism, in so far as it made any headway at all, did so only in a restricted sense. Two major factors were at work; first, the politically motivated rejection by bourgeois republics of courtly appurtenances and, secondly, the aversion felt throughout what was still a largely protestant Northern Europe for the Baroque of militant Catholicism. Here, then, such essential protestant attributes as reason, sobriety, and rejection of things sensual, went hand in hand with the striving after monumental grandeur in the Classicism of Palladio.

The era of Baroque and Rococo was also of exceptional importance where the standards of domestic life were concerned—a field in which citizens, craftsmen and manufacturers all played a vital part. The large number of rooms with specialized function, such as saloons, dining-rooms, card, music and reception rooms, libraries, cabinets for objets d'art and curiosities, wardrobes, dressing-rooms and peruke chambers, called for a great deal of new, richly decorated furniture, often available in individual suites. Besides a multiplicity of tables, upholstered chairs, sofas, chaiseslongue, etc., and cabinet furniture, there would be the vast bed which might sometimes also play an important ceremonial role. Other appurtenances such as cloth, leather or paper wall hangings, fine tableware and utensils fashioned by artist craftsmen, chandeliers, large tiled or cast-iron stoves, window curtains and pictures, were regarded as a badge of social acceptability. Much ornamental work found its way into the middle class town house, but with the Rococo and, ultimately, the Enlightenment, the inclination towards a cosy, comfortable intimacy became more strongly marked. Numerous portrayals of interiors at that time bear witness to a growing appreciation of beauty in the home, as do the dolls' houses. The nursery, too, was another innovation of these days. A seventeenth century doll's house from Nuremberg, which was a *142* centre of the toy-making industry, shows every detail of the interior of a patrician house. The process that had produced the self-confident individual now extended to the world of the child.

The Netherlands—an Exception

The contradictions inherent in the epoch as a whole take on a particularly significant form in the small, densely populated area of the Netherlands. Already a matrix, both economic and cultural, of the urban bourgeoisie, and a stronghold of middle class national consciousness, it had at the same time always been a bone of contention between neighbouring feudal powers seeking to extend their spheres of influence. In 1609, following an exemplary popular struggle, the northern provinces had wrested an armistice and de facto independence from their Spanish oppressors, though that liberation did not extend to the Flemish in the South. This combination of historical circumstances at the beginning of the Baroque era had made the Netherlands a focal point of fundamentally different artistic trends, associated respectively with the names of Rubens and Rembrandt.

However, the development of the middle class town house reflects the difference between Flemish Baroque of aristocratic complexion and the sober Classicism of Holland to an infinitely less degree than do the major works of architecture. In both regions, the legacy of the gable-fronted house with its lofty hall continued to live on in the vast majority of private dwellings. Our contemporary illustration, dating from about the middle of the seven- *143* teenth century, of the Place de Meir in Antwerp, shows that Baroque decoration played little or no part in the design of houses belonging to middle or lower middle class citizens. Yet these same small artisans, in their capacity as members of a craft guild, made use of a wealth of Baroque embellishment in their *150* communal buildings, as the Grand' Place in Brussels goes to show. Having been almost totally destroyed in a bombardment by the French Maréchal Villeroi on 13 and 14 August 1695, it was, within a few years, rebuilt as a fine, coherent whole by the guilds and fraternities. Our plate shows the guildhalls of the cabinet makers, coopers, chandlers and bakers, each of which sought to outshine the rest in the richness of its sculptural embellishment —enhanced here and there by gilding—in the style of Flemish and Italian Baroque. It might be said to exemplify many private patrician houses whose adherence to traditional forms was dictated by the restricted nature of the sites. The height of the storeys, like the opulence of the façades, was their badge of prosperity. However, the preference for palatial buildings, which is apparent in the Bakers' Hall on the right, could not often be indulged because of the lack of space. But wherever possible, the attempt was made, especially in Flemish districts, to emulate this, the most distinguished form of housing with its urbane, aristocratic connotations. No less a man than Peter Paul Rubens, the great master of Flemish Baroque painting, who had been appointed court painter to the Spanish Stadholder in 1609, endeavoured to realize these aspirations in his own house and studio in Antwerp. The years of study in Italy between 1600 and 1608 had broadened his outlook and enabled him to discover, notably in the Genoan palazzi, beauties which he made available to his fellow countrymen in the magnificent engravings he published in 1622. His home, however, still presents a peculiar contrast: On the one hand the simple façade in the vernacular tradition (asymmetrical with a dormer gable, unadorned brick walls with dressed stone bands) and, on the other, a courtyard and garden of château-like splendour. The sketch design he himself made for the garden pavilion, the façade of the studio and the portico, is, in its wealth of forms, replete with the spirit of the man. Figures, vases, balustrades, ornaments and powerful bosses are combined in a festal and vigorous harmony, lacking only, perhaps, the quality of spaciousness. This prince of painters was to achieve his heart's desire for an aristocratic style of life with the purchase in 1635 of Steen, *144–149* a country mansion. But also the numerous rooms in his town house, especially the living-rooms with their marble chimney-pieces and marble floors, leather wall hangings, pictorial carpets, paintings, objets d'art, chandeliers and heavy, richly carved furniture, combine solidity and comfort and are redolent of all the splendour of the times. By contrast, the roomy and well-lit, hall-like studio in which, with

many assistants he embarked, as in a factory, on his vast projects, is more restrained if still on a grand scale. In 1618 and 1619 one of those assistants was Jacob Jordaens, another great master of Flemish painting, who depicted popular mores and was frequently attacked for his Calvinist convictions. On achieving greater *152* recognition, he decided to remodel his house in Antwerp in accordance with the contemporary taste for palatial grandeur. The building stands with its ridge parallel to the street, while the doorway has been incorporated into a central pavilion crowned by a pediment. The powerful bands of rusticated masonry and lofty ground floor windows, however, are traditional and, though in Baroque guise, they were still retained in the Flemish middle class town house.

At the time when, like many other patrician citizens of Antwerp, Jakob Jordaens abandoned the vernacular gable-fronted type of house in favour of the international palatial type, the northern provinces, which were an established bourgeois republic, had already outstripped the South in economic terms. Founded on the pragmatic spirit of Calvinism, the republic's achievements in the cultural field reached their zenith in a new middle class art. In the economic field the republic rose to the status of a mercantile and colonial world power. Here we find little or no grandiose aristocratic architecture, since the standards both for large public buildings and for private houses in the Herengracht, Keizersgracht, or Prinsengracht were set by the burghers themselves. Economic necessity might even call for operations on an urban scale, as, for example, in Amsterdam where the vast entrepôt trade subsequent to 1610 led to the extension of the waterways to form a radial canal system, intersected by other, concentric, canals. On the 'islands' beside the *grachten* the newly rich citizens built their gable-fronted

AMSTERDAM. *Town plan, copper engraving, circa 1730.*

The city experienced a first flowering as a member of the Hanseatic League. Following the secession of the Netherlands from Spain in 1566, it became one of Europe's leading mercantile centres and a place of refuge for Flemish Protestants. By 1622 the city already numbered 100,000 inhabitants. It expanded to the size shown on the plan by successive stages—1585, 1593, 1622 and 1685. Round an insular nucleus there grew up a regular system of streets and *grachten*, reflecting a desire for orderliness at once pragmatic and typical of the Baroque era. This was all the more noteworthy for having been implemented by the burghers themselves, without any kind of intervention from above.

Types of façade in Flemish and Dutch gable-fronted houses in the Baroque era.

A = the so-called Bruges type; B–E = houses in Amsterdam (B = crow-step gable, C = in the manner of Hendrik de Keyser, D = "neck-shape", E = in the style of Philip Vinckeboons). Example F from the eighteenth century has a "clock-shape" gable.

A   B   C   D

E   F

houses and warehouses after the manner of their forefathers in compact rows on deep, narrow plots. It is evident from the elevations of the Dutch and Flemish gable-fronted houses that the type did not differ fundamentally between the two regions. Generally speaking, however, the puritanical outlook of the Dutch citizen found expression in his rejection of exuberantly florid forms. Until about the middle of the seventeenth century, when Amsterdam reached its full flowering, gables were still many-storeyed and vertically articulated, while limestone continued to be used as before in the treatment of doorways, reveals, string courses and corners. The old lay-out was also retained with a *voorhuis* (front block) and *achterhuis* (rear block). The former contained a large hall, a small reception room *(zijgkamer)* and a counting-house, the latter consisted of a small living-room and bedroom (*achterkamer*) with a stump or four poster bed, a kitchen, and a vestibule leading into a little back garden.

The buildings, between two and four storeys high, usually also had a massive cellar and staircases of sensible design leading to the upper floors which, owing to the urgent need for extra living accommodation, frequently occupied part of the roof space, though this also continued to be used for storage. At the same time, however, the tremendous wealth of the patrician class and concomitant process of social differentiation, along with the growing need for the display of that wealth, lent the houses of the upper class an elegance that derived from French and Italian forms. As a result of the stimulus provided by magnificent communal buildings such as Jacob van Campen's town hall in Amsterdam which was one of the finest achievements of Palladian Classicism, widespread use was made—in the much coveted sites in the city centre, along the main canals and in leafy squares—of the clear, flowing formal elements of the Baroque, albeit with classical modifications, notably in the work of the Vinckeboons brothers. A vivid impression may be gained of this from the patrician houses along the Herengracht. Covered for the most part by expensive dressed stone and coolly restrained in decoration, these, no less than their extravagant Baroque counterparts, proclaim the spirit of elegant, if ostentatious, self-display. The lofty basement served as a store-room, as did the lofts underneath the roof, while the gable was now accorded rather less importance. Moreover, owing to the size of the town's population and the limited amount of building space, the apartment house came to be a profitable capital investment.

The interiors depicted in many of the works of such Dutch and Flemish specialist painters as Pieter de Hooch, Pieter Janssens, Jan Vermeer van Delft and Emanuel de Witte, provide us with an accurate record of the style in which that cultivated bourgeoisie lived. Unlike the primitive dwellings occupied by the peasantry or the sumptuous, Baroque apartments of the day, they display solidity and elegance. Apart from the dining table and the four poster bed, there is little in the way of heavy furniture; on the other hand chests, upholstered chairs, pictures, household equipment and musical instruments abound.

With the decline of the power of the Netherlands towards the end of the seventeenth century, however, the independent, consciously traditional idiom that had hitherto prevailed began to disappear. Henceforward the architecture of France was to exert its influence, as 154 shown in No. 475, Herengracht, a Dutch variant of the Louis Quatorze style, which was built in the eighteenth century and bears the unmistakable stamp of Daniel Marot and Frédéric Blanchard. The presentation of the long side of the building to the street now came into favour. In place of the gable, balustrades or parapets were used to convey the desired pallatial impression, the central axis was accentuated, pilasters gave way to bosses as a means of articulation, while windows were disposed in unified and symmetrical ranges. The French ideas that found their way into the Netherlands now were not, however, altogether alien, as both countries had already displayed a predilection for classical clarity.

Western Europe and the French Example

The rise of France to the status of great European power during the seventeenth century when she became the centre of a courtly, aristocratic society and culture, ensured the survival of a tendency that had already long been in evidence, namely the approximation of the patrician house to that of the nobleman. Up till the crisis which overtook the feudal system, the mercantilism established under the aegis of Colbert within the absolutist régime had cemented the alliance between the Crown and the bourgeoisie. The Court and Paris, the capital attracted large numbers of noblemen, officials, artists and scholars, with the result that there arose a considerable demand for grandiose, domestic architecture. The vast majority of craftsmen and plebeians continued to live in cramped, timberframed houses, most of which had few rooms, but in the centre and along the principal streets there grew up palatial hôtels that contained apartments for rent to discriminating tenants. The hôtels followed the great example set by the King, notably at Versailles, in which he gave expression to an august form of Classicism. In so far as official influence did not assert itself in the design, say, of uniform streets or squares, academic norms were laid down by such architectural theorists as François Blondel, or else by institutions like the Académie d'Architecture, founded in 1671. Each

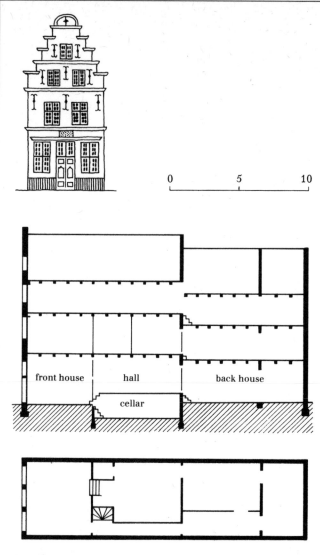

0   5   10

front house   hall   back house

cellar

FRIEDRICHSTADT *an der Eider. No. 16, Am Markt, plan, elevation and section of a hall-house of 1625.*

A typical feature is its division into a front block and a rear block. In this way full and rational use is made of the narrow plot. Because of the height of the water-table, the basement is at a higher level than usual, so that the rear chamber in the back part of the house can only be reached from the front part by way of the raised *Upkamer*. In a cramped building such as this the Baroque principles governing the axial disposition of rooms and the positioning of the staircases could not apply.

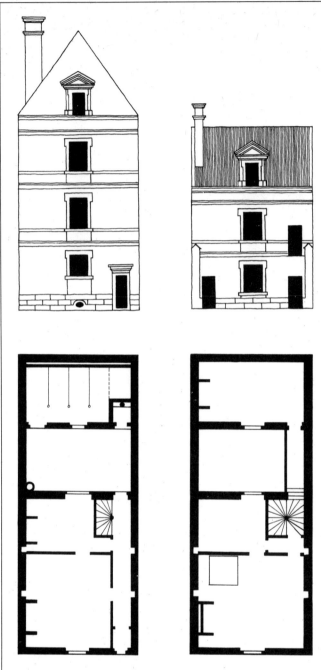

Design for a dwelling-house, from "Manière de bien bastir pour toutes sortes de personnes", by Pierre le Muet, Paris, 1647, Plate 17.

Street front, courtyard front, plan of the ground storey with living-room, kitchen, courtyard and stables, plan of the first floor with two rooms, garde-robe and corridor. In effect, the premises consist of two houses connected by high walls. The principle of order inherent in absolutist town planning also encroached upon the design of houses for simple citizens, the purpose being to achieve urban homogeneity by means of standardization. Needless to say, decorative elements are here reduced to a minimum, i.e. window frames and continuous string courses.

individual house was expected to subordinate itself to the overall effect of the town plan, and thus even palaces arose in the form of terraces, as in the Place de Victoire in Paris built between 1684 and 1687, or the Place Vendôme, completed by Jules H. Mansart between 1685 and 1701. After 1731 whole districts of Bordeaux were redesigned by Jacques Gabriel, while between 1752 and 1755 the town of Nancy underwent wholesale reconstruction.

In the Rue du Faubourg Saint-Denis the palatial upper middle class apartment complexes were so organized as to have, on each of the four floors, an apartment consisting of an ante-room, living-room, saloon, the all important *garde-robe* and sometimes, even in those days, a bathroom. But since high class hôtels of this kind sought to take account of the differing requirements of the tenants, the specifications governing the rooms varied greatly. Access from one room to another on any one floor was gained, not by a corridor, but by doors disposed along an axis to form an *enfilade* or suite of rooms, as in a château. The façades of these hôtels retained the classical style favoured by the French monarchs, in which a discreet balance between all the parts was held to be of greater importance than an abundance of individual forms. The corps-de-logis was designed as a block, while the pattern of the façade was flat and clearly rhythmical. In addition to the mansard roof, a common feature in hôtel architecture was the flat attic roof similar to that of the Palace of Versailles. Thus the verticality once so prevalent in the French middle class town house has finally been eliminated. However, since ground plans varied in accordance with the needs of the client, any uniformity in the design of façades was also precluded. In the façade of the Hôtel de Lauzun built for an army contractor in Paris, as in that of Jean-Baptiste Lully's

156 hôtel, the organization of the doorway infringes

233

the principle of symmetry. And whereas in the first, the façade is articulated solely by means of flat, pilaster strips and string courses, Lully, director of the King's Music, required that his house be given a façade in which giant pilasters rested on a rusticated, plinth-like basement storey. At a time of intellectual and convival social intercourse, almost greater importance was attached to the arrangement of the interior where the salon was the hub. The great splendour of the court, the advances made in the furniture industry in the shape of numerous new items such as chests-of-drawers, sideboards, etc., the refinement of interior decoration, notably in the sphere of wall coverings and of the applied arts, now produced in manufactories—all these served, not only as an example to the bourgeoisie, but also as an inducement to embrace a more elegant style of life. The room known as the "petit salon" *170* in the afore-mentioned Hôtel de Lauzun displays an extreme delicacy of treatment by comparison with the simple façade. On the other hand the private quarters, as distinct from the above-named reception rooms, were cosy and intimate, being expressive of an attitude, much acclaimed since the time of the Enlightenment, of rationality, common sense, and respect for the individual. Problems connected with standards of domestic life were frequently discussed in good society. The earlier combination under one roof of dwelling and place of business no longer pertained. In a series of designs for various types of artisan's house, done in 1647 by the architect Pierre le Muet, no provision is made, for instance, for a workshop—as it is for a *garde-robe*—evidently because, even at this time, the former had been rendered redundant by the existence of manufactories in which the work was carried out. The artisan had become a tenant for whose family two rooms were allotted in these plain little houses.

The unique blend of rationality and grandiosity in French upper class domestic architecture, together with the elegance of the interior appointments, was disseminated by numerous pattern books in neighbouring countries where, like French fashions, it soon became a model.

In Italy, too, the birthplace of Baroque, we may discern the influence exerted by the palatial dwellings of the now prosperous bourgeoisie. In a fragmented, economically stagnant country ruled by foreign powers, the palazzo, legacy of a great past, could not be further developed by the citizen on his own account. That task was now assumed by the nobility, and executed in splendid town palaces which, together with the churches of the Counter-Reformation, are the most impressive manifestation of the spirit of the times. Simultaneously, attempts were made to transform the principal streets and squares into imposing spaces within the framework of town planning. In no other country at that time were opulence and poverty more plainly and closely juxtaposed in the urban landscape than in Italy. Writing in 1739, the French magistrate and scholar, Charles de Brosse, sums up his impression of the famous Piazza del Popolo in Rome as follows: ". . . a magnificent edifice surrounded by a hundred mean, poverty-stricken *quartiers* . . . a few large streets of vast width serving only to lead, between the rows of entrance halls, to small, noisome alleys or to narrow, squalid crossways. . ."

During the seventeenth century the presence in the towns of large numbers of noblemen brought about a substantial increase in the price of land. The result was that the wealthy mercantile class who, though incapable of competing with the aristocratic oligarchy, wanted to bask in its reflected glory and made do by building or buying freehold apartments in palatial houses with several floors. True,

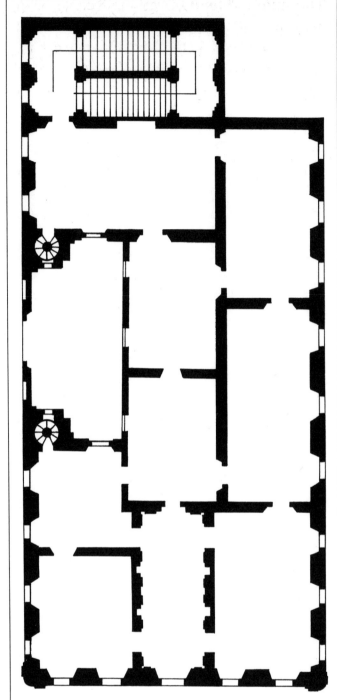

ROME. *Palazzo d'Aste (Ill. 155)*.

Plan of the ground storey.

our example, the Palazzo d'Aste in Rome reveals, in the ornamentation of the façade, an endeavour to employ the decorative vocabulary of the day, but in view of the narrowness of the plot, it was impossible either to extend it laterally by adding boldly conceived wings or to adhere to the axial principle in the preparation of the plan. Accordingly, the citizen had to swallow his pride and make do with a block-like structure and an illusion of symmetry of the façade whose grandiosity could not be repeated in the interior. In an apartment house of this description, the need for a number of separate rooms, for example saloon, dining-room, study, living-rooms and bedrooms disposed along a corridor, meant that the arrangement of the accommodation had to be varied in a manner appropriate to each individual site. In many cases a mezzanine floor was inserted and an attic with mansard roof added to provide accommodation for the servants. Each floor could be reached independently since each had its own private staircase and, even in those days, separate service stairs. Since there was no possibility of conforming to the standards set by the vast palaces of the nobility, it is understandable that the practical solutions found by the French should now have exerted an influence that also extended to the furniture and fittings. So far as the great majority of middle class town houses were concerned, that influence led, during the eighteenth century, to a sober form of eclecticism which, with the cutting down of expenditure, gave way to carefully concealed shabbiness. The only exception here was a resurgent Venice with her magnificent palaces.

In Spain, too, the appearance of middle class town houses was relatively restrained as opposed to the magnificent seats of the nobility with their exuberant proliferation of Churrigueresque architectural ornament. By and large, it was only seaports such as Cádiz and

Seville, from which trade was conducted with the colonies, that could boast private houses of more opulent design with brick corner towers and animated geometrical paintings on the façades. Most middle class dwellings still adhered to the traditional block-like form, built in brick, on which the decoration was confined to doorways and to the iron lattice-work adorning windows and balconies. In this advanced Catholic culture, a cultivar of gloomy asceticism on the one hand and boundless ecstasy on the other, the bourgeoisie struck a simpler, more down-to-earth note, not only in their houses, but also in the work of their world-famous painters and writers, men such as Miguel de Cervantes—whose house in the Calle del Rastro, Valladolid, is now a museum— Lope de Vega, Francisco Zurbarán, Velásquez *171* and Murillo.

In England the middle class town house developed in such a way as to cross the demarcation line separating it from the architecture of the nobility. In this, the decisive factor was the position of strength, both politico-economic and social, occupied by the mercantile middle classes, a position they owed not only to their victory, culminating in the Bill of Rights in 1689, over the despotism of the Stuarts, but also to the closeness of their ties with the landed aristocracy. True, it was Inigo Jones, the King's architect—appointed Surveyor to the Crown in 1615—who, with his great houses and churches, ushered in the era of Palladian Classicism which banished the stylistic chaos of the Tudor period and was to determine future developments for the next two centuries. Yet in the seventeenth century, Dutch and Flemish influence was still strongly in evidence in England. When John Smithson came to London from the provinces in 1618, he admired, and recorded in a drawing, one such building, Lady Cooke's house, which was the first to be given a tall,

JOHN SMITHSON, drawing of Lady Cooke's house, Holborn, London, done in 1619.

Completed shortly before the drawing was made, this building with its "Holborn" gable borrowed from the middle class town houses of the Netherlands, marks the transition from the Tudor to the classical phase. The latter is presaged here more especially in the austere window surrounds and string courses, while at the same time the typical national feature, the bay window carried up through several storeys, is retained. However, with the continuing trend towards a severely classical façade, the bay window began to lose its popularity.

shaped gable of Dutch provenance. This type of gable, known as the "Holborn" gable, after the district of that name in central London, combined with the strictly classical window frames and the traditional motif of projecting bay windows to form a bastard style favoured in the seventeenth century by the merchants of London and the Puritans of the southern counties. At the same time the exhaustion of the country's forests meant that brick architecture became increasingly common, as indeed it had already begun to be in the eastern counties of Norfolk, Suffolk and Essex as far back as the Middle Ages. Again the Dutch model was followed, façades being often enriched with decorative elements in soft limestone and, in some cases, stucco. Another trend in English domestic architecture betrayed Italo-Flemish influences, deriving from the Genoese palazzi by way of Rubens, in palatial buildings with low pitched hipped roofs, projecting eaves and, in some cases, balustrades and, perhaps, a central dome supporting a lantern for the illumination of the hall and stairs.

However, the greatest potential for the future lay in the type known as the terrace house whose creation was the work of Inigo Jones and his school. Despite its division into two residences in 1751/52, Lindsey House built in London in 1640 and the oldest surviving example of the type, clearly illustrates the basic principles. Dutch, Flemish and indigenous characteristics have all been dispensed with in favour of a clear, unified design based on Palladian Classicism. The structure, consisting of horizontal blocks, had a rusticated, plinth-like ground storey with, above it, an harmoniously proportioned system of articulation which was restrained yet majestic and consisted of regularly disposed windows with plain frames and a giant order of Ionic pilasters surmounted by an architrave and balus-

trade. Some buildings of this type might also be given a shallow, central pavilion crowned by a pediment. These terrace houses, miniature urban editions of the spacious royal residences in the new style, ranging along streets, parks and embankments, present a striking example of coherent town planning. The Covent Garden piazza (1630/31) was the first of Jones' designs for an ensemble of this kind, which betrays, albeit in modified form, an absolutist predilection for urban order and unity. The term applied to these developments, whether Square, Circus or Crescent, depended on the configuration of the site. In London, for example, they were to be found 184 in Great Queen Street and Lincoln's Inn Fields, while in Bath they may still be seen in Queen's 210 Square, Queen's Circus and the Royal Crescent, a nomenclature which in itself is an indication of the heights to which they aspired. However, the ambitious plan for the rebuilding of the centre of London after it had been ravaged by fire in 1666 never came to fruition.

As a type, the terrace house finally came into its own largely as a result of the definitive return to Palladian Classicism under George I. This style was employed not only by the aristocracy, but also by the well-to-do middle classes who wielded great political power in the House of Commons. The resources drawn from a powerful empire and from the epoch-making industrial revolution, which was already well under way in the eighteenth century, enabled middle class ideas and ways of life to set their stamp on future developments. The contours of urban working class districts were as yet undefined, and sober industrial architecture was still in its infancy. There emerged, alongside the classical style which was then predominant in town house and country mansion, the romantic ideas of the Gothic Revival which, however, did not at first make any real impact upon the middle class town house. Nevertheless, they gave evidence of a strongly traditional train of thought which was to assert itself at the time of the Classical Revival that was initiated by the Adam brothers, and found confirmation chiefly in the sphere of bourgeois domestic architecture. Behind the simple, classical façades, now broken up by blank containing arches, delicately wrought string courses and decorative motifs such as garlands and urns, the rooms were still disposed in the old, irregular manner. Our example, Derby House, will serve to illustrate the kind of ground plan that was to remain in force almost up to the end of the nineteenth century. The town house, which was usually narrow, had an entrance to one side which led into a typical entrance hall with an adjoining staircase, front room, and living-room or morning-room. Behind these lay other rooms, each having its own specialist function, e.g. a large dining-room, a library, cloakroom and lavatory and, perhaps, a music room. To the rear of the building was a mews where horses and carriages were kept. The kitchen and domestic offices were usually situated in the basement, with a coal cellar beneath the public pavement. Living and reception rooms were on the first floor, bedrooms on the second, while the attic floor was occupied by the servants. Towards the middle of the century, Parisian elegance began to make itself felt in the sphere of interior decoration, while the art of cabinet-making was governed by new standards of refinement, solidity and simplicity.

In the Scandinavian countries an all-important role was played by the influence of France and of the Netherlands which was often transmitted by master builders from those regions, although middle class building shows less evidence of this than do the palaces of the politically dominant nobility. Many new buildings were put up and old ones altered in

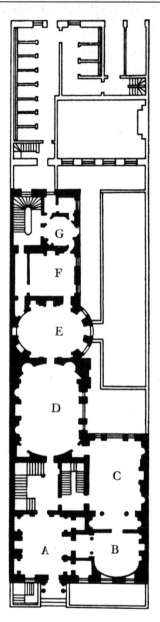

LONDON. *Plan of Derby House, No. 26, Grosvenor Square, built by Robert Adam for the Earl of Derby in 1773/74, destroyed in 1862.*

Since most of the sites were long and narrow, the tackling of a project involving a wide variety of rooms and corresponding to the domestic pretensions of the aristocracy—pretensions also shared and nurtured by the upper middle classes—inevitably called for an asymmetrical and rational plan. That plan had to take account of hallowed traditions (A = great hall), social demands (B = ante-room, C = drawing room, parlour, D = dining-room), personal requirements (E = library or music room, F = dressing room, G = water-closet) and household needs (kitchen, coach house and stables in adjoining or separate blocks). Thus. to all intents and purposes, there had ceased to be any real difference between the aristorcratic and the upper middle class style of life.

order to conform to the contemporary Classicism whose forms were for the most part of a sober, restrained character. Whereas Robert Rind's house in Stockholm, with its wide front- *157* age, strongly symmetrical fenestration, rusticated ground storey and pilaster strips at the angles, seeks to emulate a palace, the house, erected in about 1650 on the corner of No. 2, Själagårdsgatan, has bands of dressed stone *158* which recall the Dutch mode of decoration.

In Norway, long a bone of contention between Sweden and Denmark and eventually ruled by the latter from 1525 to 1814, the development of the middle class town house is of considerable interest because of the greater degree to which vernacular elements were retained. Indeed, the peasant's log house played an important role here in that it was the point of departure for the middle class citizen's timber house in towns that were for the most part small. The wooden, gable-fronted houses were usually so disposed as to form narrow, parallel alleys—in effect gutterways—with gates at either end so that they could be shut up. In the eighteenth century it became the practice to cover outside walls with boards and to make sparing use in these panelled houses of classical or Baroque stylistic forms. Few brick or stone houses were built, and then only in towns of some importance, such as Christiana (renamed Oslo in 1924), Bergen, Stavanger or Trondheim. From the sober, two-storeyed merchant's house dating from 1640, No. 5, Kongensgate in Oslo, it is apparent that, outside the mainstream of culture, the fashionable Baroque style found little acceptance. Nevertheless, in the eighteenth century, richer forms of architectural decoration and interior appointments borrowed from France and England began to be used in the houses of the wealthier merchants.

The Palace and the Terrace House in Germany

On 24 October, 1648, the bells rang out all over Germany, proclaiming the end of one of the most terrible wars Europe had ever known. It was brought to a conclusion as a result of a compromise between the utterly exhausted antagonists who, after thirty years, found themselves more or less back at the point at which they had started. The people, both peasants and citizens, had borne the main brunt and many towns and villages had been destroyed; the kings and princes, however, shared out the spoils between them. The once proud citizen, now reduced to political impotence, found himself subject to absolutism of a particularly oppressive kind, his fate being largely determined by the egoism of more than three hundred arbitrary rulers, whether petty princes or local potentates. The regional princes directed the fortunes of their middle class subjects in accordance with their own interests which were in any case of a fairly modest kind since they went hand in hand with a manufacturing system isolated from international trade. It was not long, however, before the self-confidence of the bourgeoisie found a voice in the intellectual and cultural fields. This curious contrast between submissive conformity and the new urge for self-expression is also reflected in the development of the German middle class town house during the Baroque era. It was only after the conclusion of the Thirty Years' War, which had brought all building to a halt, that Baroque and the counter-current of Classicism began to emerge, notably in church and château architecture. However insignificant the prince, he was intent on bringing to himself some of the splendour of foreign courts. Hitherto the lack of central power had favoured the development of different kinds of regional architecture and it was only natural, given the consolidation of the system of small states, that that characteristic should be perpetuated. Originally imported by foreign master masons, the Italian influence spread throughout southern Germany and Austria as did the Dutch influence in the northern and central regions of Germany and the French in the Rhineland. In the two latter areas of penetration, the classical trend predominated, while already extant racial, denominational and dynastic factors and correlations gave rise to further distinctions. As yet middle class architecture could boast few if any new communal or corporative buildings. In the construction of the patrician houses, moreover, the example was set by the local ruler if a design had not already been prescribed by the latter's planning and building regulations, as was the case in Karlsruhe, Ludwigslust, Rastatt, Oranienbaum, Arolsen, Potsdam, or Dresden.

At first there was evidence of a tendency to adhere to traditional forms. When the brewer, Heinrich Deutz, erected his house Zum goldenen Bären (Balchem Haus) in Cologne in *168, 169* 1676, he reverted to the old convention of the gable-fronted type. The roof with its storage lofts is still quite steeply pitched, while above the doorway is a small oriel window, this being a Gothic reminiscence with Renaissance features. Only the curvilinear outline of the gable is indicative of the new era. Even the spiral stair, dating from 1663 and recently removed from the Rinkenhof for incorporation in this building, is traditional. As time went on, the height of gables decreased, for the storage of goods in private houses had ceased to be the rule even in the larger mercantile cities. In Luckau in Lower Lusatia, a small town in spite of its position at the junction of major trade routes, there is a patrician house which *167* illustrates this process. During the eighteenth

century it became a general practice, in districts where houses were by tradition gable-fronted, to align the ridge with the street. Goethe's lively account of the alterations to his paternal home in Frankfurt-am-Main, when two gable-fronted houses were converted into one eaves-fronted house and given a pair of dormer gables, reveals that these changes were not dictated simply by the fashion of the day, but rather by the desire for greater comfort as well as for better lighting and ventilation. These improvements extended even to the kitchen, whose appointments, however, were still robust, practical and simple. Nevertheless, the craze for this kind of modernization and for the building of new town palaces tended to destroy the typological homogeneity of many towns.

On the other hand, there were certain towns which, as the residences of absolutist rulers, far exceeded the rest in importance and displayed a new homogeneity that resulted from Baroque town planning and drastic reconstruction. One such town was Dresden, the "Florence on the Elbe", which was largely rebuilt after the turn of the seventeenth century to become the splendid capital city of the electors or kings of Saxony. The presence of large numbers of court officials, some of aristocratic, some of middle class origin, meant that many imposing houses had to be built in the vicinity of the château. These took the form of town palaces with rentable apartments on each floor. Eminent architects, such as Matthäus Daniel Pöppelmann, Zacharias Longelune, Johann Christoph Knöffel and George Bähr, were called in to build them. They provided a model for citizens who had amassed the required amount of wealth as purveyors of luxury goods to the Court. By 1760 Dresden had become one of the most beautiful of Baroque cities. Since then the Old Town has been almost totally destroyed.

240

Preceding page

141 GDAŃSK *(Danzig). No. 41, Dlugi Targ (Long Market Place), Golden House, 1609–1617. The decorative sculpture on the gable front was executed by the Rostock stone mason Hans Voigt in 1616 and 1617. Façade reconstructed subsequent to 1945.*

After the Second World War the city's ancient nucleus was reconstructed in exemplary fahion by the Polish authorities responsible for the maintenance of historic monuments. In the sixteenth century Danzig had evolved a form of its own, a translucent towerlike structure which, however, was firmly rooted in the Hanseatic tradition of the gable-fronted hall-house. Because the frontages were of necessity narrow, sculptural decoration had to be confined to the main doorway, the pilasters and the narrow window aprons (in this case taking the form of reliefs depicting scenes from classical mythology and biblical themes). In most such houses, the gables or parapets were crowned by statues. Another feature typical of this town was the terrace (here executed in the Baroque style). Projecting into the street, it assumed a variety of forms and was reached by a small flight of seven or eight steps, inviting either for business or leisure. These raised platforms were surrounded by an iron railing or a stone parapet, the panels of which contained, on the street side, reliefs depicting mythological or allegorical scenes.

142 DOLL'S HOUSE *of 1639, in the Germanisches Nationalmuseum, Nuremberg.*

In view of the alterations made to interior appointments by each succeeding generation, this skilful reproduction of an early Baroque patrician house in Nuremberg is not without documentary value. Not only are the grander rooms plainly exposed to view, but also the secondary, more work-a-day ones, with all their equipment, of which we should otherwise have no record. The cellar which, in the doll's house is next to the front door, should in fact be thought of as situated at a lower level. It comprises the wine cellar, the larder and, somewhat inappropriately, the stable—as a sop, no doubt, to childish whimsy. Above them is a low ground or mezzanine floor containing two store-rooms as well as austere bedchambers for the servants and the children. On the next floor is a hall-like central space with a stair and cupboards, the contents of which are the housewife's pride. This room should again be thought of as forming part of an imposing ground storey, situated immediately behind the front door. On the left, there is a heated living-room, also used as a study and bedchamber and, on the right, a kitchen somewhat overlavishly equipped with pewter ware. It contains a range which also heats the panelled saloon-cum-dining-room above. Next to this is an ante-room with wall paintings, pictures and cupboards and, adjoining, another heated bedchamber with a four-poster bed.

143 *ERASME DE BIE, Place de Meir, Antwerp, circa 1650, Musée Royale des Beaux-Arts, Antwerp.*

In the Flemish metropolis the aspect of the middle and lower class houses of the mid-seventeenth century still bears the imprint of the Gothic tradition. Here we see gable-fronted hall-houses with corbie-stepped gables and unadorned façades, upon which the styles of the Renaissance and Baroque eras have left virtually no trace—hence their air of timelessness.

143

144 ANTWERP. *Rubens' House, Nos. 9–11, Rubensstraat, view from the garden side. Built between 1610 and 1617 as an ensemble consisting of dwelling-house, studio wing, courtyard, portico and garden with pavilion. Restored to its original condition between 1937 and 1947 from copper engravings by the artist Jacobus Harrewijn.*

The rear elevation of the studio wing, in which Rubens ran his workshop virtually on factory lines, is opulently decorated in the Genoese mannerist style. The appearance of the well-lit studio is also most imposing. It is a room that has seen the comings and goings of emissaries from many European potentates, all intent upon obtaining works done by the hand of the master.

145 ANTWERP. *Rubens' House, street view.*

As court painter to the Spanish Stadholder in Brussels, Peter Paul Rubens, the great master of Flemish Baroque, created for himself a palatial complex in which sumptuous display goes hand in hand with utilitarian functions behind a traditional house façade which still retains its simplicity. This synthesis would seem to reflect the components of his art—vernacular robustness on the one hand and cosmopolitan elegance on the other.

146 ANTWERP. *Rubens' House, main entrance.*

The artist felt it unnecessary to proclaim his status by giving his house a splendid façade. Accessible only to his numerous guests, the portico he himself designed in the semblance of a triumphal arch, like the pavilion in the small Baroque garden, is evidence of an intention to lead an aristocratic life, for which the great exemplar was the Italian palazzo. No less luxuriant and animated than his pictures, the forms of this decorative architecture are the expression, into which his own artistic work is organically integrated, of a spirit of festive elation.

145

147

There is an air of aristocratic grandeur, which is nevertheless not divorced from the traditional solidity and intimacy of the Flemish middle class way of life, about the appointments of the inter-connecting living-rooms and guest rooms. Marble tiled floors, Gobelin tapestries and tooled leather hangings, carved ceilings, door cases and heavy furniture, gleaming, many-branched candelabra and gilded silver ware, carpets, large chimney-pieces and the numerous pictures adorning the walls (in many cases protected by a curtain), endow these imposing rooms—as, for example, the dining-room (149)—with an air of luxurious splendour. Even the kitchen (148) is fitted out with unusual munificence and, like the studio, fits logically into the picture as a whole.

148

150 BRUSSELS. *Grand' Place, west side with the Guild Houses (from right to left) of the Bakers (No. 2) with sculptures by Jan Cosyns, the Printers (No. 3), the Chandlers (No. 4) and the Archers (No. 5).*

The square, almost entirely destroyed by the French in 1695, was rebuilt within four years by the guilds and patricians with gable-fronted houses incorporating the decorative forms of the Italo-Flemish Baroque. Since the façades are largely taken up by the typically large windows, the love of animated sculptural embellishment is brought to bear primarily on the gables. Whereas the bakers' guild house on the right, with its crowning balustrade and cupola, testifies to the strong Italian influence in the part of Belgium that remained Spanish and Catholic, the other gable-fronted houses provide living proof of the continued survival of the old type of house, albeit in a new guise.

151 AMSTERDAM. *Béguinage.*

A typically Dutch street composition which, even in the Baroque period, has retained the traditional gable-fronted house with unadorned brick walls and stone dressings round windows and doorways.

152 ANTWERP. *Jacob Jordaens' House in the Hoogstraat, completed in 1641.*

Jordaens, at one time an assistant to Rubens, is well-known for his realistic genre paintings. The house, whose palatial aspirations are revealed by the treatment of the façade and the presentation of the long side to the street, demonstrates the change in contemporary taste which, in the course of the seventeenth century, brought about the successful adoption in the Flemish region of the international type of house alongside the traditional gable-fronted form.

153 LEIPZIG. *Romanushaus, No. 23, Katharinenstrasse. The city's first palatial middle class town house, built by Johann Gregor Fuchs between 1701 and 1704 for the burgomaster, F. C. Romanus. Restored between 1966 and 1968.*

As compared with the narrow, gable-fronted house, whose façade is punctuated on doorways, windows, oriels and gable by Renaissance decoration in an additive composition, this town palace extends laterally (thirteen bays on the Brühl frontage), the whole structure being articulated by means of a rhythmically centred façade. Above a plinth-like, banded ground storey with shallow central and side pavilions, there rises a unified composition of giant pilasters and pilaster strips, with a continuous entablature and symmetrically disposed bays. Reminiscences of the past, such as oriels and gables, are integrated into the whole. In this way an aristocratic type of architecture, which was soon to become a *sine qua non* for the patrician upper class, invaded the sphere of the organically evolved middle class town house to a greater extent than ever before.

154 AMSTERDAM. *No. 475, Herengracht, late seventeenth century.*

A wealthy merchant's house of which the façade is reminiscent of the French style. After 1670 this type increasingly supplanted the traditional gabled façade. What was aimed at was a palatial effect after the manner of the hôtels, with a crowning, richly decorated parapet and a flat façade with an accentuated central axis and a unified system comprising all window and door frames and decorative elements.

155 ROME. *Palazzo d'Aste. Third quarter of the seventeenth century, from a design by Giovanni Antonio de' Rossi.*

The fact that the patrician bourgeoisie of Italy no longer played a leading role did not, one may suppose, diminish their appetite for town palaces of imposing proportions. However, they usually had to make do with one floor in a block-like, multi-storeyed house in the same neighbourhood as the sumptuous palazzi of the nobility. Because of the need for numerous rooms, the plans do not match the symmetricality of the elevations; rather, they are wholly irregular in design, on the pattern of the rationally conceived French hôtels. The various larger rooms are grouped about a central corridor. A straight stair attached to the structure and two internal spiral stairs afford separate access to the apartments on each storey, including the mezzanine floor occupied by the servants.

154

155

154 AMSTERDAM. *No. 475, Herengracht, late seventeenth century.*

155 ROME. *Palazzo d'Aste. Third quarter of the seventeenth century, from a design by Giovanni Antonio de' Rossi.*

156 PARIS. *Hôtel de Lauzun, No. 17, Quai d'Anjou, built between 1656 and 1658, probably by Louis le Vau, for the army contractor, Charles Gruyn des Bordes.*

From 1682 to 1685 this hôtel was in the ownership of the Duc de Lauzun. Since 1928 it has been used by the municipality of Paris for civic receptions. The plain, flat façade with its asymmetrically placed doorway and balcony, is little concerned with outward show, although its long frontage and typically tall windows give it an air of grandeur. The phase of the academic doctrine of *la belle architecture* in the Louis Quattorze style has not yet dawned.

157 STOCKHOLM. *No. 24, Skeppsbron, Robert Rind's House, first built in 1630 for the merchant Robert Rind, and reconstructed between 1670 and 1680 for the vintner Henrik van Santen, when it acquired the appearance it has today. Restored in 1950.*

The relief in the semi-circular pediment above the door depicting bunches of grapes is a reference to the patron. The three-storeyed, palatial building is modelled on prototypes of classical stamp in England and France and proclaims the desire of the upper middle class in Scandinavia to associate itself with the style then fashionable in Europe.

158 STOCKHOLM. *No. 2, Själagårdsgatan, corner building. A middle class town house of circa 1600, reconstructed by Hans Bartels in 1700 and restored between 1969 and 1971.*

The design of the four-storeyed corner building has been adapted to the obtuse angle formed by the street. The alternation of dark surfaces and dressed stone quoins and bands indicate Dutch and Flemish prototypes which were already playing a major role in Scandinavia at the time of the Renaissance. The doorway is the work of the sculptor Johan Wendelstam.

156

157

159 BAUTZEN. *No. 12, Reichenstrasse, middle class town house with a façade dating from circa 1720.*

The spate of building that followed the disastrous conflagrations of 1709 and 1720 has left an enduring mark on the face of this Upper Lusatian centre of Wendish culture. With its symmetrically composed façade, colossal pilasters and heavy stucco ornamentation in the form of festoons, our example, an elegant middle class town house in one of the main streets, strives after a palatial effect. Only in the doorway, which is slightly off-centre, and the three-storeyed oriel is tradition apparent.

Following pages

160 *QUIRIN GERRITZ VAN BREKELENKAM, "The Tailors Workshop", oil on canvas, 1661, Rijksmuseum, Amsterdam.*

This Leyden painter had a particular preference for scenes from the lives of handicraftsmen whose way of life was, needless to say, far more modest than that of the rich mercantile bourgeoisie. But even in workshops such as this there would be a picture—and in many cases a map—on the wall. The big work table has been moved over to the window to catch the light and also to serve as a seat, no doubt on account of the chilliness of the stone floor. On the right-hand side hang ribbons and lengths of cloth. When workshop and dwelling were combined under one and the same roof, dealings with customers formed part of the workaday milieu in a craft trade of this kind.

161 *JAN VERMEER VAN DELFT, "The Street", oil-painting, circa 1658, Rijksmuseum, Amsterdam.*

Along with the *View of Delft*, this picture is among the finest examples of Dutch architectural painting and, furthermore, is the first landscape in Holland to be done direct from nature. In some miraculous way the artist has succeeded in capturing, with his "pointilliste" technique, the colourful sensuousness and restrained atmosphere of this particular part of the street in which he shows a gable-fronted house of somewhat earlier date, and a glimpse of its courtyard. The fulfilment implicit in a quiet, everyday middle class existence, as also the unity of man, architecture and nature, momentarily come alive as though there were not a gap of three centuries between then and now.

158

159

162, 163 GOSLAR. *The Siemens family house, at the corner of Schreiberstrasse (No. 12) and Bergstrasse, built in 1692/93.*

In this, the largest and most perfectly preserved seventeenth century middle class town house in Goslar, the hall has been divided into two storeys by a beamed ceiling. In the foreground is the paved through passageway. The premises behind, which include an eighteenth century shop, are here shown in their original condition before the most recent restoration. The shop has since been moved to the warehouse wing on the Bergstrasse, which also houses the brewery with its bricked-in copper and its large chimney flue. In the far corner of the hall, a spiral stair with slab balusters, fashioned in a style borrowed from stone carving, and a carved newel depicting fabulous beasts, leads to the floor above.

164 LEIPZIG. *No. 8, Market Place, Barthels Hof, built in 1748 by Friedrich Seltendorff for the wealthy merchant and commander of the city, Gottfried Barthel, in place of a building of 1523.*

The front elevation on the Market Place was altered in 1872. A Baroque *Durchgangshaus* typical of those found in this city celebrated for its fairs, and which combines functionalism with modest display. Such houses (of which another example, dating from 1748/49, still survives at No. 19, Katharinenstrasse) are characterized by their irregular lay-out in which, as often as not, a series of courtyards used for trading purposes are connected by wide covered passageways. Merchandise was conveyed to the lofts by means of hoists, while the floors below accommodated merchants from all over the world—hence the design of these courtyards is not without architectural dignity. On the courtyard front of No. 1, Hainstrasse there is another fine two-storeyed oriel window.

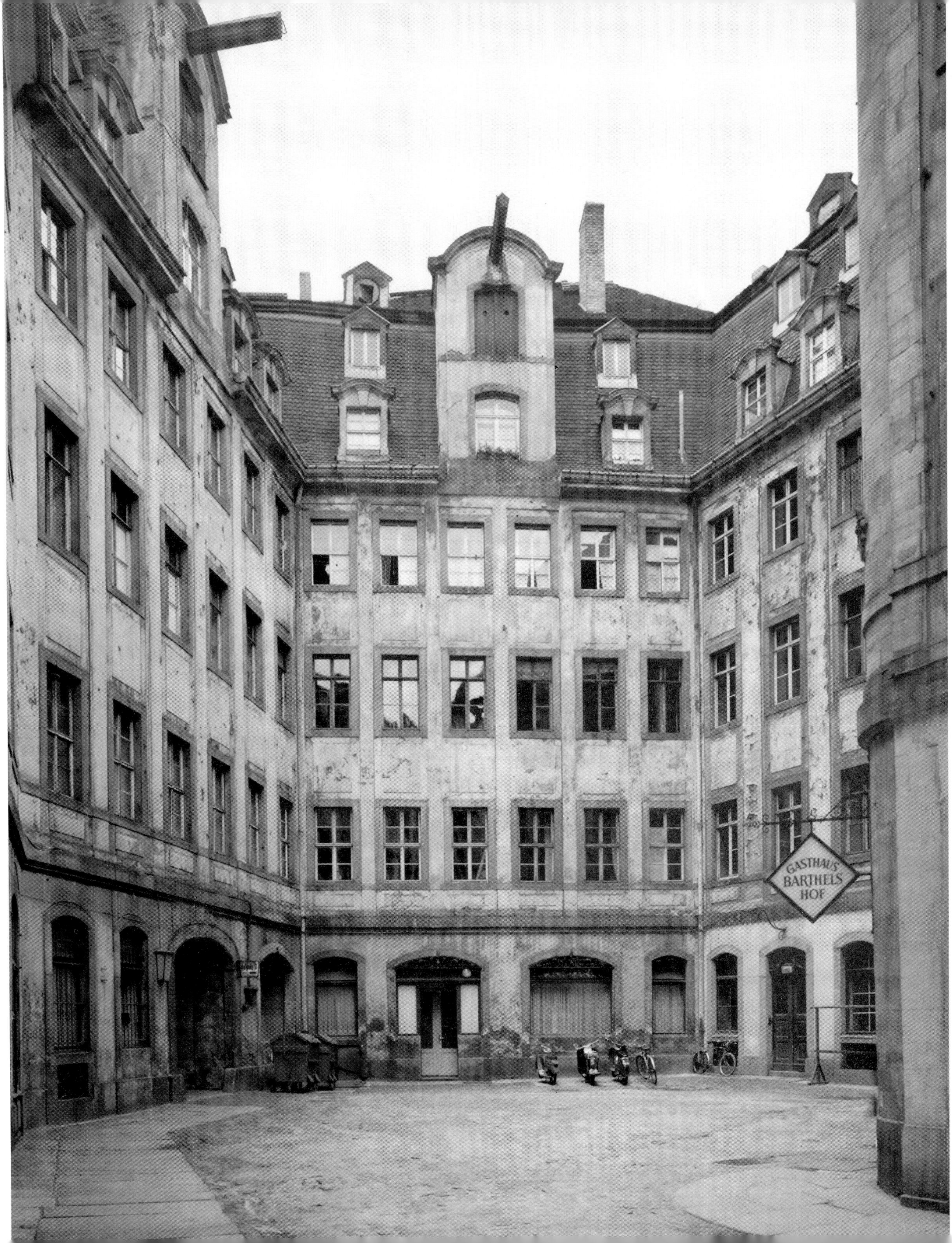
GASTHAUS
BARTHELS
HOF

165 *HANS JORDAENS, "A Cabinet of Objets d'Art", oil on wood, mid-seventeenth century. Kunsthistorisches Museum, Vienna.*

In the seventeenth century pictures formed part of the appointments of all the better middle class town houses. Hence, picture-dealing was a profitable business which in Holland was very strictly organized. Hung one above the other and displayed along with sculpture, objets d'art and such curiosities of nature as the shells on the table on the left, they recall similar collections in princely houses of an earlier date. Here, they are being offered for sale in a lofty, well-lit hall with a parquet floor, in which the atmosphere is one of refinement. Apart from the luxuriant still-lifes, the pictures are chiefly of mythological subjects in an Italian setting, which suggests that these clients preferred the exotic to the usually less costly indigenous product.

166 *FRANÇOIS BOUCHER, "The Breakfast", oil, 1739, Louvre, Paris.*

The scene depicted here by the painter of *fêtes galantes* and pastoral subjects is not, for once, piquant; rather it is an intimate and life-like portrayal of elegant middle class manners. The looking-glass above the sumptuous chimney-piece of the bedchamber does not even reveal a bed. The lady of the house is breakfasting at a small, fragile table, attended by a nurse who is feeding the baby and by her husband who is carefully placing the chocolate-pot on the mantle-shelf to keep it warm. This small corner of the room displays the all-pervading grace and charm of the Rococo style with which Boucher, as Director of the Gobelins factory, felt a close affinity. Only the shelves on either side of the chimney-piece containing toys and articles of everyday use are somewhat out of keeping.

165

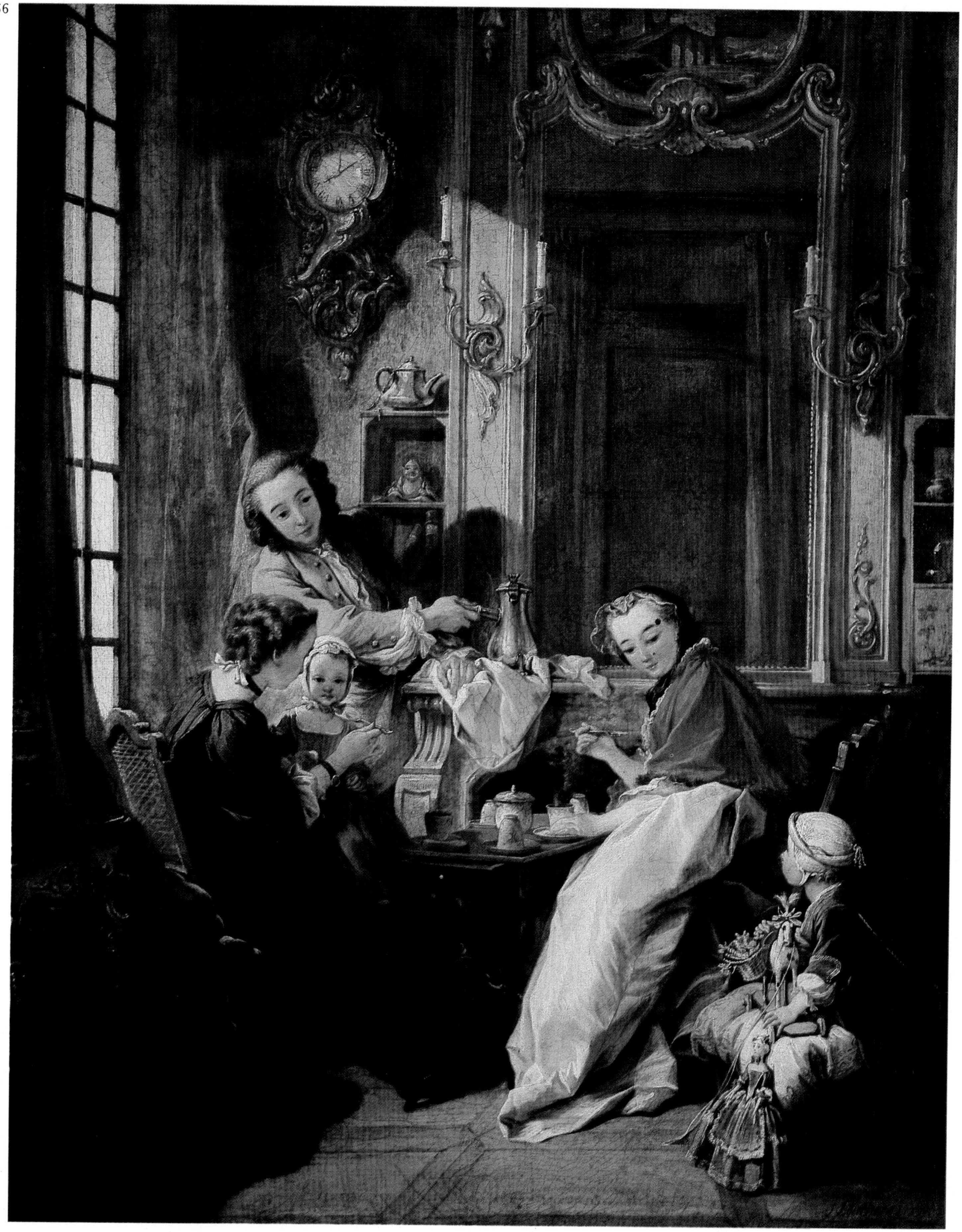

167 LUCKAU *(Lower Lusatia). No. 13, Market Place. Late seventeenth century, stucco decoration, probably by an Italian master craftsman.*

The profusely decorated façade still retains what is basically a Late Renaissance-mannerist system of articulation and a multiplicity of picturesque forms. A few of the elements are baroque as, for instance, the colossal pilasters, broken segmented pediment and crowning œil-de-bœuf.

168, 169 COLOGNE. *Balchem House (Zum goldenen Bären—The Golden Bear), No. 15, Severinstrasse, built in 1676 for the brewer, Heinrich Deutz, along the traditional lines of the gable-fronted house typical of Cologne in the Renaissance period.*

The broken pediment and the dynamic volutes are the only stylistic concessions made to High Baroque, the forms of which were late in arriving in Germany. The interior, executed in the manner of a Cologne inn, displays an original plaster ceiling as well as the spiral stair transferred there from the Rinkenhof in 1945 and dating from 1663. At the foot of the stairs there stands a victorious David holding the head of Goliath.

168

169

170

171

170 PARIS. *Hôtel de Lauzun, No. 17, Quai d'Anjou, small saloon, 1656 to 1658.*

Like the other rooms in the house, this masterpiece of interior decoration was the work of Le Brun, Le Sueur, Petel, Sébastien Bourdon and others. Gruyn des Bordes, commissary to the army, had these imposing rooms embellished with finely executed carvings and stucco ornamentation on walls and ceilings, the latter being also decorated with paintings on classical themes. A magnificent chimney-piece, a console table of the High Baroque, parquet flooring, tapestries, pictures, innumerable, delicately painted putti, fruit, flowers, masks and fabulous beasts, and overdoors with reliefs depicting the Virtues and figures from the classical pantheon—all these combine, in a town palace, to convey an impression of exceptional magnificence, the result of a schooling in courtly refinement.

171 MADRID. *Study in the house of Lope de Vega, No. 11, Calle de Cervantes, circa 1610.*

The creator of the *Judge of Zalamea* who, even in his lifetime, was recognized to be the greatest writer in Spain, lived and worked in a simple house with very functional appointments. Spain, an absolutist country, was to lose its political preeminence by the middle of the seventeenth century. On the other hand, the phase of bourgeois democratic art it now entered upon was one of universal significance, nor was it fortuitous that, here more than anywhere else, the middle class town house should have retained its simple, indigenous character.

172 *WILLIAM HOGARTH, "Marriage à la Mode", oil-painting, National Gallery, London.*

The very title of the picture is indicative of the satirical intentions of this great English portrayer of morals. The pretentious, Baroque-style surroundings underline the vapid existence of the young couple whose marriage is obviously one of convenience. Indeed, save for the good traditional furniture, the luxury here displayed is of a somewhat tawdry kind. The knick-knacks on the mantle-shelf betray a want of taste, while the pictures on the damask-hung walls in the dining-room in the background are also of dubious merit. The nearer one is partially concealed by a curtain, obviously on account of its risqué subject-matter. At all events, what can still be seen is plain enough, as are the signs of the drunken revelry in which the illustrious company has just been indulging in these rooms.

172

173 *BERNARDO BELOTTO, known as Canaletto, "The Frauenkirche in Dresden", oil-painting, 1751. Detail showing the Rampische Strasse, Staatliche Kunstsammlungen, Dresden.*

The faithful and at the same time very lively rendering by the famous Italian topographical artist who, between 1747 and 1766, was Court painter in the service of the King of Saxony, provides a record of the beauty, now irreparably destroyed, of Dresden's magnificent Baroque ensemble of aristocratic and middle class houses. Despite strict building regulations, the densely built-up streets of the capital are the product of organic growth rather than of rigid planning.

174 WÜRZBURG. *Haus zum Falken, No. 9, Market Place. Originally a Renaissance house. Converted in 1735 and embellished with Rococo decoration in 1751 to the order of the merchant Thomas Meissner.*

The damage done during the Second World War has been made good. In Catholic South Germany the Rococo is characterized by the buoyancy and superabundance of architectural ornamentation. The unknown Bavarian master responsible for this delicate, animated form of decoration has given particular importance to the dormer gables by the imaginative embellishment of their tympani.

175 WASSERBURG *am Inn.*
Once the house of the patrician
family of Kern (now a court-
house), Nos. 9 and 10, Market
Place. Johann Baptist Zimmer-
mann is believed to have created
this marvellous façade out of what
had once been two arcaded houses.

The apparent absence of architectural
articulation is compensated by the
careful blending of traditional structural members and Rococo decoration.
The dissimilar houses have been
integrated in accordance with the
principle of organic symmetry and this
also typifies what was then the main
decorative motif, namely rocaille. The
wall has been carried up to conceal the
valley roof, a common feature in the
Inn valley.

176 INNSBRUCK. *Helbling House, No. 10, Herzog-Friedrich-Strasse. In or around 1730, both façades of this Late Gothic corner house were given a mantle of magnificent stucco decoration in the form of foliate- and strapwork, probably by the Wessobrunn master, Anton Gigl, in collaboration with the Innsbruck plasterer Andrä Gratl.*

Only the external surfaces of the Late Gothic lattice-vaulted arcades have been left untouched by a decoration whose wealth of forms is without a parallel in Austria. The many-storeyed oriel towers, on the other hand, are comprised in the rich organic ornamentation, whose multiplicity of curvilinear foliate forms conceals the tectonic articulation of load-carrying and non-load carrying structural members.

177 FRANKFURT-AM-MAIN. *Goethe's House, (now a museum), No. 23, Grosser Hirschgraben, converted in 1755/56 by Goethe's father from two late sixteenth century timber-framed houses.*

Owned by the Goethe family from 1730 to 1795. After being destroyed in the Second World War, it was reconstructed between 1946 and 1951, part of it—for instance the kitchen behind the barred windows on the ground floor—being fitted out with such interior furnishings as could be salvaged. In the great poet's reminiscences of his childhood, recorded in *Dichtung und Wahrheit (Poetry and Truth)*, an important role is played by the conversion of the old, labyrinthine complex into a more fashionable and grandiose dwelling-house with its long side on to the street. The conversion plainly shows that, in the phase of Late Baroque known as Rococo, the now self-confident middle classes were intent, not only on displaying their wealth, but also and above all on attaining a higher standard of domestic comfort that was both practical and commensurate with new conditions.

178 ERFURT. *Baroque summer residence in the courtyard of No. 13, Fischmarkt, Zum Breiten Herd (The Wide Hearth), built in 1727 for the Royal Lüneburg Councillor, O. C. Schulze.*

With its strictly symmetrical bays—the central one slightly projecting—and suggestion of wings, its mansard roof, bull's-eye windows, temple-like dormer gable and windows with depressed three-centred arches, this small, two-storeyed building reiterates the vocabulary of monumental château architecture on a considerably reduced scale. As a miniature edition, it is not without charm, but already foreshadows the end of individual initiative in the architecture of the middle class town house.

177

178

179

180

179 DORNSTETTEN, *near Freudenstadt. Urban farmstead in the Market Place, seventeenth/ eighteenth century.*

In many smaller places, such as this little country town in the Black Forest, the old, well-tried types of building continued to survive. However, timber-framed architecture reached its final stage of development with the decorative enrichment of the timber structure in the Baroque era.

180 GENGENBACH *(District of Offenburg in Baden). Engelsgasse with lower middle class houses, late seventeenth century.*

These houses, occupied by lower middle class citizens, are modest both in appearance and dimensions, nor does the simple timber framing betray any hint of ambition to keep up with the times by indulging in the then prevalent love of ornamentation. Here we find the traditional projecting upper storey which precludes any attempt at a unified façade. The entrance to the cellar is outdoors, on the street side rather than within, as in the case of more opulent middle class town houses.

181 RIGA. *Dannenstern House, No. 21, Marstallstrasse, formerly two Gothic merchants' houses, converted into one between 1694 and 1698. The magnificent façade was decorated in the Dutch style by the Stockholm sculptor, Hans Walter.*

Between 1621 and 1710, then under Swedish rule, was an international trading centre and, as such, was greatly influenced by West European models in the field of domestic architecture. Today the building serves as Riga's historical and maritime museum.

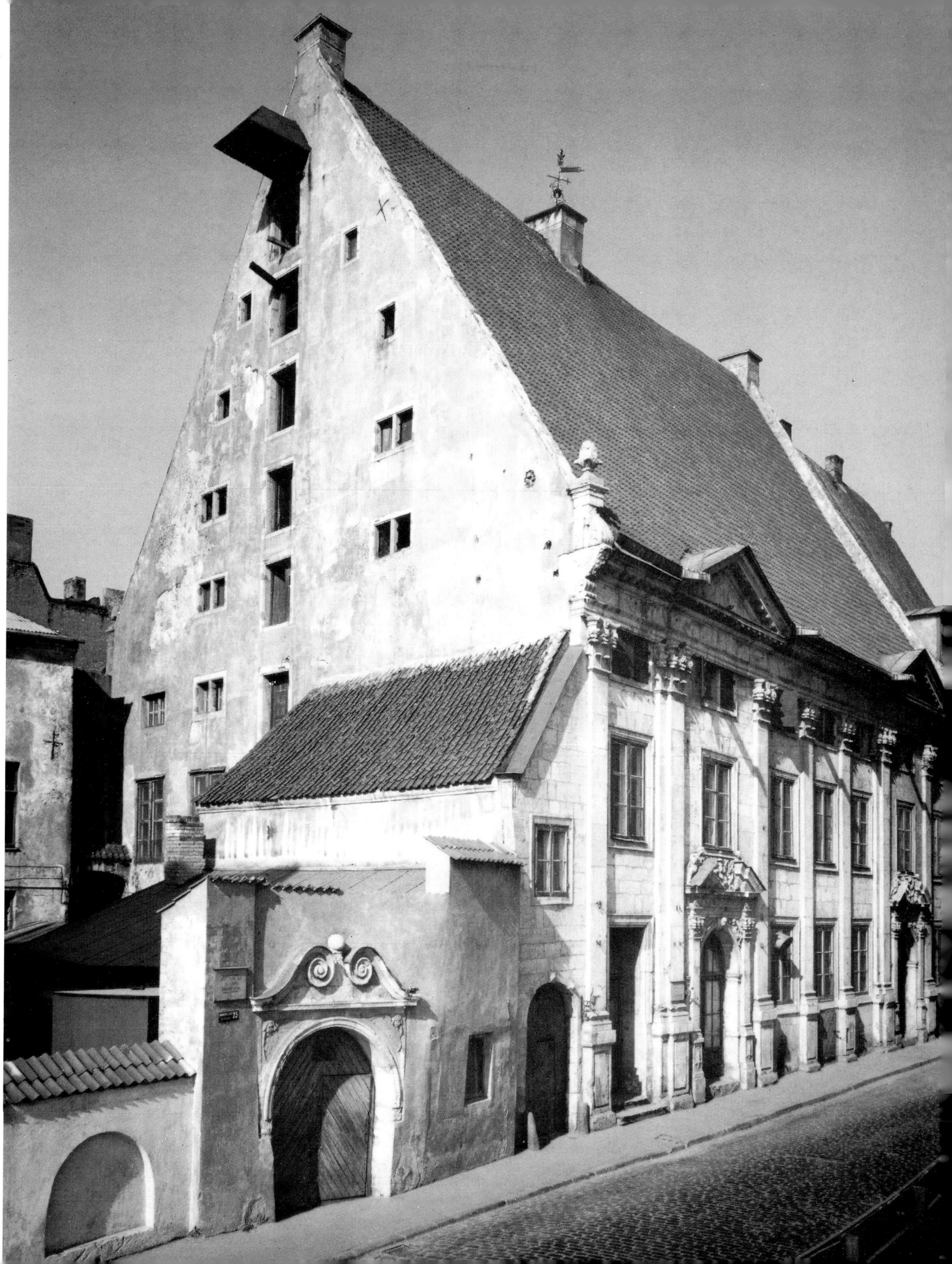

182

183

182 TORUŃ. *Palas Biskupi (once the episcopal palace of Kujawien), No. 8, Żeglarska ul., erected in 1693 above a plinth-like rusticated ground storey.*

There is no unified system of articulation by means of engaged columns, pilasters or pilaster strips. Instead the whole surface is overrun by High Baroque stucco ornamentation in the form of delicately worked foliate motifs, a characteristic feature of the Polish Renaissance with its love of decoration. This same characteristic is also evident in the Torun dwelling-house The Star (1697), a narrow, gable-fronted house in the old tradition.

183 WARSAW. *Prażmowski House, No. 87, Krakowskie Przedmieście, built between 1660 and 1667 for Dr. Pastorius, the King's personal physician and later owned by M. Prażmowski.*

Converted in 1754. At the end of the eighteenth century the façade on the Ulica Senatorska was redecorated in the classical manner. Gutted by fire in 1944, it was rebuilt in 1949 on the eighteenth century model. The elegant façade reflects, not only the resurgence of the Polish middle classes, but also their attempt to exploit for their own end the advanced courtly culture of the Rococo which had reached Poland mainly through the agency of the Saxon-Polish kings.

184 LONDON. *Lindsey House, Nos. 59 and 60, Lincoln's Inn Fields, built in 1640, probably by Nicholas Stone (formerly attributed to Inigo Jones).*

Today the sole survivor of the original development on the west side of Lincoln's Inn Fields, this early example of a terrace house, built for Sir David Conyngham, marks the belated tendency in England towards a type of town house conceived on palatial lines and incorporating the forms of Palladian Classicism. It was divided into two residences, probably by Isaac Ware, in 1751/52. The adjoining house on the left was erected in about 1730 to the design of Henry Joynes, its façade being based on that of Lindsey House. In 1795, this, too, was made into two residences. Towards the end of the seventeenth century and in the course of the eighteenth, streets and squares were to be given a monumental appearance by ensembles of terrace houses such as these.

185 RIGA. *Reutern's House, Nos. 2–4, Marstall-strasse, built between 1684 and 1688 by Ruppert Bindenschu for the councillor, Johann Reutern, previously of Lübeck.*

The carvings are the work of the Saxon sculptor H. Arnold. The severe, lucid articulation of the façade by means of colossal pilasters, architrave and an axial, pedimented gable, betrays the influence of Netherlandish Classicism.

186 BUDAPEST. *No. 3, Hess-András-tér. An inn, known as the "Red Hedgehog", with Baroque and early neo-classical iron railings on the courtyard galleries.*

Three medieval houses originally occupied the site of the early classical building, converted in 1810. Part of the former fabric survives in the barrel vault of the porte-cochère and in the door frame. The reconstructed ground plan of the house—with a wide central porte-cochère and a living-room at either side—is thought to be thirteenth century, and hence one of the earliest buildings in the Vár quarter.

187 GYÖR. *No. 12, Köztársaság tér, built of medieval materials in 1620.*

The façade was redesigned some time after 1767 and given a corner oriel like those displayed by Austrian middle class town houses in Linz and Krems. The panels above the windows are embellished with stucco strapwork and there is also stucco decoration inside the oriel and in the vestibule, giving on to the staircase. The courtyard has a columnar arcade. In this small building, the doorway, oriel and system of pilasters fit together like so many Chinese boxes.

188 PRAGUE. *No. 26, Thomasgasse (The Golden Stag), in the Little Quarter, built in 1725/26 by Kilian Ignaz Dientzenhofer. The house sign was carved in 1726 by the sculptor Ferdinand Maximilian Brokoff.*

With its strictly axial articulation by means of two doorways, this building is one of the most valuable Baroque middle class town houses in a city already rich in magnificent noble palaces.

189 ŽERAVNA. *Reception room in the house of Sava Filaretov, 1718.*

In Bulgaria, a country of extensive forests, interior appointments made of timber played an important role, the more so since notably in hilly areas, such as the reception room here illustrated, with a male preserve in the shape of a sofa or divan—a kind of raised platform—the general effect was determined by the use of decorative textiles and the highly developed art of wood carving. Walls, ceilings, niches, windows and wall cupboards were wholly clad in wood. Eastern influences are discernible in the preference shown for rich geometrical patterns as also in the Saracenic arches of the niches.

189

190, 191 BERLIN. *Ermeler-haus, No. 10, Märkisches Ufer, bought in about 1760 by P. F. Damme, supplier of uniforms and leather equipment to the Court, for 20,000 talers, and remodelled by him. The frieze and balustrade were added in 1804, in 1824 it was bought by Ermeler, a tobacco merchant.*

The building, originally at No. 11, Breite Strasse, was dismantled between 1969 and adapted to harmonize with an ensemble of historic middle class town houses then in course of erection in the Märkisches Ufer. This palatial building examplifies the Prusso-North German preference for severely classicist forms. The house, now a restaurant, contains several richly decorated smaller rooms, among them what is known as the Rose Room. The Rococo paintings, dating from about 1760 and consisting of delicately executed flowers, foliage and rocaille work, are complemented by the ceiling paintings done in 1762 by Carl Friedrich Fechhelm.

192

193

192 KALUGA. *The merchant Korobov's House, late seventeenth century.*

This richly decorated building, with a frontage of twenty metres, has the appearance of a small palace in which, however, the traditional house form, with its emphasis on width and its covered external stair, has been incorporated. What is a marked predilection for rotund, animated, richly embellished forms and for colourful contrasts in the national idiom, has successfully assimilated the West European motifs used in the articulation of the façade, such as cornices, pilaster-like elements at the angles, and window architraves of engaged columns and crowning pediments. As in all architecture that is deeply rooted in the popular imagination, the love of ebullient ornamentation often predominates over the cool, unyielding rationalism of the ruling social caste.

193 PSKOV. *House of the merchant family of Pogankin, built between 1620 and 1630. Roof and outside stair altered at a later date.*

The main building of several storeys had a covered approach to the bel étage and a variegated roof scape. Constituting an organic part of the whole is a communicating block for employees and the less important guests with, beyond it, a wing containing the kitchen and servants' quarters. Stone construction, then comparatively new in Russia, is here combined with timber, a warm material that had been employed for domestic building for centuries past, and long continued to be so used for upper storeys, where the inventively decorated living-quarters were generally situated.

194 BUDAPEST. *Nos. 5–8, Bécsi-Kapu-tér.*

In this long oppressed country, middle class domestic architecture remained comparatively modest until well into the eighteenth century, as may be seen from this small ensemble of historic town houses. There is something rustic, indeed even provincial, about the two-storeyed buildings which are not all of the same date. The corner house on the left (No. 8), is mainly fifteenth century and was altered some time after 1686 when the bowed corner oriel was added. Its immediate neighbour (No. 7) was built by János Kothl in 1741 from medieval remains, and modernized in 1807 in the classical style, when it was given allegorical and portrait reliefs round the windows. The porte-cochère was added in 1932 and, between 1950 and 1952, a general restoration was carried out. The narrow house (No. 6) next door dates from the fifteenth century, and the last one on the right (No. 5) from the eighteenth century.

195 ARBANASSI. *Hadžiiliev's House (known as the King's House), built by a well-to-do international trader in about 1800.*

One of the characteristics of Bulgarian middle class domestic architecture is its rejection of all external decoration, size and solidity (in this case the ground floor walls are 90 centimetres thick) being considered of greater importance. The small ground floor windows look more like embrasures. They illuminate, *inter alia*, the store-room with its stone-flagged floor and oak-beamed ceiling, while the large windows on the upper floor give adequate light to the living-quarters and guest chambers. The boldly projecting, tiled roof provides shade. This type of traditional and, at the same time, highly functional, house has survived in Bulgaria up till the present day.

194

195

196, 197 BRUNSWICK. *Vieweg Publishing House, No. 1, Burgplatz, built by David Gilly between 1802 and 1805 to the designs of Peter Krahe.*

In collaboration with Peter Krahe, Gilly created one of the first classical middle class town houses in Germany. The few decorative elements, such as rustication, fret mouldings, palmette frieze and dentils, are applied neatly and with economy to this cubical structure with its slightly projecting central pavilion crowned by a pediment. Shortly afterwards, between 1805 and 1808, Krahe built the house Salve Hospes at No. 12, Lessing-platz, largely borrowed from the English country mansion, thereby creating the prototype of the classical villa which was to survive until the middle of the century.

Compared with the massive grandeur of the exterior, still being influenced by the architecture of the revolutionary era, the entrance zone in the interior is more modest and restrained. The straight staircase is reminiscent of the traditional spiral staircases. The ground plan is asymmetrical, partly because of the road building line, partly because of functional considerations for this combined dwelling- und business-house.

196

197

198 POTSDAM. *Mittelstrasse in the Holländisches Viertel (Dutch Quarter), erected between 1738 and 1742 by Frederick William I for Dutch immigrants. The settlement of brick terrace houses was built to the designs of the Dutch master builder, Johann Boumann the Elder.*

Nowhere else in middle class domestic architecture does the spirit of absolutism find clearer expression than in the plans, every detail of which has been laid down. These standardized dwellings do not contain a workshop, nor do they offer much scope for individual design, though official planning took account of the architecture to which the new citizens had been accustomed.

199 POTSDAM. *No. 28, Friedrich-Ebert-Strasse.*

A charmingly designed entrance with, above it, a window with a voluted surround. It was restored in 1976. The house of which it forms part is eaves-fronted and is situated in the Holländisches Viertel (Dutch Quarter).

198

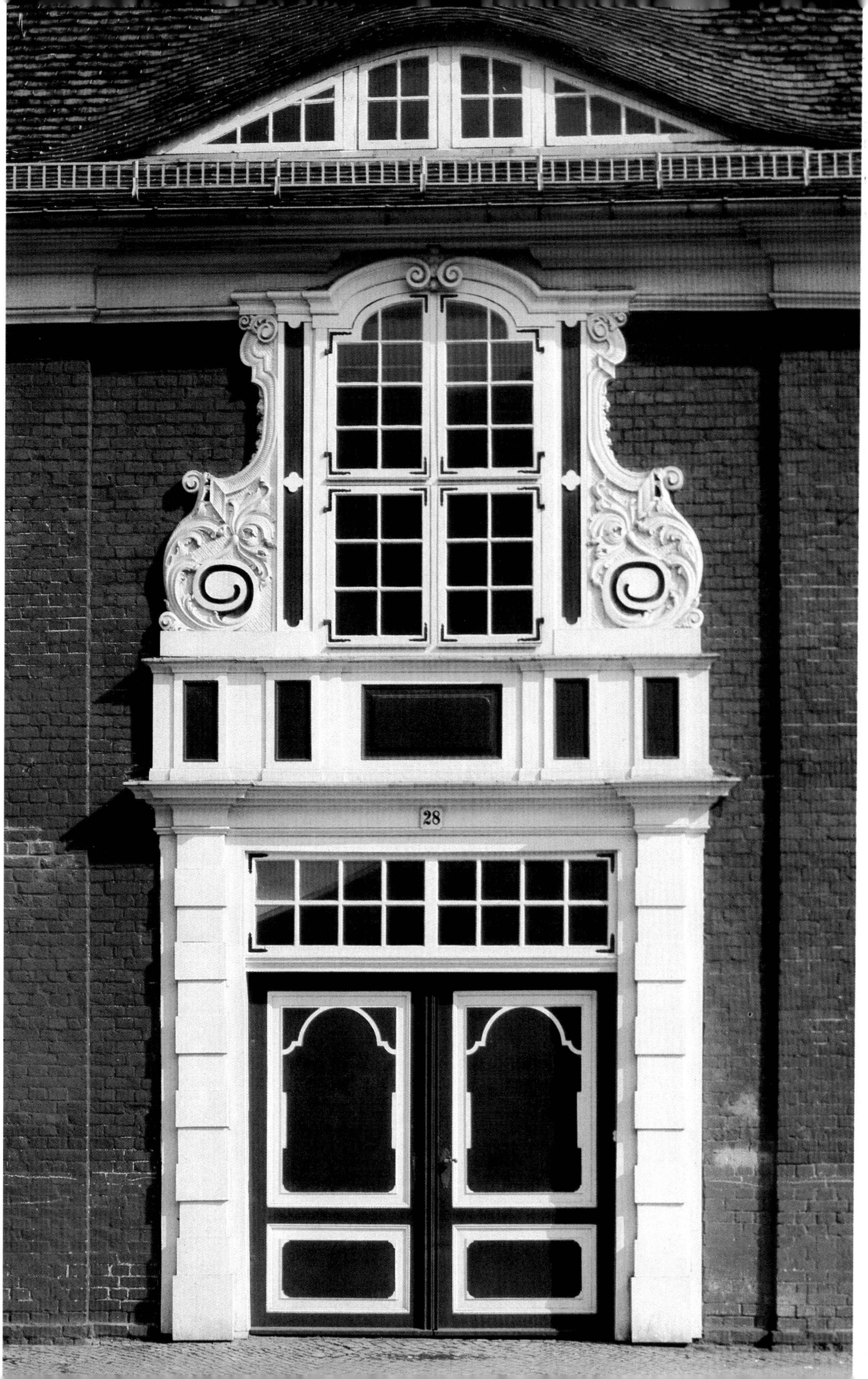
28

200 *GUISEPPE CANELLA the Elder, "Rue de Castiglione" in Paris, painting dated 1829, Musée Carnavalet, Paris.*

Napoleon Bonaparte, who became emperor of the French in 1804, intervened in town planning in an absolutist manner. He ordered the demolition of some five hundred old houses and forty streets in the area immediately to the north of the Tuileries and the Louvre, thereby making room for the creation of the Place Vendôme as a record in architectural terms of the new epoch. The proximity of the Louvre, with its vast frontage on the Rue de Rivoli, suggested the erection of similarly grandiose and monumental ensembles, this time in the form of blocks of middle class town houses of homogeneous design. Canella's picture shows the Rue de Castiglione, some two hundred metres long, with a view of the forty-four metre high Vendôme column erected between 1806 and 1810 in honour of the Grande Armée. The once narrow houses have merged to form three powerful if restrained blocks, thus making it possible to experience the street as a spatially coherent whole. Like battalions drawn up in square formation, the uniform colonnades lead the citizen to the monument of national glory.

200

201 *SEBASTIAN GUTZWILLER, "Family Concert in Basle", oil-painting, 1849, Öffentliche Kunstsammlung, Basle.*

This upper middle class living-room of the Late Biedermeier period is already overflowing with possessions. Nevertheless, it exudes an atmosphere of solidity and restraint and, like the family, here assembled with its pets, is characterized by rich and genuine relationships. Plushiness and pomposity are absent, nor do the forms of the second phase of the Rococo obtrude. What strikes one are the innumerable small objects all over the room, pictures being hung even in the deep window reveals and consisting of local landscapes and family portraits. The valuable books are kept behind glass in a recess high up on the right-hand wall. The ancient custom of suspending a bird cage from the ceiling is still followed.

202 BUDAPEST. *An apartment house with shops on the ground floor, No. 3, Bátthyány tér, built between 1793 and 1795 by Kristóf Hikisch.*

This building presents its long side to the street and, by its gridlike decoration, accentuates the divisions between storeys. Both these features are typical of the apartment house architecture that was soon to dominate the urban scene. In this early, classical building, Late Baroque decorative elements are still mingled with lively sculptural forms. Thereafter, and until the coming of historicism, architectural embellishment, whether figurative or in the form of rich carvings, was to be wholly abjured so far as the apartment house was concerned.

203 LONDON. *Woburn Walk, Bedford Place, W. C., built circa 1822.*

There is nothing strictly classical about these dwelling-houses with shops on the ground floor. Rather, unconventional ideas are assimilated into the gently rhythmical façade enlivened by small balconies and by contrasts of colour. A romantic predilection for her own history and for what had matured in the natural course of things meant that in England, in particular, the ground had already been prepared for free forms such as these.

202

203

204 BERGEN. *No. 62, Sandviksveien. House built in 1808.*

This two-storeyed brick building with its hipped roof and pilaster-framed doorway carried on the tradition of modest practicality that was already a characteristic of middle class domestic architecture in Norway.

205 KARL-MARX-STADT *(Saxony). Anger-vorstadt, Antonplatz-Brühl.*
This working-class quarter, planned as an integral whole, was laid out in about 1830 following the rapid growth of the industrial town in the early part of the nineteenth century.

The two-storeyed terrace houses, whose accommodation has been enlarged by the addition of an attic storey, are totally devoid of decoration and individuality. The architecture conferred upon the proletariat was as grey and anonymous as was the latter in the eyes of the bourgeoisie and, as an exercise in planning on the part of middle class social reformers, may be traced, along with numerous successors, back to the Fuggerei in Augsburg.

206 *CARL JULIUS MILDE, "Erwin Speckter in his Munich Lodgings", water-colour, Kunsthalle, Hamburg.*

In all probability this painting was done in 1825, when the Hamburg artist and his friend Speckter went to Munich to study at the Academy. Both the living-room and the bedchamber, of which we catch a glimpse, are sparsely furnished in the Biedermeier-neo-classical manner, though the pieces themselves are functional and well-designed. The walls, with their typical striped wall-paper, are covered with studies by Speckter himself, testifying to the way in which he has taken possession of the room. In the later Biedermeier phase the apartment would be filled with innumerable objects and mementoes.

206

207 WEIMAR. *Goethe's House, am Frauenplan, Juno Room on the upper floor.*

The reception room is imposingly if reticently embellished with stucco decoration in low relief, the straight lines and fields of which clearly demarcate each separate zone of delicate foliate ornamentation. Noteworthy features are the pictures and sculptures, amongst them the more than life-size head of the classical goddess, Juno. As a result of his travels in Italy between 1786 and 1788, the poet had become an ardent advocate of the classical view on art.

207

208 WEIMAR. *Goethe's House, am Frauenplan, study.*

The Baroque house, built between 1707 and 1709, was presented to Goethe by the Duke Karl August, in 1792. The poet in person drew up the plans for its subsequent alteration, completed in 1798. With its wide floor boards, whitewashed walls and stylishly simple furniture disposed in a practical manner, the study had a businesslike yet at the same time personal air.

209 VIENNA. *XIXth District (Döbling), Wertheimstein Villa, No. 96, Döblinger Hauptstrasse. Staircase hall with allegorical frescoes by Moritz von Schwind and arabesques by Holle, 1840.*

The villa was built by Ludwig Pichl in 1834/35 for the art collector, Rudolph van Arthaber (the staircase to the designs of Karl Rösner). In accordance with neo-classical ideas, all the decorative elements are clearly demarcated one from the other and incorporated into the architectural system, a principle exemplified at Pompeii and Herculaneum which, following the excavations, had become generally accessible. Even the figurative motifs seem to detach themselves from the surface. However, such opulent wall paintings depicting figures as well as classical landscapes are rare in middle class architecture.

208

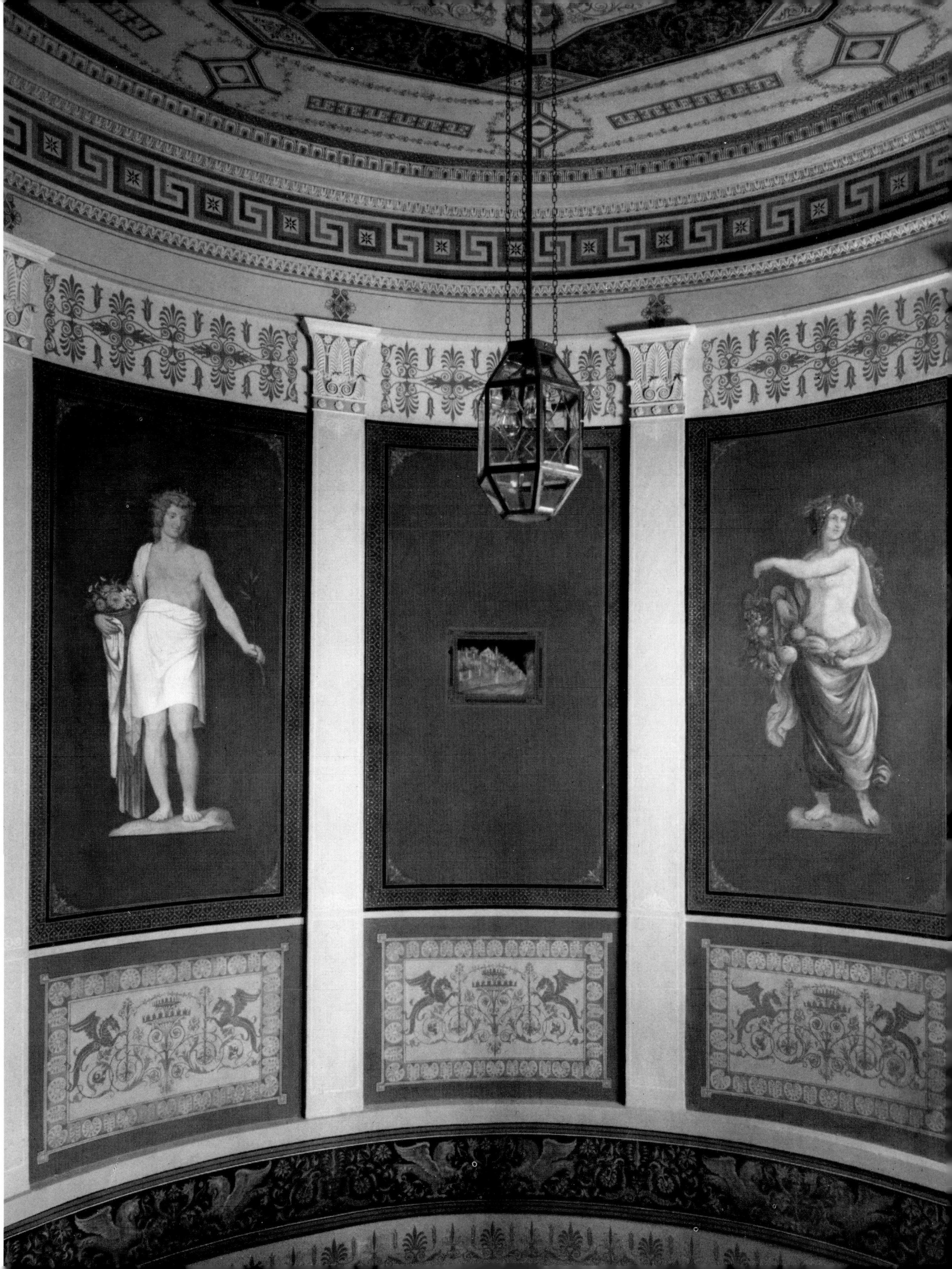

210 BATH. *Royal Crescent, built between 1767 and 1777 by John Wood the Younger.*

Even in Roman times Bath, in the county of Somerset, was famous for its thermal springs. A watering-place frequented by well-to-do citizens, aristocrats and men of leisure, it acquired in the eighteenth century a grandeur and eloquence deriving from the ensembles of white terrace houses built by the Woods. The Crescent, designed by John Wood the Younger, with its gently sloping lawns, consists of thirty houses forming a vast palatial frontage behind a façade of giant Ionic columns.

211 HAMBURG-NIEN-STEDTEN. *J. C. Godeffroy's country house (Hirschparkhaus), No. 499, Elbchaussee. Built between 1789 and 1792 by C. F. Hansen for the merchant Johann Caesar Godeffroy IV.*

The entrance front of the long, low building is axially accentuated by a central pavilion that rises through one and a half storeys. It has an air of pretentiousness reminiscent of a château, an impression that is strongly reinforced by the wide flights of steps, by the two powerful Doric columns of the recessed vestibule and by the boldly projecting cornice. Situated in the midst of an extensive, English-style park (the subsequent introduction of deer gave the house its name), the whole complex seems wholly in keeping with the patron's motto, "Peace, Prudence, Pleasure", which graces the centre of the architrave.

212 MOSCOW. *Former palace of the Stanitsky family, No. 11, Kropotkinsky Street (now the Tolstoy Museum), erected by the master builder Afanassi G. Grigoriev between 1817 and 1819.*

The plastered timber villa is a typical example of Russian Neo-Classicism with its strict adherence to forms and tendency towards spatial articulation by means of axial emphasis. The covered entrance, already a feature of Russian timber architecture, would appear to have survived in the projecting, columnar portico with its massive architrave.

211

212

213 HAMBURG-OTHMARSCHEN. *No. 50, Baron-Voght-Strasse. View of Jenisch, a country house, now a branch of the Altonaer Museum, built between 1830 and 1833 by the architect F. G. Forsmann for the Hamburg Senator Martin Jenisch and charmingly situated in a landscaped park above the banks of the Elbe.*

The initial designs for this house, which were not carried out, were made in 1829 and derived from buildings by C. F. Hansen. Work was finally put in hand in accordance with an alternative design by K. F. Schinkel, to which important alterations were made by Forsmann. Characteristic features are the almost quadrangular ground plan, the two and a half storeys with central staircase and toplight and the columnar portico on the Elbe frontage. For the most part the external articulation follows Schinkel's design. The stucco work in the interior is contemporaneous with the date of building. The vestibule contains two Ionic columns of stucco marble.

214 HAMBURG-ALTONA. *No. 116, Palmaille. House of the architect, Christian Frederik Hansen, built by him in 1803/04. Save for the later ground floor windows, the façade was reconstructed in 1952.*

German as well as English merchants and ship-owners made their home in this stately avenue built between 1786 and 1825. Although the wide house front then in fashion was precluded by the narrowness of the plots, the principle of the cubical design with emphasis on the axis was adhered to. A majestic note is struck by the aedicular treatment of the window. In the interior is a deep rectangular vestibule with a vaulted roof and a staircase hall.

213

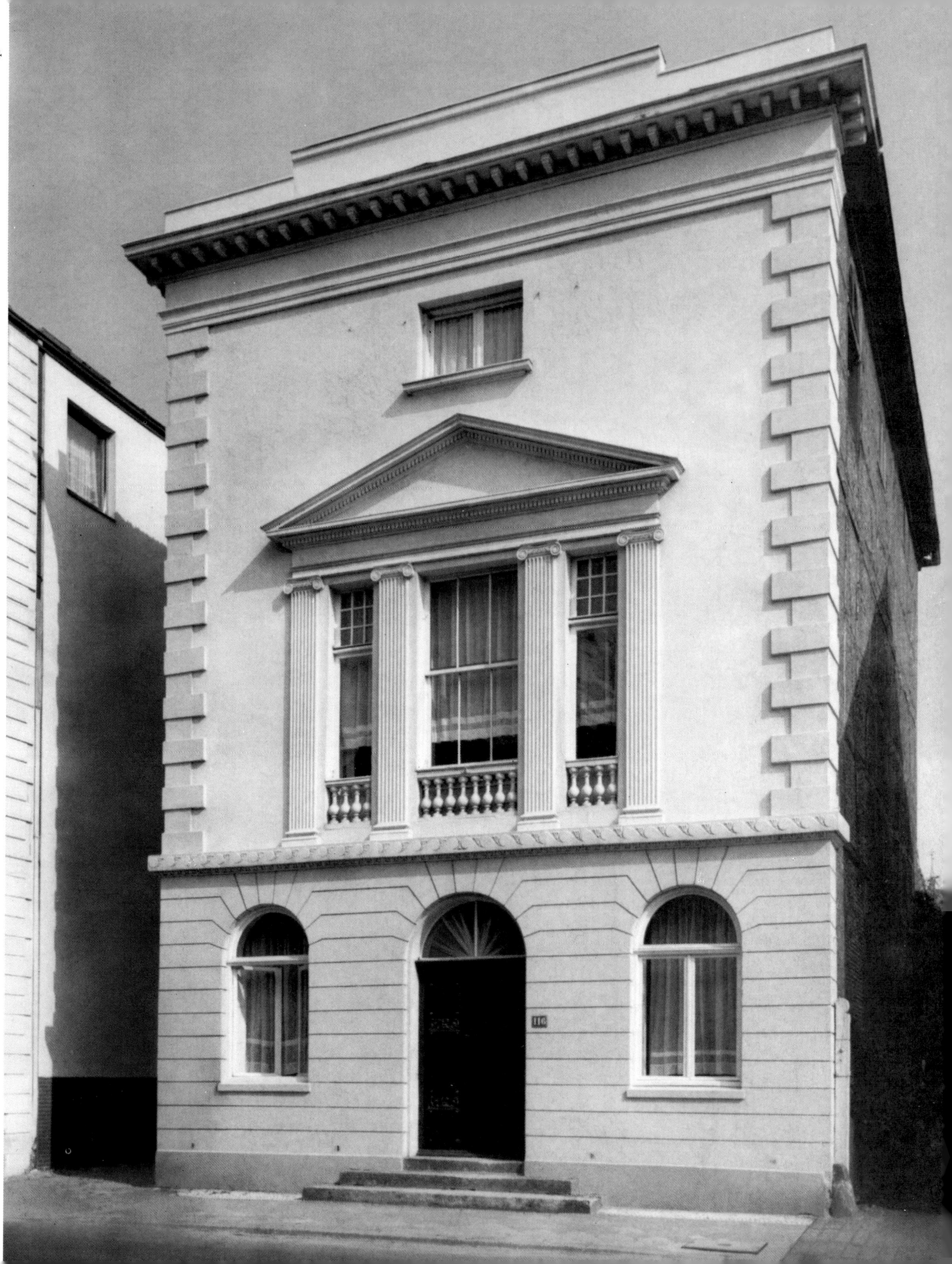

215 KOPRIVSHTITZA. *Liutova House, erected in 1854 by master builders from Plovdiv, and once used as an apothecary's shop, is now the headquarters of the Museum Directorate.*

Above the vestibule is a strongly projecting "yoke" gable (known in Bulgaria as "shoulder yoke"), which describes a convex curve and gives added emphasis to the central block of this, one of the most beautiful houses in Koprivshtitza. Baroque forms and the local traditions of a highly evolved timber architecture have amalgamated to produce what is an unmistakable national idiom.

216 PLOVDIV. *House of Argir C. Kojumdshioglu (now an ethnographic museum), No. 2, Tshomakovi Street, built in 1847 by Hadži Georgi. Restored between 1961 and 1963.*

This also belongs to the Baroque type of house. On account of the sloping site, the street side of the house rests on a masonry plinth, and it is primarily on the garden side, here illustrated, that the full wealth of its serenely buoyant forms is displayed. Between the side blocks there projects a bow-shaped central section with slender columns and a curvilinear roof, the latter reminiscent of the Byzantine-Bulgarian architecture of which it is the heir. All the rooms in the house were reserved for the owner's family and the servants were therefore housed in an annex.

217 DRESDEN. *Villa Rosa, No. 20, Holzhofgasse, built in 1838/39 by Gottfried Semper. Destroyed in the Second World War.*

Built by the great architect and devotee of democratic ideas, this house in a pleasant situation beside the Elbe was one of his greatest artistic achievements. Its influence extended not only to the later buildings of the Semper-Nicolai School, but even to the villa style of central Europe. Borrowings have been freely made from Palladio, and the well-proportioned building, with its arcaded entrance and flights of steps, exhales the temperate spirit of the early Neo-Renaissance and is a deliberate reversion to the first epoch to receive the imprint of the European middle classes. True, Antiquity was, to Semper, the *fons et origo* of natural, democratic architecture, but he regarded the Renaissance, which in its turn bore the imprint of Antiquity, as a sphere more closely related to contemporary problems.

217

218 LONDON. *Geffrye Museum. Living-room of the Victorian era.*

During the long reign of Queen Victoria, from 1837 to 1901, when England was in her heyday as an industrial and colonial power, the standards of domestic life of the wealthy middle classes were, so to speak, foundering in a welter of luxury, ornamentation and stylistic eclecticism. Nevertheless, elements ranging from the Neo-Gothic to the neo-classical were applied with some feeling for integrative harmonization, though there is no overlooking the fact that floral decoration, by now to some extent naturalistic, was not only self-defeating but also beginning to call in question the very function of the objects it adorned. The love of ornamentation here revealed still rests on a basis of sound workmanship, whereas in the lower middle class sphere it was to experience a rapid decline into cheap, mass-produced kitsch.

219 ADOLPH MENZEL, *"Weekday in Paris", oil on canvas, 1869. Kunstmuseum, Düsseldorf.*

In the nineteenth century this city of over a million, with its hectic bustle, its traffic and its crowds, tended to reduce middle class existence—and with it the private house—to a state of anonymity. Though depicted in such faithful detail, this part of the town—probably near the Opéra—is nevertheless indistinguishable from a thousand other such streets in Paris. In the eclectic town house what predominates is a boundless, but at the same time unoriginal, individualism.
Borrowings from earlier styles go hand in hand with modifications dictated by sober business sense, hence the piling up of storeys, the utilization of roof space and the clamorous advertisements on the façades, which, as may be seen from the building on the corner, often give rise to a peculiar medley.

218

220 VIENNA. *Aerial photograph of the district laid out to the west of the Lines in the second half of the nineteenth century:*

1 Early *Gründerzeit* expansion of Neuleschenfeld and Hernals
2 Partially rebuilt suburb of Neuleschenfeld
3 Early *Gründerzeit* brewery quarter of Neu-Ottakring
4 High *Gründerzeit* quarter of Schmelz
5 Former parade ground, now built over
6 High *Gründerzeit* quarter of Ottakring
7 The Lines, formerly outer girdle of fortifications
8 and 11 Allotments
9 Beginnings of sporadic peripheral development of goods depots and domestic premises
10 Twentieth century sports ground.

The photograph shows the chaotic way in which, during the second half of the nineteenth century, the larger European cities mingled industry and mass housing and overran boundaries that had existed for hundreds of years. The growth of Vienna's population (231,000 in 1800, 260,000 in 1820, 357,000 in 1840, approx. 500,000 in 1860 and 1.3 million in 1890) called for high density housing, virtually unrelieved by squares or parks, in heavily built-up areas, the more so since traffic within the city was long to remain confined to horse-drawn vehicles (after 1865, cabs were supplemented by two tramway companies) and this precluded excessive urban expansion. It was typical of the early stages of urban expansion that the effect produced by the network of streets, often based on the nuclei of former villages, should be one of organic irregularity. The houses in those streets were still of modest height, whereas the aim of late historicism (4 and 6) was a rigid, grid-like pattern of tall housing blocks. As early as the beginning of the nineteenth century, *Armengärten*, or poor men's plots, were introduced for the benefit of the masses, herded together as they were and cut off from nature. After 1860 this was to develop into the allotments movement. The attempt by the Viennese, Camillo Sitte, to give artistic shape to the industrial city in accordance with the principles governing earlier towns was doomed to failure. At about the turn of the century the well-to-do bourgeoisie found a way out of the quandary in picturesque, spacious garden cities on the lines of Letchworth in England, built between 1903 and 1904 by Ebenezer Howard, author of *Garden Cities of Tomorrow* (1896).

221 BRUSSELS. *Hôtel Tassel, No. 6, Rue P. E. Janson, built by Victor Horta in 1892/93.*

This building by the Belgian architect, Victor Horta (1861–1947), one of the most important exponents of European *art nouveau*, represents a milestone in the history of the modern private house. Incorporated in a typical street frontage of historicist apartment houses, the decoration of its façade is no longer borrowed from the past; rather it derives, with hardly a backward glance at traditional motifs, from the graceful, curving lines of flowers and foliage, as also from a mature appreciation of the aesthetic possibilities of stone, iron and glass. Everything in the interior, from wall surfaces to furniture and chandeliers, was also informed by *art nouveau* decoration, which today is already a part of history. Of far greater revolutionary import, however, were the constructional and domestic innovations of that time. From the great expanse of window it is plain that extra light was a feature of the new era, just as the part played by iron as a new and essential building material may be inferred from the grills over the windows, from the exposed iron skeleton carrying the conservatory-like ground floor, and from the iron supporting shaft upon which the boldly curving stairway rests. The latter no longer leads up from the traditional corridor, but from an octagonal vestibule, and serves rooms at different levels —a precursor of the modern split-level living unit.

220

222 VIENNA. *District XIII, Steiner House, No. 10, St Veitsgasse, built in 1910 by Adolf Loos, and since greatly altered.*

Seen from the garden side. This middle class town house, one of the first private houses to be constructed of reinforced concrete, marks an important milestone in the development of modern domestic architecture. Loos, who had gone to the United States in 1893 to spend three years there studying the new principles of rationalist architecture (to him, as he wrote in an essay in 1908, ornament was a crime), here created a structure of uncompromising logic in the grouping and spatial sequence of smooth, geometrically simple cubes. The surface of the wall is pierced by door and window openings wholly innocent of mouldings or ledges and is informed by a new, artistically creative urge directed towards a balance of structural mass and proportion.

Following page

223 WEIMAR. *Dwelling-house "Am Horn".*

This model building was erected in 1923 for the Bauhaus exhibition. It was designed by Georg Muche who drew his inspiration from Walter Gropius' and Fred Forbat's project—never in fact realized—for the Bauhaus Am Horn settlement in Weimar which was to have consisted of prefabricated houses on the modular principle. The house was altered and extended in 1926 and restored in 1974. It contains a large and lofty central living-room some six metres square with a study-alcove and a top-light. Round it is a series of small rooms—dining-room, nursery, drawing- and smoking-rooms, visitor's room, kitchen, bath and lobby. The furniture was made in the Bauhaus carpenter's shop to the designs of Benita Otte and Ernst Gebhardt.

The only reliable record of Dresden's original appearance are the townscapes of the Italian painter, Bernardo Belotto, better known as Canaletto. His view of the Rampische Strasse —formerly the most distinguished Baroque street in the Old Town—shows how, as a street composition, the four- and five-storeyed town palaces, with their mansard roofs and their façades betraying a French influence, fit harmoniously into the general scene. The retention here and there of the oriel at the centre, or rising through several storeys at the angles, testifies to the continuing influence of an earlier heritage. The building regulations issued by the Elector in 1736, which prescribed three types of design, depending on the importance of the street, were aimed primarily at producing a spatially homogeneous effect so far as the façade, height of the ridge, and the fenestration were concerned. The disposition of the rooms, on the other hand, was dictated rather by the demands of an advanced style of life. Like everywhere else at the time, the call was for larger and more diversified living-rooms and domestic offices. On the plan of a middle class town house in Dresden, the state-rooms are symmetrically disposed on the street side, while the less important units such as the nursery, servants' quarters, alcoves, dressing rooms, kitchen, privy and open newel stair are irregularly grouped about a well with a sky-light. In imitation of the aristocratic way of life, the grander part of the house was enlarged in the course of the eighteenth century by the addition of a reception room, music room and card room, a library and cabinet of objets d'art. But, inspite of all the splendour and improved amenities, bathrooms were still a rarity and, indeed, the hygienic arrangements still left a great deal to be desired.

During this period certain German towns, which were not princely residences, were given a new and dignified face by their citizens,

173

one such being Leipzig. It was no coincidence that, in an age of mercantilism, this university town, steeped as it was in tradition and famed for its fairs, should have attained a leading position in Germany at the turn of the seventeenth century. The Romanushaus, which we have already discussed, marks the beginning of a period in which patrician families sought to outdo one another in the grandeur of their town palaces. One specialist type was evolved for the purpose of accommodating a periodic influx of visitors and of large quantities of merchandise. This was what was known as a *Durchgangshaus* or *Durchhaus*, a building with a palatial front block accentuated by oriel windows, and a porte-cochère and through-passage leading to a series of courtyards at the rear which, surrounded by multi-storeyed buildings, were used for trading purposes. One of the few examples to have survived the Second World War is the Barthels Hof dating from 1748, one of the last big *Durchgangshäuser* to have been built. Of far greater interest than the front elevation in the market place is the irregular composition of the courtyard, surrounded on three sides by four-storeyed wings "as high as the heavens" which, for all their simplicity, have an air of dignity. They served a dual purpose: they provided storage space for goods as well as lodging for visitors from all over the world. Houses such as these, while conforming both to the nature of the terrain and to the demands of business, nevertheless display a sense of style and constitute the bourgeoisie's most original contribution to the architecture of the time. Such houses were also to be found in other important trading centres where fairs were held, such as Vienna and Strasbourg. Pointing the way to the future were the vaulted commercial premises, the prototypes of the shopping precinct from which the nineteenth century shopping arcade evolved.

164

 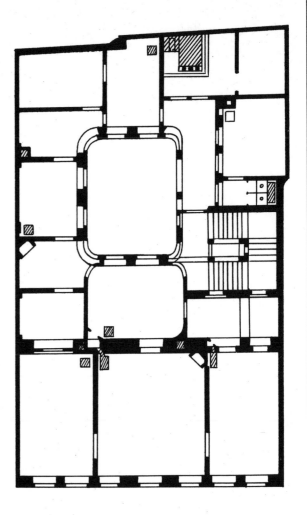

DRESDEN. *No. 19, Grosse Brüdergasse, plan and elevation, circa 1730. Destroyed by bombing, 1945.*

The site is completely built up save for a glass-roofed court. In this high quality middle class town house, which might equally well have done duty as the home of a nobleman or a high official, we may discern a lavish disposition of rooms dictated by a more pretentious way of life and new requirements such as separate rooms for individual members of the family. A characteristic feature is the division of the building into two zones, one spacious and imposing, for social intercourse (ante-room, saloon, with drawing room for the ladies and smoking-room for the gentlemen), the other, for private occasions, of more intimate proportions and irregularly disposed. Within a restricted space provision had to be made both for comfort and for the formalities.

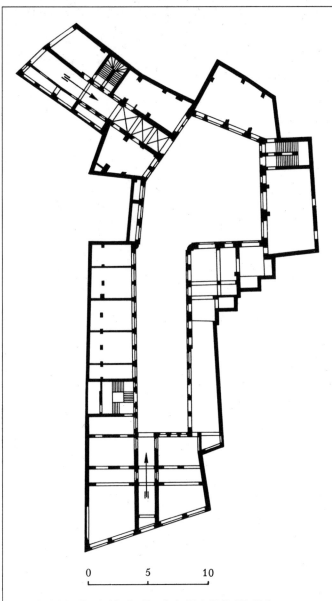

0   5   10

LEIPZIG. *No. 8, Markt, Barthels Hof, 1748 (Ill. 164).*

Plan of the ground floor. The big *Durchgangshaus* is disposed about a long, asymmetrical courtyard. Such premises, affording maximum space for people as well as merchandise, came into being in many European mercantile towns.

In a heavily built-up town centre there was, needless to say, little room for other modern forms of housing that would permit a wholesome existence close to nature. Yet, though the wealthy citizens could not afford to build a great mansion with extensive grounds and garden, he was nevertheless able to emulate the aristocratic way of life by erecting small country houses and villas with gardens on his own land outside the city walls. Leipzig was at one time famous for its many Baroque gardens. The little château built in Gohlis in 1755/6 by Caspar Richter, a merchant and town councillor of Leipzig, owes much of its lay-out and general appearance to Schloss Hubertusburg, a hunting-lodge at Wermsdorf in Saxony. As is proved by the numerous patrician art collections, wealthy citizens bestowed their patronage as lavishly as many of the petty princes. Our illustration shows one château-like summer residence in Erfurt which was built for O.C. Schulze, a Royal Councillor of Lüneburg, in 1722 on the site of an old warehouse in the courtyard of a Renaissance building, Zum Breiten Herd. **178**

In central Germany, where the numerous different trends all had a common denominator, namely a classically restrained version of the Baroque, the patrician house was used less than in South Germany and Austria as a vehicle for the ebullient, high-spirited ornamentation which also marked the region's churches and castles. Admittedly, middle class building showed none of that tendency towards majestic grandeur in which the still potent influence of the Italians, Bernini, Borromini and Guarini may be detected. Instead these block-like buildings, suggestive of palaces, were all the more receptive to the gracious, light-hearted abundance of Rococo decorative forms. Zum Falken in Würzburg, the beautiful, magnificently executed seat of the Franconian bishops, is clothed in a delicate, animated web **174**

307

BERLIN. *St Peter's Church at the end of the Brüderstrasse,*
steel engraving by G.W. Hüttmann from a drawing by Franz
Ludwig Catel, circa 1800.

Only two of the buildings (the second and fifth from the right), shown in
this old print of a typically sober Prussian street in the early classical
manner, have survived. Also characteristic of the period were the
entrances to the cellars which projected from the front of the houses
onto the pavement, a feature that was later done away with. In the
individualism of the façade articulation and the extreme restlessnes of
the skyline we may already detect the most striking characteristics of
the big city as it was later to evolve.

of sculptural decoration. The profusion of embellishment, concentrated primarily round the windows and on the dormer gables, completely masks the simplicity of the main structure; nor does one notice the absence of the typically Baroque method whereby a façade is axially articulated by means of pavilions and pilasters. The angles alone are accentuated architecturally, but for the rest what strikes the eye is the surface, upon which the decoration has run riot.

One of the glories of Bavarian Rococo domestic architecture is the patrician house Kern, at Wasserburg am Inn, consisting of two *175* arcaded houses converted into one patrician residence in which not only have the arcades been retained, but also the oriel windows and the break in alignment between the old structures. Yet the lavish stucco decoration, consisting of foliate motifs, strapwork, painted cartouches and a wide cornice, gives an organic cohesion to the whole, while at the same time the building, with its original approach to the style of the day, is informed by a vernacular delight in form and colour.

In Switzerland and Austria similar tendencies are also in evidence, although the dominant position of the aristocracy in the Austrian provinces was not conducive to the development of a grandiose middle class architecture. Individual examples of houses belonging to wealthy manufacturers or merchants have survived in Basle at Nos. 16 and 18, Rheinsprung, in Zurich at No. 5 Pelikanstrasse, and also in Vienna, notably in the west end of the town where the court officials lived. Other instances, both of them at Innsbruck, are the Neupauer-Palais, built in 1715/16 and the Helblinghaus, which retains its Gothic shell behind a curvilinear gable at the angle and a new façade embellished with acanthus, swags, putti, shell-work in stucco, relief busts and festoons, though few of the middle class town houses of

that time were given such lavish embellishment. The deep chasm of the Getreidegasse in Salzburg reveals what are predominantly smooth façades, with raised facias intended to conceal the serried ranges of pitched roofs. In the network of old, narrow streets, which still survive today, there would not, in any case, have been room for the display of sumptuous individual frontispieces.

South German exuberance was complemented in the North by a tendency to sober Classicism for which Prussian absolutism set the tone. The bourgeoisie had little of its own that could compete with these standards, for the great legacy of brick architecture had been almost entirely lost as a result of the Thirty Years' War. How completely the tradition of the gable-fronted house had been left behind *190, 191* is evident from our example, the Ermelerhaus in Berlin, a city which had been raised to the status of royal residence in 1709. In about 1760 a now affluent purveyor to the Court, one P.F. Damme, converted the building into a palatial, eaves-fronted house with a slightly projecting central pavilion. The frieze and roof balustrade were added in 1804. That the Court had served as a model is evident from the sumptuously appointed staircase and first floor living-rooms, with their wall and ceiling paintings and stucco decorations of rocaille, trellis work, flower and foliage motifs, though these display considerable restraint by comparison with South German Rococo ornamentation.

Only a few middle class town houses such as the Ermelerhaus have survived in Berlin, notably the Knoblauch'sche Haus, No. 23, Poststrasse, built in 1759/60, and the Nicolaihaus of 1709, at No. 13, Brüderstrasse. In their spaciousness, as in the opulence of their ornamentation, they express the pride of the economically independent citizen, whereas the *198, 199* standardized houses in the Dutch Quarter of Potsdam exemplify the absolutist principle as applied to the settlement of citizens who were dependent upon the bounty of the sovereign. Itself sparsely populated, Prussia at one time encouraged the immigration of groups exiled from their home countries, such as the Huguenots and refugees from Bohemia and Württemberg. When, between 1738 and 1742, part of Potsdam was laid out as a settlement for Dutch colonists, King Frederick William I decreed that this should be done in such a way as to preserve the homogeneity of the town. However, the monarch was so gracious as to permit the immigrants' vernacular tradition to live on in the plain, brick, gable-fronted houses. The uniformity of the long rows is complete, being devoid of any decorative elements save for the large volutes on the gables. The working class families inhabiting these houses were mostly employed in manufactories, and the accommodation is predictably simple, while the building material is cheap, plain brick which, being regarded at the time as inferior, would ordinarily have been faced with plaster or dressed stone. Further proof of the extent to which a sovereign might impose his own taste on small town houses such as these is provided by King Frederick II. That splendour-loving monarch did not hesitate to spend more than three million talers on giving new Palladian fronts to no less than six hundred and sixteen dwellings. In some cases several houses might share one palatial façade, built to the designs of, in particular, the architects, Georg Wenzeslaus von Knobelsdorff, Karl von Gontard and Georg Christian Unger, or else copied from famous palaces abroad. His factory operative's house of 1774, intended to accommodate two families and to be used for the development of waste ground in the town of Kholm (Chelmno) on the Vistula, was given a hipped mansard roof, bordered windows, rusticated pilaster strips and a pediment above the doorway. In comparison with this

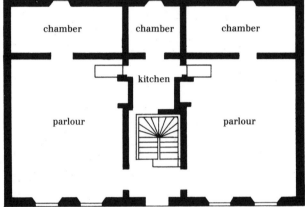

Elevation and plan of a Prussian standardized house for factory workers, 1774, in Chelmno (Kholm).

Frederick II decreed that, however lowly, each house must display a minimum of contemporary stylistic elements in order to chime in with the town as a whole. They could be applied at no great cost in the form of stucco to this two-family house, designed on a central axis. The ground plan provides for a centrally placed, communal kitchen from which the stoves in the living-rooms were stoked. Thus, for the first time the privacy of the home is infringed in the interests of economy.

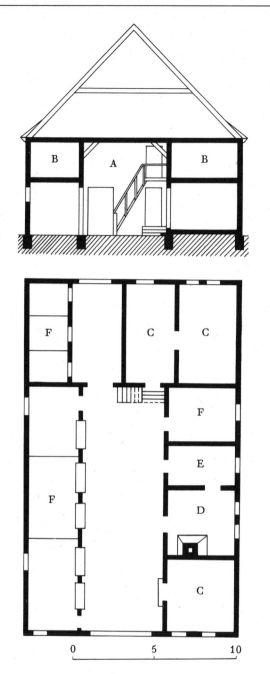

STEINHEIM *(Westphalia). No. 5, Marktstrasse, section and ground plan of an urban farmstead of 1729.*

As in a farmhouse of the North German type, men and beasts all live under the same roof, the accommodation (C = living-room, D = kitchen, E = chamber, F = stalls) being grouped round a hall (A) which rises to the full height of the house. In this case, however, a mezzanine floor (B) has been inserted all the way round to provide extra living space. Urban farmsteads of this kind have a much closer affinity to the farmhouses of their own region than to contemporary middle class town houses.

bureaucratic modernism, the outlook of the mercantile middle classes in the North Sea and Baltic towns, notably Hamburg and Danzig (Gdańsk) with their rich store of tradition, was conservative in the extreme. Their close links with the Netherlands, in particular, meant that the gable-fronted hall-houses, of which they possessed a considerable stock, were enriched by an architecture of a cognate kind. Newly acquired wealth found expression first and foremost in sumptuous and substantial internal appointments of which the halls and the state-rooms on the first floor were the principal beneficiaries. Wainscotting, heavy furniture (including the massive hall cupboard), richly carved woodwork and wide, curving staircases combined the style of an earlier day with the requirements of the new era. In sea ports such as Danzig and Lübeck a lower middle class variant came into being at the start of the eighteenth century in the shape of the so-called *Kanzelhaus* or platform house, a two- or three-storeyed, terraced building divided into apartments consisting of one room and a kitchen. Access to the upper floors was gained from the outside by way of a gallery or platform. This provided an answer in the mercantile town, as did the standardized lower middle class house in the princely seat, to the needs of the unpropertied citizen.

At this time the timber-framed house and the urban farmstead—often one and the same thing—in the smaller towns, were even more deeply rooted in tradition. Until well into the nineteenth century these houses whose character had been formed in the Gothic era, were able, without material alteration to their basic structure, to absorb all innovations by adding a few borrowed decorative elements to the exterior and by introducing a more diversified system of rooms. The sedate, timber-framed 179 houses in the market place of Dornstetten reveal a solipsistic attitude which seeks, not

311

so much to compete with the brick and stone architecture of the Baroque, as to vie with the neighbouring houses both in size and in richness of timber framing. The more modest size of the houses in Gengenbach, and the simplicity of their horizontal wooden members, of which the bressumer alone is moulded, proclaim them to be lower middle class relations of the timber-framed family which, in the course of these centuries, gave many of the towns of central Germany the picturesque character they still possess today. Here we may find a wealth of detail which, rooted as it is in the popular imagination and love of embellishment, is often combined with a predilection for lively polychrome decoration. True, the execution sometimes bears the signature of the "rude mechanic", yet it is precisely this which lends it the charm of originality. The standards of fine art no longer hold good in this, the world of the "little man". In the social framework of the town the urban farmer, as an independent producer, occupied a position that had changed little if at all. Home and byre were frequently combined under the same roof, as in the houses of the peasantry. Because of the risk of fire, however, the steadings in the yard had now been superseded by large barns outside the town.

180

The Contribution of Eastern Europe

Since the Middle Ages and the Renaissance there had been signs of the emergence in eastern and southeastern Europe of national type of middle class town house, signs that persisted in the Baroque era, but only to a limited degree. Nearly the whole of the Balkans was in the thrall of the victorious Turks. Though the Turks' sphere of influence was reduced to some extent by their defeat at the hands of a combined force outside Vienna in

1683, the advent of new rulers did not spell liberation for the countries concerned. Still held in subjugation and hampered by the changing fortunes of war, the towns developed slowly and late, as did the capitalist mode of production. Nevertheless Bulgaria comes within our purview halfway through the eighteenth century as a new country with national aspirations. Again, under Peter the Great (1689–1725), the hitherto backward Russian Empire made tremendous strides; from that period on its brick and stone architecture was to make a contribution of its own to the multifariousness of the European middle class town house. The kingdom of Poland, on the other hand, as a result of frequent wars and struggles for power, was in the throes of an acute crisis and had become a pawn in the game of European secret diplomacy, a game which, at the end of the eighteenth century, was to lead to her partition amongst her more powerful neighbours. The middle classes were unable to develop into a social force while, in the field of architecture, it is clear that, as compared with the splendid edifices of the Church and the aristocracy, the middle class town house was generally compelled to play a more modest role than was the case in other countries. However, the picture is of far greater interest in localities where traditional commercial links were still in existence or had been resumed. Amongst them, following the revival of the North Sea and Baltic trade routes, were seaports which had been towns of importance as early as the Middle Ages. The merchant princes of Riga, whose splendid façades had been converted after the manner of the classical Baroque of France and the Netherlands, were *185* at the very forefront of fashion. The Reuternhaus, belonging to one Johann Reutern, a councillor and former inhabitant of Lübeck, *181* and the Dannensternhaus, built at the end of the seventeenth century by a Dutch émigré

RIGA. *Dannenstern House, No. 21, Marstallstrasse (Ill. 181).*

The palatial façade, with its symmetrical composition of two grand
doorways and classical pediments, as also an inserted mezzanine floor,
conceals the earlier nucleus, plainly visible in section, with its irregular
disposition of rooms and multi-storeyed roof space for the storage of
merchandise.

and leading merchant, ennobled by the Swedes, are outstanding examples of the palatial type of middle class town house in the West European idiom, which was quickly taken up by the local patricians and artists. Consisting of two medieval houses, the Dannensternhaus served, not only as a home, but also as a warehouse of considerable capacity. Its façade is crowned by a mighty architrave which, however, does not blend very happily with the lofty roof.

The Baroque era saw the erection in Polish towns of numerous magnates' residences as well as the edifices of the victorious Counter-Reformation. Middle class domestic architecture, however, remained relatively unimportant until about the middle of the eighteenth century, when a new phase of economic prosperity led to the reconstruction or extension of existing premises. This was aimed primarily at adapting what were usually narrow façades to the taste of the times, and many of the squares and streets still retain today the aspect they were given then. As elsewhere, however, the richest citizens strove to emulate the new, richly decorated urban palaces. At Toruń, the palace of the bishops of Kujawien, dating from *182* the late seventeenth century, still retains the old predilection for covering wall surfaces with stucco ornamentation, while the Warsaw palace belonging to the merchant prince Praž- *183* mowski displays a façade decorated in the courtly, more refined manner of Polish Late Baroque. After their destruction in the Second World War, many of these beautiful patrician houses were restored to their original condition. Amongst them was the magnificent Uphagen House in Danzig which, as a privileged mercantile city in the eighteenth century, engendered a middle class style of life with a regional flavour of its own.

As in Poland, the aristocracy and the Catholic Church in those parts of Bohemia under Austrian rule developed a Baroque architecture so successful that even towns steeped in tradition were given a new face. In Prague, whole districts had to make way for vast and magnificent palaces, churches and monasteries. During the eighteenth century the well-to-do bourgeoisie followed suit by converting large numbers of old houses. For the most part these were simply decorated buildings of between three and five storeys. Since the width of the plots and the nature of the streets remained unchanged, it is possible to see new and old combining to form a prime example of an organic synthesis of various epochs. Few middle class town houses were able to vie with the palaces of the nobility, as did the house Zum goldenen Hirschen, built by the famous architect Kilian Ignaz Dientzenhofer between 1725 and 1726.

Hungary, depopulated and badly devastated during the expulsion of the Turks between 1683 and 1699, still remained a part of the Hapsburg Empire. Hence, save in Transylvania, Baroque middle class architecture experienced only a very modest development. The towns, most of which were small (in the first half of the eighteenth century Budapest itself could still boast no more than a few thousand inhabitants) saw the emergence of a local form of middle class architecture that owes much to the influence of Italy and even more, as time wore on, to that of Austria. Thus a characteristic feature of the townscape of *187* Györ, the corner oriels on the Baroque houses, point to exemplars in the Danubian towns of Krems and Linz. In Budapest, the houses were almost exclusively two-storeyed, their façades being articulated simply by means of cornices and string courses above and between the floors, plain window surrounds with decorative aprons benath the sills, doorways with basket arches, and niches containing effigies of saints. By the middle of the eighteenth century the *Zopfstil* had taken hold, a contemporary Rococo-neo-classical style which lacked both the elegance of Rococo and the baroque exuberance apparent throughout the Catholic countries. With the return of prosperity to Hungary in the early part of the nineteenth century, this style was to culminate in a grandiose neo-classical type of architecture.

For almost a hundred years after the Turkish withdrawal from Hungary the Slavs of the South remained under the yoke of a weak but still militant Osmanli Empire—a yoke which Bulgaria was not to throw off until 1878. But all attempts to suppress the despised rayahs or "cattle" were ultimately doomed to failure in the face of the growing movement for political autonomy which, at the beginning of the eighteenth century, had ushered in the era of "national rebirth". It is no coincidence that Slavic architecture should display a markedly national character, consisting as it does of a combination of the stylistic elements of the fine arts and of the indigenous peasant tradition. Indeed, this mingling of contemporary style and vernacular legacy has always been a determining factor in the national evolution of the middle class town house. The contribution made in the Baroque era by the rising urban middle classes of Norway, Russia and the Balkans to the multiplicity of types of European town house necessarily falls within this category. In the Balkan peninsula the evolution of the Bulgarian type is of particular interest. Here the emergent middle classes, consisting of artisans and international traders, were isolated from the influence of European Baroque and thus resorted to the indigenous type of house in which they also incorporated certain elements from Turkish domestic architecture, a fact no doubt largely attributable to the connections existing between certain of the merchants and money-lenders (known as *corbadži*) and the Turks.

The rooms, originally few in number and function—cellar and storage space on the ground floor, and living and sleeping accommodation on the first—were augmented downstairs by the addition of a kitchen and a workshop or shop opening onto the street, and upstairs by an open gallery known as a *chardak*, sometimes in the form of a projecting structure resembling a balcony. Since villages and small towns did not afford sufficient protection, the wealthier merchants, in particular, demanded a house and courtyard complex that was both strong and defensible. The result was a kind of private fortress, reminiscent of the seats of the early urban aristocracy. Bluff, unwelcoming and totally unadorned, it had a ground storey of stout rubble walls up to ninety centimetres thick whose only openings were small barred windows and narrow entrances which were fitted with heavy, iron-studded doors. Well preserved examples of this type of house have survived in the village of Arbanassi near Tirnovo. The plans of the ground storey and first floor of Konstanzaliev's house which, as a caravanserai, was situated in a courtyard surrounded by high walls, reveal a multiplicity of rooms which, scarcely though inferior to a patrician's house in western Europe, had unmistakable characteristics of their own. Thus, all the rooms on the substantial ground floor, namely the two secret cellars, the guard-room and the stables, are devoted exclusively to business and security. The timber-framed upper floor is much less solidly constructed and its rooms, save for the kitchen, pantry and servants' bedchambers, are richly appointed, with carved ceilings, wainscotting and household textiles in the reception rooms, living-rooms, dining-room, and bedrooms. As in many other countries in southern Europe (and also in the East), the unadorned exterior conceals a great degree of comfort and luxury within. It is a *195* contrast we also encounter in the Hadžiiliev house built in about 1800 by a well-to-do merchant in Arbanassi. The building, at the end of a fortified courtyard, is low and block-like, and has a tiled, low pitched, hipped roof, with wide, oversailing eaves and wooden cross-braces. The interior arrangements include two guest rooms, a fire-place in the dining-room, and a kitchen equipped with wooden balcony. On the courtyard side there is an oriel-like barred window through which the master of the house could shoot when attacked by hostile intruders.

As far as the internal fittings were concerned, especially those in the living quarters on the upper floor, carved woodwork assumed particular importance. In these hilly, well-wooded regions there was an ample supply of timber. Wood had been employed as a building material from time immemorial and, indeed, was to continue in use in towns such as Trevna, Koprivshtitza and Žeravna, until the turn of the eighteenth century. This familiarity with wood, extending back over many generations, had given rise to a highly developed form of decorative carving which could be exploited to the full when it came to fitting out the interiors of middle class town houses. An impression of one such interior may be gained from the reception-cum-living-room in the house built in 1718 for Sava Filaretov in Žeravna. *189* It is lined throughout with wood whose richness is further enhanced by finely carved geometrical motifs as well as by intarsia work and the combined use of different kinds of wood. The opulent furniture then popular in Europe is absent. Rather, the valuable coloured carpets and the abundance of floor cushions show how strong was the influence of the East on the middle class way of life. Amidst these sumptuous surroundings the master of the house would settle down comfortably with his guests on a vast sofa or divan, a kind of raised platform which was a male preserve, and devote himself to business, con-

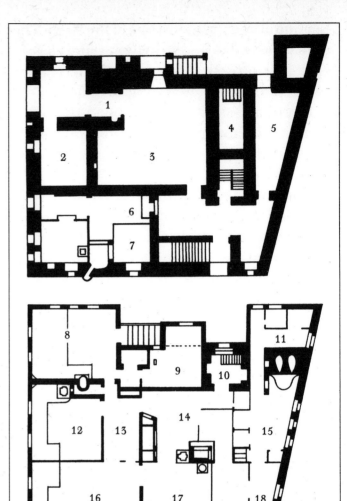

ARBANASSI *near Tirnovo. Konstanzaliev's house, late eighteenth century, plans of the ground and first floors.*

In turbulent times the thick walls on the ground floor of this isolated, fortress-like building, belonging to a Bulgarian international trader, were necessary in order to protect the lives and property of the occupants and to do so in a space which, though confined, was subdivided in a great variety of ways. As a last resort, refuge could be taken in two underground hiding-places which were reached from the first floor living-quarters by a secret stair. On the first floor were a number of rooms whose specific nature derived from an advanced style of life in which social status, morals and eastern influences all played a part. On the right-hand side of the same floor, accessible by a separate stair, were the domestic offices. The functions of the individual rooms were as follows: 1 = first underground hiding-place; 2 = cellar; 3 = storeroom; 4 = second underground hiding-place with small stairway from the first floor; 5 = stables; 6 = watchman's room; 7 = small downstairs kitchen; 8 = rest room; 9 = lying-in room; 10 = entrance to second underground hiding-place; 11 = servants' room; 12 = bed chamber; 13 = passage; 14 = dining-room; 15 = kitchen with bread oven; 16 = reception room, reached by the main staircase; 17 = living-room; 18 = serving room or pantry.

versation and the pleasures of the flesh. These pleasures were unobtrusively catered for, in that still largely patriarchal society, by the womenfolk and servants.

We shall close this survey with a brief account of some of the middle class town houses of this period which still survive in Russia. Despite the subjugation of the towns in what was a now centrally governed empire, middle-class prospects had improved as a result of the emergence of a young industry with a countrywide market. One consequence of this was the abandonment of the traditional wooden house in favour of larger, multi-storeyed brick buildings of the kind erected by wealthy merchants in important commercial and other centres such as Moscow, Yaroslavl, Pskov or Gorodok. Some of these, as may be seen from our example—a house belonging *193* to the mercantile family of Pogankin which dates from the beginning of the seventeenth century—were big homesteads capable of accommodating large numbers of people and considerable quantities of goods. Despite its lay-out, reminiscent of a *cour d'honneur*, there is nothing palatial about this building. It is constructed of stone, no doubt for reasons of safety, in view of the frequency with which earlier towns of timber houses had been ravaged by fire. No adornment enlivens its massive walls which were pierced by small, irregularly disposed windows. By contrast, the popular penchant for richly articulated forms and strong colour was all the more freely indulged in the original, upper storey, with its animated, restless roof scape that derived from Russo-Byzantine church architecture, and its projecting, outside stair—then a typical feature of Russian houses—which, being roofed-over, also served as a kind of lobby. Since these houses were built of timber, unfortunately neither the first storey nor the stair has survived.

In an account of his travels written in 1630, the Patriarch Makarios, speaking of Moscow, refers to fine, new, solidly built brick and stone houses of two or three storeys. The plaster walls of the ground floor, many of them reinforced with iron rods, were invariably adorned with painted decoration and supported a wooden upper floor. This upper floor contained the living quarters and had long galleries or balconies, as well as, in many cases, gables and turrets with onion-shaped domes. The construction of tiled stoves had been so perfected as to permit the expansion of the living accommodation. Rooms such as the saloon and the state-room which were devoted to social intercourse, assumed an important role. *192* The house in Kaluga belonging to a rich merchant by the name of Korobov which dates from the end of the seventeenth century, shows how the tradition of rich, colourful wood-carving lived on in the decoration of brick and stone architecture, and how Renaissance and Baroque motifs were borrowed from western Europe and applied to façades in a charming and altogether indigenous guise.

There can be no doubt that this process, namely an organic, constantly enriched, blending of old and new in the Russian middle class town house would have continued if the decrees of Peter the Great at the beginning of the eighteenth century had not subverted every aspect of social life, and if new standards had not been set by the opening-up of the country to the West. Such offshoots of Baroque and Rococo as reached Russia made little impact upon its architecture, a shortcoming which was more than compensated for by the rapid establishment of the neo-classical trend in mighty churches, palaces and government buildings. Here, as in other European monarchies, homogeneous town planning played an important role. Several hundred plans were submitted to the "Moscow and St Petersburg

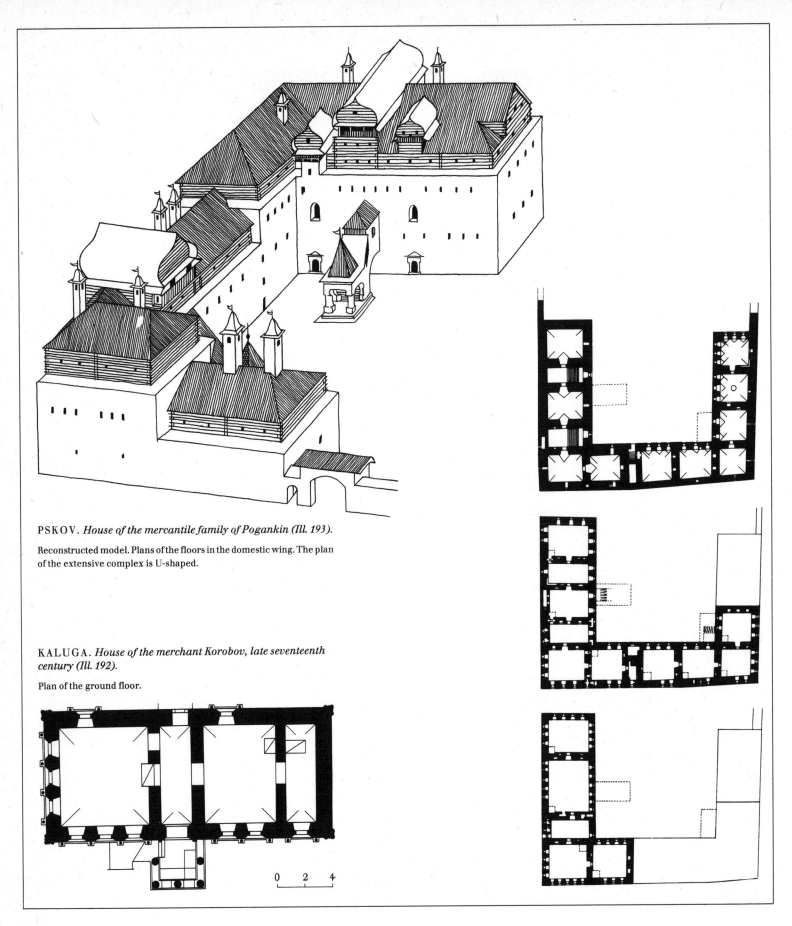

PSKOV. *House of the mercantile family of Pogankin (Ill. 193).*

Reconstructed model. Plans of the floors in the domestic wing. The plan of the extensive complex is U-shaped.

KALUGA. *House of the merchant Korobov, late seventeenth century (Ill. 192).*

Plan of the ground floor.

0 2 4

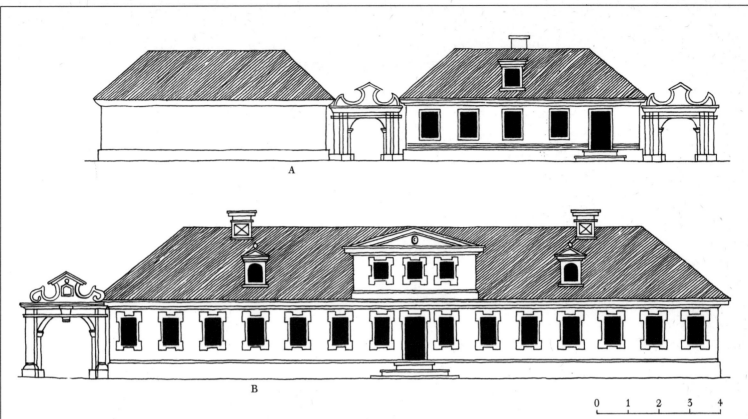

A

B

0   1   2   3   4

LENINGRAD. *Designs for the façades of three types of "model house", prepared in 1714 by Domenico Trezzini to the order of Peter I, account being taken in each case of the social status and financial situation of the client.*

A = single-storeyed timber house for the "common" people, B = single-storeyed timber house for the well-to-do, C = two-storeyed stone house for the "quality" with cellar, mezzanine floor and two entrances. When the new Russian Imperial capital was founded in 1703, Peter the Great stipulated that its domestic architecture, like that in the seats of other absolutist European rulers, should present as homogeneous an appearance as possible. Thus, the two-storeyed houses were built on the south shore of Vasilevski Island, one of the finest sites in the city, while the single-storeyed houses were confined to the central part of the island. More than four thousand almost identical "model houses" went up between 1711 and 1716. Both in regard to design and building materials (stone and brick) these houses mark a complete departure from traditional timber architecture and its sometimes rich embellishment. This is attributable to the uncompromising endeavour to overcome Russian "backwardness". However, the Baroque treatment of the façade, still plainly in evidence here, gained little or no currency in the Russian middle class town house. From the middle of the eighteenth century onwards, Russian Classicism, which was soon to establish itself in grandiose form in château architecture, exerted a decisive influence on the middle class town palace.

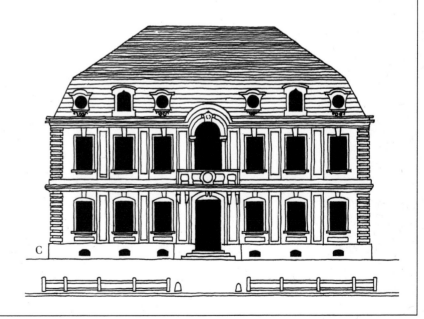

C

319

Committee for Stone and Brick Architecture",
in accordance with a decree issued in 1768
relating to the planning of each of those cities.
The control of urban development involved a
rational system of house design and, as far as
decoration was concerned, the repetition of a
few classical motifs. These fundamental reforms, directed towards homogeneity, made
possible the introduction of new and cheaper
building materials and methods, which in turn
put citizens in the position of being able to
build palatial houses. This development was
aided by industrial growth: by the end of the
eighteenth century there were more than two
thousand factories. It enabled manufacturers
and wealthy merchants to erect houses such
as that designed for a man of means, while a
house designed for a poorer man was a small,
one-storeyed building articulated only by means
of the simplest Baroque classical features in
the shape of string courses and window and
door frames.

The Eclipse of a Building Type in the Nineteenth Century

Here a huge town, continuous and compact,
Hiding the face of earth for leagues – and there,
Where not a habitation stood before,
The abodes of men irregularly massed,
Like trees in forests, – spread through spacious tracts,
O'er which the smoke of unremitting fires
Hangs permanent and plentiful as wreaths
Of vapour glittering in the morning sun.

In this astonishingly impressive picture, painted by the English poet, William Wordsworth (1770–1850), at a time when European industrialization was in full spate and the middle class ethos has emerged triumphant, there lies concealed another, almost anachronistic phenomenon—the end of the middle class town house as both an organism combining the multifarious functions of home and business and a witness to the personality of its inhabitants. True, it lived on as a building type, but what it gained in terms of quantity—and this to a hitherto unparalleled extent—it lost as time went by, in terms of architectural originality. Nor were any noteworthy results achieved in this field until the latter part of the nineteenth century, with the reforms of the English Domestic Revival. Of importance, too, were the technological advances made in the domestic sphere, namely the introduction of gas and electricity, drainage, piped water, the water-closet, central heating, the telephone, electric bell, speaking-tube and so forth which, together with the varied nature of internal appointments and developments in the furniture industry, laid the foundations of domestic comfort as we know it today. No less important was the progress made in building technology as a result of more rational construction, prefabricated parts, the use of machinery and the introduction of new materials such as iron, cement, synthetics and re-inforced concrete.

However, these civilizing innovations achieved by the bourgeoisie in the nineteenth century could do nothing to postpone the end of the middle class town house as an historically evolved form. Yet the symptoms of its end are quite the reverse of those attending its uncomplicated if ill-defined beginnings in the early Middle Ages. For neither the multiplicity of types nor the new historical circumstances contributed to the further development of this type; rather they were conducive to the disappearance of important formative elements, a process already evident in the eighteenth century and now approaching its climax. As an architectural type the middle class town house had had its day.

A vital factor was the explosive growth of the productive forces which, after the initial phase of the industrial revolution in England, rapidly did away throughout Europe with one of the essential characteristics of the early middle class town house, namely its dual function as home and business. Even the most spacious middle class mansions were no longer large enough for the accommodation of machinery, the receipt and despatch of vast quantities of merchandise and the running of commercial and industrial enterprises. The departments traditionally belonging to the middle class town house—workshop, shop, store-rooms and counting-house—were transferred elsewhere, to become separate architectural types, namely factories, warehouses, shopping precincts, department stores, market halls, office and administrative buildings and stock exchanges. The sole function still served by the middle class town house was that of a private dwelling. The more well-to-do, whose houses had now become largely independent of the fields of industry and commerce mentioned above, moved out of the amorphous urban sprawl to districts that were quieter or more suited to social intercourse.

The effect of the restructuring of society was to be no less momentous. Thousands of once capable craftsmen and independent tradesmen belonging to the middle or lower middle classes were driven out of business and ruined. Together with an incessant stream of impoverished rural labourers, they went to swell the numbers of the industrial proletariat who were compelled to live in tenements, back yard hovels, slums, inner suburbs and on company estates, often in quite indescribable conditions. In 1800 home owners constituted some sixty per cent of the citizens of a town, as compared with barely ten per cent a hundred years later. Thus the majority had now become tenants and, as such, could have no say in the design of the houses they inhabited. Anonymity engulfed the middle class town house. As objects of speculation and investment, the bulk of dwelling-houses were no longer intimately associated with their occupants who might still have considered themselves part of a community. Thus domestic architecture may be seen as, so to speak, off-the-peg housing for two groups of users—on the one hand, superior apartment blocks and private houses, detached or otherwise, standing amidst gardens in select districts, on the other, tenements and terrace houses in heavily built-up suburbs and working class districts. A stark account of the wretched living conditions of the working class (e.g. a family of eleven or more to a single room) was given by a contemporary eye-witness, Friedrich Engels, who saw in them a cogent argument for the necessity of social change by revolutionary means. The co-operative building societies that were already coming into being by the middle of the century, failed, as did their reformist successors, to find any effective counterpart to the high density architecture of the middle classes. Denied the ownership of the means of production and hence largely destitute, the proletariat, unlike the bourgeoisie in feudal times, was not yet in a position to put into practice architectural ideas of its own.

Even the bourgeois no longer had any close rapport with his house. The impassioned harangue delivered by a contemporary, Vicomte Charles de Launay, in the turbulent year 1848, testifies more eloquently to this than could any later account: "O men of the people!" he exclaimed, "who is better off than you? That proud, Parisian bourgeois, perhaps, whom you pursue with such odium? He possesses neither châteaux nor hôtels, neither woods nor meadows. He rents a cramped and dreary apartment in a so-called tenement, to wit, a beehive of plaster. There you will find none of the amenities of a prosperous existence; he has neither space, nor light, nor a view, nor air, nor calm, nor privacy, nor peace. There he lives, in company with people with whom he is not acquainted; he knows nothing of them, save their shortcomings; he knows not whether his neighbours are honest, kind-hearted or friendly—all he knows is that they are pleasure-seeking and obtrusive, that they slam doors, return home at a late hour and that, at meal-times, they eat curious foods whose nauseating smell permeates the corridors. But then, you may well object, that uncomfortable apartment is richly furnished and, if he does not own the house, he does at least own the furniture ... and what furniture! ... a dreadful hotch-potch of hideous objects, reflecting the bad taste of every period ... O men of the people, did you only know how ugly is that which you envy him, you would forgive the bourgeois his good fortune ..."

Hence a detailed examination of the course up to the present day of this different kind of urban middle class domestic architecture, in all its variety of types, does not properly fall within the province of what is an historical survey. The development we have described,

along with its transitional manifestations, a development which had been ushered in by historicism, was to culminate in Classicism with its universal tendency to erode the multiplicity of regional types of middle class town house. The private house now experienced an eclipse, for the standards were set by the big new building types emanating from communal and national bodies as a result of expansion in the fields of culture (museums and theatres), education and science (universities, schools and libraries), civil administration (houses of parliament, town halls, law-courts, etc.), communications (stations, post offices, hotels), social services (hospitals), social and leisure activities (clubs, meeting houses, pump-rooms, exhibition halls, baths), and national pomp (monuments, halls of fame, etc.), to which might be added the continued building of châteaux and churches. To the despairing question "In what style shall we build?", posed by the architect Heinrich Hübsch in 1828, this period whose principle was "architecture means embellishment", could provide all too many answers drawn from a new and more profound knowledge of past epochs. However, it is symptomatic that the middle class town house's own antecedents should only be invoked when clothed in the stylistically rich garb of advanced cultures such as that of the Renaissance and the Baroque. The demand for the modishly up-to-date made greater inroads on the existing stock of private town houses than in any previous century. Against the background of a hitherto unparalleled population explosion, towns burst out of their constricting walls and continued to expand unchecked. Almost everywhere the heart of the big city was sacrificed to the development of the modern commercial centre, and only where industrialization was either absent or slow in establishing itself did a town retain something of its former aspect. It was not until the nineteenth century was drawing to a close that a maturer and more profound comprehension of the beauty of what was old gave rise to the endeavour, not only to improve the state of modern architecture, but also to preserve the existing stock of historic houses whose full value seems to have been appreciated only in our present century of high density industrial building.

True, it was no longer possible to inject new life into the old middle class town house. But in the chapters that follow we shall endeavour to portray the decline of what was a fascinating building type by citing examples of its progeny. It will be seen that, even in the era of historicism, so eminently important an impulse as the crystallization of national consciousness in certain parts of Europe was able to produce remarkable results in the field of domestic architecture.

The Standardizing Influence of the Classical Revival

The epoch of the Classical Revival in the second half of the eighteenth century, in which the Antique was ever more frequently invoked—this time based on systematic archaeological knowledge—contributed more than any other to the standardization of the middle class town house throughout Europe. The rapid abandonment of national and regional diversity in favour of an eaves-fronted building of cubical clarity, with a few, austere, decorative features and a monumental, symmetrically placed portico or pavilion surmounted by a pediment, is attributable to a number of reasons to which allusion has already been made. Among them we might further cite the complete disappearance, even at this stage, of the multi-functional nature of the middle class town house. Of equal importance was the contemporary en-

deavour to offset the bombast of Baroque and the decorative elegance of Rococo with the restrained neo-classical ethic of "noble simplicity and quiet grandeur", as propounded by J. J. Winckelmann. "In the classically rigorous traditions of the Roman Republic," wrote Karl Marx, "the bourgeoisie found the ideals and the artistic forms, the self-delusion which they needed if they were to conceal from themselves the limited bourgeois implications of their struggles and maintain their passions at the level of great historical tragedy." Indeed, the middle class town house, reduced for the most part to the function of a dwelling, whether villa, town palace or apartment house, was at very least a badge of militancy in the above sense. Neo-classical tendencies which were, moreover, of a markedly aristocratic, absolutist cast, had long since established themselves in domestic architecture, more especially that of northern Europe. The sober spirit of Neo-Classicism, as manifested in the transitional phases of the Louis-seize style in France and the *Zopfstil* in Germany, permeated the whole of architecture to assume, in the French Empire style of the Restoration period after 1815, an imperial character that corresponded in German middle class domestic building to the modest world of Biedermeier.

The grandiose Utopia of a new architecture—the so-called revolutionary architecture—produced by, amongst others, Boullée, Ledoux, Lequeu and Desprez in France after the momentous events of 1789, was of short duration. Though most of these men had been royal architects whose point of departure had been Neo-Classicism, they succumbed to the spell of the Enlightenment and to the Utopian socialist ideas of, for instance, Rousseau's *Contrat Social*, and evolved on paper bold visions of a future architecture based on stereometric forms. At the time, however, most of these projects proved incapable of realization, a case

PARIS. *Rue de Chartres, from a contemporary pen drawing by Friedrich Gilly made in 1793.*

The German architect, a fervent supporter of the French Revolution, considered the twisting Rue de Chartres, situated outside the Cité (the Gare du Nord has since been built in the vicinity), to be a worthy subject for his pen. In this quarter of artisans and petty bourgeois it was not imperial grandeur that determined the character of the architecture, but rather the juxtaposition of the indigenous, the neo-classically modern and the startlingly new. This last may be descried in the background where there is a building that contains both shops and apartments. Here the grid-like pattern formed by the railed loggias is strongly suggestive of a modern façade. The concept of apartments that were structurally practical and afforded an equal amount of external space to each tenant marked a first step towards a high density architecture tailored to the needs of the occupants. As a programme, however, it remained without a sequel at that time.

in point being Ledoux's design—two horizontal, interlocking cylinders—for a tyre-maker's house in the "ideal city" of Chaux. For this architect paid scant heed to existing structural techniques or to the functional aspects of a building, and chose to ignore, not only cherished notions of domestic architecture, but also the reality of a handicraft in process of decay. As in other examples of his designs for artisans, merchants, artists and officials, his "modernity" lies in his radical rejection of all that is traditional, and in his invention of symbolic forms (*architecture parlante*) for the house. Nor was the artist's imaginative extravagance in any way dictated by the need, say, to eliminate social differences, as is indeed borne out by one of Boullée's sayings: "The modest exteriors of houses of the poor help to enhance the grandeur of the rich."

It would be useless to speculate on the direction in which architecture might have developed had those ideas borne fruit. What is noteworthy, however, is the fact that so radical a subversion of all existing notions should have taken place against a background of a mighty social upheaval whose aims (liberty, equality and fraternity), were unattainable even in those days. The architectural reality was another matter, being as replete with contradiction as the bourgeois ethos that was then prevalent. A severely monumental form of Neo-Classicism in which Egyptian elements were comingled had already gained ground at the time of the Directory and was to continue unchecked into the Napoleonic era of the Empire style. Like his absolutist predecessors, Napoleon I wanted to invest the French metropolis with the greatest possible degree of splendour. In accordance with a unified plan, magnificent streets such as the Rue de Rivoli, the Rue de Castiglione and the Rue des Pyramides were lined, as in the past, with fine if uniform palatial apartment houses occupied

325

by middle class tenants. A decree of 1804 forbade the erection of workshops for artisans in this imposing quarter near the Louvre. Irrespective of their function, the houses were given a continuous colonnade on the ground floor. Flat roofs were forbidden and gables banned. Arcades, plain window frames, straight pediments above mansard windows and continuous cornices with dentillated friezes were the components of the economical vocabulary used to express the desire for a monumentality that impresses by reason of the size of the composition as a whole and of the reiteration of similar motifs. However, the small sketch of the Rue de Chartres in Paris, made by the German architect Friedrich Gilly (1772–1800), testifies to the existence, away from the big boulevards, of an apartment house architecture of a very practical, indeed almost modern, kind, and one hardly touched by considerations of style. The drawing, dated 1793, already presages the typically irregular street front of days to come. Here we have a palatial building side by side with houses devoid of adornment, amongst them, where the street bends, one with a grid-like pattern of loggias, which might well have been built today. It was undoubtedly this practical, lucidly articulated structure which led Gilly to make the drawing in the first place, for as an architect deeply impressed by the events and the architecture of the Revolution he, too, was in pursuit of simple and rationally determined forms. Yet this promise of a domestic architecture based on function and practicality was doomed to frustration, so deeply engrained was the doctrine that embellishment was essential to this form of art.

For a century or more there was a gulf between practical requirements on the one hand and this or that simulacrum of style on the other. Not that the more intelligent were unaware of that gulf but, confronted by a society which craved prestige, they were unable to bridge it. It was only in the underrated, less centrally situated functional buildings erected by engineers and anonymous builders, e. g. factories, warehouses, bridges, conservatories and, later, railway stations and exhibition and market halls, that the seeds of a modern aesthetic based on function and materials were able to germinate. When, in 1826, Karl Friedrich Schinkel, the leading German neo-classical architect, paid a visit to England, at that time the most advanced of all industrial countries, he was particularly intrigued by the mighty edifices of the new industrial architecture, as depicted by Joseph Wright of Derby in his romantic painting of Arkwright's cotton spinning mill: "Boxes like these," Schinkel wrote, "are eight or nine storeys high and sometimes long enough to have forty windows to a row. The columns are of iron, as are the beams above them . . . From a distance a host of such boxes, standing in very elevated positions . . . make a wonderful sight, especially at night when thousands of windows are aglow with the brilliant light of gas . . . These vast piles, executed in red brick by a foreman, without heed to architecture and solely for reasons of bare necessity, create an impression that is exceedingly awesome."

Needless to say, "without heed to architecture" also applied to the brick working men's houses sited either haphazardly or in ordered rows in the gloomy purlieus of industrial towns—a fact rarely noted, and then only by realistic writers such as Charles Dickens. From this anonymous mass the middle class town house was at ever greater pains to distinguish itself. In Bath, the watering-place of the *beau monde*, we encounter the neo-classical type of the English terrace house in what is probably its finest form, both from the point of view of monumentality and from that of town planning. Conventions of a taste shared in common

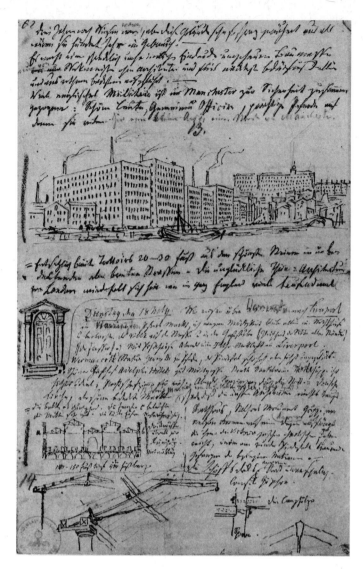

KARL FRIEDRICH SCHINKEL, "Factory Buildings in Manchester", sketch from the journal of his travels in England, dated 17 July, 1826. Staatliche Museen zu Berlin (Collection of Drawings).

Schinkel's written account of the nature of this English manufacturing town is here illustrated with a sketch of a long range of factory buildings —for the most part spinning-mills—on the bank of a canal. These vast edifices, described by Schinkel as "awesome" and "executed without heed to architecture", are seven to eight storeys high and wholly devoid of architectonic articulation, the only features being the rows of windows and the flat roofs.

and not despotic decrees that induced the prospective owners of the thirty houses in the 210 Royal Crescent, erected by John Wood the Younger between 1767 and 1777, to renounce individual designs in favour of the imposing overall effect of a semi-elliptical, château-like frontage. Indigenous forms, not all of them by any means strictly classical, go to make up what is an exceedingly varied domestic architecture in the towns of an England whose population had grown from a bare seven million in 1760 to twelve million in 1820. Traditional features, such as the bay window and the gable, were retained, while the design of façades, as is borne out by the houses built in 1800 in Bedford Place, London, was exceedingly animated, if not actually restless. Light balconies and galleries with elegant cast iron railings, plaster rendered in various colours, and curvilinear parapets, serve to enliven the whole. The integration of nature and historic forms was early apparent in the land that gave birth to Romanticism and from which would emanate before very long the first reformative ideas in the field of domestic architecture.

For almost a century the character of the wealthy citizen's town house in Tsarist Russia was to be determined by a strict, if somewhat ponderous, form of Neo-Classicism which, having made rapid headway, and being further aided and abetted by pernickety buildings regulations, had become all but universally established by 1760. The difference between the numerous mansions of the nobility, most of which were erected in Moscow after the fire of 1812, and the houses of the bourgeoisie was one only of degree.

Owing to a shortage of stone and brick, timber long continued to predominate in the simpler forms of domestic architecture. With its projecting, columned portico, the small 212 wood and plaster palace of the Stanitsky family testifies to the national predilection for a struc-

327

tural design that was strongly articulated spatially, but was nevertheless compact, with a marked axial emphasis. The plan, too, reveals the lucidity of the system, the rooms being disposed along intersecting corridors. The larger rooms on the street side were chiefly reserved for social occasions, while those at the back served the everyday needs of the family. Shortly after the middle of the nineteenth century the apartment house of several storeys also gained a footing as a contemporary type of high density architecture in the larger Russian towns.

It need hardly be said that, despite formal similarities imposed by international Neo-Classicism, traditional building customs and subtle national differences continued to exist. Thus the middle class domestic architecture of the Scandinavian countries was characterized by a Neo-Classicism of a markedly sober kind. When Copenhagen was being rebuilt after the disastrous fire of 1807, C. F. Hansen evolved a style of domestic architecture which adhered rigidly to Doric forms. In distant Norway, which finally attained complete independence in 1814, the remarkable simplicity of buildings such as the brick middle class town *204* house in Bergen bears witness to the country's meagre economic resources. Finland, a Russian possession since 1809, also fell in with the general stylistic trends then current in Europe. True, in Helsingfors, elevated to the status of capital city in 1812, Neo-Classicism was adopted only for the high density communal buildings designed by J. A. Ehrenström and C. L. Engel. The detached one- and two-storeyed timber dwelling-houses, on the other hand, were richly decorated with carvings after the pattern of the houses of Finnish farmers, whose way of life they also reflect, whereas in the majority of European towns, the private house already denoted privileged status in an age of high-density architecture, as is evident in particular from the vast increase in the building of villas.

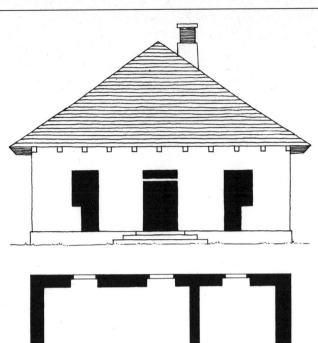

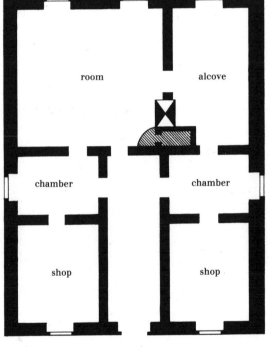

Design for standard houses in small Polish towns, from P. Aigner, 1791. Plan and elevation of a tradesman's house.

The design is suited to the needs of the future occupants, while the severely symmetrical façade articulation is devoid of all embellishment.

This grand and exclusive form of individualism could be indulged only by the wealthier members of the bourgeoisie who were in a position to buy large plots at a time when land was already at a premium. At the same time, the function of the private house as workshop or place of business was steadily dwindling in importance. True, the detached, palatial house of several storeys which David Gilly was commissioned to build in 1802 for the publisher Vieweg on a prominent site in the Burgplatz *196, 197* in Brunswick, still combined the functions of publishing house and home behind its simple, dignified façade. But the retreat—already in evidence by the end of the eighteenth century—of the commercial and industrial middle classes to villas in "non-commercial" suburbs, is one of the significant characteristics of social polarization. In the last quarter of the eighteenth century, a select "garden city", inspired by the English country house, was built alongside the Elbchaussee between Altona and Blankenese. Most of it, however, was destroyed during the Second World War. Of the few fine, neo-classical middle class houses to have survived, we would cite that of a merchant, J. C. Godeffroy, which is surrounded by large *211* grounds landscaped in the manner of an English park. It was the first important work to be executed by the architect Christian Frederik Hansen between 1789 and 1792. No longer was the merit of a building defined by its height or the richness of its decoration. In the central block, no more than one and a half storeys high, the effect is achieved by noble proportions and the few monumental elements of the façade, such as the Doric columns of the portico and the narrow, projecting cornice. However, the marked symmetry of the exterior is out of keeping with the interior, in much the same way as the ponderous front façade is at variance with the lighter, garden side and its projecting oval vestibule. True,

214

the rooms are planned on a grand scale, but their irregular disposition is hardly conducive to convenience. Indeed, the staircase, so important a feature in Baroque, leading to the mezzanine floor has been relegated to one side. When the Palmaille, a stately avenue in Hamburg-Altona, was laid out by C. F. Hansen and his nephew J. Hansen between the years 1786 and 1825, each of the two-and-a-half storeyed houses retained its elegant individualism—already so plainly in evidence in Godeffroy's country house—despite the connecting arched gateways and the uniform height of the storeys and cornices.

Thus we have on the one hand a marked tendency towards individualism in villa architecture and, on the other, the uniform effect produced by the dovetailing of the apartment house into square and street frontages, two extremes which, between them, led to the loss, at this time, of the factor which had once preserved an harmonious balance between original individual structures and communal responsibility. The process of de-individualization was by no means exclusively confined to the architecture of the middle and lower middle classes, a fact borne out by the examples already cited of monumental square and street compositions in Paris and Bath, to which may be added the transformation of Karlsruhe by Friedrich Weinbrenner between 1800 and 1825, perhaps the most impressive instance of such a development in Germany. For like the free-standing, palatial villa, the unified ensemble of luxurious apartment houses on a prominent urban site was able to satisfy what was a deep-seated desire for the grandiose.

Shops frequently formed part of the ground floor of buildings that were as a rule the work of architects of little originality who, in the case of middle class apartment houses, would embellish the façades more or less lavishly in accordance with set designs. Up to the middle of the century, however, this form of high density architecture continued to benefit from the neo-classical legacy of proportion and clarity, though the leading architects of the day did not generally regard the apartment houses as a worthwhile assignment. Indeed, it was to become increasingly rare for such buildings to display any original sense of style, as does, for instance, the house, No. 3, Bátthyány tér, built towards the end of the century in Budapest by Kristóf Hikisch, in which the influence of a number of regional traditions is still apparent. Similarly in Czechoslovakian towns, neo-classical merchants' houses may be found which still retain inner courtyards with covered walks. Towards the end of the eighteenth century an attempt was made in Bratislava to make better use of building plots by erecting wings containing rentable apartments which could be reached by means of galleries (known as *pawlatschen*). The advent of the apartment house marks the beginning of a new chapter in the history of European domestic architecture, a chapter whose end cannot yet be foreseen.

We shall make no more than a brief allusion to the interior appointments of the middle class town house at this time. They bore the imprint both of the Enlightenment and of Classicism, for it was in the hundred years between 1750 and 1850 that they experienced their golden age and acquired the characteristics of restrained simplicity and idiosyncratic style. When Goethe came to Leipzig in 1765 to visit A. F. Oeser, the director of the Academy of Painting, he was deeply impressed by Oeser's "inner closet": "The whole was arranged with taste," he wrote, "simply and in such a fashion that the little room contained a very great deal. The furniture, cupboards, portfolios were elegant, without ornamentation or superfluity. Indeed, the first thing he commended to us, and to which he constantly reverted, was simplicity in all those things which it is the business

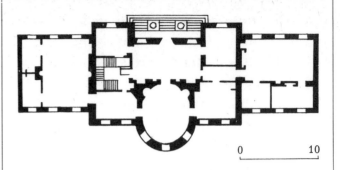

HAMBURG-*Nienstedten. Plan of a country house, No. 499, Elbchaussee, built between 1789 and 1792 by Christian Frederik Hansen for the merchant, J. C. Godeffroy (Ill. 211).*

Typical of the Danish architect's early buildings is the austere grandeur borrowed from English Palladianism which elevates this middle class house to the status of an aristocratic country seat. The clear, cubical forms of the all-white building contrast effectively with the luxuriant vegetation of a park romantically landscaped in the English manner.

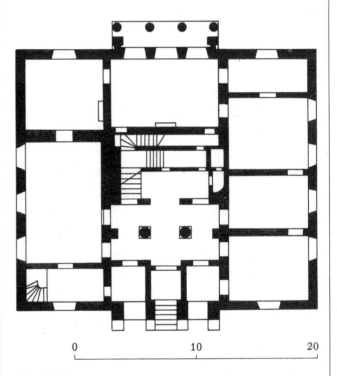

HAMBURG-*Othmarschen. Ground plan of the Jenisch country house, No. 50, Baron-Voght-Strasse, built between 1830 and 1833.*

The villa, a cubiform structure, was executed in the style of the Italian Renaissance. The rooms are situated round a central staircase lit by a toplight.

of art and handicrafts to produce between them. As the declared enemy of volutes and rocaille and of Baroque taste in general, he showed us things of this sort etched in copper, and drawings of old patterns, contrasting them with the better ornamentation and the simpler forms of the furniture as well as of the other appurtenances of the room and, because everything round about him accorded with these maxims, his words and precepts made upon us an impression that was both good and enduring." (Goethe, *Aus meinem Leben (From my Life)*, Vol. 8). Later on, as minister to the Grand Duke of Weimar, the great poet was to adhere to these maxims when fitting out his Baroque house in the Frauenplan, for he gave instructions that the whole of the interior should be redesigned in accordance with neo-classical ideas. The colour of each room harmonized in subtle fashion with its function. The grey-blue of the reception room was intended to convey an impression of space and distance, the yellow tones of the dining-room, warmth and snugness, the green of the study calm and equanimity. Here the author of the *Farbenlehre* (*Theory of Colour*) applied his theoretical findings to his own sphere of existence. Devoid of all ostentation, equipped with comfortable, practical furniture, simple and intimate in atmosphere, his study proves to be the most personal of all the rooms. The so-called Juno Room on the other hand, was, as a reception room, elegant if restrained, being adorned with stucco decorations, painted overdoors, a trelliswork design up to the level of the dado, window curtains and works of art. In an age when men rejoiced in the belief that the human race could be ennobled by culture and aesthetic education, this house, as the home of an important art collection and the expression of a personality, was intended to contribute "not only to a good life," as Goethe told Duke Karl August in a letter of 1806, "but

207, 208
209

also, perhaps, to the dissemination of art and science." If, in our example, we have chosen to lay stress on the home background of one of the most outstanding intellects of the day, this is because it is representative of the general development of the middle class style of life which, for the first time, was also to find widespread acceptance amongst the aristocracy. That development, in the shape of the intimate, exclusive, middle class sphere of existence, was to attain its finest flowering during the Biedermeier period between 1815 and 1850, when there was a revivalist phase. However, there were few original contributions to the art of interior design, such as may be seen for instance in the Wertheimstein Villa in Vienna. Here the lavish murals by Schwind and Holle for a rich art collector were exceptions at a time when appointments already bore the unmistakable stamp of industrialism and became increasingly influenced by lower middle class taste. The appointments, however, which a banker like Geymüller could afford, for instance, were of a superior, aristocratic quality. Yet solidity and simplicity still acted as correctives in a development which was soon to degenerate into vulgar eclecticism, bad taste, rapid changes of fashion, and general tawdriness and kitsch.

In what Style shall we build?

In the year 1828, the German architect Heinrich Hübsch published a pamphlet bearing the above title and containing the replies of several of his colleagues. The work reflects their utter perplexity in the face of a superabundance of new assignments, but it also contains valuable pointers as to how those assignments might be tackled. Hübsch had been a pupil of the confirmed neo-classicist Friedrich Weinbrenner who, as chief architect for the wholesale transformation of Karlsruhe, had founded his own school of architecture. Hübsch, who had travelled widely, was now thirty-three years old. Realizing that he stood at a parting of the ways, he fell in with the view of the best minds of the day, who held that the new style should largely reflect the needs, functions and truth of a structure, its materials and the techniques employed. However, it proved impossible to realize these forward-looking theories which, had they been consistently adhered to, would even then have laid the foundations of modern architecture. Under the spell of historicism men sought an answer in the past. As far as Hübsch was concerned, the fact that the structurally impractical, trabeated system had been favoured by the neo-classicists, was reason enough to turn him into an ardent advocate of the arcuated style with its self-supporting vaults and arches. Other architects—Schinkel, for instance—considered that the Hellenic style was perfect enough to cope with any assignment, while the Gothic was also held by some to be a worthy exemplar. Revolutionary views such as those expressed by Friedrich Engels who, in 1840, saw in historicism "a retrograde sign of the times", elicited no response. The uncertainty of the architects was compounded by that of the clients who belonged to an extraordinarily wide variety of social groups, including the bourgeoisie, the nobility and the Church. All these invoked history when seeking to have their own ideas incorporated in their architecture. Thus an unbounded individualism governed only by fashion and personal taste began to gain ground, a development that was reflected in the buildings of the bourgeoisie, whether private residences, profitable apartment houses, and even factories. It was in the second half of the nineteenth century that the curious amalgam of down-to-earth profit-seeking and idealistic meretri-

ciousness came to a head as a result of personal megalomania and nationalist bragadocio. What can only be described as a craving for ornamentation ultimately extended even to the peasant farmhouse. Virtually the only spheres to remain exempt from this craving were the simple, urban farmhouses which lay off the beaten track, and the dismal, high-density housing of the working class.

All in all, this development is an expression of the inability to take full advantage of the new possibilities of the "truthful" architecture which had grown out of the industrial revolution and had already held out a promise of things to come. But as historical perspective lengthens, we may discern ever more clearly that, within the limits of this period, many creative architectural works of genuine artistic merit were produced. Since only a few areas have been opened up by recent research, our concluding remarks will have to be confined to a discussion of the broad outlines.

In the neo-classical period it was already apparent that the middle class town house was ceasing to serve the dual function of home and place of work which was an unmistakable indication of the approaching demise of this traditional architectural type. At the same time there were signs of the break-up of the old, closely knit community of several generations that lived under the same roof. The individual began to retreat in his own lair, and the house itself was systematically divided into two parts, one, the grander part, being used for social occasions, the other for the everyday life of the household in which the servants were assigned the humblest sphere of all. The three architectural types which came to predominate were the middle and upper middle class detached villa, the small, lower middle class terrace house and the multi-storeyed, purpose-built apartment block which catered for all classes, though its character varied greatly

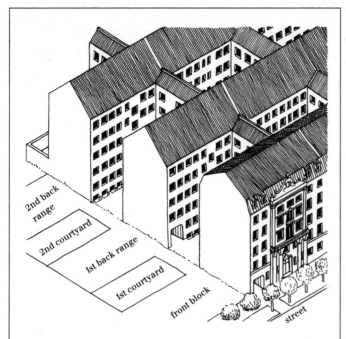

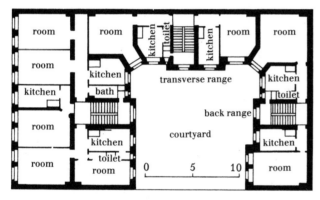

BERLIN. *Tenement houses of the Gründerzeit, circa 1880. Plan and schematic projection.*

Hitherto the apartment block had occupied a rectangular site bounded by streets. Now, however, in the interest of profit and in accordance with the depth of the site, the latter was subdivided into a grid-like pattern of rear blocks and lateral connecting ranges, grouped round narrow courtyards accessible by means of passageways. The courtyards were barely larger than a room, having a minimum area of 28.52 square metres, and were, for the most part, surrounded by four- or five-storeyed buildings, so that the majority of those inhabiting the rear blocks were virtually deprived of light and fresh air. Because of the high price of land, landlords sought to erect housing of maximum possible density (it was at this time that the U.S.A. saw the first skyscrapers). In this they were restrained only by police regulations governing fire precautions and the circulation of traffic.

as far as status, design and amenities were concerned. The middle class town palace, which had still been the predominant type in the Baroque era, had now become largely obsolete.

The heterogeneity and decay that characterized the microcosm of the home may also be seen on a larger scale in the urban scene. 220 Our aerial photograph showing the development of the western part of Vienna reveals that, when confronted by the population explosion, the age of liberalism lost the urge for bold, purposive urban composition. Indeed, the demolition by imperial decree of the city's fortifications and their replacement by the Ring-Strasse, an imposing boulevard lined with public buildings, exhausted whatever impetus there may have been. Further west, suburbs and villages were indiscriminately engulfed by mixed residential and industrial quarters, unrelieved by trees or grass and laid out in an unimaginative, standardized grid-pattern in which the main and side streets intersect at right angles. The Janus face of this epoch becomes clearly apparent if we take a closer look at the kind of residential block which, with minor variations, was to be found in all the larger towns of Europe, including Berlin, the capital of imperial Germany. On the street side, the "select" front block, its palatial façade embellished with stucco features, contains apartments for middle class citizens. Each apartment has a number of specialized rooms, including a bathroom, and being adequately lit because it is adjacent to the street. But the contiguous side, the back and transverse ranges which are grouped round small courtyards, are neither ornamented nor well-lit. Here large, lower middle and working class families are herded together in a minimum amount of space, their numbers as often as not swollen by the inclusion of individual lodgers.

As a rule such groups of apartment houses were put up quickly and cheaply by big speculative builders in accordance with a set design, and only in exceptional cases were they regarded by architects as a worthwhile assignment. For instance, in 1841 the Berlin Association of Architects refused to participate in a municipal competition involving workers' flats on the grounds that "an assignment of this nature has little to offer in the way of architectural interest". The character of many districts in the town was determined by the speculators' greed which building regulations were scarcely able to contain. Thus, while the alignment of frontages in squares and streets in Berlin was governed by a fire regulation issued in 1853 by the Chief of Police the design of the façades was affected only to the extent that outside steps might not project more than 0.58 metres beyond the prescribed frontage, while balconies, if situated at or above a height of 3.14 metres, might not oversail the pavement by more than 1.88 metres. The important clause relating to the height of a building was extremely elastic in practice; on principle, no building in any street might exceed the height of 11.30 metres. Despite the ruling that rooms must be at least 2.51 metres high, an entrepreneur who wanted the maximum possible number of living units in view could, in a building of regulation height, accommodate no less than five storeys including the officially authorized basement apartment. Moreover, the occupants of the premises at the back were condemned to a permanently twilight existence because courtyards did not have to be more than 5.34 metres square (the minimum necessary for the manipulation of fire hoses) and because the stipulation that the apartments must "have adequate light and air, be dry and not injurious to health" was susceptible to subjective interpretation. The builder's only obligations, so far as the occupants were concerned, were to ensure that fire-resistant material was used for staircases and that the entrances to courtyards were 2.81 metres wide and 2.85 metres high to permit the passage of fire fighting equipment. Though the apartment blocks were not supposed to be more than 120–150 metres wide and 75 metres deep, in practice they often far exceeded these limits.

Sad though it is to see one field of urban domestic architecture reduced to the abject status of money-spinner, this should not be allowed to blind us to the very real achievements of historicism in more exalted spheres. True, the private house had become one of the very lowliest of building types, especially in comparison with public building but, as has already been shown, the role played by villa architecture was a not inconsiderable one. Here we find reflected, to some extent mixed in with other ideas, the general development of the many aspects of historicism during its two principal phases. The first of these, lasting until about the middle of the century, was characterized by the retention of clear, well-proportioned forms, while the later phase that tended towards exuberance, opulence and academic perfectionism, was brought to an end round about 1900 with the advent of Art Nouveau, *Sachlichkeit* (an early form of functionalism), and the Neo-Classical Revival.

During the early phase, from 1830 onwards, the stylistic trend that predominated in the domestic architecture of central and western Europe was that of the Renaissance Revival. Allusion has already been made at the beginning of this chapter to the structural advantages, emphasized by H. Hübsch, of the "arcuated style", though these had little or no part to play in domestic architecture. Of greater significance, especially in the design of multi-storeyed apartment blocks, was the additive use of Renaissance elements in façades. Gottfried Semper, one of the most important Liberal-

Democratic architects of the day, whose Villa Rosa, built in Dresden in 1839 and destroyed in the Second World War, was based on Palladio's Villa Rotonda, maintained that architecture and revolutionary social development were indissolubly linked. The decades that followed the revolution of 1848, in which Semper had actively participated, engendered a universal climate of compromise that involved the abandonment of this meaningful concept in favour of extensive, spectacularly inflated decoration, which would soon incorporate Neo-Romantic and Neo-Baroque forms.

Nevertheless, this enrichment was not wholly devoid of meaning, for national impulses, as they became more widely disseminated, took the place of their anti-feudal, democratic predecessors. With the creation of the Empire in 1871, nationalist, post-victory euphoria conjured up a Renaissance Revival of a specifically German character. The revival manifested itself particularly in the villa and the apartment house furnished in a picturesquely asymmetrical manner with turrets, dormer gables, oriel windows and a superabundance of sculptural ornament. France harked back to her indigenous Renaissance, as did Holland and Belgium to the lively variants of their own Late Renaissance.

In many countries an intensified desire for display and a predilection for splendour and sensual opulence inevitably resulted, shortly after the middle of the century, in the revival of Baroque, once so bitterly combatted under the banner of national self-expression. In pale imitation of large public buildings, the Neo-Baroque or Wilhelmine style, combined with that of the Neo-Renaissance, began to impose itself on the façades of apartment blocks in Germany, ousting the Neo-Rococo which had prevailed in the domestic sphere in the years between 1830 and 1860. In Austria the so-called *Reichsstil*, or Empire style, conjured

217

up the vision of a glorious past; in France the Second Empire looked back to the imperial grandeur of the Roi Soleil and his successors; while in Belgium, Flemish Baroque carried all before it. Generally speaking, other styles, such as Neo-Gothic and Neo-Romanesque, were of no more than secondary importance as far as urban domestic architecture was concerned. In the early part of the nineteenth century these styles were primarily employed by the Church and the aristocracy, but after 1850 their use spread to public secular architecture. More or less extensive borrowings of decorative and structural elements from these early periods are everywhere apparent in domestic architecture. But there was never any general revival, characterized by genuine understanding, of the wide variety of types of middle class town house that had evolved during the Gothic period. However, in the Victorian era Neo-Gothic assumed greater importance so far as the English private house was concerned. Yet, in the country which gave birth to Romanticism, the "Gothic" of the early eighteenth century was largely confined to an aristocratic élite. It was not until the Gothic Revival and the building of the Houses of Parliament, begun in 1834, that it became a movement pervading the entire country, inspired to some extent by reformative ideas. There was a renewed delight in picturesquely asymmetrical house design, typical bay windows, and high pitched roofs with timber-framed gables and carved barge boards. However, as may be seen from our example of a *218* Victorian interior, the middle classes favoured an astonishing medley of styles. No more than twenty or thirty years ago such exuberance would unhesitatingly have been dismissed as bad taste; not so now, when caution is enjoined by the current wave of nostalgia. Whatever the case, the objective observer cannot but admit the existence of an original if unifying common denominator in this predilection for an eclectic, busy, highly coloured décor.

The extent to which historicism contributed to the discovery of national identity, particularly in the case of the hitherto oppressed peoples of Europe, is discernible, for instance, in the "Bulgarian Renaissance", although similar aspirations were also harboured by other Balkan nations. After 1838 even the Russian Czar sought national self-expression in a reversion to traditional buildings in the Byzantine-Old Russian mode. In contrast to this deliberate process, the representatives of the Bulgarian mercantile and industrial bourgeoisie resorted spontaneously to indigenous stylistic forms, as well as to those of their West European neighbours, in an attempt to set themselves apart from the Turks who continued to occupy the country up till 1878. Increasing prosperity and greater needs went hand in hand with the formative development of the Bulgarian middle class house which, with its several storeys and wide variety of rooms, had cast off the image of the rustic, private fortress. The single-storeyed Lyutov house built in 1854 in Koprivshtitza, boasts a façade and portico whose lively, symmetrical regularity testifies to the influence of the Baroque. The carved wooden ceiling of the elliptical salon at the centre of the dwelling-house displays a rosette symbolizing the sun. The plan of the Kableshkov house in Koprivshtitza, erected in 1845, is an example of the further development of the so-called Baroque house. Both storeys are almost symmetrical with an axial emphasis, being disposed in accordance with the typically Baroque principles of curving, inter-penetrating spatial compartments and of an imposingly accentuated staircase. Curvilinear forms are also to be seen on the façade, sides and roof. The Kojumdshioglu house in Plovdiv, dating from 1847, is another

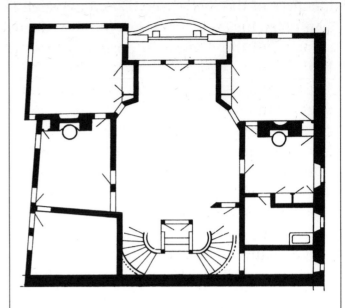

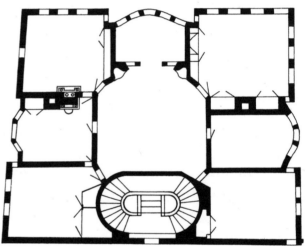

KOPRIVSHTITZA. *Kableshkov's house, 1845 (Ill. 215). Plans of the ground and first floors.*

The interior disposition of this so-called Baroque house—a type which first gained acceptance in Plovdiv, Koprivshtitza and Samokov, subsequently reaching the districts north of the Balkan massif—recalls the principles of Baroque château architecture in its axial lay-out, the introduction of a double staircase, and the curvilinear spaces of the vestibule and salon which interpenetrate, not only each other, but also the adjoining areas.

instance of the same type. Elements such as symmetry, the undulating roof, the bow-shaped centre and the columned portico are in the Baroque-Byzantine style yet they are expressed in the colourful and decorative idiom of the country in which the traditional art of wood-carving plays so essential a role. One of the finest examples of the Bulgarian Renaissance —in fact a vernacular interpretation of the Baroque—is the Sarafski house in Samokov. For the execution of the carved and painted ceilings the rich banker of that name called in in the leading Bulgarian wood-carvers of the day, Peter and Georgi Dashin and Stojtsho Fandakov.

Today we see clearly that, though historicism failed to achieve homogeneity in the field of domestic architecture, we should be wrong in taking a merely negative view of its achievements. These were, of course, dismissed out of hand by the advocates of reform when this movement began to take shape in England just after the middle of the century. Initially it was a romantic movement based on the restoration of the old handicrafts, and went hand in hand with concepts of social reform, for William Morris saw the Domestic Revival to some extent as an ethical problem. He strove to revert to the simplicity of an earlier age. These views found systematic expression for the first time in the Red House at Bexleyheath, a private residence built to William Morris's order by Philip Webb in 1859/60. Constructed of brick, it derives its name from that material which, instead of being concealed wherever possible, as was then the custom, has been left exposed. In accordance with the client's requirements, the building is designed with all the emphasis on the interior. Save for a few Neo-Georgian elements, the house is totally unadorned and, thanks to the almost pedantic avoidance of symmetry, has a somewhat rustic air.

The subsequent course taken by the reformative movement in combatting historicism, and its struggle for an architecture that was functional and straightforward, would call for a study of its own. This development is represented by two buildings in a modern, plain 222 style—the Steiner House in Vienna built by 223 Adolf Loos and the Haus am Horn in Weimar by Walter Gropius.

Appendix

BIBLIOGRAPHY

A selection of works of the specialized literature; only in some cases inventories of architectural and art monuments, art topographies and town monographs are mentioned.

GENERAL LITERATURE

Arthaud, Claude: *Welt der Genies. Wie grosse Künstler wohnten.* Munich, 1968.

Bernt, Adolf: "Bürgerhaus." With a detailed list of literature. In: *Reallexikon zur deutschen Kunstgeschichte.* Vol. III, columns 180–221. Stuttgart, 1954.

Camesasca, Ettore (Editor): *Storia della Casa.* Milane, 1968.

Fayet, M. de, Buffet-Challié, L., and Wittkopp, U.: *Raumkunst des 18. Jahrhunderts.* Düsseldorf, Lausanne, 1964.

Hähnel, Joachim: *Hauskundliche Bibliographie.* Vol. 1. 1961–1970. First part. Münster, 1972 (= *Beiträge zur Hausforschung*).

Hansen, Hans Jürgen (Editor): *Holzbaukunst. Eine Geschichte der abendländischen Holzarchitektur und ihrer Konstruktionselemente.* Oldenburg, Hamburg, 1969.

Hinz, Sigrid: *Innenraum und Möbel.* Berlin, 1977, 2nd edition.

Meier-Oberist, Edmund: *Kulturgeschichte des Wohnens im abendländischen Raum.* Hamburg, 1956.

Norberg-Schulz, Christian: *Holzhäuser in Europa.* Stuttgart, 1979.

Savage, George: *Die Wohnkultur. Eine Stilkunde der Innenarchitektur.* Vienna, Munich, Zurich, 1971.

Schultz, Alwin: *Das häusliche Leben der europäischen Kulturvölker vom Mittelalter bis zur 2. Hälfte des XVIII. Jahrhunderts.* Munich, Berlin, 1903.

Stiehl, Otto: *Der Wohnbau des Mittelalters.* Leipzig, 1908, 2nd edition; 1st edition by August von Essenwein (= *Handbuch der Architektur,* part 2, vol. 4, No. 2).

Veltheim-Lottum, Ludolf: *Kleine Weltgeschichte des städtischen Wohnhauses.* Heidelberg, 1952.

Violett-Le Duc, Eugène Emanuel: *The Habitation of man in all ages.* (From the French edition of 1876.) Ann Abor Michigan Gryphon Books, 1971.

Waetzoldt, Stephan (Editor): *Bibliographie zur Architektur im 19. Jahrhundert. Die Aufsätze in den deutschsprachigen Architekturzeitschriften 1789–1918.* Vol. 7, *Wohnhaus.* Nendeln, 1977.

WORKS REFERRING TO MUNICIPAL ARCHITECTURE

Benevolo, L.: *Storia della città.* Bari, 1976.

Braunfels, Wolfgang: *Mittelalterliche Stadtbaukunst in der Toskana.* Berlin, 1953.

Bunin, A. W.: *Geschichte des russischen Städtebaus bis zum 19. Jahrhundert.* Berlin, 1961.

Czok, Karl: *Die Stadt. Ihre Stellung in der deutschen Geschichte.* Leipzig, Jena, Berlin, 1969.

Ennen, Edith: *Frühgeschichte der europäischen Stadt.* Bonn, 1953.

Ennen, Edith: *Die europäische Stadt des Mittelalters.* Göttingen, 1972.

Grote, Ludwig (Editor): *Die deutsche Stadt im 19. Jahrhundert. Stadtplanung und Baugestaltung im industriellen Zeitalter.* Munich, 1974.

Gruber, Karl: *Die Gestalt der deutschen Stadt. Ihr Wandel aus der geistigen Ordnung der Zeiten.* Munich, 1952.

Herzog, Erich: *Die ottonische Stadt. Die Anfänge der mittelalterlichen Stadtbaukunst in Deutschland.* Berlin, 1964.

Hiorns, Frederick Robert: *Town-building in history.* London, 1956.

Junghanns, Kurt: *Die deutsche Stadt im Frühfeudalismus.* Berlin, 1959.

Mauersberg, Hans: *Wirtschafts- und Sozialgeschichte zentraleuropäischer Städte in neuerer Zeit.* Göttingen, 1960.

Münter, Georg: *Idealstädte. Ihre Geschichte vom 15.–17. Jahrhundert.* Berlin, 1957.

Planitz, Hans: *Die deutsche Stadt im Mittelalter. Von der Römerzeit bis zu den Zunftkämpfen.* Graz, Cologne, 1954.

Platt, C.. *The English medieval town.* London, 1976.

Radig, Werner: *Die Siedlungstypen in Deutschland und ihre frühgeschichtlichen Wurzeln.* Berlin, 1955.

Roerig, Fritz: *Die europäische Stadt und die Kultur des Bürgertums im Mittelalter.* Göttingen, 1958, 3rd edition.

Roerig, Fritz: *Wirtschaftskräfte im Mittelalter. Abhandlungen zur Stadt- und Hansegeschichte.* Vienna, Cologne, 1971.

MIDDLE CLASS TOWN HOUSES IN VARIOUS REGIONS

Central Europe (Germany, Austria, Switzerland)

Aepli, Hubert: *Der westschweizerische Profanbau der Renaissance 1550–1680.* Freiburg, 1960.

Bach, Anita: *Wohnhausbau von 1775 bis 1845 in Weimar.* University thesis, Hochschule für Architektur Weimar, 1960.

Baumeister, S.: *Das Bürgerhaus in Warendorf. Ein volkskundlicher Beitrag zur Geschichte des Profanbaues in Westfalen.* Münster, 1974.

Becker, H.: *Das Landhaus Hamburgs in der Zeit vor 1800.* Hamburg, 1931.

Berger-Schäfer, Hans: *Das Frankfurter Bürgerhaus.* University thesis, Technische Hochschule Berlin-Charlottenburg, 1919.

Bernt, Adolf: *Deutsche Bürgerhäuser.* Tübingen, 1968.

Brandt, A.: "Deutsche Bürgerhäuser vom Mittelalter bis zur Neuzeit." In: *Tagungsbericht der Deutschen Gesellschaft für Hausforschung.* Münster, 1951.

Ebinghaus, H.: *Das Ackerbürgerhaus Westfalens.* Dresden, 1912.

Eckardt, Götz (Editor): *Schicksale deutscher Baudenkmale im zweiten Weltkrieg. Eine Dokumentation der Schäden und Totalverluste auf dem Gebiet der DDR.* Berlin, 1978.

Eicke, Karl: *Das bürgerliche Wohnhaus in Cottbus.* Berlin, University thesis, Technische Hochschule, 1917.

Erdmannsdorffer, Karl: *Das Bürgerhaus in München.* Tübingen, 1972.

Erffa, W. von: *Das Bürgerhaus im westlichen Oberfranken.* Tübingen, 1977.

Farenholtz, Christian: *Entwicklung im Lübecker Profanbau.* Brunswick, University thesis, Technische Hochschule, 1956.

Freckmann, Klaus: *Das Fachwerkhaus an der Mosel.* Cologne, 1975.

Fricke, Rudolf: *Das Bürgerhaus in Braunschweig.* Tübingen, 1975.

Geyer, Bernhard: *Das Stadtbild Alt-Dresdens. Baurecht und Baugestaltung.* Berlin, 1964.

Giersberg, Hans-Joachim: *Das Potsdamer Bürgerhaus um 1800.* Potsdam, 1965.

Götzger, Heinrich: *Das Bürgerhaus der Stadt Lindau im Bodensee.* Tübingen, 1969.

Griep, Hans Günther: *Das Bürgerhaus in Goslar.* Tübingen, 1959.

Griep, Hans Günther: *Das Bürgerhaus der Oberharzer Bergstädte.* Tübingen, 1975.

Gruber, Otto: *Deutsche Bauern- und Ackerbürgerhäuser. Eine bautechnische Quellenforschung zur Geschichte des deutschen Hauses.* Karlsruhe, 1926.

Haubenreisser, Wolfgang: *Der Erker als Architekturmotiv in der deutschen Stadt. Seine Typen, Formen, Entwicklung und architektonische Bedeutung unter besonderer Berücksichtigung der Erker in Leipzig.* Tübingen, University thesis, 1961.

Hauke, Karl: *Das Bürgerhaus in Ost- und Westpreussen.* Tübingen, 1967.

Hauke, Karl: *Das Bürgerhaus in Mecklenburg und Pommern.* Tübingen, 1975.

Heinitz, Oscar: *Das Bürgerhaus zwischen Schwarzwald und Schwäbischer Alb.* Tübingen, 1970.

Helm, Rudolf: *Das Bürgerhaus in Nordhessen.* Tübingen, 1967.

Henning, R.: *Das deutsche Haus in seiner historischen Entwicklung.* Strasbourg, 1882.

Hübler, Hans: *Das Bürgerhaus in Lübeck.* Tübingen, 1968.

Jacob, Frank-Dietrich: *Die Görlitzer bürgerliche Hausanlage der Spätgotik und Frührenaissance. Studien zur Problematik der Wechselbeziehungen zwischen sozialökonomischer Struktur und bürgerlichem Hausbau im Zeitalter der frühbürgerlichen Revolution.* Görlitz, 1972.

Jericke, Alfred: *Das Goethehaus am Frauenplan.* Weimar, 1958.

Kaiser, Gerhard, and Möller, Roland: "Erfurter Bürgerhausfassaden der Renaissance." In: *Denkmale in Thüringen. Ihre Erhaltung und Pflege in den Bezirken Erfurt, Gera und Suhl.* Weimar, 1973, pp. 94–129.

Kreft, Herbert, and Soenke, Jürgen: *Die Weserrenaissance.* Hameln, 1964.

Kretzschmar, Frank, and Wirtler, U.: *Das Bürgerhaus in Konstanz, Meersburg and Überlingen.* Tübingen, 1977.

Kühnel, Harry: *Denkmalpflege und Altstadtsanierung in Krems a. d. Donau 1959 bis 1974.* Krems a. d. Donau, 1974.

Kuhn, Waldemar: *Kleinsiedlungen aus friderizianischer Zeit.* Stuttgart, 1918.

Ladenbauer-Orel, H.: "Archäologische Bürgerhausforschung in Wien." In: *Archäologisches Korrespondenzblatt* 3 (1973), pp. 371–378.

Lauffer, O.: *Das deutsche Haus in Dorf und Stadt.* Leipzig, 1918.

Löffler, Fritz: *Das alte Dresden. Geschichte seiner Bauten.* Dresden, 1955.

Mayer, Eugen: *Das Bürgerhaus zwischen Ostalb und oberer Tauber.* Tübingen, 1978.

Mielke, Friedrich: *Das Bürgerhaus in Potsdam.* Tübingen, 1972.

Oberg, Peter: *Der Beischlag des deutschen Bürgerhauses.* Danzig, 1935.

Peters, O: *Das barocke Bürgerhaus in den Rheinlanden. Die Entwicklung der Fassade des Barockhauses am Rhein.* Bonn, 1924.

Pevsner, Nikolaus: *Leipziger Barock.* Dresden, 1928.

Pfaud, R. *Das Bürgerhaus in Augsburg.* Tübingen, 1976.

Phleps, Hermann: *Deutsche Fachwerkbauten.* Königstein im Taunus, *1953.*

Pinder, Wilhelm: *Bürgerbauten aus vier Jahrhunderten deutscher Vergangenheit.* Königstein im Taunus, Leipzig, 1929.

Radig, Werner: *Frühformen der Hausentwicklung in Deutschland. Die frühgeschichtlichen Wurzeln des deutschen Hauses.* Berlin, 1958.

Ropertz, Peter Hans: *Kleinbürgerlicher Wohnbau vom 14.–17. Jahrhundert in Deutschland und im benachbarten Ausland.* University thesis, Aachen, 1976.

Rudhard, Wolfgang: *Das Bürgerhaus in Hamburg.* Tübingen, 1975.

Sage, Walter: *Das Bürgerhaus in Frankfurt a. M. bis zum Ende des Dreissigjährigen Krieges.* Tübingen, 1959.

Sauer, H.: "Bürgerhäuser des 16. Jh. in Freiberg." In: *Sächsische Heimatblätter.* 19 (1973), pp. 63–68.

Schmerber, Hugo: *Studie über das deutsche Schloss und Bürgerhaus im 17. und 18. Jahrhundert.* Strasbourg, 1902.

Schuster, Max-Eberhard: *Das Bürgerhaus im Inn- und Salzachgebiet.* Tübingen, 1964.

Schwemmer, Wilhelm: *Das Bürgerhaus in Nürnberg.* Tübingen, 1972.

Sittel, Walter: *Das mittelalterliche Wohnhaus in Trier. Ein Beitrag zur westdeutschen Wohnhaus- und Stadtforschung.* Aachen, University thesis, Technische Hochschule, 1958.

Stein, Rudolf: *Das Bürgerhaus in Schlesien.* Tübingen, 1966.

Stein, Rudolf: *Das Bürgerhaus in Bremen.* Tübingen, 1970.

Stender, Friedrich: *Das Bürgerhaus in Schleswig-Holstein.* Tübingen, 1971.

Stephan, E.: *Das Bürgerhaus in Mainz.* Tübingen, 1974.

Stephani, K. G.: *Der älteste deutsche Wohnbau und seine Einrichtung.* Leipzig, 1902/03.

Stier, W.: "Das Lübecker Bürgerhaus zur Zeit der Renaissance." In: *Der Wagen.* Lübeck, 1969, pp. 79–95.

Strobel, R.: *Das Bürgerhaus in Regensburg.* Tübingen, 1976.

Suhr, P.: *Der Backsteingiebel des norddeutschen Bürgerhauses im Mittelalter.* Berlin, 1935.

Völckers, Otto: *Deutsche Hausfibel.* Bamberg, 1949.

Vogt, G.: *Frankfurter Bürgerhäuser des 19. Jahrhunderts. Ein Stadtbild des Klassizismus.* Frankfurt-am-Main, 1970.

Vogts, Hans: *Das Bürgerhaus in der Rheinprovinz.* Düsseldorf, 1929.

Vogts, Hans: *Das Kölner Wohnhaus bis zur Mitte des 19. Jahrhunderts.* Neuss, 1966.

Wagner-Rieger, Renate: *Das Wiener Bürgerhaus des Barock und Klassizismus.* Vienna, 1957.

Wagner-Rieger, Renate (Editor): *Die Wiener Ringstrasse. Bild einer Epoche. Die Erweiterung der inneren Stadt Wien unter Kaiser Franz Joseph.* Wiesbaden, 1975, vol. V.

Weiss, Richard: *Häuser und Landschaften der Schweiz.* Erlenbach, Zurich, Stuttgart, 1959.

Wilhelm, Rolf: *Die Fassadenbildung des Dresdener Barockwohnbaues.* Leipzig, University thesis, 1939.

Winter, Heinrich: *Das Bürgerhaus zwischen Rhein, Main und Neckar.* Tübingen, 1961.

Winter, Heinrich: *Das Bürgerhaus in Oberhessen.* Tübingen, 1965.

Wulz, Fritz C.: *Stadt in Veränderung. Eine architektur-politische Studie von Wien in den Jahren 1848 bis 1934.* Stockholm, 1977, 2nd edition.

Southern and western Europe (Belgium, England, France, Italy, Netherlands, Spain)

Achere, Jules van: *Baroque and classic art in Belgium (1600–1789).* Brussels, 1972.

Acton, Harold: *Villen der Toscana.* Berlin, 1973.

Addy, Sidney Oldall: *The evolution of the English house.* London, 1933.

Arslan, Edoardo: *Das gotische Venedig. Die venezianischen Profanbauten des 13.–15. Jahrhunderts.* Munich, 1971.

Barlay, M. W.: *The house and home.* London, 1963.

Bassi, E.: *Palazzi di Venezia. Admiranda urbis Venetae.* Venice, 1976.

Baudouin, F.: *Das Rubenshaus.* Antwerp, 1955.

Bentmann, Reinhard, and Müller, Michael: *Die Villa als Herrschaftsarchitektur. Versuch einer kunst- und sozialgeschichtlichen Analyse.* Frankfurt-am-Main, 1970.

Braun, Hugh: *The story of the English house.* London, 1941.

Breffny, B. de, and Ffolliott, R.: *The houses of Ireland. Domestic architecture from the medieval castle to the Edwardian villa.* London, 1975.

Cállari, Luigi: *I palazzi di Roma e le case d'importanza storica e artistica.* Rome, 1970.

Cereghini, Mario: *The oriel in alpine architecture* (Italian). Milan, 1962.

Chierici, G.: *Il palazzo italiano dal secolo XI al secolo XIX.* Milan, 1952 ff.

Chueca Goitia, E.: *Historia de arquitectura española. Edad antigua y edad media.* Madrid, 1965.

Cook, O.: *The English house through seven centuries.* London, 1968.

Courtens, A.: *Romanische Kunst in Belgien.* Vienna, Munich, 1969.

Craig, M.: *Irish houses of the middle size.* London, New York, 1976.

Devliegher, L.: *De huizen te Brugge.* The Hague, 1968.

Devliegher, L.: *Les maisons à Bruges. Inventaire descriptif.* Amsterdam, 1975.

Evans, Joan: *Art in mediaeval France. 987–1498.* London, New York, Toronto, 1952.

Frommel, Christoph Luitpold: *Der Römische Palastbau der Hochrenaissance.* Tübingen, 1973.

Gaunt, William: *Flämische Städte. Brügge, Gent, Antwerpen, Brüssel. Geschichte und Kunst.* Cologne, 1970.

Goldthwaite, R. A.: "The Florentine palace as domestic architecture." In: *The American Historical Review,* 77 (1972), pp. 977–1012.

Haug, Hans: *L'Art en Alsace.* Strasbourg, 1962.

Haupt, Albert: *Palastarchitektur von Oberitalien vom 13. bis 17. Jahrhundert.* Berlin, 1930.

Hautecœur, Louis: *Histoire de l'architecture classique en France. I, 2 La Renaissance des humanistes.* Paris, 1965.

Hewett, C. A.: "The development of the post-medieval house." In: *Postmedieval Archaeology,* 7 (1973), pp. 60–78.

Jordan, Robert Furneaux: *A picture history of the English house.* London, 1959.

Junecke, H.: *Der französische Wohnbau von 1500 bis 1650.* Halle, 1937.

Kubelik, M.: *Die Villa im Veneto. Zur typologischen Entwicklung im Quattrocento.* Munich, 1977.

Lloyd, Nathaniel: *A history of the English house.* London, 1931.

Mariacher, Giovanni: *Ambienti italiani del trecento e quattrocento.* Milan, 1963.

Masson, Georgina: *Italienische Villen und Paläste.* Munich, Zurich, 1959.

Meischke, R., and Zantkuijl, H. J.: *Het Nederlandse woonhuis van 1300–1800.* Haarlem, 1969.

Moos, Stanislaus von: *Kastell, Palast, Villa. Studien zur italienischen Architektur des 15. und 16. Jh.* Zurich, 1967.

Oulmont, Charles: *La maison au 18ᵉ siècle.* Strasbourg, 1970.

Pobé, Marcel: *Das klassische Frankreich. Die drei Jahrhunderte vor Ausbruch der Revolution.* Vienna, Munich, 1963.

Pobé, Marcel: *Splendeur gothique en France.* Paris, 1960.

Pignatti, Terisio: *Ambienti italiani del seicento e settecento.* Milan, 1964.

Ramsey, S. C., and Harvey, J. D. M.: *Small Georgian houses and their details 1750–1820.* London, 1972.

Richardson, A. E. and Gill, C. L.: *London houses from 1660 to 1820.* London, 1911.

Schmid-Burgk, Max: "Das mittelalterliche Bürgerhaus im Hennegau." In: *Belgische Kunstdenkmäler* (Editor Paul Clemen). Munich, 1923, pp. 179–202.

Smith, J. T.: "Lancashire and Cheshire houses: some problems of architectural and social history." In: *The archaeological Journal,* 127 (1970), pp. 156–181.

Smith, P.: Houses from the Welsh countryside (Wales). London, 1975.

Staatsmann, Karl: *Das Bürgerhaus im Elsass.* Berlin, 1925.

Thompson, A. Hamilton: "The English house." In: *Social Life in Early England* (Editor G. Barraclough). London, 1969, pp. 144 ff.

Van de Walle, A. L. J.: *Gotische Kunst in Belgien.* Vienna, Munich, 1972.

Vitry, Paul: *Hôtels et maisons de la Renaissance française.* Paris, 1911.

Vogts, Hans: "Das flandrische Wohnhaus seit der Mitte des 17. Jahrhunderts." In: *Belgische Kunstdenkmäler* (Editor Paul Clemen). Munich, 1923, pp. 281–318.

Wood, Margaret: *The English mediaeval house.* London 1968, 2nd edition.

Northern Europe (Denmark, Finland, Norway, Sweden)

Ambrosiani, Sune: *Haustyper i Skandinavien.* Riga, 1930.

Andersson, Henrik O., and Bedoire, Frederic: *Stockholms byggnader. En bok om arkitektur och stadsbild i Stockholm.* Stockholm, 1974.

Bjerknes, Kristian: *Gamle borgerhus i Bergen.* Bergen, 1961.

Elling, Christian: *Danske borgerhuse.* Copenhagen, 1943.

Elling, Christian: *Palaeer og Patricierhuse fra Rokokotiden.* København, 1930.

Engquist, Hans Henrik: "Über die Gestaltung und Disposition des Bürgerhauses in Dänemark um 1500." In: *Acta Visbyensia,* V. Visby, 1976, pp. 173–190.

Faber, Tobias: *A history of Danish Architecture.* Copenhagen, 1963.

Hauglied, Roar (Editor): *Byborgerens Hus i Norge. Fra middelalderen til idag.* Oslo, 1963.

Kavli, Guthorm: Norwegian Architecture. Past and present. Oslo, 1958.

Kavli, Guthorm: *Trønderske trepaléer. Borgerlig panelarkitektur nordenfjells.* Oslo, 1966.

Langberg, H.: *Danmarks bygningskultur.* København, 1955.

Lundberg, Erik: *Herremannens Bostad. Studier över nordisk och allmänt västerländsk bostadsplanlägnning.* (With comprehensive bibliography.) Stockholm, 1935.

Paulsson, Thomas: *Scandinavian Architecture. Buildings and society in Denmark, Finland, Norway and Sweden from the iron age until today.* London, 1958.

Rentzhog, Sten: "Den svenska trästaden – en inventering." In: *SJU Uppsatser i Svensk Arkitektur Historia* (Editor U. G. Johnsson). Uppsala, 1970, pp 147–174.

Svahnström, Gunnar: "Häuser und Höfe der handeltreibenden Bevölkerung im Ostseegebiet und im Norden vor 1500." In: *Acta Visbyensia* V. Visby, 1976, pp. 9–28.

Wickberg, Nils Erik: *Finnische Baukunst.* Helsinki, 1963.

Wickberg, Nils Erik: *Historiske huse i Helsingør.* København, 1973.

Eastern Europe (Bulgaria, Poland, Romania, Soviet Union, Czechoslovakia, Hungary)

Bičev, Milko: *Bulgarski barok.* Sofia, 1955.

Bitschew, Milko: *Die Architektur in Bulgarien.* Sofia, 1961.

Bruns, D. W., and Kangropool, P.: *Tallinn. Leningrad, Moscow* (Russian). Moscow, 1971.

Chrościcki, Juliusz A., and Rottermund, Andrzej: *Architekturatlas von Warschau.* Warsaw, 1978.

Csatkai, Endre, and Dercsényi, Deszö: *Sopron és környéke müemlékei.* Budapest, 1953 and 1956.

Döpmann, Hans-Dieter: *Das alte Bulgarien. Ein kulturgeschichtlicher Abriss bis zum Ende der Türkenherrschaft im Jahre 1878.* Leipzig, 1973.

Dostál, O., et al.: *Československá historická mešta.* Prague, 1974.

Dražan, V.: "Gotický a renesančni městský dům z jižnich Čech a Meravy." In: *Zprávy památkové péče,* X (1950), pp. 129–160.

Gasiorowski, E.: "Toruńska kamiennica mieszczańska." In: *Zeszyte naukowe UMK Nauki Humanistyczno společzne.* Z. 16. Torun, 1966.

Genthon, István: *Kunstdenkmäler in Ungarn.* Leipzig, 1974.

Gerevich, László: *The Art of Buda and Pest in the Middle Ages.* Budapest, 1971.

Gerö, László: *Gotische Bürgerhäuser in Buda.* Budapest, 1966.

Grabar, Lazarew, Kemenow (Editors): *Geschichte der russischen Kunst. Von den Anfängen bis zur Gegenwart.* Dresden, 1975.

Horler, Miklós, and Pogány, Frigyes: *Budapest müemlékei.* Budapest, 1955.

Ionescu, Grigore: *Ištoria Arhitecturii in Rominia.* Bucharest, 1963/65.

Kožucharov, Georgi: *Bulgarskato kusta prez pot stoletija.* Sofia, 1967.

Libal, Dobroslav: *Alte Städte in der Tschechoslowakei.* Prague, 1971.

Lorentz, S.: *Die Renaissance in Polen.* Warsaw, 1955.

Matějková, Eva: *Kutná Hora.* Prague, 1962.

Mencl, Václav: *Praha.* Prague, 1969.

Mencl, Václav: "Vývoj studia středověkého měsť anského domu." In: *Monumentorum tutela,* 7 (1971), pp. 5–28.

Merhautová, Anežka: *Raně středověká architektura v Čechách.* Prague, 1971.

Peev, Christo: *Alte Häuser in Plovdiv.* Mainz, 1968.

Pišá, V.: "Románské domy v Praze." In: *Monumentorum tutela,* 7 (1971), pp. 85–174.

Rokyta, Hugo: *Die böhmischen Länder. Handbuch der Denkmäler und Gedenkstätten europäischer Kulturbeziehungen in den böhmischen Ländern.* Salzburg, 1970.

Šamánková, Eva: *Architektura České Renesance.* Prague, 1961.

Sebestyén, G. and V.: *Arhitectura Renasterii in Transsilvania.* Bucharest, 1963.

Stamov, Stefan (Editor): *The architectural heritage of Bulgaria.* Sofia, 1972.

Tic, Aleksei A.: *Russian architecture of stone dwelling-houses in the 17th century* (Russian). Moscow, 1966.

Čarek, J.: "Z dějin stároměstských domů." In: *Pražský Sbornik historický,* 10 (1977), pp. 5–50.

Üprus, Helmi: *Tallinna etikukivid.* Tallinn, 1971.

Üprus, Helmi: "Das Wohnhaus in Tallinn vor 1500." In *Acta Visbyensia* V. Visby, 1976, pp. 141–164.

Vaga, Voldemar: *Das mittelalterliche Wohnhaus in Tallinn.* Tartu, 1961.

Wasilew, M.: *Riga* (Russian). Riga, 1971.

Zachwatowicz, Jan: *Polnische Architektur bis zur Mitte des XIX. Jahrhunderts.* Warsaw, 1956, 2nd edition.

Zaryn, S.: *Trzynaście kamienic staromiejskich Strona Dekerta.* Warsaw, 1972.

Zlatew, Todor: *The Bulgarian house in the period of the Bulgarian Renaissance* (Bulgarian). Sofia, 1955.

INDEX OF PLACE NAMES

Unitalicized numerals refer to the text, numerals in italics refer to the numbers of the illustrations.

INDEX OF PROPER NAMES

Unitalicized numerals refer to the text, numerals in italics refer to the numbers of the illustrations.

A.C.L., Brussels 11, 147, 220
Alinari, Florence 55, 56, 57, 58, 61, 62, 63, 68, 155
Amplicationes y Reproducciones Mas,
  Barcelona 171
Antikvarisk-Topografiska Arkivet,
  Stockholm 10
Bavaria Verlag, Gauting near
  Munich 7, 42, 47, 71, 86, 140, 141
Bayerische Staatsgemäldesammlungen, Alte
  Pinakothek, Munich 51
A. de Belder, Antwerp 39, 152
Belgisches Verkehrsamt, Düsseldorf 150
Klaus Bergmann, Potsdam 199
Bertram-Luftbild, Munich-Riem 13 (Freigabe
  Reg. v. Obb. G 4/30.745)
Klaus G. Beyer, Weimar 22, 59, 60, 98, 105, 167,
  208, 223
G. Beygang, Karl-Marx-Stadt 205
Bibliothèque Nationale, Paris 69
Britische Zentrale für Fremdenverkehr,
  Frankfurt/Main 210
British Tourist Authority, London 121, 184
British Travel Association, London 34, 120, 122
Bundesdenkmalamt, Vienna 27, 77, 83, 209
Wilhelm Castelli, Lübeck 5
Walter Danz, Halle 95
Deutsche Fotothek, Dresden 92, 93, 114, 217
dpa – Bild, Frankfurt/Main 94
Lajos Dobos, Budapest 28, 30, 186, 187, 194, 202
John Freeman, London 50
Foto Marburg, Marburg 15
G. Galinsky, Berlin 82
Geffrye Museum, London 218
Germanisches Nationalmuseum,
  Nuremberg 142
Photographie Giraudon, Paris 8, 156, 170, 200
Gotland's Historical Museum, Visby 9
Ruth Hallensleben, Wuppertal-Elberfeld
  3, 168, 169
Harry Hardenberg, Stralsund 1, 19
Teodor Hermanczyk, Warsaw 123, 126, 127, 128,
  131, 133, 183
Hans Hinz, Basle 201
Humboldt-Universität, Berlin, Hochschulfilm-
  und Bildstelle 222
V. Hyhlik, Prague 2
Institut für Denkmalpflege, Berlin 43, 44, 78,
  79, 80, 81, 87, 88, 89, 90, 96, 99, 100, 159, 162, 163,
  164, 190, 191, 196, 197, 198, 207
Krzysztof Jablonski, Warsaw 130, 182
M. Jeitner, Aachen 23
Rolf Kleinhempel, Hamburg 206
Landesbildstelle Rheinland, Düsseldorf 219
The Metropolitan Museum of Art, New York 40
Photo Meyer, Vienna 113, 165
R. Meyer, Dresden 12, 32
Municipal Museum, Stockholm 109, 157, 158
Musée Royal des Beaux Arts, Antwerp 143, 160
Musées Royaux des Beaux-Arts, Brussels 112
The National Gallery, London 172
Nationalmuseum, Copenhagen 33, 107, 111
Novosti, Moscow 16, 17, 18

Österreichische Nationalbibliothek, Vienna 221
Österreichisches Fremdenverkehrsamt,
  Vienna/Markowitsch 106
Preiss & Co., Albaching 118, 119
Publishers' archives 6, 14, 97, 129, 138, 181, 185,
  203
Gerhard Reinhold, Mölkau near Leipzig 52, 172
Rijksdienst v/d Monumentenzorg, Zeist 108, 116
Rijksmuseum, Amsterdam 160, 161
Riksantikvaren, Oslo 204
Jean Roubier, Bourges 35, 36, 37, 38, 101, 102, 103
SCALA, Florence 46, 48, 49, 53, 54, 64, 65, 66,
  144, 145, 146, 148, 149
Ernst Schäfer, Weimar 178
C. Schildknecht, Lucerne 84
Toni Schneiders, Lindau 24, 31, 45, 72, 174, 175,
  179, 180
Schweizerisches Landesmuseum, Zurich 115
Service de documentation photographique de la
  Réunion des musées nationaux, Paris 166
Staatliche Landesbildstelle, Hamburg 211, 213,
  214
State Museum of Architecture, Moscow 192,
  193, 212
Stadtbildstelle, Augsburg/Beisser 85
Werner Starke, Dresden 4, 124, 125, 132
Statni ustav Památkové Péče a Ochrany
  Prirody, Prague 25, 26, 134, 135, 136, 137, 139,
  188
Süddeutscher Verlag, Munich 67
László Szelényi, Budapest 29
Assen Tschilingirow, Berlin 189, 195, 215, 216
Gudrun Vogel, Leipzig 153
VVV – Amsterdam 110, 117, 151, 154
R. Wessendorf, Schaffhausen 73, 74, 75, 76
Walter Wolff, Görlitz 91
ZEFA, Frankfurt/Main 20, 21, 70, 104, 176, 177